Statistics for Real-Life Sample Surveys

Non-Simple-Random Samples and Weighted Data

Samples used in social and commercial surveys, especially of the general population, are usually less random (often by design) than many people using them realise. Unless it is understood, this 'non-randomness' can compromise the conclusions drawn from the data. This book introduces the challenges posed by less-than-perfect samples, giving background ___ ___dge and practical guidance for those who have to deal with them. It explains ___ ___les are, and sometimes should be, non-random in the first place ___ ___-randomness; when correction by weighting is ap ___ ___tistical treatment of these samples m ___ ___ the techniques at work. This is a book for prac ___ ___ for the methods and formulae needed to deal with commonly encountered situations and, above all, a source of realistic and implementable solutions.

The authors are from Roy Morgan Research, Australia's best-known market and social research, public opinion and political polling organisation.

Sergey Dorofeev is Technical Director of Roy Morgan International, the global arm of Roy Morgan Research.

Peter Grant was Research and Development Manager in the Melbourne head office.

Together they have more than 50 years' experience of commissioning and conducting survey research.

Statistics
for Real-Life Sample Surveys

Non-Simple-Random Samples and
Weighted Data

Sergey Dorofeev and Peter Grant

Roy Morgan Research, Melbourne, Australia

CAMBRIDGE
UNIVERSITY PRESS

CAMBRIDGE UNIVERSITY PRESS
Cambridge, New York, Melbourne, Madrid, Cape Town, Singapore, São Paulo

Cambridge University Press
The Edinburgh Building, Cambridge CB2 2RU, UK

Published in the United States of America by Cambridge University Press, New York

www.cambridge.org
Information on this title: www.cambridge.org/9780521858038

First published 2006

Printed in the United Kingdom at the University Press, Cambridge

A catalogue record for this publication is available from the British Library

ISBN-13   978-0-521-85803-8 hardback
ISBN-10   0-521-85803-8 hardback

ISBN-13   978-0-521-67465-2 paperback
ISBN-10   0-521-67465-4 paperback

Contents

Preface

Yet another book on the statistics of samples: what can there be left to say? Indeed there is a very large choice of titles on statistics and sampling and most of what is in this book can be found somewhere in the published literature. There are two main kinds of book in this area. One kind presents the statistics of simple samples in a simplistic way, based on the application of pure probability theory, and is inclined to gloss over the fact that reality is rarely that simple. The other kind deals with the complexities of complex samples, but often in a way that anyone but a specialist mathematician will find daunting. Our purpose is to provide an appreciation of the statistical issues involved in real-life sample surveys and practical guidance on how to cope with them, without losing sight of the need to remain comprehensible to the non-mathematician.

Qualified professional statisticians, particularly those whose interest lies mainly in the assessment of sampling and non-sampling survey error, may find this book too superficial. But it is intended primarily for practising researchers whose main concern is to extract meaning from survey results and to apply it in the formulation of plans and policies, and who may have only basic formal statistical training. We assume a reasonable level of numeracy, but those who are not mathematically inclined should not be put off. Our first aim is to impart an understanding of the issues and the principles involved, for which only rudimentary mathematics is required. The more advanced formulae and the proofs are there for those who can make immediate use of them and as a source of reference for those who may need them in the future or who may need to refer others to them.

The content of this book is intentionally selective. We do not intend it to be a general introduction to the very broad subjects of sampling or statistics. We assume that readers are already familiar with the basic principles of the statistics of samples from other texts, but stand in need of some help in applying what they have learned in the more complicated 'real world', where practical problems loom so much larger than they did in the textbook examples.

Our experience provides us with two specific stimuli to write. Firstly, we have lost count of the researchers we have met, many of them with formal qualifications which include statistics, who were ignorant of some of the fundamental issues involved in any deviation from simple random sampling because they had never seen them explained in practical terms. For these researchers a compact source of reference which covers the basic, and some of the not-so-basic, principles of sampling and evaluation of sample-based data can be of value. This should be especially true because we explain the mathematical and mechanical processes of sampling and data analysis, and try to show the reasoning behind them, some of their implications and some of the pitfalls.

Secondly, and more importantly, there are two subjects of considerable practical importance that are not well served by the more accessible literature. In general, our experience is that basic textbooks are inclined to present an unreasonably optimistic picture of the quality of the samples with which their readers will have to work. We aim to provide a review of the problems associated with the evaluation of real-world sample-based data and practical guidance on coping with them. In particular we examine the related questions of the treatment of samples other than simple random ones and the practice and implications of weighting data.

Weighting is a subject which is mentioned briefly if at all in the main textbooks and about which many researchers appear to know very little. However, in practice very many surveys have the data weighted at the analysis stage, for a variety of reasons. Weighting has important implications for the assessment of results, especially in the calculation of confidence intervals and in significance testing. Users of popular statistical software packages are often unaware of some of the things that these may do with weighted data.

This book brings together in a compact form the essential material for understanding and coping with the most salient problems of non-simple-random samples. Almost all of the theoretical material it contains is available from other sources, but much of that is to be found in specialist books and journals that may not be readily accessible, even to those who know what to look for. We aim to provide an awareness and understanding of the main factors in sample design and planning and the practical realities of sample selection and recruitment, their likely effects and the allowance that should be made for them in interpreting results. We particularly aim to provide the practising researcher with a source of reference for the methods and formulae necessary to deal with the most commonly encountered situations and above all with practical, realistic and implementable solutions.

We have also included a short review of some of the more common analytical tools used with survey data. If we seem slightly less than enthusiastic in our endorsement of these it is because experience has taught us to be cautious in applying sophisticated mathematical procedures to data that may be considerably less sophisticated. It is understandable that researchers should be keen to exploit any technique that will squeeze more information out of a data set amassed with much trouble and expense, but there are pitfalls to be avoided. We seek to temper that enthusiasm rather than to blunt it.

We could not have produced a book such as this unaided. We express our thanks first of all to Roy Morgan Research of Melbourne, Australia, for providing the support and facilities which made this book possible. Parts of the text have been developed from material originally produced for in-house training and reference and we appreciate the opportunity to expand these in a wider ranging text. Results from a genuine large-scale survey are very valuable in providing illustrations and we are fortunate in being able to use examples from the Roy Morgan Single Source survey. This is a large-scale, wide-ranging, national continuous syndicated survey that has been operating in Australia for many years. It includes the Australian industry-currency print media survey and a number of other 'industry monitors'. The annual sample size is over 55 000 adults. It also operates in the USA, UK, New Zealand, and Indonesia.

We also thank the Australian Institute of Health and Welfare for their permission to use the case history of the 1998 National Drug Strategy Household Survey.

Like all practising researchers, we owe a great debt to the many other researchers who over the years have shared their accumulated experience. Above all, we are indebted to Michele Levine, CEO of Roy Morgan Research, for her unfailing encouragement of our efforts, and for her constant willingness to share her knowledge and experience with us. In addition, we must make special mention of George Rennie with whom we have worked on a number of projects and whose ideas and insights have often helped us to clarify our thinking.

1 Sampling methods

This book is about the statistical aspects of sample surveys. However, it is mainly concerned with the statistics of samples that are not of the simplest kind and therefore an appreciation of the process of sample design and of the realities of sampling is an essential requirement for assessing the statistical approach necessary for any given survey. Before proceeding to the methods of dealing with data from samples which are not of the simplest and most straightforward kind, we must first understand why this additional complexity may be necessary, desirable or inevitable in the first place.

Accordingly, we devote this chapter to a brief review of the main methods of sampling and in particular to the thinking that underlies them. We do not intend to be comprehensive in scope or to be prescriptive. We shall cover only those issues affecting the statistical side of survey sampling, and not matters of data collection procedures, fieldwork administration or processing. For a fuller understanding there is a wide range of readily available texts on both the theory and the practice of sampling (see Appendix B for suggestions for further reading).

Survey sampling in the real world is frequently an imperfect process, and we must come to terms with its imperfections, not pretend that they do not exist. No sample used in commercial, scientific or academic studies will be a perfect representation of the whole from which it is drawn.

Correct procedures in the selection of samples will minimise the problems but they will not eliminate them. There is a temptation to think that, because a sample has been drawn according to the best advice and theory and using the best information available about the population or mass which the sample is supposed to represent, it can then be taken as a perfect (or even the best possible) microcosm of that population or mass. Similarly, the fact that a sample can be shown to be atypical in some respects does not necessarily invalidate the conclusions drawn from it, though it may prompt some re-examination of those conclusions.

In short, to use sample-based estimates properly we need an understanding of the factors at work in the sampling process, in theory and in practice, and at both the design and evaluation stages. We also need practical ways of assessing the effects of variations from the 'ideal' of the simple random sample.

Simple random sampling as the benchmark

The simple random sample lies at the heart of most teaching about statistics. It is the simplest form of sample to deal with mathematically; the associated formulae are generally compact and uncluttered. It has many elegant and desirable characteristics. It forms an excellent starting point for teaching the principles of statistical interpretation, reasoning and inference. Our concern is that, in the real world, the samples likely to be encountered by former students of statistics, and by researchers whose principal concerns and skills are not statistical, will not in practice be simple random samples. And many of these people will be ill prepared to deal with them except by treating them, incorrectly, as random.

The 'simple random sample' on which most statistics teaching is based implies that each and every unit in the population which that sample is to represent has an equal chance of selection, that each sample member is selected totally independently and that all selected members of the sample provide full information.

Many research projects call for a sample which is not 'simple' because the research has objectives for which 'simple' sampling is not the optimum. Except in artificial and controlled situations, most samples are not truly random because of the practical difficulties of selecting them and extracting the necessary information from them. This is particularly true of samples of the general human population. It is generally not possible to start with a comprehensive list or sampling frame of the population from which to make our random selection; it is often not possible to contact all the randomly selected members within the inevitable constraints of time and resources; and those contacted may not be willing or able to cooperate in the survey (an increasing problem). In a very large number of cases, therefore, we end up with a non-random sample even if we set out to select a random sample.

Even where a sample has been selected purely randomly, there is no guarantee that it will be representative, or comparable with another similarly randomly selected sample, in all respects, and some corrective action may be needed. Researchers who have set out to take a simple random sample may be tempted to feel that they have done their best and that they are absolved from responsibility for any shortcomings it may have. They have, however, an obligation to make themselves aware of any such imperfections and to deal with them appropriately.

The fact that a sample is not fully random, or is imperfect in its execution, and that the basic random sample statistical tools are not strictly applicable, should not be a cause for despair. There are ways of dealing with data from such samples in a professional and realistic manner and these are presented in the present volume. Nor should the fact that a sample has imperfections be in itself a reason for dismissing the results of a study using such a sample. The important things are to recognise what needs to be allowed for and to ensure that any interpretation and presentation of results makes a realistic allowance for the effects of non-randomness or unrepresentativeness.

This book is intended to complement rather than to replace the many books that deal with the standard and straightforward statistics of random samples. In this chapter, and in those that follow, we assume familiarity with the basic elements of probability theory and the simpler calculations involved with the evaluation of sample based estimates. (However, Appendix A contains a brief recapitulation of the fundamentals.)

1.1 Accuracy and precision

It is appropriate at the outset to stress the distinction between 'accuracy' and 'precision'. These words are sometimes used loosely or even regarded as interchangeable in the context of sample surveys. However, they are quite distinct concepts and researchers must be careful not to confuse them. In particular they should be aware which aspects of the conduct of a sample survey are likely to affect the accuracy of a survey's results and which will affect the precision – and which will affect both.

It must be remembered that sampling errors are not the only sources of uncertainty in survey based estimates. Results can be affected by other factors such as the wording or sequence of questions, respondent reaction to the subject matter (guilt, prestige), respondent fatigue, or even external influences such as the economic situation or the weather. These can have a greater and less predictable effect than sampling errors.

The 'accuracy' of an estimate denotes how well it corresponds to the true reality. Most surveys are carried out, naturally, to measure things where the true value is not known. The survey may provide the only estimate available. However, surveys also generally include measures where the true value for the population is known, even if these are only such basic facts as the age and sex of the sample members, and a comparison of such results with the known, true values may give some guide to the likely accuracy of other results.

Some measures for which the population value is known are used in the process of post-stratification and weighting, described later. Weighting is normally used to counter known biases, whether deliberate, as part of the survey design, or accidental as a result of imperfections in the sampling process. The variables used to determine the weighting are therefore forcibly brought into line with reality. Comparisons with population values for other variables should therefore generally be made after any weighting has been done. The variables used for post-stratification (explained in section 1.10) may also be compared with the true population values in their unweighted state, as a measure of the 'raw' sample quality, provided that due allowance is made for any differences arising purely from a deliberately disproportionate sample design.

Precision and repro-ducibility

Accuracy relates to closeness to reality and is largely dependent on the degree of bias involved. Precision on the other hand relates to the reproducibility of results. The precision of an estimate is largely dependent on the sample size, or, more strictly, on the *effective* sample size (a term that will be explained shortly). With a knowledge of the effective sample size it is possible to estimate how close to the present result a repeat of the survey would be likely to come, provided it was carried out in the same way and on the same scale. More specifically, we can predict how variable the estimates would be if the survey were to be repeated many times.

Precision can thus be more readily measured or estimated than accuracy. Merely repeating the sampling a number of times (or dividing the sample into matched replicates) will give some indication of the amount of variation to be expected in estimates and thus of the precision likely to apply to any individual estimate, even if we know nothing about the true population value. We can examine the size of

differences between an estimate from an individual sample and the mean of that estimate across all the samples. However, if we do not know what the true population
value is from some other source, we have no way of estimating how far away from
it our sample estimate is, whether from an individual sample or from a series of
replicated samples.

Statistical theory gives us ways of estimating the likely variation between sample estimates using evidence derived from a single sample, but it provides no help
with estimating how far any such sample estimate is from the true (but unknown)
value. For that we may have no other recourse than to a judgemental identification of
likely sources of measurement error and an equally judgemental assessment (where
possible) of their likely direction and magnitude and of their relative importance,
based solely on experience, logic and common sense.

As precision is predominantly a question of scale, it is possible for an estimate to be very precise, but also very wrong due to biases in the sample or in the
method of data collection. Conversely it is also possible to be very close to the true
result by chance with a small, poorly designed and ill executed survey – though not
reliably so.

Sometimes precision may be needed more than accuracy. If the key measures in
a survey are 'soft', for instance customer satisfaction (what does 'satisfied' actually
mean?), then there is no way of assessing whether the result is 'accurate'. However,
if a survey is be repeated over time the important thing is to ensure consistency of
measurement so that whatever 'satisfaction' means we can be sure that we are measuring it the same way each time. Changes observed from one survey to another can
be assessed to determine how likely they are to be indicative of genuine changes
among the population rather than just part of the natural variation to be expected
from repeated sampling. To do this we need to know what level of variation would be
expected from survey to survey, and this should, ideally, be low relative to the magnitude of the changes observed. Here adequate sample sizes and above all consistency
of methodology can be more relevant than strict purity of sample design.

At other times accuracy may be all-important. Predicting voting at an impending
election, for instance, requires accuracy as well as consistency, because it really
matters whether the final figure is 49% or 51%. Survey researchers are judged, rightly
or wrongly but very publicly, on their ability to get such numbers right. A consistent
difference of five percentage points may be acceptable in a customer satisfaction
survey, but would be unacceptable in such a voting intention survey.

1.2   Design effect and sample size

The precision of any sample based estimate is determined by both the size of the
sample and the way in which the sample was selected. The sample as used may
provide a less or (occasionally) more precise estimate than a simple random sample
of equivalent size would have done. In assessing the effect of sample design the
variance of an estimate from the actual sample is compared with the variance of an
estimate from a simple random sample of equal size.

Two terms that will be used extensively in this book are introduced at this point. The *effective sample size* is the size of a simple random sample which would yield an estimate with the same precision as the one we have. The *design effect* is the ratio of the variance[1] of the actual estimate to the variance of an estimate from a simple random sample of the same size. It may be more helpful to think of it in terms of the ratio of the actual sample size to the effective sample size.

A further term that may occasionally be encountered elsewhere is the *design factor*. This is the ratio of the *standard error* of an estimate to that which would have been yielded by a simple random sample of equal size. As such it is simply the square root of the design effect. The similarity of the name invites confusion without providing any great benefit and the term will not be further used in this book.

The design effect is a measure of the precision of an individual estimate. It is not a general measure of the precision of all estimates produced from a sample: every estimate produced by a sample has its own design effect and these can vary widely within a single survey data set. Nor should the design effect necessarily be viewed as a measure of the 'quality' of a sample. Samples that yield high design effects may do so because a complex design was required to achieve specific objectives. Nevertheless, where a simple sample design turns out to produce high design effects there is a case for asking why this might be.

The design effect is determined by estimating the variance of an individual estimate, and the estimation of variance is the subject of Chapter 3.

1.3 Defining the objectives

Designing the sample is one of the most important operations in conducting a survey. The principal decisions must be taken at a very early stage in the planning process. There is no single set of rules for designing samples and the design adopted in any instance will be the result of reconciling a number of often conflicting demands and constraints.

The design is (or should be) determined by the objectives of the survey. It is essential to have an agreed explicit statement of objectives in advance, and to ensure that these are realistic and appropriate. Project briefs for surveys are often written by people who do not understand the complexities of sampling. They may be insufficiently specific, lack essential information or be unrealistic in the implied expectations. This is not necessarily a criticism: the author of the brief may be someone very familiar with the subject matter and the issues and with the processes of policy-making or the management of a business, rather than a researcher. The main requirement, however, is to state why a survey is being done and what use is expected to be made of the results. It might be asked what business this is of the researcher; all the researcher needs is to

---

[1] The term 'variance' in this book is always used in its statistical sense of the mean squared difference between individual observations and their mean, and not in the sense used by accountants, of the (signed) difference between a reference value and an actual value (e.g. budget and expenditure or previous and current year).

be told what information is required from the survey. However, the researcher should be in a position to judge the extent to which the survey is likely to be able to meet the need of whoever initiates the project. A clear and agreed statement, in advance, of the background to the project, the objectives, the constraints and the means to be used to achieve the objectives will allow all parties to understand and think clearly about the practical issues. It may also bring to light any areas where different parties have different interpretations and hence different expectations, and it is helpful for all if these can be resolved before rather than after the survey is carried out.

Documenting the objectives   Even where the project is initiated by the researcher responsible for carrying it out, such a statement is essential to allow anyone examining the project in later years to see how and why the survey was conducted and, perhaps more pertinently, to assess the relevance and comparability of the results to other evidence. Re-analysis of existing data is often valuable and cannot be undertaken confidently without adequate documentation of the sampling process.

Where sample selection and fieldwork are to be contracted out it is essential that the potential contractors be given all possible relevant information. They need to know what they are expected to do and deliver and must be aware of anything known to the 'client' that is likely to affect the difficulty, cost or timing of the project. An experienced contractor may be able to contribute to the sample design process, if only in practical suggestions for making the process more cost efficient. Above all, a contractor must be certain that what is contracted for can be delivered on time and within budget.

It is therefore the researcher's task to ensure that before a survey is begun, the brief is set down as, or translated into, a clear plan which will allow the right decisions to be made about the sampling. Such a plan should set out:

- the objectives of the survey and the decisions likely to be affected;
- a definition of the population that the results of the research are intended to represent;
- the method of selecting the sample and, where appropriate, the sampling frame(s) to be used;
- the planned size of the sample;
- constraints of timing and budget, either or both of which may be negotiable to some extent;
- the nature of any important subgroups in the population who must be specifically represented;
- the subject matter of the survey;
- the time likely to be required by a respondent to complete the interview or questionnaire;
- the degree of accuracy or precision required in the principal measures;
- whether this survey is related to any other survey carried out in the past or simultaneously elsewhere, or planned for the future.

It may be thought that some of these matters have no bearing on sample design, let alone on the process of statistical evaluation of the results. But the subject matter of the survey, for instance, may indicate or preclude some kinds of data collection method (thereby limiting the sampling options). Both the subject matter and the workload to be taken on by the respondent may influence the degree of cooperation obtained from those approached, also a sample design issue. Many of these matters need to be borne in mind when the precision of any estimate yielded by the survey has to be assessed. The design of the sample, particularly the method of sample selection, has a considerable bearing on the methods that can be used to calculate the variance of those estimates.

Reconciling priorities

Where there are multiple objectives, the priorities should also be determined. Sometimes the different objectives set out in an initial project brief may indicate different sampling approaches. If so, some objectives may have to be abandoned or relegated in priority or a compromise may be required. In reaching a compromise the relative priority of the different objectives should be indicated.

An essential factor, sometimes overlooked, is the general question of sample 'quality'. How good a sample do we need? It may sound heretical to suggest that we should ever accept, or even aim for, anything but the best, but in practice it is not always essential to strive for perfection. This is not a condonement of slipshod or incompetent work but a recognition that other factors may outweigh the requirement for top quality. The important thing is to match the quality of the sampling to other aspects of the task. If the principal information we are gathering is inherently imprecise (depending on the interpretation of question wording, for instance), then to strive for disproportionate accuracy in the sampling process may in some cases be less important than maximising the sample size.

There are times when a rough and ready sample is justified. In a pilot survey, the main concerns are often to establish whether the questionnaire 'works', whether respondents understand the questions and find them relevant and easy to answer, and to see what broad kinds of answers are given. Here getting a quality sample may be less relevant than ensuring that a good variety of people are interviewed. A pilot survey may, on the other hand, sometimes be used to see how well the proposed sampling method works in practice.

In other cases only a rough estimate of the incidence of some attribute may be needed; it may be sufficient to establish that the incidence of an attribute is so low in the population that it can be ignored or discounted, or sufficiently high that it cannot. Where a survey is intended to repeat a similar exercise done in the past so that the results can be compared and the degree of change estimated, then matching the previous method of sampling may be more important than doing it 'right', and the precision of comparisons will always be limited by the size of the initial survey. In such circumstances the method chosen to meet the objectives might be different from what would be chosen if there were no prior survey.

For some purposes, however, a correctly designed, carefully planned and rigorously executed sampling procedure is essential. Where crucial decisions of investment or policy hinge on the results, or where the results are to be subject to public or hostile scrutiny, we must have confidence in the results, and that confidence is founded on knowing that the survey has been carried out to high standards. Sampling is largely under our control and we cannot afford to allow it to be the weakest link in the chain.

Probability and non-probability sampling

There is a fundamental division in sampling between 'probability' and 'non-probability' sampling methods. The division centres on whether or not it is possible to estimate the probability of a sample member's being selected. 'Probability' methods do not require that every member of the population have an *equal* probability of selection, but rather that the probability, or the relative probability, of selection of each member be known, either in advance or once the selection has been made. Whatever the actual process of selection, which can take many forms, knowing the probability of selection provides us with more confidence in the statistical treatment of the results. Statistical theory rests on known probabilities and a sound theory based approach is only possible for data sets where probabilities are known with at least reasonable certainty.

Non-probability methods should not be dismissed out of hand. Often there may be no practical alternative. If the objectives of a survey determine a method of data collection that makes a probability sample impossible, then a non-probability sample will have to do, and will often do very well. A farmer taking a sample of wheat to determine its moisture content does not laboriously select each grain individually or even ensure that all parts of the heap in the barn are sampled from. A scientist carrying out an experiment on sheep may allocate his batch of sheep randomly between treatment and control groups but he may have had little say in how that batch of sheep were selected from the total population of sheep. The difference (whether in money, resources or time) between the cost of a probability sample and a pragmatic non-probability alternative may be so great as to render the former unacceptable. A requirement to carry out all fieldwork within a critical and very narrow time-span may preclude full probability sampling methods. Where experience shows a method to be reliable, or where the overall method of selection can be shown (or even reasonably presumed) to have no or little bearing on the objectives, a non-probability sample may yield valuable and valid information.

What is certainly true is that more care and caution are needed in the interpretation of results derived from non-probability samples, and the precision of estimates derived from them is more difficult to estimate. However, the operative word is *more*. Results from even the best probability sample require care in interpretation and a constant awareness that samples are fallible.

There is a great danger in supposing that because a sample is a pure random sample it is therefore an accurate representation of the population it represents. The researcher may have done everything possible to ensure that no non-random influences have occurred, but should not on that account be complacent about the quality of the results. The most carefully drawn sample can still turn out to be noticeably biased through sheer bad luck. Two identically drawn random samples will invariably yield different results, so at least one of them is 'wrong'. There is also the question of non-sampling errors, which this book does not attempt to cover, and which can apply to probability and non-probability samples alike.

1.4   Defining the constraints

Sample surveys are practical exercises and have to be carried out in the real world. The theory of sampling and sample design has to be tempered with the practicalities of locating and extracting information from the prospective sample members.

A sampling plan put together without an understanding of the limitations of the materials available, and most particularly of the real operating conditions under which fieldworkers collect the data, is likely to lead to unrealistic expectations on the part of those commissioning the survey. It is also likely to lead to failure on the part of those conducting the survey to deliver in accordance with the (unrealistic) specifications. At worst it may result in hasty corrective action being taken mid-way through a research project, as problems become apparent, to modify the methods being used.

It is therefore in everyone's interest to ensure that the constraints within which a survey will be carried out, over and above those implied by the project plan, are understood in advance. The sampling plan should therefore contain statements of the assumptions made in arriving at the recommended design, and the constraints within which the plan has to be executed. Such constraints may include:

- limitations imposed on the choice of data collection methodology by the objectives or subject matter or by logistic restrictions;
- the availability of sampling frames, the extent to which these are comprehensive, up-to-date and reliable, and the level of detail they offer;
- where relevant, the information available against which the results delivered by the sample can be assessed;
- any legal, ethical, cultural or similar considerations affecting or restricting the conduct of the survey;
- the need to conform to any precedent, or to follow the design or methodology of another piece of work to allow comparisons to be drawn.

Cost and quality: the trade-off

Some apparent constraints may be negotiable (e.g. time and budget) or otherwise less firm than they may appear, where it can be shown that relaxing them would lead to a 'better value' end result. It is often advisable to consider, and possibly to table for discussion, more than one plan before a decision is made about the sample design. It is certainly essential to know how variations in the elements of the design or in the assumptions affect the final costs as well as the quality of the survey. For instance a response rate 5% below what was planned will probably have an adverse effect on both cost and quality, while requiring one additional interview per cluster (see section 1.12) may save money but could reduce the precision of estimates.

The issue of the trade-off between cost and quality is too complex to be covered systematically in this book. Most kinds of survey errors related to sampling can be reduced, at a cost. For a wide-ranging review of the questions of errors and costs see Groves [24].

But assessing the extent of such reduction is not a simple matter. The cost and the likely degree of reduction have to be weighed carefully, both against each other and against the objectives of the survey and the kinds of measures made by it. Striking a balance is not easy and researchers with different priorities or interests may differ considerably in their judgements of what should be sacrificed to what. It is very easy to criticise a sample (usually someone else's) for being inadequate in design quality or insufficiently rigorously executed, or even for being 'over-engineered'. The poor researchers responsible for making these decisions are at the mercy of both the ivory tower academic and the accountant, but should at least be satisfied in their own minds that their decisions with respect to sampling are guided by the principle of 'fitness for purpose', however they see that purpose.

1.5 Defining the population

At an early stage in the planning of the project a decision must be taken about the population to be studied. The *population* (sometimes referred to as the *universe*) is the totality that our sample is to represent. This is often made up simply of people, but it could also be a population of households, businesses, institutions, ships, shops, sheep or cars, or of events such as journeys or admissions to hospital. It is important to define the target population precisely. Is it just 'all people' or 'all adults' (if so, what defines an adult?) or some more specific group, such as 'persons aged 18–64 living in private households'. The target may of course be a very specialised population, such as 'all practising dentists' or 'all dental practices'.

Existing information about the size and nature of the defined survey population should be reviewed, as this may provide guidance for sample design. Are its members disproportionately concentrated in certain regions, or likely to be found in certain neighbourhoods? Can they be readily distinguished from other members of the population? Is there, in extreme cases, an available list of its members?

The 'survey unit' should also be defined. Are we surveying individuals about themselves, for instance, or are we surveying households or businesses but obtaining the information from one person in each?

In reality it may not be possible to ensure that the target population can be fully covered in a survey. There are groups in the general population which in any given survey it may be impractical to reach adequately or at all. These may include, depending on the circumstances:

- people in remote or sparsely populated areas (for logistical and cost reasons);
- people not in private households (people in hospitals, prisons, convents, boarding schools, at sea, etc.);
- people who are regularly away from home for long periods;
- people without telephones;
- people too mentally or physically incapacitated to undertake an interview;
- people with insufficient command of the language in which the survey is conducted or, where appropriate, inadequate literacy skills.

There is also the increasingly large group in the general population of people who simply *refuse* to cooperate in a survey. Unlike many of the other groups, this one may vary widely in size within whatever target population is defined, depending largely on the nature of the survey and the way in which potential respondents are approached.

A judgement must be made about the importance of such groups to the survey and the effect their omission or under-representation is likely to have on the results. The results from the sample can strictly be applied only to the sampled population. Can the excluded or under-represented groups be assumed to be sufficiently similar to the sampled population that they can be safely ignored, or should some attempt be made to include them? Is a surrogate respondent admissible (for instance, a relative answering on behalf of a severely ill person)? Can and should some of these groups be covered in a separate sample with a separate sample design and methodology? Or should we re-define the population to be covered? Should we, in short, have a formal separate definition of the 'survey population'?

1.6 Sampling frames

Having defined the population we must now work out how the sample is to be selected from it. For this we need a list, in some form, of all the potential sampling units. This list is known as the *sampling frame*. The ideal is to have a complete list of all members of the defined population, from which a sample can be selected in an appropriate way. This is occasionally encountered. In a survey of employees of a company commissioned by its management, a comprehensive, up-to-date and accurate list of all employees, with sufficient classificatory information, may reasonably be expected.

1.6.1 Population registers

In some countries a comprehensive and up-to-date population register may be available as a sampling frame. The information available about individuals may be limited, to perhaps name and address only, but it can be relied upon as a source of a true random sample of the population at a (current) point in time. As an example of this, the Swedish National Address Register (Statens Personaddressregister, SPAR) allows a sample of a user-specified number of names and addresses to be provided within defined bounds of geography, date of birth and gender. For face-to-face interviewing the sample can be effectively clustered by specifying small geographic units such as postal code areas. SPAR is used by the direct marketing industry for mailing lists and is also available for survey purposes. Because of the sensitive nature of the information held, such samples are provided subject to strict conditions of use. Surveys being by their nature more intrusive than direct mail campaigns, use of SPAR for this purpose may be subject to greater scrutiny. Specific approval has to be obtained for each survey from the authority controlling the register, and an application to use the register must state the scope and objectives of the survey.

Where such registers are available for commercial purposes, there may be a facility for individuals to insist that their names not be made available for marketing purposes and that they be excluded from any lists issued to direct marketers. For bona fide surveys it may be possible to have such people included in the sample of names provided. However, the benefits of this may be partly negated if such people turn out to be more reluctant to participate in the survey. Whether or not it is worth any extra effort or expense involved in including such people may depend on the proportion of the population they represent.

Other countries may have registers of households (such as SIFO in the Czech republic) or dwellings (like the British Postcode Address File).

In view of the general trend towards greater formal protection for the privacy of the individual, it is possible that the availability of such registers as currently exist may be restricted or withdrawn in future.

Where no full list is available as a sampling frame, a workable alternative must be sought which preserves as far as possible the spirit of unbiased selection, even though in practice not every individual in the population would be eligible for selection. For surveys of the general population, publicly available lists like electoral registers and telephone directories may be used. These lists, like most others in practice, are defective, and the reasons may vary from country to country. Electoral registers, even where they are available for sampling purposes, may be incomplete (depending largely on whether enrolment is compulsory or voluntary, and on the qualifications for enrolment), out of date because they may only be updated periodically or shortly before an election, or in some cases subject to political manipulation. Telephone directories are inevitably out of date even when they first appear and may be substantially (and increasingly) incomplete because subscribers insist on being omitted. Often the listed names are predominantly male. In spite of these shortcomings, both lists can often serve as a starting point for sampling from the general population.

1.6.2 Surrogate lists

An electoral register can serve as a list of *addresses* if duplicates can be removed (relatively easy if the list is available in electronic form). A popular method of sampling from the electoral register involves the assumption that dwellings containing no registered electors are randomly distributed, at least within neighbourhoods. If this is so, the addresses next door to addresses selected from the register should form a reasonable sample. The assumption can certainly be challenged, but there may be no preferable alternative.

Telephone directories have a particular deficiency when used as a sampling frame for telephone surveys. The availability of home telephones varies. In some developing countries coverage may be low and patchy. In advanced countries it may now be almost universal. However, in recent years in advanced countries the old problem of a large proportion of households not having telephones has been replaced by that of the increasing proportion of residential numbers not included in the published telephone directories. The extent of the problem will vary from country to country and reliable estimates of the proportion are usually hard to come by, but figures of up to 30% have been quoted. This has led to a more frequent insistence on a form of sampling that includes a proper proportion of unlisted numbers. Many surveys are carried out with samples drawn from the directories, but if people with unlisted ('silent', 'ex-directory') numbers are known or suspected to be materially atypical in some crucial respects, then to omit them could weaken, or at least erode confidence in, the sample.

Unlisted telephone numbers

Methods of allowing for including unlisted numbers in samples generally rely on the fact that residential telephone numbers have been allocated within narrow ranges (if a number exists, other numbers sharing all but the last few digits are also likely to exist) and that unlisted numbers are interspersed with listed ones. Where numbers are selected manually from printed directories (typically by selecting a random page, column and sequence within column) a randomising element can be introduced. Typically the number may be increased by 1 or the last digit may be replaced by a randomly selected one.

While perhaps open to objection on the grounds that they are not strictly random, these methods yield a sample with a reasonable proportion of unlisted numbers.

Where residential telephone directories are available in a usable electronic form (Electronic White Pages, or EWP) more sophisticated computerised methods may be used. The term 'random digit dialling' (RDD) is frequently used, in spite of its doubtful correctness.

Modern telephone systems generally have many more possible numbers than there are people in the population they serve so that the great majority of possible numbers are not in use. It is clearly beneficial to reduce as far as possible the proportion of unconnected numbers in the randomly selected sample to be used.

The usual procedure is to determine what ranges of numbers are actually in use for residential subscribers, and therefore the ranges within which other, unlisted, numbers should lie. A list of all EWP numbers is compiled and sorted into numerical order. If the *potential* numbers are regarded as a series of 100-number blocks (within each of which all numbers have all but the last two digits in common) it can then readily be seen which blocks are in use, and how many listed residential numbers are in each. Blocks with a specified minimum number of numbers (usually, but not necessarily, one) then form the sampling frame for practical purposes. (Blocks of sizes other than 100 can, of course, be used.)

A file is generated of all possible numbers within those blocks. This file can be compared with the EWP and listed residential numbers flagged. It can also be compared with the Electronic Yellow Pages to remove known business numbers (there will still be some unlisted business numbers). The proportion of non-existent numbers, though still high, is now generally manageable. How high this proportion is will depend on the telephone company's policy and practice of allocating numbers and may vary considerably. If the numbers are dialled by a computer and the telephone exchange equipment is modern, unallocated numbers can be detected and discarded by the computer very quickly, so that the additional unproductive interviewing time is minimised.

There are three complications inherent in the inclusion of unlisted numbers. Firstly, calls to unlisted numbers are less likely to be answered. A number may be dedicated to a fax machine or modem, which can usually be detected. But the number may be unlisted, perhaps for security reasons, precisely because there is generally no-one there to answer it, or the subscriber may be using a call-screening device, or the number may be an unlisted business number and unattended during the evening or weekend when much interviewing of the general public takes place. There is, of course, no way of reliably telling which applies, and only the last of these should not be considered as affecting the response rate.

Secondly, if an answer is obtained from an unlisted residential number, a higher rate of refusal (or at least reluctance) to be interviewed may be expected. People who do not want their numbers generally known are often suspicious about and unreceptive to an unsolicited approach from strangers. 'Where did you get my number from?' is often the first response, from those who have not already hung up.

Thirdly, increasing numbers of households have multiple telephone lines, often only one of them being listed. This means that such households have a higher probability of selection. Where a sampling procedure involves unlisted numbers it is advisable to include in the questionnaire a question to determine the number of separate numbers (not handsets) used by the household for voice calls, and to ensure that this is allowed for at the analysis stage (see section 1.14).

A further, related problem is the emergence of a sector of the population that no longer has a fixed home telephone line but relies on mobile telephones. These may or may not be included in directories and there has in the past been a general reluctance to make calls to mobile phones (where these can be recognised from their number) for survey purposes, if only because owners might be charged for incoming calls and codes of practice generally prohibit any procedure that 'adversely affects' a respondent.

In an increasing number of countries telephone subscribers may apply to have their number added to a register of numbers that are not to be used for direct marketing purposes ('do-not-call lists'). Such registers may be maintained by government bodies, telephone companies or by direct-marketing trade bodies. Telephone sales organisations are expected to ensure that these numbers are not called. The degree of enforceability and the effectiveness of the registers in providing protection from unwanted sales calls may vary. There is also variation in who is expected to take account of such lists. Charities, political parties and religious bodies may or may not be exempt from any restriction, though bona fide survey organisations are generally not restricted. As with the use of population registers, the situation in any country is subject to change.

Loosely defined populations

In many cases, the definition of the survey population may not permit any reasonably exact prior estimate of its incidence among the general population, or any short cut to locating its members. For a survey among 'prospective buyers of new cars', for instance, we could not necessarily rely on prior information. Part of the trouble lies in the necessary vagueness of the definition, and indeed of the possible alternative ways of expressing it. Do we mean 'people who have decided to buy one (and are perhaps only weighing up which and when)' or 'people who are thinking about whether to buy one'? In either case there will be no list available. Individuals may vary over time in the firmness of their intention with changes in their family or financial circumstances or in the general economic climate. The person with no intention of buying a car today may be a prospect next week after the current car breaks down in the middle of a rainy night.

We may have to identify such people by contacting a more widely defined group and interviewing only those who qualify – a process generally known as *screening*. In practice we are surveying a broad population, but perhaps asking only one question of most of the people contacted. Usually, and preferably, the opportunity would be taken to ask a few more questions of those people screened out, to provide at least some basic information about the quality of our overall sample and about how our survey population differs from the wider population. It should be noted that variations in the definition or in the questions used to determine whether a respondent matches it may have more effect on the estimated incidence of this group than variations in sampling methodology.

In attempting to locate small minority groups it is sometimes possible to identify people who have taken part in a previous large-scale survey as fitting the requirements. If a sample of these is used it must be remembered that the quality of the new sample cannot be greater than that of the original sample and, because of a further element of non-response, will almost certainly be less. There is a potential problem of non-sampling errors if respondents' answers are coloured by their experience of being interviewed before. On the other hand, the elimination of a time-consuming and expensive screening process may allow a much larger sample to be achieved. However, the re-use of samples in this way is likely to be subject to restrictions imposed by Codes of Practice and in some cases by legislation.

Where a formal sampling frame is used it is often essential that it contain information that allows the survey units to be classified, if only geographically. Stratified and clustered sample designs (see below) require that the sampling frame be divisible into smaller units so that the selection of the sampling units can be made appropriately.

1.6.3   Surrogate procedures

In many cases the sampling frame will not contain the final survey units. A *multi-stage* sampling design may be used, with formal sampling frames not being used in all stages. In the first stage, for instance, the sampling frame may consist of medium sized geographic areas. Within each selected area there may be another sampling frame of very small areas, and within each selected small area there may be no formal sampling frame available so that another method must be used to select the final sampling units.

In some cases it is possible that the sampling frame may be, in part, constructed as one stage in the survey process. A sample of small areas may be selected, and in each small area a complete list of all dwellings is made by fieldworkers covering the whole area exhaustively (*enumeration*), and this would be the sampling frame for the next stage.

A review of the issues of using sampling frames is to be found in many books on the conduct of survey research and some on statistics. Moser and Kalton [44] is particularly down-to-earth and practical.

1.7   Simple random sampling

The 'purest' form of sample, and the simplest, is what is generally termed the 'simple random sample'. This is the kind of sample with which much of statistical theory and most statistical textbooks are concerned. It requires the simplest formulae and presents the fewest problems in interpretation of results.

Let us first consider what makes a sample a 'simple random' one. A simple random sample fulfils two requirements:

- the sample is 'random' because *every* member of the defined population has an *equal* chance of selection; and
- it is 'simple' because each member of the sample is selected independently of all others.

To these might be added a third requirement that each selected sample member should yield information of equal quality, that is, that the selected members should all be used, should all cooperate and should all contribute to the required extent. This is a subject of considerable practical importance to which we shall return later.

The first requirement implies that each member of the defined population must be known about, directly or indirectly, in other words that we have a complete and accurate sampling frame. He or she must either be individually listed in a source from which a selection can be made using a demonstrably random selection process, or be unambiguously identifiable through a process that produces an equivalent result.[2] Alternatively some subset to which he or she belongs must be capable of being selected with probability proportional to its size and the individual can then be selected within that. A multi-stage selection of a sample member does not in itself preclude randomness provided that the principle of equal probability is preserved. Multi-stage processes are discussed in more detail below.

Independence of selection means that groups of sample members should not be related to each other more closely than chance would permit and that no sample member is selected, or has his or her probability of selection increased or decreased, by the selection of any other member. By extension it implies that any multi-stage sampling process must be applied separately and independently for each selection.

The difficulty of meeting our two requirements, except in the most artificial and circumscribed situations, will be immediately evident. When we also consider the

---

[2] If, for instance, a sampling frame contains only a list of households and the number of persons in each, a selection might be made of 'the second person in household x', the ordering criterion, such as alphabetical order or ascending or descending order of age, having been agreed in advance.

problems presented by the third requirement, it should be clear that very few sample surveys can claim to have a true simple random sample.

A simple random sample is unbiased. There are other forms of sample selection that are also random and unbiased but that do not meet the criteria for a 'simple random' sample. There are also sampling methods that are unbiased but not truly random.

1.8 Multi-stage sampling

In selecting the members of a sample it is permissible, and often expedient, to use a more complex method of selection than simply picking individual entries from a single complete list. It is possible that the only list available is of groups or subsets of the population, so that initially a group has to be selected and then an individual within the group. The final sample is drawn in multiple stages. A sample drawn in this way could still be considered as a simple random sample as long as all the requirements of simple random sampling have been met. Specifically, the groups must not be selected in a way that upsets the principle of equal probability of selection of the individual sampling units. This means that any inequalities of probability arising at any stage must be compensated for at another stage.

Consider the case where a sample of dwellings is to be selected and the only sampling frame available is a list showing the numbers of dwellings in each of a number of small geographical areas. The individual dwelling is selected in two stages: first an area is randomly selected, but with a probability proportional to the number of dwellings it contains; then a list is made of all dwellings in the area and a single dwelling is selected strictly at random (with equal probability) within that small area. A large area has a better-than-average chance of selection, but if it is selected, each dwelling has a lower chance of individual selection than it would have had if it had been in a smaller *selected* area. The net result is that the chances of selection of all dwellings remain equal, irrespective of the sizes of the areas in which they are located.[3]

The probability of the selection of a sample member in a multi-stage sample design is the *product* of the probabilities of selection of the unit within which the member is located at each stage. Strictly these are conditional probabilities: the probability of selection of a unit given that the previous-stage unit has been selected.

The same principle may be applied to sampling involving more than two stages, and if at each additional stage the principle of selection with probability proportional to size is applied, the sample may still be considered a simple random sample. However, in this example the procedure was used to select one sample member only. To preserve the principle of true simple random sampling each member would have to be selected individually by the same process. In practice multi-stage sampling is generally employed when *multiple* selections are to be made at each stage. In the example above, for instance, some large areas may be chosen, then several small areas within

---

[3] If there are N dwellings in the population and n_a dwellings in an area then that area should be given a probability of selection of n_a/N. The probability of selection of the dwellings within the area is $1/n_a$ so the overall probability of selection remains $1/N$ whatever the size of the area.

each and finally several persons or households within each selected small area. As long as the principle of selection with probability proportional to size is preserved (which in this case means choosing the same number of small areas within each large one and the same number of households within each small one) the sample can still be said to be random, but it is no longer a *simple* random sample. Now the final sample members are not selected independently. If A and B are households in the same small area and A is selected, B has a higher probability of selection than if the households were selected individually by a multi-stage process. The effects of this 'clustering' are discussed later.

1.9   Stratification

Where the objectives of the survey require it, the population to be sampled is often divided into a series of mutually exclusive identifiable groups. Usually this is done if these are to be sampled differently or if it is felt essential to control the proportions of the sample that they represent. This process, *stratification*, is equivalent to splitting the population into a series of sub-populations (*strata*), each of which is sampled separately. The number of interviews to be conducted in each stratum is normally determined in advance. The sub-populations are then recombined at the analysis stage. Stratification requires a separate sampling frame for each stratum. Depending on the circumstances, the sub-populations may be sampled in proportion to their sizes or disproportionately.

1.9.1   Proportionate stratification

Proportionate stratification imposes a measure of control over the composition of the sample. It ensures that the sample has the same characteristics as the population in respect of one attribute (or combination of attributes). If that attribute is materially related to the objectives of the survey, this can be beneficial.

If, for instance, it is known or expected that certain of the principal attributes being measured by a survey will show a high level of variation between strata, then those estimates will be made more precise by stratifying the sample: measures not showing such variation will not be made more precise but neither will they be adversely affected. Proportionate stratification generally has no adverse effects, relative to a simple random sample: it may increase the precision of some estimates but will not of itself reduce that of any others.[4]

---

[4] The standard error of an estimate of a proportion from a proportionately stratified random sample is estimated by (5.2) in Moser and Kalton [44]:

$$\text{s.e.}(\hat{p}) = \sqrt{\frac{\sum_i n_i \hat{p}_i(1 - \hat{p}_i)}{n^2}},$$

where n is the total sample size, n_i the sample size in the ith stratum and $\hat{p}_i$ the estimated proportion in the ith stratum having the attribute concerned, and where the n_i are reasonably large. This value is maximised when all the $\hat{p}_i$ are equal.

In estimating the standard error of a proportion from a proportionately stratified random sample, the estimated proportions in each of the strata should be taken into consideration. In our experience this separate calculation is often overlooked and no allowance is made for the effect of stratification in assessing the confidence limits of an estimate or the significance of differences. This is our first example of the dangers of treating any sample data as though they were from a simple random sample. It will certainly not be the last.

The ratio of the estimated standard error allowing for stratification to that without allowance is itself a useful measure. The square of this ratio is the *stratification effect*. This is a component of the *design effect*, and is used as a measure of the improvement brought about by stratification. It must be remembered that the stratification effect, like the design effect, applies only to the estimate for which it was calculated and each measure yielded by a survey will have its own design effect, to which the stratification effect will make a varying contribution. Design effects can be estimated for a range of more complex survey designs and this will be explored in detail in Chapter 3.

Defining the strata

The selection of the strata must be considered carefully and based on some knowledge of the issues involved. Variables selected for stratification must be those for which reliable information is available. In surveys of the general population, geography is often used as a stratifier. The overall area to be covered by the survey is divided into a number of areas of *known* population, which is often administratively convenient as well as statistically beneficial. For instance, in a survey measuring newspaper readership, estimates for regional newspapers may benefit significantly from increased precision while estimates for national newspapers would probably also benefit to some extent. A sample of employees of a company may be stratified by function or grade (e.g. production, sales, administration), or perhaps by function within location. The most important thing is that the proportions of the population represented by the various strata should be known with certainty. Stratification may be unrelated to respondent type: where the survey relates to short-term behaviour, it may be appropriate to stratify interviewing equally by day of week to avoid a source of potential bias.

Note that this is not the same as *quota sampling* (see section 1.16). For stratification, the stratum to which any potential sample member belongs must be known before selection, that is, that sample member must be selected *from* one of the designated populations. This does not preclude the use of quota sampling in conjunction with (usually geographic) stratification, though a stratified quota sample is still essentially a quota sample and subject to all the limitations that presents.

1.9.2   Disproportionate stratification

Disproportionate stratification, the effect of which is normally corrected by weighting at the analysis stage, can be employed for a number of reasons, depending on the objectives of the survey. As an example we will consider a survey designed principally to explore the differences between people in three kinds of area, metropolitan, other urban and rural.

- If maximum precision of the estimates of differences between the three groups is the sole objective, then if nothing is known about them the objective would probably be best achieved if each of these three area types were made a stratum and had an equal sample size, irrespective of the proportions of the overall population in each. This would maximise the sensitivity of the comparisons but (unless the three strata had equal populations) at the expense of some loss of precision for overall estimates taking the three strata together.

- Disproportionate stratification can be used to ensure that adequate sample sizes are available to allow certain important subgroups to be examined in appropriate detail if they are of particular importance to the objectives of the study. For instance one particular metropolitan area might be considered as being of particular interest, be made a fourth stratum and be allocated additional interviews to provide additional precision for estimates based on that stratum alone.

- It can be used to ensure that the greatest possible overall precision is achieved for the most important measures in the survey, though often at the cost of a loss in precision for other measures. If it is known in advance that the variance of the principal attributes the survey is seeking to measure is different in different strata, then suitably over-sampling the strata within which those variables have higher variance will yield more precise overall estimates. For example, personal income may be known to be more variable in metropolitan areas than in rural areas and over-sampling the metropolitan areas may be considered appropriate. This also applies to proportions: proportion estimates closer to 50% have a higher variance than those closer to 100% or to zero. For each stratum the sampling fraction (that is, the sample as a proportion of the population it represents) should be proportional to the *standard deviation* of the estimate to provide the most precise estimate overall. If our strata contained equal populations and the three estimated incidences of an attribute were 40%, 30% and 20%, then the strata should contain approximately 36%, 34% and 29% respectively of the sample to minimise the standard error of the overall estimate.

- It can improve efficiency where the direct cost of interviewing varies from stratum to stratum. Rural areas may incur much higher costs per interview because of additional travelling time for interviewers. Saving money through a reduced number of rural interviews may allow more than that number of additional interviews in urban areas with an overall gain in precision. The stratum sampling fraction should be inversely proportional to the square root of the cost per interview in that stratum for maximum efficiency.

Sampling units of different sizes

Where the sampling units vary in size, stratification can be used to minimise the variance of estimates. This does not usually apply to consumer surveys but for surveys of retail establishments, farms or businesses, where there is often a wide range of sizes, stratification by size and disproportionate sampling of the 'large units' strata can improve the precision of turnover related estimates. For instance, in a survey designed to estimate total sales of margarine, sampling a disproportionately high number of supermarkets and a correspondingly lower number of corner shops would produce a more precise estimate.

Disproportionate stratification will only fully benefit such measures as it is *designed* to benefit. If a sample is designed to improve the precision of one measure it may improve the precision of related measures in the same survey but it may equally make others less precise. As will be noticed from the examples quoted, there can be a number of reasons for disproportionate sampling. Several of them may operate together in the case of any single survey, but they might point in different directions. The final decision on the sampling fractions to be employed for each stratum will then be the result of a series of compromises and above all judgemental decisions about the priorities of the survey.

There are established mathematical methods for optimising the allocation of samples between strata when the survey concentrates on a group whose incidence (or mean) varies from stratum to stratum, and these are discussed at some length by Kish [35] and Cochran [9] among others. However, it appears that except where great variation between strata is expected the use of these formulae is unlikely to be very helpful, for the following reasons.

- The decisions, which must be made at the planning stage, presume accurate foreknowledge of such matters as the incidence of the attributes to be measured, the pattern of variation in that incidence and the actual costs of fieldwork. If the assumptions made prove to be incorrect the 'optimised' sample may prove to be less than optimal or even disadvantageous. Experience of past surveys on similar topics and with similar samples will of course be helpful.
- There is inevitably a large measure of personal judgement in determining the relative priorities of conflicting requirements, especially when there are several interested parties in the planning of the survey. Balancing the relative needs of overall precision and precision of comparisons between important subsets of the sample is itself a difficult task and one on which the theory sheds no light.
- Optimisation can only be done in respect of one or a few variables and will often result in reduced precision for others. Losses in precision of non-priority estimates may be unacceptable. Adverse effects of disproportionate stratification on some parts of the survey should always be considered.
- Business or policy considerations may over-ride objective statistical considerations in respect of some measures or some particular subset of the population. In a national survey on health issues, for instance, regional health authorities may insist on minimum (or equal) sample numbers in their areas, irrespective of the population distribution.

In any case, the optimised allocation is frequently not very different from proportionate sampling and even when it is, the increase in precision it yields can be surprisingly small. In any attempt to optimise the allocation the likely change in precision should be calculated for both the key measures and for selected others.

The one case where formal optimisation is likely to be consistently beneficial is where there are large differences in 'size' between the sampling units. However, even here some adjustment of the optimised scheme will often be made to take other considerations into account.

1.10 Post-stratification

In stratification proper, the strata are predefined and sampled separately: it is possible to allocate each person selected to a stratum prior to the interview. However, there are many cases where information about the composition of the population is available and where it would be desirable to allocate potential respondents to a stratum but where there is no information available in advance about the individuals to allow this. For example, an age-within-sex distribution of the population may be available, but there may be no indication of the age or sex of individuals in the sampling frame.

Given that the distribution of the population is known and that the age and sex of each respondent is known after interview, age/sex strata can be defined and each respondent allocated to the appropriate one following the interview (hence the term *post*-stratification). The strata have not been sampled separately and the number in each age/sex group has not been fixed in advance, but the known distribution gives us the number of interviews to be 'expected' in each stratum if the sample fully represents the population.

The actual number of interviews in each stratum can be expected to differ from that predicted by the known age/sex distribution of the population. The differences would ideally be randomly distributed, but any shortcomings and biases in the execution of the sampling may mean that there is more variation than expected and some of the differences may be systematic as a result of systematic variations in the response rate (e.g. higher for women and older people than for men and the young).

Balancing strata by weighting

Post-stratification is applied so that material differences between actual and 'expected' numbers of respondents per stratum can be countered by 'weighting' the individual respondents. In its simplest form this means giving each respondent in a stratum a weight that ensures that the sum of those weights is the same as the 'expected' number of interviews. When analysing the data the weights of respondents are summed rather than the actual numbers of respondents being counted. This subject is covered in the following chapter. For the moment it is sufficient to remember that the weighting process may increase the accuracy of estimates but also has the side-effect of increasing their variance, and thus of reducing their precision.

The weighting used to redress the deliberate imbalances introduced into a sample by deliberate disproportionate (pre-)stratification is also a form of post-stratification. This is a special case, however, which does not necessarily reduce the precision of estimates, provided the calculation is done properly.

Post-stratification has the advantage of removing some biases, but as with strat-ification proper it can only align the composition of the sample with that of the population for those characteristics that define the strata. It also requires that reli-able information be available for defining the strata and the size of each. Appropriate choice of post-stratification variables is important: experience of working with a particular population may provide information on which variables are likely to pro-vide the greatest measure of control, in terms of being regularly related to response rates.

Post-stratification will almost invariably be done to bring the (weighted) sample composition into line with the population. Only under exceptional circumstances would it be used to force the sample to some different composition.

1.11   Systematic (interval) sampling

Rather than simply selecting units from a sampling frame individually at random, it is often beneficial to make the selection in a way that ensures that the selected sample reflects the distribution of some attribute that may be felt to be relevant to the survey. We may for instance wish to select a sample from a list of people in a way that accurately reflects the range of environments in which they live. To do this we should sort the list by some suitable indicator such as the population density of the area in which the individual lives. The list is now ordered to represent the spectrum of environments and by spreading selections evenly throughout the list we can ensure a reasonably representative spread in the sample.

Suppose that a sample of n is required from such a population with N members. Then on average each of the n sample members can be considered to represent k members of the population, where $k = N/n$. Where n is small relative to N, k is usually in practice rounded to the nearest integer. If the population members are listed in ascending or descending order we can select at random one of the first k members and every kth thereafter. The selections will be spaced at equal intervals down the list and k is the *sampling interval* (hence the name *interval sampling* also given to this method).

Where n is a high proportion of N, k is unlikely to be an integer, and a fractional value should be used for the interval. The initial selection would be made by taking as a starting point a random real number x greater than zero and not greater than k and selecting the population member whose sequence number is the integer equal to or next greater than x. x is then replaced by $x + k$ and the next member selected in the same way, and so on until n members have been selected from the list. This is like dividing the sample up into a series of n 'ranges' of as equal a size as possible and selecting a constant number (in this case one) from each. This is somewhat akin to stratification, though membership of the 'strata' is arbitrary.

Systematic sampling is random in that each member of the population has an equal chance of selection. It is not a 'simple random' process in that the selections are not made independently: selection of the first determines the selection of all others. However, the difference is negligible for practical purposes and this is a small price to pay if a dangerous source of potential bias can be neutralised. Depending on the circumstances, systematic sampling could be used as an alternative to stratification, or it could be used within strata as a further way of controlling the composition of the sample.

However, there are possible pitfalls. If n is small and there is considerable variation in density (in the above example), there is a possibility of bias. In this example, if x is small relative to k, *all* the members selected will tend to have higher densities within each range, or where x is large, all the members selected will have lower densities. Where this is likely to be a problem, an independent selection can be made within each range (so that the sampling interval is no longer constant but should have a mean close to k). It has also been suggested that $k/2$ should be taken as the starting point.

Systematic sampling can also be used where it is appropriate to select sample units with unequal probabilities and this is covered in section 1.14.

1.12   Cluster sampling

A randomly selected sample taken from the general population would result in the selected sample members being distributed across the whole area, with very few of them being close together. If the survey is being conducted by telephone or by post this may not matter. If it is to be conducted face-to-face the amount of unproductive but costly travelling required of the fieldworkers may make the project impracticable. A pragmatic solution is to arrange the sample so that interviews are physically grouped into workable areas. Typically, a multi-stage sample design, usually involving geographical stratification, is employed to select workably small areas, or sampling points, within which the final selection of a set number of respondents is to be made, the number being determined in part by what is considered to be a reasonable work-load for an individual interviewer. Depending on the size of the area selected, respondents may be more or less tightly 'clustered'. Clearly, the closer together they are the less time the fieldworker has to spend moving between them to move on to the next interview or to return to make call-backs on the hard-to-reach selections.

Sometimes interviewers are provided with a single selected address (a *starting address*) and required to follow a set of rules for selecting addresses at which to interview (relative to the starting address) and respondents within households. This is the lowest-cost option but it has the disadvantage that the resulting interviews are concentrated in a very small area. How much this matters will vary depending in part on the subject matter of the survey, but it is always a potential cause for concern.

The advantage of such clustering is that it allows a greater number of interviews to be achieved within a fixed budget, and the increased precision from the greater number may very well more than offset any loss in precision resulting from the clustering. The statistical effects of clustering are discussed in more detail in Chapter 3. See Harris [26] for a discussion of the trade-off between cost and precision. It should also be borne in mind that field costs, even with field overheads, are not the only costs of a survey and that the costs of stages of a project other than fieldwork may not be affected by the choice of sampling method.

Cluster sampling may also make practicable what would otherwise be impracticable. For example, consider a survey of international air travellers departing from a major airport. Sampling among all passengers with no sampling frame would be haphazard rather than random and extremely difficult to administer. Sampling a small proportion of flights and a high proportion of passengers on each selected flight gives a reasonable measure of probability of selection, though at the expense of a clustering effect. If adequate passenger and flight statistics for that airport can be obtained (they would certainly exist, but may not be easy to get), then the probability of a flight's selection can be ascertained. If the number of passengers travelling on the selected flight is known, an estimate can be made of the individual's probability of selection. There remains, of course, the question of how the individual passengers are best selected from all those travelling on the flight, but at least part of the problem has been brought under control.

Clustering is a part of sample design normally associated with face-to-face surveys. Where interviewing is conducted by telephone there is normally no need to cluster the interviews. Selected telephone numbers can be randomly spread over the geographical area being covered and randomly assigned to the different interviewers. However, at the analysis stage of a large survey it may be worth treating the *interviewers* as clusters. This may help the process of overall field quality monitoring by indicating whether there is more variation than would be expected between the results of individual interviewers' work.

1.13   Complex samples

Stratification, multi-stage selection and clustering are often used in combination, but with the object of, as far as possible, preserving the principle of selection with 'known' probability. Figure 1.1 illustrates pictorially the way these may be applied, singly or in combination. It represents a hypothetical town in which twenty dwellings are to be selected. (The town may of course be one part of a much larger sample.) It is divided by main roads into five areas containing, conveniently, roughly equal numbers of dwellings. These areas may be regarded either as strata or as Primary Sampling Units. These areas may be further subdivided if necessary. In reality it is unlikely that a single town as part of a larger sample would be treated in the more complex ways illustrated.

1.14   Selection with unequal probability

So far we have been dealing with samples in which each unit in the population has an equal probability of selection, at least within its stratum of the population. Frequently it is appropriate to design the sample in such a way that members are selected with

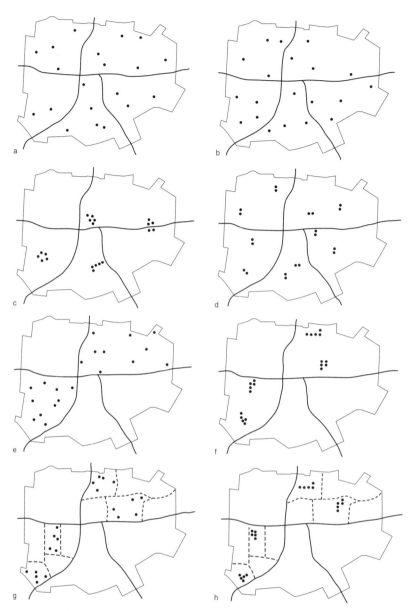

Figure 1.1   Alternative sampling schemes. Each panel shows a sample of size 20 that diverges from simple random sampling but still preserves the principle of equal (or at least known) probability of selection. (PSU, primary sampling unit.) (a) Simple random sample: 20 individual selections. (b) Stratified random sample: four random selections in each stratum. (c) Cluster sample: four randomly selected clusters of five. (d) Stratified clustering: two randomly selected clusters per stratum. (e) Two-stage selection: two PSUs selected, with 10 random selections in each. (f) Two-stage cluster sample: two PSUs selected, with two randomly selected clusters of five in each. (g) Three-stage selection: two PSUs selected, two secondary units selected from each, five random selections within each secondary unit. (h) Three-stage cluster sample: two PSUs selected, two secondary units selected from each, one cluster of five in each secondary unit.

unequal probability, because that is part of the research design. Often it is unavoidable because of the nature of the available sampling frame.

Selection with known probability is more fundamental than selection with equal probability. It is often thought that the most important requirement for a sample is that it should be representative. In practice what is important is that it should be *projectable* to the population it purports to represent.

1.14.1   Selection with probability proportional to size

The concept of selection with probability proportional to the value of some quantitative attribute is one that will be met with frequently in practical sample selection. For practical purposes only we will call this attribute 'size', though size could mean physical length, area or volume, turnover or quantity of goods produced (of a business), number of members (of a household) or any such measure.

For instance, if we want to measure the sales of brands of margarine through retail outlets we would ideally sample retail outlets with probability proportional to their total margarine sales. Since that is one of the things we would presumably be trying to measure, some other objective measure would be needed such as total store turnover, if available, or some more readily observable surrogate such as estimated floor area or number of checkouts. The reason for selecting with probability proportional to 'size' in this case is that we are in effect sampling and counting the sales transactions made by the selected stores, not the stores themselves. The sample is a sample of the retail 'business' rather than of the stores. By selecting the stores with probability proportional to 'size' the probability of selection of each transaction becomes at least approximately equal.

Similarly, in a survey of shareholders of a company with a view to predicting the likely support for a resolution to be put to the shareholders at an Annual General Meeting it would be appropriate to sample shareholders from the company's share register with probability of selection proportional to shareholding (or voting power), as such resolutions normally require the support of holders of a majority of the shares. This is efficient, as the simple proportion of *selected* shareholders in favour would represent an unbiased estimate of the proportion of shares held by shareholders in favour. The most extreme alternative, of selecting shareholders with equal probability, would require each shareholder's response to be weighted in proportion to the number of shares held, the weighting producing a marked reduction in the precision of the estimate. Companies generally exhibit a very high variation in the number of shares held by individual shareholders, with a small number of the largest shareholders accounting for a considerable proportion of the issued shares. It would be very easy for this small number of very influential shareholders to be badly over- or under-represented in a sample. An intermediate strategy, of stratifying the shareholders by size of holding and separately sampling, say, small, medium and large shareholders separately, with equal probability *within stratum*, would still require weighting by size of holding, and thus would involve some loss of precision.

The simplest way of selecting one item from a set with probability proportional to size is to use a variation of the 'interval sampling' method described in section 1.11. A list is prepared in which each item appears with its individual size, and also with the *cumulative* or running total of sizes shown. A random number between zero and the cumulative total for the whole list is selected. The item in the list with the lowest cumulative total equal to or greater than this random number is selected. The probability of selection is therefore proportional to the size of the difference between successive cumulative values. Notice that the order in which the items are listed does not influence the probability of selection.

Use of systematic sampling

Where, as is more usual, multiple selections have to be made from the list, systematic sampling can be used. The list can be ordered, either by the size itself or by some other relevant measure, to ensure an appropriate spread in the selections. Suppose the objective is to select local government areas as part of a multi-stage sampling procedure. Instead of just listing the areas, they are listed with their individual 'sizes' and a cumulative total is built up, working down the list. N is now the overall cumulative total of 'sizes'. k is calculated as before, and a number x between zero and k is selected randomly (both x and k can be real). The area is selected whose cumulative total is equal to x or is the smallest greater than x. x is then replaced by $x + k$ and the next member selected in the same way, and so on until n members have been selected from the list, in essentially the same way as for sampling with equal probability.

Figure 1.2 shows an example of using an interval selection method to select a set number of schools with different numbers of pupils from a list. The list in this case is arranged alphabetically but could be ordered in some other appropriate manner such as size of school, age of school or social deprivation index of the catchment area. The presumption is that equal numbers of pupils will then be selected from each selected school.

There is the possibility that, where the size of members of the population varies greatly and where a relatively large number must be selected, some units may be chosen more than once. A unit whose 'size' is greater than k *must* be chosen at least once and one whose size is greater then $2k$ must be chosen at least twice. The most appropriate course of action depends on what kind of units are being selected, but there are a number of options.

- If the selected unit can itself be suitably subdivided it may be appropriate to replace that unit with its various subdivisions (for instance, a local government area could be replaced by its constituent wards).
- In multi-stage sampling it may be appropriate to increase the number of selections within that unit at the next stage.
- The population could be stratified into two or more sub-populations based on size and the strata (each with less variation in size) could be sampled separately, with different sampling fractions, and balanced by weighting in the final results.

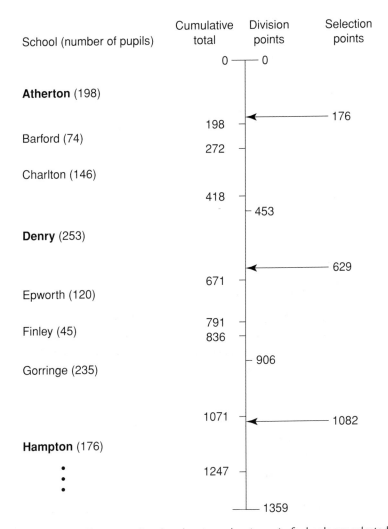

Figure 1.2   Selection with probability proportional to size. A number ($n = 10$) of schools are selected from a list of schools with a total of $N = 4530$ pupils, with probability proportional to the number of pupils. The sampling interval is $k = N / n = 453$. The first selection point x is a randomly selected number in the range 1 to k (in this case $x = 176$). The ith selection point is $x + k(i - 1)$. Boldface indicates selected schools.

- If the unit is a final sampling unit and cannot be subdivided (for instance, a shareholder in the example above) it may be used once, but the results from it can be weighted by the number of times it was selected.

The choice of measure to determine the probability of selection is not necessarily automatic. A survey of companies might select firms in proportion to annual turnover, profit, expenditure on research and development, number of employees, number of apprentices, market capitalisation, electricity usage or some other measure, or with equal probability, depending on the objectives of the survey. It is possible that multiple and conflicting objectives might require that a sample be looked at in more than one way. For instance, in a survey of retail grocery stores it may be important to estimate both what proportion of stores have a particular attribute and what proportion of business they account for – indeed the comparison of the two estimates can itself be enlightening. The first measure would suggest that the sample should be drawn with all stores in the population having an equal chance of selection and the second that they should be selected with probability proportional to turnover. In such a case the probability of selection of individual units is unlikely to be strictly in accordance with either principle; the sample would follow a compromise design aimed at satisfying both requirements to the best possible extent. The essential thing is to ensure that enough is known about both the population and the sample members to assess the relative probability of selection of the individual store in relation to each of these measures.

1.14.2   Selection with probability not known in advance

Unequal selection probability may arise when the probability of selection is not known in advance. In some cases it may be possible to introduce a mechanism at the point of selection to avoid such imbalance, but often this is not possible, and the inequality has to be accepted as part of the selection process. Once again, the important thing is to know as precisely as possible what the probability of selection of each member of the sample was.

A similar situation arises where individuals are being sampled directly but their probability of selection may be determined by circumstances. Members of a sample drawn from patients in a hospital at an arbitrary point in time would have probabilities of selection proportional to their lengths of stay. The longer they are there the more likely they are to be included. Had the sample been drawn from *admissions*, and thus with equal probability of selection, the characteristics of the sample might be quite different. Which method is appropriate depends on the objectives and subject matter of the survey.

Sampling individual persons by initially sampling households is a very frequently encountered case where differential selection probabilities come into play. Frequently we may have a sampling frame of households and not know how many eligible persons are to be found in each household until the household is approached ('eligible' persons are those who fall within the definition of the population being sampled). If a random sample of households is selected with equal probability and one eligible person is then selected in each selected household, then clearly those in small households will have a disproportionately high probability of selection. The probability will be inversely proportional to the number of eligible persons in the household.

There are field procedures that can be used to overcome this and to equalise the probabilities of selection in such a situation. One involves compiling a single list of all the eligible persons in each selected household in turn and using every kth person on the list or those whose names correspond with pre-designated randomly selected sequence numbers. These procedures clearly remove the household size bias but they present operational difficulties. They assume that it is possible to obtain the necessary information from each selected household. Some households may be uncontactable or uncooperative and the number of eligible persons may not be otherwise ascertainable. The procedure may result in households containing eligible persons remaining unused, which is wasteful of the time spent in contacting that household. It may also result in more than one person within the same household being interviewed. This is generally to be avoided, partly because it can be difficult to keep the separate interviewees from influencing each other's responses and partly because it may introduce or exacerbate a clustering effect (see Chapter 3). Any saving in interviewer time is likely to be small.

Within-household sampling

Often the simplest course is to accept the variation in selection probabilities and to allow for it at the analysis stage, provided the probability of selection is known. If, as above, we have selected households with equal probability but we decide to select one person from each, we need a method of randomly selecting that person. There are, once again, a number of methods. Those of Kish [34, 35] and of Troldahl and Carter [57] require a list to be compiled of all eligible persons in the individual household in a predetermined sequence (e.g. in descending order of age within sex), and an individual is selected from the list by a procedure outside the control of the fieldworker, based on the sequence of the names.

A simpler method is to determine the number of eligible persons and then, when there is more than one, to seek to interview the (eligible) person who is the next (or last) to have a birthday. This is not strictly a *random* procedure since in any household the probability of selection of individuals is determined by how their birthdays are distributed throughout the year. However, it is unbiased and does not leave the fieldworker any discretion. It has also been found to perform as well as the more systematic methods in practice. A further advantage of the 'birthday rule' is that it is less invasive. In an age when people are increasingly suspicious of anything that looks like a threat to their privacy, a method that can be explained as, and seen to be, simply a selection mechanism is likely to provoke less resistance than what may look like the collection of private information for unknown and possibly nefarious purposes.

There is anecdotal evidence suggesting that the proportion of initial contacts claiming to be the 'next birthday' person is not always what it should be. For instance, in households with three people eligible for interview a reasonable expectation would be that one-third of the initial contacts should claim to have the next birthday. If it is more than this, the implication is that the contact persons may sometimes be deliberately putting themselves forward for interview, perhaps either out of curiosity or to 'protect' other household members. Or the interviewer, having established a contact, may unconsciously (or otherwise) be encouraging the contact to provide him or her with a completed interview. If the birthday rule is used its performance should be monitored and corrective action taken if it shows this kind of bias. This means, of course, ensuring that the appropriate information is recorded, preferably on the questionnaire or at least on some field document.

If such a bias is found it may be possible to counter it by disguising the consequences of the answer until it has been given. For instance a form similar to the Kish
form can be used to determine whether the 'next birthday', 'last birthday', 'second-
next birthday' person is to be selected (depending on the number of eligible persons)
but the selection is not revealed until the contact has indicated what position he or
she has in the sequence.

Both the enumeration methods and the birthday rule have a major problem in common, however. The initial contact has cooperated to the extent of providing the information necessary for selection. If that person is selected, then (assuming eligibility)
there is a good chance that a successful interview will ensue. Where the initial contact
is not selected, the selected person may not be available and/or may be more likely
to refuse cooperation. The result is an increased non-response rate from households
where the initial contact is not selected and a consequent over-representation of initial
contact persons in the sample. As the people who are most likely to answer the door-
bell or telephone may not be typical of the population of interest this is a potential
source of bias that should be monitored. It may be one of the factors that have to be
allowed for in 'design' weighting (see section 2.1.1).

1.15   Non-response

Selecting the sample members is one thing; obtaining the desired information from
them is another. Ideally all intended sample members will be available and will
cooperate in the survey. In practice, however, this rarely happens. In surveys of the
general population there can be a variety of reasons why intended participants fail to
end up in the final sample, including the following.

- Where addresses are selected these may turn out to be non-residential, unoccupied,
  demolished or otherwise incapable of yielding an interview.
- It may prove impossible to make contact with any resident at a selected address or
  telephone number, even after repeated calls.
- A selected respondent may be away for an extended period, beyond the duration of
  the fieldwork.
- A selected respondent may be too infirm or ill, or be unable to speak the local
  language.
- Access to a selected respondent may be barred by other persons in the household.
- Cooperation may be refused, either by the initial contact or by a selected resident.

In some societies there may be a range of culture-dependent reasons for non-response
and response rates may vary widely between different sections of the community.

Codes of Practice governing the collection of sample survey data from the general
population (which may be reinforced by legislation) generally require that respondents
must be permitted to decline to participate in a survey, and must be free to withdraw
their cooperation at any point. Some government statistical organisations may have
statutory powers to *compel* persons or organisations to provide information but they
are generally reluctant to exercise these to the full.

The result is that some people who should have been in the sample are excluded from it. In the nature of things these people are unlikely to be typical of the population as a whole, though of course, it is normally very difficult to determine in what ways and to what extent. How much this matters may depend on the subject and objectives of the survey, but a high *response rate* (the proportion of intended respondents actually providing information) must be regarded as a very desirable attribute of a sample.

Unfortunately, in many more materially advanced societies it is becoming increasingly difficult to achieve high response rates in surveys of the general population. There is a variety of reasons for this. Many people are busier and out of the home more than they would have been in previous decades. In many countries a higher proportion of women work full-time or part-time than formerly.

Non-contact   Ways of allowing for inability to contact selected respondents have been suggested, but are not necessarily helpful. Politz and Simmons [45] suggested that, under suitable conditions, the 'not-at-homes' could be allowed for without making multiple attempts at contact. Respondents interviewed at the first call are asked on how many of the previous five days they would have been available for interview at the same time of day as the actual interview. The probability of interviewing a respondent is determined by the number of days out of *six* (the current day plus the previous five) on which that respondent would have been successfully interviewed. Put simplistically, respondents at home every day are deemed to be adequately represented, while those interviewed on the one day of the six on which they happened to be at home have only a one-sixth probability of selection and thus represent a category six times as prevalent in the population as in the sample. A weight, the inverse of that probability, is applied to each respondent to compensate. Although the idea is attractive, subsequent experimental work (see [59]) indicated that gains in accuracy were marginal at best but that the loss in precision of estimates, resulting from the wide range of weights applied, was very considerable.

Bartholomew [3] suggested that where two attempts to contact each selected respondent were made, those not contacted after the second call could be regarded as similar to those interviewed on the second call (i.e. to those *not* available at the *first* call). Respondents interviewed at the second call would therefore be weighted up to represent all those not interviewed at the first call. Unfortunately, these days the proportion of selections not interviewed after two (or more) attempts is often very high, resulting again in very high weights being applied to a small proportion of the sample and a consequent loss of precision.

Both these methods, of course, deal only with the 'not-at-home' problem and not with what is these days a more pressing problem: reluctance or refusal to be interviewed. Increased concerns for physical security lead to the use of screening devices for callers, both at the door and by telephone. Increased concern at the growing opportunities technology gives to governments, businesses and others to capture, manipulate and exploit personal information causes greater wariness. Previous approaches by salespersons under the (fraudulent) guise of survey research may have made some individuals reject a later approach to take part in a genuine survey. Being asked for one's opinion in a survey is no longer necessarily a novelty; indeed some areas have been so heavily surveyed that it is becoming a nuisance.

Reluctance to be interviewed can be reduced in many cases by establishing the bona fides of the fieldworker and reassuring the respondent about why the information is being collected, how it will be used, what purpose it will serve and of the confidentiality, anonymity and security of any personal information given. Where circumstances permit, an initial contact through an explanatory letter or telephone call may help. For unlisted telephone numbers in random-digit-dialling telephone surveys, where they would perhaps be most beneficial, they are of course not an option. Financial or other incentives are increasingly being resorted to in order to gain cooperation. However, the general downward trend in response rates is such that survey research practitioners are questioning the benefits in practice of probability methods over non-probability methods in more and more cases.

Non-response is a fact of life. It can be minimised but not avoided. In setting up field procedures it has to be allowed for. We cannot simply tell an interviewer to approach ten people and expect ten interviews to result. There are, however, a number of possible approaches to minimising the adverse effects. They all rely on a set of procedures and rules aimed at maximising the proportion of potential interviews that are converted into successful interviews. Central to these is a rule determining the minimum amount of effort that must be made before abandoning a name or address that might yield an interview.

If interviewers are given specific names (or addresses), such as from a list of customers or employees or from a population register, they can be given more names or addresses than the number of interviews required and rules for how these are to be used.

One possible approach, if the response rate can be estimated with reasonable confidence in advance, is to provide the interviewer with the number of names or addresses estimated to yield the required number of interviews and to instruct the interviewer to endeavour to obtain as many interviews as possible, sticking strictly to that list. There will of course be variations in the response rate from interviewer to interviewer; some will end up achieving more interviews than others, and allowance should be made for this in the weighting of the final sample.

More frequently an interviewer is given a number of names or addresses greater than the number of interviews required. The list may be divided into 'primary' and 'substitute' addresses, the substitutes to be used only when there is no longer any possibility of achieving any further interviews with those on the primary list. A similar procedure applies when interviewers are given a 'starting address' and rules for selecting subsequent addresses. The general principle is to keep to a minimum the number of addresses at which contact is attempted but at which no interview results.

Strict interpretation of this principle can be time consuming and can increase considerably the cost of fieldwork, with interviewers spending large amounts of time in making call-backs and waiting for appointments. It certainly means that ample time has to be allowed for the fieldwork phase of the survey. Where time and budget are limited or sample quality requirements are less pressing, less strict call-back rules are often applied.

The above remarks apply predominantly to face-to-face surveys. For telephone surveys there is generally less of a problem with 'unproductive' interviewer time so that cost may be less of a consideration. On the other hand surveys are often done by telephone for speed so time may not permit the extended period necessary for an intensive call-back regime.

Declining response or cooperation rates are perhaps the biggest single problem confronting the survey researcher today. While the highest possible response rate remains a very desirable objective it is important to be realistic in our expectations. The high response rates taken for granted in the 1960s and 1970s (when some of the classic sampling texts were published) can still be achieved, but only with greatly increased effort and expense.

Response rates

So far we have used the term 'response rate' without formally defining it. Because surveys vary in complexity there is no simple formula that covers all cases. The broad principle is that the response rate is the number of usable interviews achieved as a proportion of the number of cases where an interview could have been possible, but the definition of 'possible' may depend on the circumstances. Some flexibility is needed in what is to be included in the numerator and, particularly, the denominator. In some cases there will be areas of uncertainty (such as whether a household that could not be contacted contained any persons eligible for the survey) and there may be cases where partially completed interviews are counted as successes rather than failures. Whether a person unable to speak the language of the survey is included in response rate calculations or excluded as 'out of scope' may depend on the definition of the target population. A useful set of standards and a range of definitions of 'response rates' for different circumstances has been published by the American Association for Public Opinion Research [1]. Other related definitions such as 'refusal rate', 'cooperation rate' and contact rate are also used. These statistics, as well as indicators of sample quality, may be used by field management in identifying problem localities or under-performing interviewers.

Item non-response

We have been considering non-response as relating to the failure of selected respondents to participate in the survey. However, respondents may also fail to respond to individual questions or parts of a survey. A person may agree to take part in a survey but be unwilling to answer certain questions. This is generally referred to as 'item non-response'. It is an issue that affects all forms of sample, but we will consider it here in outline. It is a particularly difficult issue to deal with for several reasons. It is not always clear or possible to infer in an individual case why a question is unanswered. It is not always possible to identify genuine refusals. In a self-completion questionnaire questions may be skipped unintentionally, as a result of misunderstanding, fatigue or inattention on the part of the respondent, or of poor questionnaire design on the part of the researcher.

In some cases a 'don't know' response to a question is a polite and non-confronting form of refusal to answer. There is therefore no way of distinguishing between the genuine 'don't know' and the 'won't say'.

A detailed treatment of methods of dealing with item non-response is outside the scope of this book, but they vary widely in complexity and sophistication. The crudest method is simply to present the numbers of 'missing' responses with all the other results and to leave the end user to decide how to interpret them. Slightly less crude is the method of assuming that the missing respondents would have answered in the same way as those who did answer the question ('missing at random') and re-scaling the aggregate results to keep the proportions the same. This may be expedient but it must be made clear to the user of the results that this is what has been done. A variation on this is to assign or impute a response at random to each respondent with a missing answer such that the proportionate distribution of actual responses is unchanged. The introduction of a random element into the responses recorded for each respondent has also the unfortunate side-effect of adding an element of randomness to the degree of association between variables, and thereby causing the strength of this association to be underestimated in the data.

Where the incidence of item non-response is low, such imputation methods might be justified on the grounds that the convenience of preserving internal consistency outweighs the slight distortion they introduce.

More complex methods attempt to impute missing answers to an individual respondent by using other information provided by the same respondent and/or by other 'similar' respondents to estimate which response the respondent would have been most likely to give, possibly also placing constraints on the overall distribution of imputed responses.

Where responses are imputed, by whatever method, it is essential that this practice is made clear to the user. The method(s) used and the extent of their use must be explicitly stated. Imputed responses should be identified so that the original data set, without imputation, can be reconstructed if necessary.

Prevention is better than cure, however, and minimising item non-response by sensitive questionnaire design must be the first line of defence against non-response.

The whole issue of non-response is raised here because it is a factor that can undermine the quality of the sample. A very theoretically correct sampling plan is of little benefit if the response rate is dismal. The additional cost of extra sophistication in the sampling may be magnified further if response rates are low. Given the increasing difficulty of achieving high response rates in surveys of the general population, it is becoming increasingly difficult to operate full probability sampling methods in practice.

1.16   Quota sampling

So far we have been considering 'probability sampling', a form of selection where the probability of an 'individual' inclusion in the sample can be estimated, preferably in advance, but at least in retrospect. However, other methods of sampling are in common use and these will be reviewed briefly. Some of them are sufficiently lacking in any form of plan or control to be dismissed out of hand as serious attempts to represent fairly the population of interest (see section 1.17). Others represent a serious attempt to achieve a reliable sample and must be taken seriously. Of these, the most popular method is 'quota sampling'.

In quota sampling the respondents are not pre-selected. In surveys of the general population typically interviewers are sent out to specified locations and told to conduct interviews with a specific number of people. They are told that certain numbers of these must each possess a certain attribute, perhaps that half must be men and half women, that they must interview a certain number aged 18–35, etc. A *quota* is set for each attribute and interviewers are expected to adhere to this as closely as possible. The quotas are set so that they represent together the known distribution of the control attributes across the known population.

Normally a master set of quotas is set for the whole area to be covered or for individual geographic regions or strata, typically based on census information or on some other reliable source as appropriate. This is then broken down to separate quotas for each sampling point or interviewer. Ideally they will be varied from one interviewer's assignment to another to represent any known geographical variation.

Generally these quotas are set in terms of simple and obvious attributes such as the sex and age of respondents, but other relevant attributes may be used, depending on the population being surveyed and the subject matter of the survey, such as working status and broad occupation type, ethnicity or education level. 'Relevant' here means that they are likely to be related to, or to be useful predictors of, measures to be collected in the course of the survey. The choice will be influenced by the researcher's knowledge (or anticipation) of the attributes liable to be biased in uncontrolled sampling and/or liable to affect the overall estimates if not controlled. Almost invariably, however, they are attributes that can be readily determined before the initial contact is made, or at a very early point in the interview.

In some cases quotas may be set deliberately to over-sample or under-sample certain categories of the population, for the same kinds of reasons already discussed for probability sampling.

The targets may be set for the individual attributes independently (half men, half women, half 18–35, half older) with no requirement that any interaction between the attributes be controlled. These are known as 'parallel' quotas. Often, however, the control attributes are 'interlaced'; a target number of interviews is set for male white-collar workers aged 18–35, and each other combination (or quota 'cell'). Interviewers are expected to complete the required number of interviews for each cell and to reject any potential respondent who falls into a cell where the quota has already been achieved.

Sometimes a mixture of approaches may be used. An interlaced quota may be set for each sex/age combination with an overall (non-interlaced) quota for full-time employed and other respondents. The choice depends on the circumstances of the survey, as described above, but also on the total number of interviews required of the interviewer. An interviewer required to complete 50 interviews may have a more elaborate quota (with more cells or more interlacing) than one required to do ten.

Quota sampling tends to get short shrift in the more academic textbooks. Cochran dismisses it in half a page. Kish devotes more space to it, and reviews the reasons for its use and its shortcomings. It is easy to see why it should be held in low esteem. The lack of control, the amount of discretion allowed to the interviewer, the absence of documentation on persons approached but not interviewed, all mean that the precision of estimates cannot be estimated using the conventional statistical formulae. In no way can a quota sample be considered as equivalent to a simple random sample in statistical terms. This is the essence of the problem as far as the purposes of this book are concerned. It is simply not possible to apply any theoretical approach to the estimation of the design effect and thus of the effective sample size. All estimates have to be pragmatic ones. This is discussed further in Chapter 3.

The discretion allowed to the interviewer in the selection of respondents is perhaps the greatest single criticism levelled at the method. Interviewers are given assignments requiring a certain amount of work and will naturally tend to do this in what they perceive as the most efficient manner consistent with the instructions they have been given. This does not imply that they do anything improper, simply that once in the field they use their initiative and experience to ensure that they do not spend unnecessary time on unproductive tasks. An interviewer will use visual and other clues to increase efficiency of contact. For instance an interviewer with separate quotas of high and low socio-economic status respondents to fill will make for more affluent and poorer areas respectively in which these quotas may be more efficiently filled. Towards the end of an assignment an interviewer will be positively looking out for certain types of people only. If interviewing in public places is permitted, potential respondents who would fall into already filled quota cells can often be spotted without any need for formal contact and ignored.

When interviewers are working independently, generally no documentation is produced that allows any realistic assessment of response rates. In door-to-door surveys there is usually no requirement to make further calls where no response is obtained on an initial call. The result is that samples tend to be biased towards people who are *accessible*. For this reason quota controls are often used which go some way towards mitigating this bias, such as a requirement for a certain proportion of interviews to be with full-time workers of each sex and for a proportion of interviews to be done in the evening or at a weekend.

But in spite of its apparent unattractiveness, quota sampling is firmly established and very widely used in many countries and particularly in 'commercial' research. There are a number of reasons for this, which may vary in importance from country to country, but undoubtedly the principal ones are that quota sampling is quicker and cheaper per interview than full probability sampling. The ability of interviewers to get through an assignment with the minimum of unproductive time, the typical lack of recalls and the reduction in effort at the sample planning and sample drawing stages will combine to cut the costs. They may also make it possible to compress the interviewing into a very short space of time and make it possible to complete fieldwork and report results very quickly. And at all events the only real alternative may be to exercise *less* control over the sample selection.

Cost and
precision

The cost-per-interview argument is less attractive than it looks on further consideration. Sample sizes are determined according to the degree of precision required of the survey estimates. The lower cost per interview of quota sampling makes it superficially attractive relative to full probability sampling: a larger sample size can be obtained within the budget. But this larger sample size may in reality yield little additional precision or indeed less precision. What it does is to provide the *appearance* of greater precision. Surveys may be costed and commissioned on the basis of the number of interviews rather than of the degree of precision in the estimates. This is accepted simply because, one suspects, many users do not realise the statistical implications of the sampling method and are applying, incorrectly, the standard textbook formulae for estimating variances and hence standard errors which strictly apply only to simple random samples. On the other hand it has to be said that these same formulae are often uncritically misapplied to probability samples that are not simple random samples.

There is, however, little room for argument about the timing advantage. Where time is critical there is no point in proposing a superior sampling method that will only deliver results too late for them to be used. There are occasions when only admittedly inferior sampling methods will meet the objectives of the survey.

The popularity of quota sampling in 'commercial' research should not be taken to mean that those conducting 'commercial' surveys are not concerned with quality while those doing public sector or academic research are. Many practitioners and commissioners of survey research do or have done both. Rather, they are likely to have different priorities and to be subject to different constraints. Quality of sample is, after all, only one of the factors that determines the overall quality of a survey research project.

Many surveys are principally concerned with 'soft' measures, which have no *absolute* validity. Measures of attitudes, perceptions and opinions generally cannot be compared with any authoritative external measure. There is thus no way of saying that such measures obtained from a full probability sample would be more *accurate* than those from a quota sample. Looking at the relationships and the strength of association between variables covered by the survey is frequently of greater importance than the absolute values themselves in providing insight into the issues the survey is intended to explore. Biases and additional imprecision arising from the use of quotas may be of less importance than where a verifiable factual measure is to be obtained. Where the survey is carried out repeatedly or continuously, consistency of methodology may be of much greater value and concern than strict accuracy.

Voting
intention
surveys

It may, therefore, seem surprising that so many political voting-intention polls rely on quota sampling. The measurement of voting intention, especially in the approach to an election, is (rightly or wrongly) interpreted by the media and the public as a prediction of the outcome. The polls are therefore open to be judged very publicly by the accuracy of their 'predictions', and sometimes they are found wanting.

A conspicuous instance of this was the British general election of 1992. The major face-to-face polls (all with quota samples) were generally very consistent in their findings, both over time and between companies. Their results did differ from poll to poll but no more than would be expected of separate samples and given that there were some small differences in methods. Collectively they suggested that the Labour Party would receive slightly more votes than the Conservatives. Even the four polls carried out in the two days immediately before voting showed on average that Labour would receive a little under 1% more of the vote than the Conservatives. In the event the Conservatives won with a margin of 7.6%. The difference was far too great to be explained as any form of statistical aberration. In addition the polls had committed the cardinal sin of not picking the winner.

A major investigation was commissioned by the Market Research Society. Its report [42] covered a very wide range of methodological aspects of the polling process and also external social factors that may have affected the polls. It criticised some aspects of the operation of the quota sampling but found that there was no evidence that replacing it with probability sampling would have affected the outcome materially.[5] Historical analysis of the polls' performance at elections back to 1945 indicated that probability-sample polls were no more accurate as predictions than quota-sample polls. If anything they were less accurate, but the quality of the probability sampling itself may have been low as a result of the pressures affecting any political poll. These very pressures are the main reasons for the continued use of quotas. Polls, especially those close to an election, have to be carried out within a very short time span, partly to reflect shifts in opinion over a short time period, partly often to meet publication deadlines.

Quota sampling may also be used in conjunction with methods that retain at least some element of probability sampling. To improve the degree of control over quota sampling, interviewers may be restricted in the areas in which they are allowed to work. In conventional quota sampling the interviewer may be allocated a whole town, suburb or electorate and may be free to select respondents anywhere within that area. Alternatively, an interviewer may be allocated only a very small area, of perhaps 100–200 households, and required to work wholly within that. If these small areas are selected by a probability method they may collectively represent a reasonable cross-section of the population in terms of dwelling types, income, employment type and other factors associated with locality. Quotas may then be applied, perhaps with respect to sex and age, within each area. The use of such small areas may also introduce the problem of clustering, discussed earlier, compounding the problems of quota sampling.

Where fieldwork can be very closely coordinated, as for instance in the case of computer assisted telephone interviewing (CATI), quotas are sometimes imposed as an adjunct to probability sampling. CATI systems frequently provide centralised real-time reporting and allow supervisors to monitor and direct the progress of the survey. A random sample of telephone numbers may be used but quotas may also be set,

[5] The inquiry found that the main reasons for the discrepancy were: a late 'swing' (subsequent research revealed a large number of people making up or changing their minds close to the election); a higher than expected turnout among Conservative supporters; some inadequacies in the application of quotas and weighting; and a greater reluctance by Conservative supporters to declare their intentions.

usually with some tolerances. The quota is not imposed on an individual interviewer but is applied overall. Each answer is entered into the computer as it is given and when the system detects that a respondent falls into a quota cell that is already full the interviewer is directed to terminate the interview politely. There is at least some documentation of contacts that do not result in an interview. However, if no call-backs are made to numbers where no response is obtained at the initial call, and quota controls are used as a way of giving the sample the appearance of representativeness, the resulting sample cannot be considered a probability sample.

Quota sampling may also be used where there is no adequate sampling frame, but where the general characteristics of the population being sampled are known. It is also routinely used where no sampling frame can be applied. For instance, some surveys have by their nature to be conducted in fixed locations. 'Blind' paired-comparison taste tests may require facilities for food preparation and other non-portable equipment and are often carried out in shopping centres where a sample is recruited from whoever happens to be passing by. As the passers-by at any location are extremely unlikely to be representative of the required population, quotas are imposed to remove the most obvious biases. Experience and circumstances may dictate what kinds of quotas are imposed. The resulting sample, while not adequate as a general survey sample, may be quite adequate for the purposes for which it is needed.

Quota sampling cannot realistically be regarded as being as good as probability sampling, though it may be more appropriate in some circumstances. In practice it can sometimes deliver accurate results, especially where these can be calibrated against known values. An organisation using quota sampling of the general population regularly, with trained and experienced interviewers accustomed to the practice, may be able to adjust and stabilise its methods to ensure that key measures correspond with known reality and thus provide some assurance that other measures are also likely to be reasonably accurate. It would obviously be more difficult for anyone organising a survey for the first time with inexperienced field staff to operate a quota sampling design satisfactorily.

It must also be remembered that probability sampling is itself frequently far from perfect. The problems of non-contact and non-cooperation, described already, under-mine the quality of probability samples, however well they may be designed. A proba-bility sample is only as good as its execution. With generally declining response rates the average difference in quality between probability sampling and quota sampling may be becoming less marked.

1.17   Other non-probability sampling methods

There are other methods of sampling in use, generally in smaller scale survey work, but they are not generally used when there is any requirement for great quantitative accu-racy or to estimate the precision of the estimates they yield. These may be classified as:

- convenience sampling, where sample units are selected purely on the basis of avail-ability or for the convenience of the researcher;

- judgement sampling, where the researcher makes a selection that he or she judges to be representative of the population being researched;
- purposive sampling, where the sample is made up of units that are deemed to be important to the study.

'Convenience sampling' may be resorted to where a strictly numerical 'quantitative' outcome is not required and/or where research is purely exploratory or preliminary, or where it is believed that the population being sampled is either so homogeneous or has the characteristics being measured so randomly distributed that the outcome would not be materially affected by more sophisticated sampling. Nevertheless, the researcher must be aware of the fact that the sample is *not* properly selected and must interpret the results in that light.

Judgemental and 'purposive' sampling may be justified in surveys of small populations, particularly in business-to-business surveys, where it might, for instance, be unthinkable to allow certain major companies not to be included. It is rarely appropriate, necessary or even practicable for consumer surveys.

A word must be said in passing about surveys (of whatever kind) with very low response rates. A sample which is the result of only a very small proportion of those selected returning useful information must be regarded as self-selecting and highly suspect as a source of quantitative information. Among the worst examples of this are the 'phone-in polls' conducted by TV shows and print media. Here the response rates are both low and unknown. Such polls, usually on controversial issues, are likely to provoke a disproportionate concerted response from vocal, organised or threatened minorities rather than to reflect overall public opinion. They are the more reprehensible because the results are made public, and because the organisations conducting them frequently employ professional researchers who presumably would not endorse them. They should not be treated as serious research.

However, surveys with low response rates should not be dismissed totally, as they can often yield usable information. The self-completion customer satisfaction questionnaires found in hotel bedrooms may be returned by only a small proportion of guests, but they may provide a valuable though incomplete picture, if only of negative aspects of guests' experience. As an objective measure of quality or performance they may leave much to be desired. However, by identifying problems and indicating where specific corrective action can be taken they may, with all their methodological deficiencies, be guiding the management decision process in a timely and cost-effective way – which is what surveys should be doing.

1.18 Sampling small populations

In the overwhelming majority of surveys the sample used consists of a very small proportion of the total population. How small that proportion is is not normally a matter for concern; it is the absolute number of interviews that determines the precision of estimates. The standard formulae for variance and related measures assume that the sample is drawn from an infinite population (or in practice that the *sampling fraction* is so small as to be negligible).

However, when the sampling fraction becomes appreciable, it does have a beneficial effect on precision. Mostly this is small, but it is also readily and easily calculable. The *finite population correction* is a number between 1.0 and zero and is the square root of the complement of the sampling fraction. If, for example our sample contains 40% of a particular limited population the sampling fraction is 0.4 and the finite population correction is $\sqrt{1.0 - 0.4}$ or about 0.775. The standard error of any estimate should be multiplied by this.

Where sampling fractions are small the finite population correction is close to 1.0 and thus has little effect. In most surveys the sampling fraction is very small, and the finite population correction is so close to 1.0 that it can be safely ignored. Advice in textbooks varies slightly but generally the advice is that unless the sampling fraction is over 5% (some say 10%) the correction need not be applied. A sample containing one-tenth of the population would have a finite population correction of 0.949, and the standard errors of estimates would thus be reduced by only 5% of their value. Even when half the total population is included the standard errors are reduced by only some 30%.

On those rare occasions where we can conduct a survey in which the *whole* of a population participates, the question of 'sampling' does not arise. Such a survey would normally be called a census, and here there can be no sampling errors and the estimates have no variance or standard error. It could perhaps be said that we have a sampling fraction of 1.0 and a finite population correction of zero, but logically it is clear that with complete coverage of the population there can be no question of any errors due to the selection of participants. As in any sample survey there can, naturally, be non-sampling or measurement errors in the estimates a census yields. It should not be imagined that census estimates are automatically accurate just because no sampling issues are involved.

1.19   Some final thoughts

Before leaving the subject of sampling we should consider two interesting issues.

If an attribute whose incidence is to be estimated is truly randomly distributed throughout a population then, as long as the attribute itself (or anything correlated with it) does not enter into the sampling process, the method of selecting a sample has no effect on the accuracy of the estimate. A rough and ready selection method can give the same result as a strict simple random sample of equivalent size. The sampling method and its application only become important as the distribution of the attribute departs from strict randomness. Few attributes, of course, are truly randomly distributed. But for many it can be hard to predict which individuals in a population will possess that attribute, even with detailed knowledge of their other attributes. Sometimes it can be easy to identify a segment of the population within which an attribute will occur (or occur disproportionately) but difficult to find any predictors within that segment. If we cannot identify anything that such an attribute is related to, how can we be sure that the time and trouble we take over getting the sampling right has really resulted in a better quality result?

The degree of error (difference from the true value) will also vary from estimate to estimate. If a randomly drawn sample is used to measure a large number of uncorrelated attributes, the degree of error will vary. One in twenty of them can be expected to be 'wrong' by an amount at least equivalent to the 95% confidence limits. We usually have little idea which estimates are close to reality and which are very different, but it should be a constant reminder to us that 'perfection' in sampling is unachievable and that with the best of samples we must not dismiss from our minds the fallibility of the estimation process.

2 Weighting

2.1 Principles

For some reason little has been published on the subject of weighting. It is generally ignored in texts on statistics and on survey research. However, its prevalence, particularly in larger surveys, makes it essential that practising researchers be familiar with the purposes, principles and methods of weighting and with its implications.

Ideally a survey sample has all the characteristics of the population it represents, and the results it yields can be used as they stand after a straightforward count of the number of respondents falling into each designated category. In practice, however much effort may be put into the execution of a well planned sampling exercise, the sample will never be representative in all respects. A sample intended to be a 'cross-section' of the population may prove to be biased or deficient in some way. Or particular groups may be deliberately over-represented in the sample, as described in the preceding chapter.

The imbalances may be corrected at the analysis stage by a process known as 'weighting'. Increased emphasis is given to the information from under-sampled groups and less to the information from over-sampled groups in calculating the final estimate. In practice it is normally done by attaching a 'weight' to each respondent in the survey. The weight is proportional to the relative contribution that respondent's information is to make to the final estimate. Respondents belonging to an under-represented group will have a higher weight than those belonging to an over-represented group. A sample designed so that it is representative without weighting is called a *self-weighting sample*.

Weighting, as practised in survey research, may be defined as:

the application of a constant multiplying factor to the data provided by a respondent to vary the contribution that respondent's results make to the overall estimates.

In analysing the weighted survey data, the size of a defined group is represented not by the number of respondents it contains, but by the *sum of their weights*.

Before proceeding further there are three things that must be clearly distinguished.

- The purpose of the weights, as described above, is to balance the contribution individual respondents make *relative to each other*. The absolute numerical value of the weight is not important.
- Sometimes a survey, or an individual question, is intended to estimate not the number or proportion of people who meet some criterion, but the amount of some quantitative variable that describes these people. For instance, we may want to determine not how many people drink tea, but *how much* tea they drink in total. Our estimate of this will be based on an estimate from each person of the amount he or she individually drinks. The sum of these amounts (weighted as appropriate) will form the basis for our estimate for the population. The quantity associated with the individual sample member is what is being accumulated in a tabulation. Note that the *quantity* and any *weight* applied to an individual are separate and multiplicative.
- The results from a sample are sometimes multiplied by a single constant (often referred to as an *expansion factor*, *inflation factor* or *grossing-up factor*) to relate them directly to the population. The sum of the weights for the whole sample or any subset of it, multiplied by this constant, can then be read directly as an estimate of the size of the corresponding part of the population.

It is important to discriminate the separate natures and functions of weights and quantities, particularly as the term 'weight' is sometimes loosely applied to what is here described as a quantity. In this book the term 'weight' is used solely as defined above.

Combined weighting and expansion factors

Expansion factors are often incorporated in the weights themselves, so that the sum of the weights represents the population (often scaled down by a factor of perhaps 1000 to keep the numbers manageable). The weight thus contains two components, the balancing component and the scaling component. The scaling component is statistically neutral: it should not influence the estimation of precision or affect significance testing. However, in practice popular statistical software packages may not deal correctly with weighted data and may be particularly liable to produce misleading results if the weights are scaled. We shall examine this in some detail later, in section 3.3.8.

A sample, especially as used in surveys, is a selection made from a larger population about which conclusions are to be drawn. The very fact that it is a sample, usually a very small fraction of the population from which it is drawn, means that at best it is subject to sampling variation. A perfectly random sample of 100 people, drawn from a typical adult population, might ideally contain 49 men and 51 women. However, if we took a large number of such samples we would find that the number of men in the sample would vary. In almost a quarter of the samples there would be 45 men or less and in a further quarter there would be 53 or more. This is an inevitable part of the sampling process.

Apart from random and therefore uncontrollable fluctuations there may be biases within resulting from the sampling method or from its execution. The way in which the sampling is done may itself affect the composition of the sample. To take an extreme example, if interviewing has to be carried out in people's homes and only on weekdays during the daytime, the sample is likely to be deficient in full-time workers. Even with the strictest of interviewing regimes there are likely to be sectors of the population who are under-represented (those who are chronically sick or who travel a lot, for instance) for purely practical reasons. The resources required to cover such anticipated problem minority groups adequately are normally beyond what is affordable. It is a matter for judgement whether their omission materially affects the quality of the information.

Imbalances may also have been introduced deliberately into the sampling plan for reasons connected with the objectives with the survey, as has been discussed earlier.

In summary, there are many reasons why even the best of samples may be unrepresentative in some respects. To correct for known and quantifiable biases the estimates derived from the sample may be adjusted by giving extra weight to the information from groups that are under-represented in the sample and less to those that are over-represented.

The imbalances in the sample may be complex. Persons of a defined type, such as 'men', may not be under-represented as a whole, but certain kinds of men, such as 'men under 30', may be under-represented, and perhaps particularly in certain geographical areas. The first task is therefore to identify which groups are not in the sample in their correct proportions. Often this can be anticipated: experience may show that with a particular method of sampling certain biases tend to occur each time. The nature and extent of bias can only be determined by comparing the sample figures with some other authoritative estimates.

Reasons for weighting

There are five main situations in which weighting is (normally) used. These are not mutually exclusive. The conditions of the survey may mean that two or more of the situations apply in a particular case.

- Controlled differential sampling or disproportionate stratification involves deliberately including more of certain kinds of people (or whatever is being sampled) in the sample than would be indicated by their incidence in the population. It can be done for a variety of reasons that were explained in Chapter 1 (section 1.9). Whatever the reason, differential sampling usually involves a penalty in the form of a loss of statistical efficiency if weighting is employed. Differential sampling and post-weighting are employed where the benefits outweigh the penalty.
- Selection of individuals with unequal probability. In some cases there may be a systematic and predictable divergence from the ideal of selecting among all potential respondents with equal probability. A frequently met case is where a sampling method selects households with equal probability but then selects one individual with equal probability *within* each selected household from among those members of the household who are within the definition of the population being sampled (eligible persons). In such a case the individual's chance of selection is lower in large households and higher in small ones. For each eligible person the chance of his or her household being selected is equal, but once that household is selected the individual's probability of selection is *inversely* proportional to the number of

eligible people in it. In such cases the procedure is to record as part of the interview the number of eligible people living in the household and to use that as part of the weighting process.

- Uncontrolled differential sampling occurs where the probability of selection of an individual is partly determined by factors that are only revealed in the course of the interview itself. For instance, visitors sampled at a holiday resort may have a higher probability of selection the longer they are there, but their length of stay may not be known until they are interviewed.

- Restoration of a sample to a known profile. Even the most perfectly planned random sample may contain chance deviations from expected proportions that are too big to go uncorrected. And even a planned fully random sample often cannot be perfectly executed in practice. Not everyone who is selected can be contacted or agrees to cooperate. These people are almost certain to be atypical in material respects and this introduces biases into the sample.

- Samples involving non-probability methods may be partly controlled (e.g. by setting quotas for certain types of respondents), but other biases may subsequently be evident. It may not be practicable to allow for all anticipated biases in setting quotas for individual interviewers because of the limited number of interviews each is to undertake. Known biases can be counteracted by weighting. Where the characteristics of the population are known reliably (e.g. there are official or authoritative estimates for guidance) the sample can be weighted to conform to those estimates.

For other non-probability sampling methods similar considerations apply, and in addition it must be noted that, whatever the type of sample, weighting does not eliminate non-visible biases that arise out of the selection procedure itself.

Strictly speaking, the use of weights implies that causes of bias are being eliminated. In the case of disproportionate stratification this is true. Otherwise, in practice only the symptoms are being treated directly. By eliminating one manifestation of bias we assume, or at least hope, that the action we take is also reducing the root bias. By eliminating several such manifestations together we hope that we are reducing that underlying bias to a greater extent. This is probably not an unreasonable assumption, but there is no guarantee that it is true in any particular instance. Removing the obvious, quantifiable superficial biases does not necessarily remove, or even reduce, the *unknown* biases – those in characteristics for which no correction was made. However, being aware of material biases and not making some attempt to improve the situation by applying weights requires a good explanation.

2.1.1   Design weighting and non-response weighting

In summary, weighting serves two purposes in the process of preparing a sample to provide estimates of the attributes of the population it is to represent. These two purposes represent conceptually two stages in the weighting process. They are often treated as two separate operations, and this is helpful as it ensures that due attention is given to each.

Firstly weighting serves to remedy biases that were introduced by the sampling design and which can therefore be said to be deliberate. The probability of a respondent's selection is subject to a number of factors which individually or collectively may be said to be *design* or *a priori* biasing factors. The weighting needed to correct these biases may be similarly described as design weighting or *a priori* weighting. Where multiple forms of design bias affect a respondent the net correction required is usually the product of the individual correction factors that must be applied for each source of bias treated.

Such kinds of bias include the following.

- Disproportionate stratification, already discussed, means that all respondents in an under-sampled stratum must be up-weighted and those in an over-sampled stratum down-weighted to restore the correct balance.
- Selection of households with equal probability and of one eligible person in each with equal probability means that a weight proportional to the number of eligible persons must be applied to allow for this.
- With random-digit dialling (RDD) telephone samples a household with more than one telephone number on which it can receive voice calls is more likely to be selected and should be weighted in inverse proportion to the number of such telephone lines. The incidence of this will vary from country to country but is probably on the increase generally. Fortunately it appears that multiple lines are more common in larger households so that the combined effect of this correction and the 'number of eligible persons' correction will tend to be less than the product of the two individual effects.
- In a face-to-face survey each interviewer is usually allocated a sampling point and told to conduct a specified number of interviews there. Whether because of the nature of the interview process or because of unpredictable outside circumstances it may happen that fewer (or even more) usable interviews are achieved. The sampling point may thus be under-represented or over-represented to the extent that the number of interviews achieved falls short of or exceeds the expectation, and should be up-weighted or down-weighted accordingly.[1]
- Where the respondent's chance of selection is only revealed by information gathered in the course of the interview that information should be used to determine the relative *a priori* probability and an appropriate correction factor.
- The process of selection of an individual within a household is normally carried out with the initial contact, the person who answers the door or telephone. There are two possibilities of bias here, which can both be assessed if suitable field records are kept. The proportion of initial contacts selected for interview in households containing a specific number of eligible persons may not be appropriate. In addition, where the

---

[1] If the population of interest for a survey is a subset of the general population, its incidence may vary between sampling points. If, for instance, in a survey of dog-owners a sampling point contains mainly high-rise flats, fewer than average interviews with dog-owners may be expected. It may be more appropriate here to judge the representation of the sampling point by the number of completed screening interviews rather than the number of completed interviews.

person selected is someone else, an interview may not be achieved with that person in all cases. (See discussion on page 31.) Such biases should ideally be monitored and corrected for.

Which of these or other biases apply to any particular survey is usually obvious with a little thought. Which ones should specifically be corrected for is to some extent a matter of judgement. The likely benefits and improvement in accuracy of estimates to be obtained from each individually or in combination must be considered in the light of the likely effect on the precision of those estimates. Particularly with relatively small samples, excessive complexity may not be warranted. Where doubt exists and circumstances permit, it may be worth experimenting with alternative weights to examine the effect of selective or more comprehensive design weighting on both the estimates and their precision.

Inferred patterns of non-response

In an ideal world, when sample members have received their design weights the weighted sample will be representative of the population. In practice, however, things are rarely this simple. The design-weighted sample may show differences when compared with the population. These differences may be presumed to have arisen because the execution of the sampling process is less than perfect as a result of the practical difficulties of dealing with our fellow humans. A second layer of weighting is therefore needed to bring the design-weighted sample into line with the population. This may be conveniently (if somewhat loosely) described as 'non-response' weighting, since variations in the response rate are the prime cause of the differences to be ironed out. It can be difficult to establish the effect of variations in non-response as such. Very often we know little about the attributes of the people who should have been in our sample but are not, even when we have made initial contact with them. We are therefore generally thrown back on inferring patterns of non-response from the differences between the profiles of the design-weighted sample and the population. The question of the relative effects at this stage of non-response and other causes is at all events philosophical, since it is the overall difference between the design-weighted sample and the population that we have to compensate for.

In practice, the two stages of weighting are often not segregated but are mixed together or even carried out as a single process. This is perfectly possible, and it is legitimate as long as it is done properly. For instance, correction for differential sampling of strata strictly speaking belongs to design weighting, but if weighting is done within stratum and the strata are balanced as a final stage or integrated with the 'non-response' weighting no harm is done.

All too often the design weighting is ignored and the profile of the unweighted sample is adjusted in the simplest way to fit the population profile without taking the design biases into account. When the two stages are integrated into a single process their separate natures and purposes should not be lost sight of. A common form of this neglect, perhaps the most common and possibly the most damaging, is failure to allow for the effect of the number of persons in the household eligible for interview when sampling individuals by means of a sample of households. Sometimes the information necessary to determine the design weight, for instance the number of eligible persons in a selected household, is not even collected.

One reason for not physically separating the two stages is that it can be difficult to separate totally design biases from non-response biases. The information being used to assess the effect of design biases may itself be tainted by non-response factors (for instance, where a sampling point has a shortfall of interviews this could be due to excessive non-response that could not be overcome within the time available).

Even if no population figures are available against which to judge the composition of the sample, design weights should still be applied if the method of selection makes it appropriate.

2.1.2 Representing multiple populations

A sample is sometimes required to represent multiple populations. This can occur, for instance, in samples that have to represent both individuals *and* the households in which they live. We may need to know both the proportion of households with, say, central heating, and the proportion of *people* in such households. If households have been selected with equal probability and the sample is also to represent individuals within them, then if only one individual is interviewed per household, those individuals interviewed have a probability of selection inversely proportional to the number of eligible people within the household. Weights (usually a second set of weights) would have to be employed to restore the imbalance. Typically two weights would be attached to each sample member, and the appropriate weight would have to be selected, depending on whether respondent or household totals are being accumulated.

A survey of retail stores may be given two sets of weights to allow it to represent the stores either in proportion to their numbers *or* in proportion to their turnover. The relationship between the results using the two sets of weights is often of great importance for understanding the nature of distribution problems. If an item is out of stock in 10% of stores but these represent 30% of all sales of that product category, these are clearly the bigger stores and the problem probably has to be tackled at the account management level. If it is out of stock in 30% of stores representing 10% of all category sales, these are the small stores, probably mainly independent, and the problem will have to be approached quite differently.

In such cases the units may not have been sampled either in proportion to their numbers or in proportion to their size but using some compromise sampling scheme. This was discussed in section 1.14.

2.2 Methods of weighting samples

It is not the authors' intention to present a comprehensive review of all weighting methods in use, but to describe those most commonly encountered and the principles that guide them. Other methods may be appropriate in certain circumstances, but whatever the method used to calculate weights much of the underlying thinking remains the same and many problems and pitfalls are common to all methods.

There are two principal methods used in the weighting of samples. They have the common aim of ensuring that the composition of the weighted sample matches, in specific respects, the composition of the population it is to represent. They differ in their approach. One takes a direct route, with a simple, one-step process transforming the profile of the original sample, but there may be limits in any given case to the complexity of the corrections that may be made, or rather to the number of require-ments that may be imposed, determined principally by the sample size. The other method involves a more complex process. It allows more controls to be applied, but it is less 'tidy' and has its own limitations. The choice of method will be determined by the circumstances and the characteristics of the sample involved. There may be a clear case to be made in favour of one or the other, but a mixture of the two is also possible, perhaps if different parts of the sample require different treatments or if a multi-stage weighting process is indicated.

Whatever method is eventually chosen it is essential that the data first be carefully examined and checked against as much population data as may be available, reliable and comparable.

2.3   Cell weighting

Single-stage cell weighting is the most usual and most straightforward form of weight-ing and requires very little explanation. The small number of pages devoted to it here is a measure of its simplicity rather than of its importance. In the days of manual and electro-mechanical processing of survey data it was the only really practicable form of weighting and its ease and transparency of implementation continue to make it the almost automatic choice for relatively uncomplicated samples.

One or more variables are selected as *weighting variables*. For each of these the sample is divided into a number of mutually exclusive and exhaustive categories (that is, each respondent falls into one and only one category) which are non-overlapping with respect to that variable (e.g. men and women, age 18–24, age 25–49, age 50+, etc.).

Where, as is usual, there is more than one weighting variable, the respondents are implicitly divided into mutually exclusive and exhaustive categories ('cells') in respect of the combinations of categories they fall into on each weighting variable. The number of cells is thus the *product* of the numbers of categories identified for each of the weighting variables. For each cell we know how many sample members it contains.

For each cell a *target* value is specified. The targets represent, or are proportional to, the sizes of the respective cells in an ideal sample, that is, one which has the same characteristics as the population. The target is the desired sum of weights for the cell. As explained previously, the sum of weights for the total sample need not be the same as the unweighted sample size.

Where respondents have been selected with (nominally) equal probability, and no design weighting has been applied, the weight for each cell, or more correctly for each respondent in each cell, is calculated by dividing the cell target number by the actual number of respondents in the cell. Where there has been design weighting, it should be divided by the sum of the weights resulting from any previous stages of weighting.

In the following hypothetical example a sample of 100 respondents is weighted using a simple 2×2 age/sex matrix. It is assumed that the population is equally divided into the four types, so that the target for each cell is 25 respondents. The actual numbers of respondents in the sample for each cell differ quite markedly from the targets.

	Men			Women			Total		
	Target	Actual	Weight	Target	Actual	Weight	Target	Actual	Weight
Under 35	25	16	1.56	25	24	1.04	50	40	(1.25)
35+	25	27	0.93	25	33	0.76	50	60	(0.83)
Total	50	43	(1.16)	50	57	(0.88)	100	100	(1.00)

Each individual respondent is assigned a 'personal' weight, but within any cell these are the same. The mean weights in parentheses for the column and row totals are for reference only.

Subject to practical constraints (see below) the matrix may have any number of dimensions and any number of categories in each dimension. A 'dimension' for this purpose is a variable, which may be categorical or numeric (see section 5.1.1), or possibly a combination of variables, with respect to which a respondent can be assigned to a category or to a range of values, and which serves to identify two or more mutually exclusive subsets of respondents who are to be grouped together for weighting purposes.

The choice of dimensions is determined by:

- biases apparent in the sample;
- availability of reliable population estimates (reliable target sums of weights must be set for each cell, i.e. for each combination of characteristics); and
- relationship between number of cells and sample size (the need to avoid having too many empty or very small cells).

This is a one-step process. The calculation of weights for any one cell is independent of the calculation for any other cell and has no effect on any other cell in the matrix. The calculation is extremely simple and can generally be done manually.

There is no requirement in principle for the definition of weighting cells to be uniform throughout the sample. For instance, the choice of weighting variables could vary from one stratum to another, or respondents might be divided into more categories in larger strata than in smaller ones, as long as the two fundamental requirements are met: each respondent is assigned to one and only one cell; and the population that cell represents is known. Some flexibility in defining weighting cells is desirable, and a diligent detailed examination of the sample characteristics relative to the population *before* the weighting scheme is established may reveal areas where particular additional correction is required.

Empty cells and extreme weights

Where the average cell size is small, some cells may contain no respondents at all. A target sub-population is defined but has no respondents to represent it. This usually implies excessive complexity in the weighting scheme, poor choice or poor partitioning of weighting variables or a poor sample to start with. In these cases there are several alternatives.

- Sample numbers and targets of adjacent cells may be combined. Usually this is done using just one dimension, but theoretically it should be done on *all* dimensions to preserve all the marginal totals. Choice of which cells are to be combined is a matter for judgement in the individual circumstances.
- The weighting scheme may be revised to use fewer categories per variable and/or different combinations of variables.
- If the cell is of very limited individual significance it may be ignored and a minor imbalance in the weighted sample accepted.
- An alternative method of weighting may be employed in the area around the defective cell (see hybrid methods, below).

If there are many empty cells the only solutions may be to reduce the number of dimensions or the number of categories on one or more dimensions, or to adopt a different weighting method altogether.

Where cell sizes are small but not zero care must be exercised to avoid extreme weight values being applied to individuals. The variance of weights has an effect on the precision of estimates, as the next chapter will discuss in some detail, and extreme individual weights can make this 'weighting effect' particularly marked. These can cause rogue results when analysing small groups within the sample. A limit may be set on the maximum value a respondent weight may take, and any cell exceeding this maximum value would need to be treated in some way. The solutions are as for empty cells, above. There is no need to set an arbitrary threshold for minimum cell sizes: what matters is not the number of respondents in the cell but the value of the weight required relative to the overall (or, if applicable, stratum) mean.

Where cell weighting is employed as the second or subsequent stage of a multi-stage process, the principles remain the same. The initial 'actual' respondent counts (as in the table on page 53) are replaced by the sums of the weights assigned to the respondents in each cell in the previous stage(s) of weighting. The weights are calculated by dividing the target sum of weights for each cell by the corresponding sum of these 'prior weights'. The respondents in any one cell will then not necessarily have identical weights. (Multi-stage weighting is discussed further in section 2.6.)

In the days before computers were in widespread use for processing survey data the information recorded was usually transferred to punch-cards and the cards were physically counted by machines. Where weighting had to be applied, it was customary to determine the number of respondents in each cell of the 'ideal' sample and to scale these such that for the most over-sampled cell the target number corresponded to the actual number of interviews. Therefore for each cell the target was equal to or greater than the actual number. In each cell where the actual number was less than the target a sufficient number of respondents were selected at random and their cards were physically duplicated, to create new 'virtual' respondents. Where the cell had less than half the desired number, all respondents were duplicated once and some twice, and so on. Each (real) respondent thus received an integer weight, the sums of the weights for each cell (in effect the number of real and virtual respondents) corresponding closely to the ideal. Where cells were heavily over-sampled, randomly selected respondents from those cells were sometimes even discarded to help balance the sample.

This primitive (though at the time effective) method of weighting has nothing to commend it when fractional weights can be used and it has two specific dangers. Firstly, the use of varying integer weights rather than a constant fractional weight within each cell adds unnecessarily to the variance of the weights and thus increases the weighting effect. Secondly, the production of additional 'virtual' or dummy respondents makes it difficult to identify the true unweighted sample size and to calculate weighting and overall design effects.

This historical relic is mentioned here only because one occasionally comes across references to it. In at least one textbook published in the twenty-first century the methods of duplication and discarding of respondents are described as still in use. It may also be related to some of the odd things that some statistical packages do with weighted data, a subject that will be discussed further in section 3.3.8.

2.4 Marginal weighting

In some cases we may know how the population is distributed on each of a number of variables *independently*, but not know how these distributions are related in detail. We may know, for instance, the proportion of the population that is male and the proportion that falls into each of a number of age categories, but we may not know the age distribution among men and women separately. We know of course what the age distributions of men and women are for the sample, but we have no way of setting targets for individual age/sex combinations. As with cell weighting we can build up a matrix of all the combinations of weighting attributes possessed by the sample, but in this case we must resort to matching the marginal totals only, hence the name of the process. (It is also sometimes referred to as 'rim-weighting'.) Marginal weighting involves a form of post-stratification. However, the sample is stratified on several different variables simultaneously without any consideration for how these may be inter-related.

The objective is to provide each respondent with a weight such that the sums of those weights for specific subsets of those respondents agree with predetermined targets. Typically there is no unique solution, and so there is generally a requirement to minimise (or at least to keep to as low a level as is practical) the effect of weighting on the variance of the estimates.

Marginal weighting can also be extended to redress the effect of different probabilities of selection. If, for instance, households have been selected with equal probability but one respondent was selected from each selected household, then target marginal weight totals may be set according to the numbers of eligible persons living in households of different sizes, where this is known (see also section 2.6).

If we attempt to weight by cells using many weighting variables and many categories per variable, with the result that the mean number of sample members per cell is very small, we may find that many (or even most) cells are empty or contain very few respondents. Cell weighting then becomes highly problematical, if not meaningless. *Marginal weighting*, which adjusts only on the basis of marginal distributions for selected variables without calculating specific cell weights, may be a useful alternative.

This may seem intuitively unsatisfactory. We are correcting some of the overall sample imbalances, but leaving uncorrected some of the detailed ones we know about. However, there is nothing to stop us setting targets based on *combinations* of attributes as well as on individual attributes. Another answer to this may be to weight the sample in stages instead and this is discussed in section 2.6.

There are several methods of marginal weighting and we describe three of these. While the calculations for cell weighting can be done on the back of an envelope, marginal weighting is almost invariably carried out by computer. The computer program should contain adequate checks for error conditions and should produce a comprehensive report enabling any problems to be identified.

The process of marginal weighting can be represented as a system of equations for which a solution has to be found, and for which additional constraints may apply. Instead of giving a general formula, we will illustrate marginal weighting in the case of three variables. Let $(P_i)_{i=1}^{n}$, $(Q_j)_{j=1}^{m}$ and $(R_k)_{k=1}^{l}$ be the target sums of weights[2] for the first, second and third variables, respectively. Therefore, the total target sum of weights is

$$\sum_{i=1}^{n} P_i = \sum_{j=1}^{m} Q_j = \sum_{k=1}^{l} R_k.$$

[2] Care should be taken to ensure that the sums of specified targets are the same for each variable. Even quite small discrepancies (usually rounding errors) can be troublesome in practice.

The sample is then naturally divided into ijk-cells according to these three variables, each cell consisting of respondents with the corresponding three values. The ijk-cells are exactly those used in the conventional cell weighting described above. The difference is that the cells are treated in related groups rather than individually, so that occasional empty or very small cells do not pose a problem.

For an ijk-cell, denote by $n_{i,j,k}$ the unweighted (or design-weighted) number of respondents (which may be zero in some cells) and by $w_{i,j,k}$ its weight (which we have to find). Therefore, the weights should be such that we get the correct marginal distributions for the three variables. In mathematical terms, it means that we have the following system of linear equations:

$$\begin{cases} \sum_{j,k} w_{i,j,k} n_{i,j,k} = P_i, & i = 1, \ldots, n \\ \sum_{i,k} w_{i,j,k} n_{i,j,k} = Q_j, & j = 1, \ldots, m \\ \sum_{i,j} w_{i,j,k} n_{i,j,k} = R_k, & k = 1, \ldots, l. \end{cases} \tag{2.1}$$

In addition, the weights are usually required to be non-negative.

Hence, the total number of equations is $n + m + l$ while the total number of weights ($w_{i,j,k}$) to be calculated is usually greater (it is $n \cdot m \cdot l$ minus the number of cells where $n_{i,j,k} = 0$). Consequently, this system has, in general, many solutions if there are no other requirements. There are several methods that impose extra conditions on the weights which allow us to choose a unique solution. Below we consider three such methods.

There are established techniques for solving systems of linear equations, which need not be described here. There is also a wide selection of software available for this purpose.

Notice that *not* every system (2.1) has a solution if the weights are required to be non-negative – the marginal distributions may impose incompatible demands on the data. Consider a simple (if extreme) example where there are two variables, each with three categories (the target marginal distributions are in the right column and in the bottom row):

5	7	10	25
3	0	0	15
9	10	1	5
10	15	20	

The requirements in this example are clearly contradictory. The three respondents in the second row *must* have a total sum of weights of 15, but all of them are in the first column whose sum of weights should be 10. This means, in consequence, that other respondents in the first column must have *negative* weights, in order to compensate for the excessive sum of weights of these three respondents. To avoid negative weights, an obvious solution in this example would be to combine the second category of the 'row' variable (with three respondents) with one of the other two categories. While this may be 'satisfactory' in avoiding negative weights, the loss of separate control over the second row category is itself unsatisfactory in view of the significant proportion of the target total it accounts for and the distorted nature of the data set. Mere avoidance of negative weights is not enough. The presence of negative weights may indicate that the sample is (as here) so distorted that it cannot realistically be pulled back into shape.

This simple example shows that even with marginal distributions care must be taken when choosing variables for marginal weighting. The variables should be 'reasonable' in the sense that there should be enough respondents for each category of each variable and not all of them should have the same value for another variable.

Negative weights

Any system of weighting which is capable of producing negative weights should incorporate checks and reporting facilities to warn the user of their occurrence. The user must then decide what to do about them. The existence of negative weights can cause serious problems. The existence of negative weights also probably means that the range, and thus the variance, of the weights applied is excessive. If negative weights can be generated, so can very large weights. A check for the variance and range of weights should be a part of every system of weight calculation (irrespective of the method) and closer examination of these is essential before any set of weights is accepted for further work.

The existence of negative weights also poses problems of interpretation. Users of the data may baulk at the concept of negatively weighted respondents. Such weights cannot be dismissed as a useful fiction (like $\sqrt{-1}$) as they may be visible in the tabulated results. If our sample is to represent a population, and we happen to select for examination a subset the sum of whose weights is negative, are we to ask our users to accept that there may be a negative proportion of people in the population with some attribute? If each such respondent is associated with some (non-negative) quantity, what is the user to make of the suggestion that this part of the population has a negative (weighted) total, but of course a positive mean? The authors cannot help feeling that users of survey data (unless they happen also to be quantum physicists) may find this a little confusing, and suggest that solutions that involve the use of negative weights should be avoided if at all possible. They would also suggest that a result involving negative weights is an indication that more has been asked of the data than they can reasonably bear, and that the weighting process may be making things worse rather than better. The cure may be worse than the disease.

There are two advantages of marginal weighting: the range of weights applied is (generally) less than that generated by cell weighting, with a consequent reduction in the statistical loss (see Chapter 3); and a greater number of dimensions can be used relative to the sample size.

The disadvantage, and it is potentially a severe one, is that limited or even no account may be taken of interactions between dimensions overall. For instance the sexes and all the age groups may be in their correct proportions, but the (weighted) number of *young men* may remain over or under what it should be. In the example below we might have hoped for equal numbers of respondents in each cell, whereas there is a serious internal imbalance (a shortage of younger men and older women).

But the marginal totals are already correct in both dimensions, so marginal weighting can have no effect on the imbalances in the cells.

	Men	Women	Total	Target
Age 18–34	3	7	10	10
Age 35–49	4	6	10	10
Age 50+	8	2	10	10
Total	15	15		
Target	15	15		

It is, however, possible to define a 'dimension' as a combination of two (or more) logically different variables (e.g. an 'age/sex' dimension consisting of 'younger men', 'younger women', 'older men', 'older women') where such interactions are known to exist and, of course, where reliable information is available to allow targets to be set for each combination. If marginal weighting is contemplated, such interactions must be checked for before and after the weighting process.

It is also possible, though fortunately rare, for marginal weighting to fail to produce a convergence between the sums of weights and the targets. When this happens it is often because a small number of respondents dominate two different groups, one of which is over-represented and the other under-represented. In such cases, which may be quite difficult to pin down, the weighting plan must be revised.

We now describe three methods of solving this general system (2.1) which meet the objectives but do not necessarily produce identical results.

2.4.1 Iterative marginal weighting

This process, also known as 'raking', involves comparing target sample sizes with actual achieved sample sizes on a number of dimensions *independently* and sequentially. Theoretically any number of dimensions could be used, but realistic targets can generally be set confidently for only a very limited number. Respondents are initially assigned a weight of 1.0 each (unless they already have some other weight from a prior stage in the process – see section 2.6). The sample is compared with the targets on the first dimension. A correction factor (denoted C.f. in the following tables) is calculated for each category in that dimension based on the category targets and category totals. In its simplest form this would be the quotient obtained by dividing the target by the actual (weighted) total. However, it may be beneficial to apply a correction factor closer to 1.0, perhaps the square root of the quotient, to draw the figures into line more gently. This will require more iterations but may result in a slightly smaller final sum of squared weights. Each respondent is then assigned a revised weight by multiplying the existing weight by the correction factor for the category to which the respondent belongs.

It is possible, and sometimes desirable, to place limits on the range of weights to reduce the statistical loss (see Chapter 3). A maximum (and minimum) weight may be specified, and each adjusted weight that falls outside the range is replaced with the maximum (or minimum) value. This may increase the number of iterations required. If applied too severely it may also prevent the weights from converging altogether. If this happens, either the limits must be relaxed or the cause must be identified and an alternative approach sought. The number of respondents whose weights have been limited in this way should be reported and examined as part of the checking procedure.

This method will be illustrated with a simple example with two variables, say age (three categories) and sex (two). Assume that we have thirty respondents with the following cell distribution:

4	3
5	8
4	6

The marginal totals and targets are the following:

	Men	Women	Total	Target
Age 18–34	4	3	7	10
Age 35–49	5	8	13	10
Age 50+	4	6	10	10
Total	13	17		
Target	20	10		

We begin with the dimension that shows the greater difference between targets and actuals (sum of squared differences), in this case sex. All the respondents in the first column are given a correction factor (here 20/13, or 1.54) and all those in the second a correction factor of 10/17:

	Men	Women	Total	Target
Age 18–34	6.15	1.76	7.92	10
Age 35–49	7.69	4.71	12.40	10
Age 50+	6.15	3.53	9.68	10
Total	20.0	10.0		
Target	20	10		
C.f.	1.54	0.59		

The revised weighted totals are then compared with the targets on the second dimension, the rows. Similar correction factors are calculated and applied to individual respondent weights. Thus those in the first row (age group) have a correction factor of 10/7.92 and so on.

	Men	Women	Total	Target	C.f.
Age 18–34	7.77	2.23	10.0	10	1.26
Age 35–49	6.20	3.80	10.0	10	0.81
Age 50+	6.35	3.65	10.0	10	1.03
Total	20.32	9.68			
Target	20	10			

The process is repeated alternating the dimensions. In the present very simple example the weighted marginal totals are already very close to the targets even after one complete iteration. In more complex cases, with more categories per variable, this does not always happen.

The process continues repeatedly ('iteration') until no difference in respect of any category exceeds a predetermined maximum value. A limit should be set to the number of iterations permitted. This can be generous, as the process is not time consuming with modern computer hardware. Failure to bring all weighted totals within acceptable limits after the set number of iterations should be investigated.

Monitoring the iteration
After each iteration the squares of the differences between targets and corresponding actual weighted totals should be summed. This gives a measure of the amount of adjustment still required. This sum should decrease asymptotically towards zero with each successive iteration. Failure to decrease is an indication of a problem and the unweighted and (partially) weighted figures should be re-examined to determine the nature of the problem.

The final weights applied in this example are:

1.9194	0.7762
1.2148	0.4913
1.5544	0.6286

The total sum of the squared weights is 37.87. This is a measure of the effect of weighting and will be discussed in detail in Chapter 3.

Where more than two dimensions are involved the sequence in which the dimensions are used should not make any difference to the final result. However, it seems appropriate that at each stage the dimension should be selected that exhibits the biggest sum of squared differences between target and current sums of weights. This should make monitoring progress towards the final solution simpler.

The final weight applied to each respondent is the *product* of the initial weight assigned (here 1.0) and *each* of the correction factors applied to that respondent at each stage. The iterative method has two particular advantages. Firstly, it copes well with situations where there are many weighting variables and many categories per variable, so that equation systems such as (2.1) become very complex. The authors have seen it used successfully (with large samples) for a system with four weighting dimensions with over 200 categories between them. Secondly, because all the adjustments are multiplicative it cannot produce a solution that includes negative weights. The multiplicative process can on the other hand generate excessively high weights. Setting upper limits for the values of the weights, perhaps relative to the mean (or stratum mean) weight, may be appropriate.

Iteration can of course fail to produce a solution at all, but this may serve as an effective message to the user that something needs to be changed. A common symptom of failure to produce a solution is 'hunting' between two configurations of weights, the changes made for one weighting variable being reversed by those made for another. A good weighting program will detect this and terminate with a warning.

Setting independent targets

In some cases targets may be set for a number of independent categories, which may overlap and need not include all members of the sample. This may be treated as an extension of iterative marginal weighting, with each attribute for which a target is set forming a binary variable with its complement. The categories for which targets are set may cover complete dimensions ('men', 'women', all the age groups) but may include individual subsets of the population (e.g. cat-owners, registered electors) for which reliable targets can be set. Each respondent is initially assigned a weight of 1.0 (or the weight from the prior stage if multi-stage weighting is used). The weighted totals for each attribute are compared with the targets and the biggest absolute difference is identified. In the example below this is 'cat-owners' (Stage 1).

	Target	Stage 1		Stage 2		Stage 3	
		Actual	Difference	Actual	Difference	Actual	Difference
Men under 35	25	18	−7	22.1	−2.9	23.3	−1.8
Women under 35	25	22	−3	26.1	+1.1	**27.4**	**+2.4**
Men 35+	25	27	+2	23.2	−1.8	24.4	−0.6
Women 35+	25	33	+8	**28.6**	**+3.6**	25	0
Cat-owners	35	**44**	**+9**	35	0	33.9	−1.1
Work full-time	40	41	+1	42.4	+2.4	41.6	+1.6
Anglican	25	22	−3	23.6	−1.4	24.0	−1.0
Catholic	27	29	+2	29.2	+2.2	28.6	+1.6
Other religion	48	49	+1	47.2	−0.8	47.4	−0.6

The *absolute* difference should always be used, never the percentage or relative difference. The absolute difference will not only cause the weighted estimates to converge more quickly on the targets but also, more importantly, will reduce considerably the chance that the data set will 'hunt' or fail to converge altogether.

A correction factor is calculated (35/44, or 0.795) and applied to the existing weights of all respondents in the 'cat-owner' group. Similarly a correction factor is applied to all respondents *not* in the group, of $(100 − 35)/(100 − 44)$ or 1.161, to preserve the sample's weighted total. This gives the 'Stage 2' weighted totals.

Down-weighting cat-owners (in this example) will change, if only marginally, all the other categories. All these other categories are likely to contain a mixture of cat-owners and non-cat-owners; the cat-owners among them will be down-weighted and the non-cat-owners up-weighted.

The net effect is likely to be that the other categories will be on average closer to the target than before. We can take the sum of the absolute differences (i.e. neglecting the sign) between targets and actuals as a (rough) measure of the imbalance of the sample. Initially these totalled 36. After correcting the cat-owners at Stage 1 this has reduced to 16.2. Notice that the reduction is greater than the 9 accounted for by the correction of the 'cat-owner' group as such.

The weighted totals for each attribute are again compared with the targets and the largest difference identified (women 35+). A correction factor is applied to the current weights of respondents in this category to bring their sum of weights into line with the target, and a different factor is applied to the current weights of non-members of this group to maintain the total sum of weights at the overall target. Notice that the weighted total of cat-owners will now almost certainly not remain exactly the same as the cat-owner target. However, the weighted totals in general will be closer to the targets. The sum of absolute differences is now down to 10.7.

This is done repeatedly, using the largest difference each time. On each iteration the weighted totals should get generally closer to the targets. The process continues until some acceptance criterion is met. Typically this would be that either the max-imum difference between any target and its corresponding sum of weights, or the sums of differences or squared differences between all targets and the actual sums of weights, should not exceed a stipulated value. Note that it is perfectly possible for the same cell to have the biggest difference more than once in the course of this process.

It is perfectly possible to apply marginal weighting using a combination of multiple dimensions (where each respondent falls into one category on each dimension) and one or more independently set targets.

2.4.2   Minimisation of variance

This method was kindly communicated to us by George Rennie. The idea is quite simple – the weights should have the minimum possible variance consistent with satisfying system (2.1). Because the sum of weights is fixed (it is equal for each of the equations in (2.1)), this can be reformulated to say that we should minimise the sum of *squared* weights. In mathematical terms, for three weighting variables as in our previous example, the function to minimise is the following:

$$f = \sum_{i,j,k} w_{i,j,k}^2 n_{i,j,k}.$$

The solution to this problem can be obtained, for example, by the Lagrange multipliers method. More precisely, one more variable per dimension is introduced.

$(\lambda_i)_{i=1}^n$, $(\mu_j)_{j=1}^m$ and $(\nu_k)_{k=1}^l$ are found from the following linear equations (see Appendix D for details):

$$\begin{cases} \sum_{j,k}(\lambda_i + \mu_j + \nu_k)n_{i,j,k} = 2P_i, & i = 1, \ldots, n \\ \sum_{i,k}(\lambda_i + \mu_j + \nu_k)n_{i,j,k} = 2Q_j, & j = 1, \ldots, m \\ \sum_{i,j}(\lambda_i + \mu_j + \nu_k)n_{i,j,k} = 2R_k, & k = 1, \ldots, l. \end{cases} \quad (2.2)$$

The final weights are then computed by the formula

$$w_{i,j,k}n_{i,j,k} = 0.5(\lambda_i + \mu_j + \nu_k)n_{i,j,k}$$

or

$$w_{i,j,k} = 0.5(\lambda_i + \mu_j + \nu_k) \text{ if } n_{i,j,k} > 0. \quad (2.3)$$

(If $n_{i,j,k} = 0$, the weight $w_{i,j,k}$ is not defined because it is not needed.)

The total number of equations in (2.2) is $d = n + m + l$ with the same number of variables so that a $d \times d$-matrix must be inverted to solve the system. In practice, the number d is usually not large so the method should be quick to compute. Of course, the formulae and the number of equations should be adjusted accordingly when the number of dimensions is different from the three given in the example.

As has been mentioned earlier, there is no guarantee that weights will always be non-negative. When this happens, in most cases the reason is that the marginal requirements are contradictory and one or more must be relaxed, for instance by collapsing some categories. It can also happen (not often) that the matrix in (2.2) is singular so that there is more than one solution to the system. This means that one of the conditions in (2.1) is redundant: either the selection of marginal variables must be modified or one of the solutions must be chosen by an additional criterion.

Because this method seeks to minimise variance of the weights employed it is not suited to multi-stage weighting as it may largely nullify the effects, for instance, of design weighting. The generalised regression method described below is more appropriate when prior weighting has to be preserved.

To illustrate this method we will use the same simple example as before, with two marginal variables. Assume that we have thirty respondents with the following cell distribution:

4	3
5	8
4	6

The marginal requirements are the following:

4	3	10
5	8	10
4	6	10
20	10	

The weights $w_{i,j}$ ($i = 1, 2, 3$, $j = 1, 2$) to be found should therefore satisfy five equations

$$\begin{cases} 4w_{1,1} + 3w_{1,2} = 10 \\ 5w_{2,1} + 8w_{2,2} = 10 \\ 4w_{3,1} + 6w_{3,2} = 10 \\ 4w_{1,1} + 5w_{2,1} + 4w_{3,1} = 20 \\ 3w_{1,2} + 8w_{2,2} + 6w_{3,2} = 10. \end{cases}$$

There will be five new variables $\lambda_1, \lambda_2, \lambda_3, \mu_1, \mu_2$ and the system (2.2) for them will be the following

$$\begin{cases} 7\lambda_1 + 4\mu_1 + 3\mu_2 = 20 \\ 13\lambda_2 + 5\mu_1 + 8\mu_2 = 20 \\ 10\lambda_3 + 4\mu_1 + 6\mu_2 = 20 \\ 4\lambda_1 + 5\lambda_2 + 4\lambda_3 + 13\mu_1 = 40 \\ 3\lambda_1 + 8\lambda_2 + 6\lambda_3 + 17\mu_2 = 20. \end{cases}$$

This system may easily be solved and the (unique) solution is

$$\lambda_1 = 5.8337, \quad \lambda_2 = 4.8496, \quad \lambda_3 = 5.2836, \quad \mu_1 = -2.2090, \quad \mu_2 = -4.0$$

so that the weights can be computed by formula (2.3). For convenience, they are shown in a table form:

1.8123	0.9169
1.3203	0.4248
1.5373	0.6418

The total sum of squares (the value of function f) for these weights is 37.74. Notice that this is slightly smaller than the sum of squares produced by the iterative method described earlier. The weights in each cell are slightly different, though of course the marginal totals remain the same.

2.4.3 GREG (generalised regression)

A more general method is to choose weights which have the minimal possible distance to *initial* or *desired* weights. Let (w_i) be the final weights and (v_i) be the initial/desired weights. The function to minimise is then

$$\sum_i \text{dist}(w_i, v_i), \tag{2.4}$$

with the condition that (w_i) must satisfy system (2.1). The distance $dist$ could be any distance function such as the square of the difference or any other non-negative function. This problem may arise, for example, when initial weights have been allocated but now additional weighting has to be done to correct the sample with respect to certain population benchmarks. The correction should be such that the distortion from the original weights is minimised. Quite often the initial weights are the *probability* weights, i.e. weights which are inversely proportional to the respondent's probability of selection within some intermediate sampling unit such as a household.

If the distance function is simply the square of the difference and $v_i = 1$ for any i, this method coincides with the previous method of variance minimisation because

$$\sum_i (w_i - 1)^2 = \sum_i w_i^2 - 2 \sum_i w_i + n$$

(n is the unweighted sample size). The sum $\sum_i w_i$ is constant so that in this case we will really minimise the sum of squared weights.

Clearly, the mathematical algorithm to solve the general minimisation problem depends on the distance function and includes, in many cases, regression techniques. We will not go into further details here but several papers [6, 11, 12, 13, 19, 31, 60] can be recommended in which various techniques are discussed.

2.5   Aggregate weighting

At the beginning of this chapter we stressed the difference between weights, used in varying the contribution of individual respondents to the final estimates, and quantities, used (in conjunction with weights) in incrementing tables where something other than numbers of people are being accumulated. It is sometimes necessary to adjust the results from a sample to ensure that the *sums of the weighted quantities* match target figures. Such targets may be established from official or industry statistics or from other reliable sources. It must also be borne in mind that the adjustment of the summed quantities may need to be carried out in conjunction with, but normally after, the weighting of respondents to match the known population.

The first task is to establish how any mismatch between the sample estimate and the target might have arisen. This involves judgement about the nature and quality of the sample data (and possibly the target figures).

Discrepancies of this kind may arise from both sampling errors and non-sampling errors. Non-sampling errors relate to discrepancies between the reported or observed values for individual respondents and the corresponding true values. If the reported values cannot be regarded as individually accurate it is very questionable whether weighting of respondents is a suitable way of countering the discrepancies. If a discrepancy arises to any great extent from non-sampling sources of error, is it reasonable to try to compensate for this through weighting, or what other form of correction can be made?

Among the principal sources of bias are culture-based social pressures (prestige, guilt, 'political correctness', etc.). It is well known, for instance, that in some cultures respondents severely understate their expenditure on tobacco, alcohol, confectionery and gambling, though they are unlikely to deny totally their involvement in these. In other instances respondents may systematically over-report. In cases like this it may be felt appropriate to assume that any respondent with a non-zero value is understating and simply to adjust all the non-zero values upwards or downwards. Or perhaps some respondents deliberately omit or conceal non-zero values.

This is a judgement issue and the researcher has the duty to make a considered judgement. Weighting should not be used as a fix for inconvenient or untidy numbers. It is too easy to use a mechanical weighting process as a substitute for a considered judgement and thereby avoid responsibility. **Only with very strong justification should weighting be used to correct non-sampling errors.**

Examination of data and targets should include the following considerations.

- Are we sure the target figures relate solely to the survey population? If our survey is among consumers are we sure that the target figures do not include business activity? (This check should not be necessary, of course, but experience suggests otherwise.)
- Are we confident that amounts have not been misrecorded? A few numbers misaligned in the data file, and therefore out by a factor of a power of ten, can have a noticeable effect. If sound verification procedures are in force at the data entry stages this should not happen – but it is not unknown.
- How reliable and accurate are the quantities being reported by individual sample members likely to be? Is it something that can be precisely verified by the respondent (such as the amount of the most recent electricity bill) or is it a best guess from memory ('average number of cinema visits per month')?
- Does the information provided by the respondent relate to the respondent alone or does it cover others (perhaps the family)? Is this appropriate, is it done consistently and could this affect the estimates?
- Does the shape of the distribution of the quantity suggest any obvious cause? Do we know anything about the population distribution? Where a high proportion of the aggregate is likely to be accounted for by a small number of cases with large values of the quantity, have we got too many or too few of these?
- Has there been a lot of rounding? Examination of the first and last significant digits may help: is there an unreasonable number of (non-zero) values ending in zero, for instance, and should the distribution of first significant digits follow Benford's law [5, 27, 28]?
- Is there any indication from elsewhere that respondents are likely consistently to overstate or understate, consciously or unconsciously, the quantity concerned?
- Are there too many or too few zero values? Are respondents likely to have omitted or concealed positive values?

The decision to be made at this stage is: are the quantity values of individual respondents to be changed, or is the balance between them to be changed by weighting? If the quantity values can be changed, by ascribing or imputing new values as some function of the old, then re-weighting the sample (other than that needed to balance the sample) should be unnecessary.

Alternatives to weighting This book is not mainly concerned with non-sampling errors, or with the design of questionnaires. But before considering the ways of correcting aggregates by weighting we should digress to look at the alternatives of imputing adjusted values to some or all cases. This may be appropriate and justifiable and, if so, is likely to have fewer adverse side-effects than weighting. The principal benefit is that the effects are localised. If the value of a quantity is changed for a specific respondent the remaining quantities are not (usually) affected. If the respondent's weight is unchanged, the weights of all other respondents are similarly unaffected. This would probably be the preferred course of action if many quantities are involved and the differences between actual and target sums of weighted quantities are considerable.

The choices available depend on how the values have been obtained or recorded. The simplest form of recording is as an exact numerical value. It may be reasonable to expect this in some cases, but often we have to be content with an estimate, or more realistically a 'best guess'. To encourage respondents to make that best guess some form of stimulus, often in the form of a list of ranges of possible values, may be needed. The coarseness or fineness of the gradations will depend on the subject matter. The resulting responses will be inexact and we have to interpret them in order to make any aggregated estimate. But this is often preferable to accepting a high level of 'don't knows' (as well as heavily rounded estimates) if respondents are pressed to name a specific figure.

If the information has been collected in terms of approximate numbers or ranges, and we are confident that our sample is sufficiently representative of the population, we may feel justified in inferring some consistent response bias and imputing values to such responses so that the aggregate or mean and the shape of the distribution correspond to what is *known* about the population.

Imputation here is rather different in its purpose (and method) from the case of missing data (see section 3.4) in that we are claiming to infer an 'improved' value for a respondent based on external benchmarks rather than on other information provided by the respondent.

If after careful consideration of the alternatives we are still convinced that weighting is appropriate, a number of decisions have still to be made before the method of applying the corrections is chosen.

The weighting of aggregates in this way can put considerable stress on the sample. If sums of *quantities* associated with the respondents are being adjusted by applying weights to *respondents*, the profile of the sample respondents will also be changed. Assuming that the sample of respondents (as individuals) is also required to match targets of sums of weights, then a further set of constraints is imposed. Sums of weights and sums of weighted quantities must both correspond to the targets set. If this is not done there is a risk that serious biases may have been introduced into the composition of the sample itself.

Zero
quantities

Correcting quantity aggregate sums by weighting means that some respondents are up-weighted and some down-weighted to change the shape of the distribution of quantities. If the sum of quantities is below the target, respondents with high values will have to be up-weighted and respondents with low values down-weighted to match. This raises the question of what is to be done with zero quantities. Where only a small proportion of respondents has non-zero values it may be acceptable to apply a single adjustment constant to the existing weights of all such respondents and to down-weight all those with zero values accordingly.

But many quantity measures have a high incidence of zero values for good reasons. For instance, a quantity 'expenditure on dog food' is likely to be zero for most non-dog-owners. Are we satisfied that the zero-value cases are represented in the sample in their correct proportion? Is the correction only to be made among respondents reporting non-zero values or should we allow the zero-value respondents to be up-weighted or down-weighted as well? In the example given above, that would undoubtedly change the estimate of the incidence of dog-ownership unless a constraint is applied to keep this fixed.

Preliminary examination of the distribution of values should be undertaken to assess the likelihood of a successful adjustment. As a routine measure the difference between the target mean and the observed mean should be standardised (divided by the standard deviation of the observed values). A simpler measure to take is the proportions of observed values falling above and below the target mean. The greater the absolute standardised value, or the lower the lesser proportion, the greater is the distortion likely to be introduced by the adjustment. If the target mean lies wholly outside the range of observed values, of course, no adjustment of weights can produce the desired result without resorting to the use of negative weights.

Adjusting multiple quantities

Where there is more than one quantity to be reconciled with a target the situation is more complicated. In many cases respondents will have non-zero values for more than one quantity. Conceivably all respondents will have non-zero values for all quantities. The adjustment to weights will therefore be made individually for every respondent and will be a function of the position of the respondent in the distribution of each quantity. Note that if more than one quantity has to be corrected by weighting it may be very difficult or even impossible to preserve the weighted numbers of zero-value cases. A zero-value respondent for one quantity may have a non-zero value for another.

Consider the case of a data set with two quantities which both need to be adjusted upwards in aggregate, and a respondent with non-zero values of both of these. If this respondent has a below-average value for one quantity (implying down-weighting of that respondent) but an above-average value for the other (implying up-weighting) the net result is likely to be that that respondent's weight will not be changed greatly. Weight changes will be predominantly among respondents whose values for the quantities are either both below or both above the respective quantity means. The greater the number of quantities to be adjusted in this way, the greater is the potential for distortion of the results.

If such aggregate weighting is undertaken, particularly with multiple quantities, it is essential to inspect the composition of the sample after weighting and to compare it with the pre-adjustment sample, in respect of the following.

- The means and variances of the quantities should be calculated and the shapes of the distributions should be plotted. Visual comparison of the pairs of (weighted) distributions should reveal any major distortion. If the shape of any distribution has changed noticeably is there reason to think that the adjusted distribution is more consistent with reality?

- Correlations (weighted) between the quantities should be compared. If there has been a general strengthening or weakening of correlations, does this make sense in terms of other background knowledge? If correlation within one or more particular groups of quantities has changed, does this also make sense?
- The distribution of weights should be examined. Has aggregate weighting changed the variance of the weights and their distribution unduly? What effect is this likely to have on the precision of estimates (see the following chapter)? Are there any negative weights, and if so, what is to be done about this?

Such examination will reveal the price that has to be paid for bringing the aggregate estimates into line with benchmarks through weighting. Whether this price is worth paying must be left to the judgement of the researcher but it is a judgement that should be explicitly made.

If the changes introduced by aggregate weighting are felt to be unacceptable, consideration should be given to alternatives: imputation, as discussed above, or just accepting that the sample under-estimates or over-estimates by a known amount.

We now consider some practical methods of applying aggregate weighting. Aggregate weighting typically uses techniques similar to those employed in marginal weighting as described earlier. The principal difference is that we are dealing with continuous distributions rather than with discrete groups of respondents.

Assume that there are m variables for which the weighted sample estimates should coincide with population benchmarks. Denote by $(B_j)_{j=1}^m$ the target figures. These variables might, for instance, be volumes of brands within a product category for which there is a reliable source of information about their population totals. For respondent i and brand j, denote by $a_{i,j}$ the 'brand' value, that is the amount respondent i purchased of brand j. The set of requirements for aggregate weighting is then the following

$$\sum_i a_{i,j} w_i = B_j, \quad j = 1, \ldots, m, \tag{2.5}$$

where w_i is the weight for respondent i.

Just as in marginal weighting of respondents, not all requirements are necessarily compatible with each other (especially if individual brand values are zero for many respondents) and the result may include negative weights if there are contradictions.

As well as requiring that the weighted values of the (quantity) variables should sum to known totals it is also reasonable, in most cases, to require that the sums of weights of respondents, in total and in defined subsets, should be held to fixed totals. Weighting to match quantity targets should ideally not be allowed to distort the profile of the sample of respondents.

Again, the system (2.5) usually has many solutions because the number of equations is simply the number of quantities for which we wish to correct the totals, and this number is normally less than the number of respondents. Therefore, there are several ways of choosing a solution of (2.5). We will consider four methods of aggregate weighting of which the first three are very similar to the methods of case weighting described in section 2.4.

2.5.1 Rim Weighting

The procedures for calculating (or adjusting) weights iteratively are similar in principle to those described earlier for adjusting respondent proportions, but with differences appropriate to the kind of data being adjusted.

The simplest procedure in this case is to treat each quantity as a weighting variable or dimension. However, instead of the numbers in each of the categories being compared with corresponding targets, for each dimension or quantity the weight correction factor applied to the respondent is a function of that respondent's value of the quantity relative to the quantity mean.

The requirements for transforming the weights would follow two principles.

- Respondents with a value relative to the target mean in the direction in which the mean is to be adjusted should have their weights increased (e.g. if the mean is to be increased, those with a value greater than the target should have their weights increased while those below the target should have their weights decreased).
- Respondents with values distant from the target mean should have their weights adjusted more than those close to the target mean. This would concentrate the adjustment of weights where it would most affect the mean.

There are many different ways of adjusting weights so that the mean weighted quantity will match the target mean. However, it would also be preferable to keep the sum of weights constant as well as to minimise the disruption in weights. Fortunately, there is a mathematical solution to this problem. The procedure may be applied to the whole data set or it may be restricted to, and therefore performed wholly within, some defined subset. This may be defined by some outward attribute (geographical area, sex, etc.) or by some attribute related to the task in hand, for example, only respondents with non-zero values. Let n be the number of respondents involved. For respondent i, denote by x_i the quantity value and by w_i the respondent's current weight. Let W be the total sum of current weights in the sample and t the target quantity mean.

The objective is therefore to find a new set of weights $(w_i')_{i=1}^n$ satisfying the requirements

$$\sum_{i=1}^n w_i' = W, \qquad \sum_{i=1}^n w_i' x_i = t W$$

and for which the total discrepancy from the current weights

$$\sum_{i=1}^n \left(w_i' - w_i \right)^2$$

is minimised.

The (unique) solution to this problem is given by the following formula (see Appendix D for a proof):

$$w_i' = w_i + \frac{(t - \bar{x})W}{n \cdot \mathrm{var}(x)} \cdot (x_i - \bar{x}_0), \tag{2.6}$$

where $\bar{x}$ is the actual weighted mean quantity, $\bar{x}_0$ is the actual *unweighted* mean quantity (i.e. $\bar{x}_0 = (x_1 + \cdots + x_n)/n$) and var($x$) is the unweighted sample variance:

$$\text{var}(x) = \frac{1}{n} \sum_{i=1}^{n} x_i^2 - \bar{x}_0^2.$$

Notice that if, for instance, $\bar{x} < t$, the new weights will be greater (than the current weights) for respondents with value x_i greater than the mean value $\bar{x}_0$, and the new weights will be smaller for respondents with values less than the mean value $\bar{x}_0$. However, the adjustment process is additive and accordingly there is no guarantee that all new weights will be non-negative. As in conventional marginal weighting, aggregate requirements can be contradictory.

This adjustment of weights is repeated for each variable where the target quantity is required. When adjustments are made to the weights in respect of any one variable, the weighted totals for the variables previously adjusted will almost certainly become different from their targets. When all have been adjusted the cycle will have to be repeated, though the discrepancies between actual and target sums of weighted quantities will (or at least should) be less with each iteration. Iterations of the cycle continue until an appropriately low level of discrepancies is reached.

It is also a very straightforward matter to include the 'conventional' weighting dimensions in this process, thus allowing the composition of the sample itself to be controlled and reducing the whole process to a single stage. However, it is probably preferable in general to apply the non-quantity weighting first and then to weight by quantities in a second stage, with the original (non-quantity) targets being included to hold the composition of the sample constant. This has the advantage that it allows the contributions of the conventional and quantity weightings to the overall change to be assessed separately.

As an alternative, the quantities can be treated in the same way as the overlapping categories described on page 62, where instead of considering each dimension in rotation the largest single discrepancy is always tackled next. The problem here is in determining which is the 'biggest' discrepancy as the quantities may all have different units and hence different scales. Expressing the differences between actual and target values for both means and proportions relative to the standard deviations of the actual values (the standard deviation of a proportion being $\sqrt{p(1-p)}$) is probably the simplest solution. In discussing iterative marginal weighting in section 2.4.1 we advised selecting the variable to be selected for correction on the basis of the biggest absolute difference between the sum of current weights and the target. Because the scaling of the quantity values can vary widely and arbitrarily, this is not feasible here. Some form of standardisation is probably inevitable. (This is a minor concern relative to the other problems likely to be encountered in aggregate weighting.)

In both cases iteration should continue until the greatest remaining difference does not exceed some suitable threshold value.

2.5.2 Minimisation of variance

The problem is formulated in the same way as for marginal weighting – minimise the variance of weights while ensuring that they satisfy equation (2.5). For simplicity, we also require that the total sum of weights should be fixed:

$$\sum_i w_i = P. \tag{2.7}$$

The mathematical problem is then exactly the same as for marginal weighting, that is to minimise the sum of squared weights $\sum_i w_i^2$.

The solution can again be obtained by the Lagrange multipliers method. The new $m + 1$ variables $(\lambda_j)_{j=1}^m$ and μ should satisfy the system of $m + 1$ linear equations

$$\begin{cases} \sum_{j=1}^m \lambda_j \sum_i a_{i,l} a_{i,j} + \mu \sum_i a_{i,l} = 2B_l, & l = 1, \ldots, m \\ \sum_{j=1}^m \lambda_j \sum_i a_{i,j} + \mu n = 2P, \end{cases} \tag{2.8}$$

where n is the unweighted sample size.

This system can be solved by standard linear system techniques and then the weights are calculated by the formula (see Appendix D)

$$w_i = 0.5 \left(\sum_{l=1}^m \lambda_l a_{i,l} + \mu \right).$$

2.5.3 GREG (generalised regression)

System (2.5) may also be solved by choosing the solution which is the closest possible to the initial or desired weights. Again, this is very similar to marginal weighting and particular techniques depend on the way the distance between weights is calculated.

2.5.4 'Quantity weights' approach

Finally, one more approach to solving system (2.5) may be useful where all the quantities are closely related, for instance where they represent the volumes of different 'components', for instance brands of a commodity, such that the sum of the component quantity values within each respondent is itself a meaningful number (volume of the total commodity associated with the respondent). This approach introduces what may be called *quantity weights*. These weights are then used to calculate the respondent's weights. In mathematical terms, let $(v_j)_{j=1}^m$ be the quantity weights of the m components. Then the assumption with this method is that there is the following relationship between the quantity weights and the respondent's weights (w_i):

$$w_i = \sum_{j=1}^m c_{j,i} v_j, \tag{2.9}$$

where $C = (c_{j,i})$ is an $m \times n$ matrix (n is the unweighted sample size). One particular way to get matrix C is to obtain each respondent's *shares* of each aggregate quantity, so that $c_{j,i}$ is simply $a_{i,j}$ divided by the total of the jth column in matrix $A = (a_{i,j})$. Therefore, in this case a respondent's weight will depend on the 'mix' of values of the quantities for that respondent. However, there is no predetermined formula for C and there could be other ways to define it.

The respondent's weights are then relatively easy to compute. In matrix terms, the equations (2.5) can be written as

$$A\bar{W} = \bar{B},$$

where $\bar{W} = (w_i)$ and $\bar{B} = (B_j)$ are the corresponding columns. According to formula (2.9), $\bar{W} = C\bar{V}$, where $\bar{V} = (v_j)$ is the column of quantity weights. Hence,

$$AC\bar{V} = \bar{B}. \tag{2.10}$$

The matrix AC is quadratic, with dimensions $m \times m$, and its inversion then gives us the solution in terms of quantity weights:

$$\bar{V} = (AC)^{-1}\bar{B}.$$

Now the respondent's weights are calculated by formula (2.9).

In practice, there are two requirements for matrix C: (a) the matrix AC should not be singular, i.e. equation (2.10) should have a unique solution, (b) the weights should in most cases be non-negative.

A disadvantage of this method is that it does not fix the overall sum of respondent weights so that the final sum of weights could, therefore, be different from any meaningful figure.

2.6   Multi-stage and hybrid weighting systems

In some cases it may be appropriate to apply weights in more than one stage. An instance would be where households have been sampled with equal probability, and one individual has then been selected randomly from each household, but the sample is to represent individuals. Then an initial design weight may be applied to each sampled individual inversely proportional to his or her probability of selection *within the household*. This weight then becomes the initial weight ('prior weight') attached to the respondent at the start of the next stage of weighting, whether this is cell weighting, marginal weighting of respondents, aggregate quantity weighting or some other method.

Or in a multi-country survey each country's sample may be weighted appropriately for the respective country, and at the coordination stage a further weight applied to balance the various countries, in proportion to their respective populations.

The final weight applied to each respondent is then the product of the weights and correction factors applied at each stage.

The various alternative weighting procedures all have as their common object the matching of results from a sample to values derived from external knowledge about the population the sample is to represent. It is possible that in some circumstances no single method is appropriate. We have already touched on the use of different weighting methods sequentially at different stages. It is also possible to use different methods within the same stage. Apart from the trivial case where different methods are applied in different strata, the main reason for requiring this is the need to use cell weighting to ensure the correct sums of weights for combinations of weighting variable categories but also to apply additional controls independent of some or all of the cell weighting variables.

The simplest option is to perform the cell weighting and further marginal weighting in cycles until all the sums of weights are acceptably close to the targets. This is in fact equivalent to making the cell weighting matrix into a single weighting dimension in a conventional marginal weighting procedure.

However, it is not possible to be certain in advance whether this method will result in convergence, especially if the weighting systems we want to combine are very different from each other. In general, more research is needed about convergence in marginal weighting.

A much more efficient approach is, we believe, to write all equations from several weighting systems together and then to *solve them simultaneously*. For example, to combine cell and marginal weighting, more equations are added to the system (2.1). The new equations should state that sums of weights from the corresponding cells should coincide with target figures. This method means, in particular, that *respondents within the same cell may now have different weights*. Once all requirements have been obtained, the new system of equations can be solved using one of the methods already described. The total number of equations should still be reasonable so that there should not be problems from a computational point of view.

The advantages of this method become even more obvious if we want to combine, for example, marginal and aggregate weighting. The problem with aggregate weighting is that it does not normally take account of sums of respondent weights, whether in cells or marginally. This is a case where there could be problems with convergence of rim weighting. But if we write all equations from (2.1) and (2.5) together, we can still solve the new system and, therefore, obtain the weights which give both the correct marginal totals and the correct aggregate totals. Clearly, any of the methods described above can be chosen to achieve this. It is possible that different methods would otherwise have been used for marginal weighting and aggregate weighting. Now, of course, a single method is used for both of them. But this compromise is a small price to pay for the opportunity to meet both marginal and aggregate requirements simultaneously.

2.7   Statistical considerations

In this chapter we have examined the reasons for applying weighting and the methods of doing it. Broadly, weighting is aimed at improving the *accuracy* of sample-based estimates.

The following chapter is devoted to the estimation of the effect of both sampling and weighting on the *precision* of estimates. But to round off this discussion of the processes of weighting it may be appropriate to summarise (even at the risk of some repetition) the effects of the weighting itself. The price of increased accuracy is (normally) a loss in precision. This loss may be small and affordable, and the net effect can (and should) be an improvement in the overall quality of the information yielded by the sample. But if the weighting is not carried out with some discrimination and with care the result will not necessarily be an improvement.

Weighting involves a calculable increase in the variance of estimates and thus a widening of confidence limits and a loss of discrimination in significance testing. The loss of precision is related to the range of weights applied. The greater the range of weights, the greater the loss.

For any sample-based estimate, a measure of the overall loss of precision can be obtained by calculating the 'effective sample size'. This is, as it were, the size of the 'pure' sample which would have the same degree of precision as the weighted actual sample. It is this figure, rather than the unweighted sample size, that should be used in significance tests and in estimating confidence limits. Where a subset of the sample is chosen the same formula is applied within that subset. If the subset corresponds to one cell in a cell weighting matrix, for example, all the respondents will have the same weight so the weighting will have no effect on the effective sample size.

The weighting effect

The ratio of actual sample size to effective sample size is known as the 'design effect'. Design effects are typically (but not always) greater than 1.0 (i.e. the results are less precise than the unweighted sample size suggests). However, the design effect is not a constant for the whole survey. It can vary from question to question and even for different answer categories within a question as well as within different subgroups of the sample. The weighting effect, however, remains constant for all questions within any one subsample. Where weighting has been employed the contribution of the weighting process to the overall design effect can readily be calculated. The 'weighting effect' is a component of the design effect that can be independently estimated. Fortunately the calculation is a simple one involving just the sum of the weights and the sum of their squares.

Calculation of the weighting effect will give exactly the same result whether the weights are calculated to average 1.0 or are scaled to represent a population total or sum to some other arbitrary total. The scaling of weights has no effect on the statistics. However, some statistical packages do not deal correctly with weighted data when performing significance tests and may treat the sum of the weights as though it were the (unweighted) sample size. If the sum of the weights is greater than the effective sample size such packages will overstate the significance of results. If their sum is smaller, the significance will be understated. The usual, but unsatisfactory, response in these cases is 'run significance tests using unweighted data'. As weighting was presumably done to redress biases or imbalances, the difference being tested for may be greater or smaller in the unweighted data than in the final weighted data and the weighted difference is presumably the better estimate. As will be demonstrated in Chapter 4 the most commonly used significance tests *can*, with care, be performed satisfactorily with weighted data. However, for potential problems with statistical software see section 3.3.8.

The picture is more complicated where the sample has been stratified and/or clustered. Stratification may benefit some estimates. Clustering erodes the effective sample size. Calculation of the combined effects of stratification, clustering, non-response weighting, etc. is a complex issue, discussed in some detail in Chapter 3, but the more complex the sample, by and large, the greater will be the design effect. However, it is worth repeating that the combined effect of all these design parameters is not constant across the survey but can vary from question to question.

Whatever method of weighting is applied it is essential to check what effect the weighting process has had. Design effects and weighting effects should be calculated for some of the principal measures. Methods of assessing the design effect are discussed in Chapter 3.

Even simple checks such as the variance of the weights (within strata if appropriate) will give an indication of the likely loss of precision caused by the weighting process. In a multi-stage weighting procedure this should be done at each stage so that the contribution of each stage to the variance of weights can be assessed. This should be a part of the output of any weighting software.

And finally, how much has the weighting actually changed the original estimates? How different are the weighted from the unweighted estimates? If the weighting is so complex that it broadens the confidence intervals of our estimates out of all proportion to the changes it imposes on them, then it may be positively unhelpful. An estimate of $50\% \pm 2\%$ may be of more use than a probably more correct estimate of $49\% \pm 4\%$.

2.8 Ethical considerations

There is nothing unethical in weighting as long as it is carried out objectively, it is done for good reasons and it is fully disclosed.

However, weighting is a process that modifies the data as collected. The weighted results are therefore not the same as the pure sum of what the survey respondents reported. There are (or should be) good reasons for this, as weighting is used to reduce imbalances in the final sample and therefore to improve the overall quality of the results. The critical concern is that the inclusion of weighting in the processing of the data must always be declared and/or obvious.

When results are reported details of weighting should be provided. If only a summary of the procedure is provided in a published report, fuller details should be made available to anyone with a legitimate interest. When presenting weighted results in tabular form it is good practice to give at least some indication of the numbers of interviews on which the figures are based. This is particularly necessary when the weights do not have a mean value of 1.0.

Documentation of weighting procedures is essential. Future analysis of the same data set should yield identical results. Because weight calculation algorithms can differ, as we have seen, it may not be possible for a later user without access to the software that did the original weighting to reproduce exactly the weights applied in the originally released data set. Any weights allocated to a respondent should be embedded in that respondent's data so that it can be re-used later without the need to recalculate. Adequate details both of the procedure itself and of any benchmarks, target sums of weights, population estimates and other reference material should be preserved and archived with the data set.

Above all it must be remembered that weighting is not a *remedy* for any problem. Weighting should not be thought of as repairing deficiencies in a sample and should not be relied on as a solution for inadequacies of sample planning or execution. It is, perhaps, all too easy to regard weighting as yielding an unconditional improvement. If that is so, the thinking goes, then the more we do the better. True, used wisely and with discrimination, weighting should be capable of improving the accuracy of sample-based estimates, but the distinction and the balance between accuracy and precision which was discussed at the beginning of Chapter 1 should not be lost sight of. Above all, weighting should not be allowed to induce complacency, and worse still self-delusion, any more than the use of simple random sampling.

3 Statistical effects of sampling and weighting

This chapter presents a subject often overlooked in statistical books: sampling and weighting methods may have a very strong and usually adverse effect on the statistical tools used in the evaluation of sample-based data, such as the standard error and confidence limits. Simple random sampling is rarely used in practice, except in limited or artificial situations. Even if it is used, the final sample may still turn out to be biased and may require some weighting to remove obvious imbalances. As a result, the usual simple formulae for standard errors and confidence limits become inadequate in most surveys and may lead to wrong conclusions.

The estimation of the variance of an estimate lies at the heart of any attempt to assess the confidence limits of that estimate or to apply any significance test to it. The term 'variance' is frequently misused and has a very precise and specific meaning here. The term is sometimes used loosely where 'variation' or 'variability' would be appropriate. It is also used elsewhere to mean a difference between an observed value and a reference or expected value. But in the context of statistics it is a measure of how individual observations vary around their mean value.

Within its statistical sense there are two kinds of variance with which we may have to deal. Both are measures of dispersion or scatter of observations. The first has to do with the variation that occurs within the sample: how much, for instance, the height of individual sample members varies around the overall mean (see page 230). But it is the second with which we are more immediately concerned. This relates to the extent to which estimates of the same thing would vary *from sample to sample*. It therefore gives us our indication of how precise our estimate is likely to be. As we rarely have the opportunity to examine multiple 'identical' samples we normally use statistical theory to estimate this from the variation within the sample. This 'variance of the estimate' is then used to calculate the standard error and 'confidence interval' of the estimate.

A realistic estimate of variance is therefore essential. We should say 'realistic' rather than precise: even with a simple random sample the estimate of the variance of the population, derived from the variance observed in the sample, is itself an estimate and subject to a margin of error because independent samples all drawn to the same specifications would yield different estimates of the variance. Where the sample is not a simple random one, it is still often possible to obtain a reasonable estimate of the variance, even in cases where no detail of how the sample was selected may be known. Where details of the sampling method are available, better, or at least simpler, procedures may be available.

At all events, there is no reason to ignore the question of calculating variance. To act as though a sample were a simple random one when it clearly is not is both reprehensible and unnecessary. It may not always be practicable for individual researchers to undertake the necessary calculations with the tools at their disposal, but they should at the very least be aware of the nature of the effects of sample design and weighting. They should also be able to make reasonable assessments of at least the direction and preferably the likely magnitude of these effects and to make at least some allowance for them in the assessment of results, even if this means no more than a cautious interpretation of significance tests.

Detailed discussion of the statistical effects of sampling is beyond the scope of this book. There is an extensive literature on sampling theory for interested readers. Instead of presenting the full theory, we give several common formulae and algorithms for calculating variance, which should cover a wide range of actual situations. We also present a useful pragmatic approach that allows us to estimate all effects by a simple formula based only on weighting. Finally, the statistical effects of missing data in a sample are discussed. All necessary proofs are given in Appendix E.

This chapter will of necessity have more mathematical formulae because we need to deal with variance estimation. Several technical results are placed in boxes, so that readers who wish to can skip them.

3.1   Calculation of variance

The formula for calculating the variance of an estimate depends on the sampling method and on weighting as well as on the estimate itself. In other words, there is no one formula that would be appropriate for all situations.

The more complex the sample design, the more difficult it is to compute the variance of an estimate. Post-sampling correction (weighting) adds further to the complexity. This affects both the difficulty of obtaining the estimate and the confidence we can have in its accuracy. As we get away from the simplest sample designs, the amount of computation required increases rapidly and it becomes more burdensome to calculate an estimate of variance for every estimate generated. So too the degree of uncertainty in the estimate of variance itself increases, as it may be more difficult to judge whether the calculation method being used is adequate, optimistic or over-conservative for the specific characteristics of the particular estimate.

In any but the simplest cases there is usually no simple answer to the problem of choosing the appropriate formula. In practice there is often no standard formula that fits the situation exactly and an approximation should be used. Most books on sampling theory discuss variance calculations for the effects of stratification and clustering. In practice, however, these techniques are almost always combined with various weighting methods. Weighting may be used to compensate for pre-stratification, non-response and known, designed-in or *a priori* variations in probability of selec-tion, and there are very few formulae that match modern weighting techniques. For example, post-stratification itself can be very complex, e.g. setting sum-of-weights targets for *several variables simultaneously*, marginally and/or within cells, using different mathematical tools. Potentially, any method of weighting would require its own formula or method to calculate the variance. In general, much more research is required in this area.

We first discuss ways of computing the variance in simple cases, where only one sample design factor is influencing an otherwise simple random sample. We then give several general formulae that can be used as an approximation in a wide range of practical situations. An assumption we use (and which is justified in most practical cases) is that the sample size is very small compared with the population so that we can ignore the sampling fraction.

In the following, $\bar{x}$ is a sampling mean and $\hat{p}$ is a sampling proportion. Capital letters will be used for totals rather than average values.

3.1.1 Stratification

The population is first divided into m sub-populations called strata and the sampling is conducted in each sub-population separately. The final sampling mean is then estimated as the corresponding average of strata means:

$$\bar{x} = \sum_{s=1}^{m} \lambda_s \bar{x}_s, \tag{3.1}$$

where λ_s is the proportion of the population represented by stratum s.

The variance of $\bar{x}$ is then easy to compute in terms of strata variances:

$$\mathrm{var}(\bar{x}) = \sum_{s=1}^{m} \lambda_s^2 \mathrm{var}(\bar{x}_s). \tag{3.2}$$

The same applies to a proportion, with $\hat{p}$ substituted for $\bar{x}$ in formula (3.2). If the sampling within each stratum is simple random, the standard formulae can be used to estimate the variance of strata means/proportions. However, the formula above is valid for *any* sampling and weighting design inside individual strata as long as each stratum's variance can be calculated correctly.

The strata may or may not be represented in the sample in the same proportions as they occupy in the population. When the sampling is proportional and simple random in each stratum (called *stratified random sampling*), the variance is generally less than the variance of the overall simple random sampling (see Cochran [9], Theorem 5.8) although reductions in variance are usually small. However, when the incidence of an attribute varies considerably between strata the gain (or, occasionally, the loss) in precision can be appreciable (see page 18). If the strata have been disproportionately sampled and the variances in the over-sampled strata are higher (which in the case of proportions means estimates closer to 50%) then there should be some gain in precision. Otherwise there is likely to be some loss.

In general, whether stratification has a beneficial effect or not depends on the sampling strata proportions, on the difference between strata estimates and on survey priorities. This is illustrated in the next section.

3.1.2   Clustering

Cluster sampling is a very common survey technique and is a generalisation of simple random sampling: instead of individual respondents, *clusters* of respondents are randomly chosen. Clusters often do not all have the same size. Even if the *intention* was to have them equal, it is often impossible to achieve this in practice. They are also very unlikely to be equal in size if any subset of the sample is analysed, unless this is defined purely in terms of whole clusters.

We present here just one useful variance formula for cluster sampling (see Theorems 9A.3, 9A.4 in Cochran [9]): assume that a sample of m clusters is drawn from a population, with selection probabilities of the cluster members proportional to their sizes. Let $\bar{x}_i$ be a mean estimate of cluster i and let $\bar{x}$ be the mean of cluster means:

$$\bar{x} = \frac{1}{m} \sum_{i=1}^{m} \bar{x}_i. \tag{3.3}$$

Then the variance of $\bar{x}$ is estimated similarly to simple random sampling, but as the variance of the cluster *means*:

$$\text{var}(\bar{x}) = \sum_{i=1}^{m} \frac{(\bar{x}_i - \bar{x})^2}{m(m-1)}.$$

Notice that we do not consider post-stratification as a separate case simply because the existing formulae are not applicable to many of the more complex post-stratification techniques. For instance, post-stratification is usually done using several variables simultaneously. For some variables, it could simply be an adjustment of marginal proportions while for others the adjustment could be within cells, not necessarily all of them, formed by intersections of these variables. Furthermore, there is a variety of techniques for achieving this including matrix inversion, with or without minimisation of the variance of weights, and iterative approaches, to name but two. Therefore, any theory should consider various techniques and derive the best variance formula for each of them. A more practical approach, however, is to do all weighting first, derive all the weighted estimates and then apply a general variance formula assuming that weighting will automatically reflect itself in the formula. Although not perfect, this is a common practical method and will probably remain so until an appropriate theory is developed.

3.1.3   Ratio estimates

For many surveys we have to deal with *ratio* estimates. This happens where the total sum of weights is not necessarily the same when sampling is repeated. Even the common estimate of a mean as the weighted count divided by the sum of weights will become a ratio estimate in a survey where the sum of weights is not constant. This typically occurs when both the numerator and the denominator in a calculation are estimates that could vary from sample to sample, so that both have their own margins of error. It may sometimes appear confusing because the final weights are often *scaled* to give a fixed total figure (e.g. population) so that the final sum will always look constant. In order to assess whether an estimate is a ratio estimate or not, the scaling should be temporarily excluded from consideration.

For example, a sample of individuals may be selected by initially sampling households, one respondent in a household being randomly chosen for an interview. Respondents are then weighted in proportion to the number of eligible persons in the household to compensate for the unequal probability of selection. The mean estimate (as the weighted count divided by the sum of weights) will then be a ratio estimate because a repetition of the sample may produce a different sum of weights (before the scaling). On the other hand, post-stratification usually does not change the total sum of weights; it only adjusts the relative proportions of population groups in a sample.

A more frequently encountered occasion for using ratio estimates is where an estimate is based on a *subsample* whose size (sum of weights) is not controlled by stratification or post-stratification. Clearly, it is impossible to achieve the correct sampling proportions for all population groups within the sample. Even if the sum of weights is constant for the whole sample, it may be highly volatile for small subsamples (e.g. left-handed dog-owners with blue eyes). Estimates of proportions within such groups would clearly be ratio estimates.

A familiar formula for the variance of a ratio estimate is the following (see Kish [35], formula (6.3.1)): if $r = X/Y$ is a ratio estimate, then

$$\text{var}(r) = \frac{1}{Y^2}[\text{var}(X) + r^2\text{var}(Y) - 2r\text{cov}(X, Y)], \tag{3.4}$$

where $\text{cov}(X, Y)$ is the covariance between variables X and Y. The covariance can be estimated for a clustered sample according to another formula from Kish ([35], formula (6.3.2)): if $X = \sum_{i=1}^{m} X_i$ and $Y = \sum_{i=1}^{m} Y_i$, where X_i and Y_i are the corresponding totals for *cluster i*, then

$$\text{cov}(X, Y) = \sum_{i=1}^{m} X_i Y_i - \frac{XY}{m}. \tag{3.5}$$

A slightly more complicated case is when r is a *ratio of ratios*, that is $r = r_1/r_2$, where $r_1 = X_1/Y_1$ and $r_2 = X_2/Y_2$ are ratio estimates themselves. The above formula for the variance can still be applied. Then the variance of r_1 and r_2 can be computed by the same formula once again, while the covariance between r_1 and r_2 can be obtained by formula (6.6.9) in [35]:

$$\text{cov}(r_1, r_2) = \frac{\text{cov}(X_1, X_2) + r_1 r_2 \text{cov}(Y_1, Y_2) - r_1 \text{cov}(X_2, Y_1) - r_2 \text{cov}(X_1, Y_2)}{Y_1 Y_2}.$$

It is frequently necessary to consider the *difference* between two ratios r_1 and r_2. A well established formula for the variance of the difference can then be applied:

$$\text{var}(r_1 - r_2) = \text{var}(r_1) + \text{var}(r_2) - 2\text{cov}(r_1, r_2), \qquad (3.6)$$

where the covariance is estimated in the same way as before.

Finally, *stratified ratios* are also common in practice. In other words,

$$r = \frac{X}{Y} = \frac{\sum_s X_s}{\sum_s Y_s},$$

where X_s and Y_s are the corresponding totals in stratum s. An astute reader may ask: why do we consider the stratification again? Did the stratification formula (3.2) not guarantee that we can first estimate the variance in each stratum and then get the combined variance? The answer is very simple: the estimate can be based on a subsample for which the sampling strata proportions may disagree with population proportions and which may be different when sampling is repeated. Ideally, for each variable of interest we ought to use a separate estimate based on the correct population proportions. However, this is often not done in practice due to computational limitations and because the true population proportions may be unknown. Assuming strata independence, we can modify an established formula to derive the variance of the stratified ratio:

$$\text{var}(r) = \frac{1}{Y^2} \left[\sum_s \text{var}(X_s) + r^2 \sum_s \text{var}(Y_s) - 2r \sum_s \text{cov}(X_s, Y_s) \right]. \qquad (3.7)$$

3.1.4   Ratio estimates for stratified clustering

A common sampling method is a combination of stratification with clustering, where clusters are chosen randomly with probability proportional to their size. A ratio estimate of a mean value can then be computed as

$$r = \frac{X}{W} = \frac{\sum_s \sum_{i=1}^{m_s} X_{s,i}}{\sum_s \sum_{i=1}^{m_s} W_{s,i}}, \qquad (3.8)$$

where $X_{s,i}, W_{s,i}$ are totals in cluster i within stratum s and m_s is the number of clusters in stratum s. The variable X usually corresponds to weighted counts while W corresponds to the sum of weights. Notice that the weighting is assumed to be finished and all estimates are weighted. To calculate the variance, let $X_s = \sum_{i=1}^{m_s} X_{s,i}$ and $W_s = \sum_{i=1}^{m_s} W_{s,i}$ be the corresponding stratum totals. Then the variance of ratio r can be estimated by formula (6.4.4) from [35]:

$$\text{var}(r) = \frac{1}{W^2} \sum_s \frac{1}{m_s - 1} \left[m_s \sum_{i=1}^{m_s} (X_{s,i} - r W_{s,i})^2 - (X_s - r W_s)^2 \right]. \qquad (3.9)$$

This formula can be applied in many practical situations. Note, however, that it is a requirement that each cluster be wholly within a stratum.

Another general formula should be applied when the clusters are chosen by *systematic sampling*. The estimate r is exactly the same while the variance formula is obtained as a combination of that given by Kish [35], formula 6.5.7, and the stratified ratio formula (3.7):

$$\text{var}(r) = \frac{1}{W^2} \sum_s \frac{m_s \sum_{i=1}^{m_s-1} [(X_{s,i} - r W_{s,i}) - (X_{s,i+1} - r W_{s,i+1})]^2}{2(m_s - 1)}. \quad (3.10)$$

The systematic sampling formula should be applied with caution because it relies on differences between *consecutive* clusters in the original selection. A change in the cluster order from that which was used for the systematic sampling may give a different variance estimate.

Remember that these formulae could be applied to the ratio estimate above. If, however, we know the population proportions, the stratification estimate is more precise:

$$\hat{r} = \sum_s \lambda_s r_s,$$

where $r_s = X_s / W_s$ is the ratio within stratum s and λ_s is the population proportion of stratum s. We use the notation $\hat{r}$ to emphasise that it is a different estimate. To compute the variance of this estimate, we can apply the stratification formula (3.2) and formula (3.9) for *one* stratum. Hence, in the case of random selection of clusters with probability proportional to size the variance will be

$$\text{var}(\hat{r}) = \sum_s \frac{\lambda_s^2 m_s}{W_s^2 (m_s - 1)} \sum_{i=1}^{m_s} (X_{s,i} - r_s W_{s,i})^2. \quad (3.11)$$

For systematic sampling, the variance of the stratification estimate $\hat{r}$ is computed by the following formula:

$$\text{var}(\hat{r}) = \sum_s \frac{\lambda_s^2 m_s \sum_{i=1}^{m_s-1} [(X_{s,i} - r_s W_{s,i}) - (X_{s,i+1} - r_s W_{s,i+1})]^2}{2 W_s^2 (m_s - 1)}. \quad (3.12)$$

It is illustrative to see what happens to the ratio estimate when the weighted sampling proportions are correct, i.e. they coincide with the population proportions. Notice that in this case both estimates r and $\hat{r}$ are the same. In other words, for the same estimate we get two different variance formulae (3.9) and (3.11). Although $\hat{r}$ can be considered as a particular case of r, formula (3.11) is *not* a particular case of (3.9). Of course, in this case the stratification formula (3.11) is correct. This simple example again shows that there is no universal formula and that it is important *first* to decide which estimate to use and *then* to look for a variance formula.

3.1.5   Keyfitz method

Keyfitz [33] has developed a simple method to estimate variance in the case when there are two clusters in each stratum. The ratio estimate (3.8) in this case is

$$r = \frac{X}{W} = \frac{\sum_s (X_{s,1} + X_{s,2})}{\sum_s (W_{s,1} + W_{s,2})},$$

and its variance can be estimated by the following formula:

$$\text{var}(r) = r^2 \sum_s \left(\frac{X_{s,1} - X_{s,2}}{X} - \frac{W_{s,1} - W_{s,2}}{W} \right)^2 \qquad (3.13)$$

(see also Kish [35], formula (6.4.8)). The formula should clearly be applied only if there are exactly two clusters per stratum. In the case when there are more than two clusters in the strata, one might try to divide the original strata into smaller strata that would contain exactly two clusters. The problem could be, of course, that if the sampling procedure is repeated, the substrata may not have two clusters each time. This means that if the assumption about having two clusters in each substratum is not true, the variance may be underestimated. It is therefore desirable that if the Keyfitz method is to be used the sample should be planned with this in mind and the allocation of clusters and strata arranged accordingly.

Keyfitz also gives a generalisation of this formula for a post-stratified estimate. This is not given here for the reason we have already discussed: Keyfitz's post-stratified estimate supposes that all proportions to be adjusted come from values of *one* variable. Even if there are initially several variables, say age, sex and region, it is always assumed that the adjustment is done in all age–sex–region cells which still means that there is only one combined variable. In modern surveys, however, there are often *several* variables for which marginal proportions are adjusted (simply because if all possible cells are considered, many of them may not contain any respondents). In such a case it would be very difficult to construct an estimate that would explicitly incorporate all these variables. Therefore a practical approach is again to apply post-stratification as well as other weighting procedures and then still to use formula (3.13) assuming that all estimates are weighted.

3.1.6   Jackknife and bootstrap

At this point it is appropriate to introduce two interesting and pragmatic alternative techniques for estimating variance: the intriguingly named jackknife and bootstrap methods. The techniques have become popular relatively recently as computing resources have become more readily available but there is already an extensive literature on this topic, from among which just two books may be mentioned. A good conceptual introduction to bootstrap methods is given in Efron and Tibshirani [17]. A more theoretical monograph on jackknife and bootstrap methods is Shao and Tu [51]. Both books have an extensive bibliography where further references can be found.

The traditional approach to variance estimation is to obtain the true population variance corresponding to a sample estimate and then look for a formula based on sample data that would approximate this population variance. As we have seen, this may be an onerous and exacting task and it becomes increasingly difficult to match the more complex sampling and weighting methods. The alternative approach is to use *resampling*. In other words, the sample we have is considered as a *population* from which further subsamples are drawn and similar estimates are computed to replicate the original estimate. Both jackknife and bootstrap are resampling tools dealing with subsamples of a given sample.

The *jackknife* was originally introduced by Quenouille [46], to estimate bias of estimates for simple random sampling. Assume that $\hat{z}$ is an estimate based on n observations $x_1, \ldots, x_n$. The main idea is that each observation x_i is excluded in turn from the data and a similar estimate $\hat{z}_i$ is computed from the remaining $n-1$ observations $x_1, \ldots, x_{i-1}, x_{i+1}, \ldots, x_n$. The jackknife estimate of variance is then given by

$$v_{\text{jack}} = \frac{n-1}{n} \sum_{i=1}^{n} \left(\hat{z}_i - \hat{z}_{(\cdot)} \right)^2,$$

where $\hat{z}_{(\cdot)} = (\sum_{i=1}^{n} \hat{z}_i)/n$. This expression is reminiscent of the sampling variance formula for $\hat{z}_i$ except that the factor is $(n-1)/n$ instead of $1/n$ (or $1/(n-1)$).

The formula above is, of course, only for simple random sampling. As with the traditional approach, there are many different jackknife tools for various sampling techniques and there is no universal procedure that would be suitable for all surveys. We mention here just one general jackknife procedure presented in Shao and Tu [51], section 6.2.1. When the sample is obtained by stratified clustering, the resampling is done by excluding *clusters*, one at a time, instead of individual respondents. For simplicity, we consider only the weighted mean estimate (weighted count divided by sum of weights). When a cluster i in stratum s is excluded, the weighted counts and sum of weights are recomputed with the only difference that in stratum s, the weighted counts/sum of weights are both multiplied by factor $n_s/(n_s - 1)$ (n_s is the number of clusters in stratum s) before being added to the weighted counts/sum of weights from other strata. Denote by $\hat{z}_{s,i}$ the new mean estimate obtained when cluster i in stratum s is excluded and let $\hat{z}_s = (\sum_{i=1}^{n_s} \hat{z}_{s,i})/n_s$. Then the jackknife variance estimate is calculated by the formula

$$v_{\text{jack}} = \sum_{s=1}^{m} \frac{n_s - 1}{n_s} \sum_{i=1}^{n_s} (\hat{z}_{s,i} - \hat{z}_s)^2,$$

where m is the number of strata.

Unfortunately, there is little information available about the performance of this formula for a range of surveys. The assumptions in Shao and Tu [51] for an asymptotic convergence are too theoretical to check for any given survey, and in any case there are several variants of the jackknife procedure with different performance for different types of surveys. It is possible, for instance, to exclude only *part* of a cluster rather than the whole cluster. There are also other practical questions. For instance, what is the performance effect of various weighting methods, and how do the jackknife variance estimates compare with the traditional variance estimates? The formula, therefore, should be applied with caution and ideally there should be prior research into whether it is accurate for a given survey or not.

The *bootstrap* was introduced in 1979 by Efron [16] and is in fact a generalisation of jackknife. The main idea is that for a given sample with n values $x_1, \ldots, x_n$, we consider it as a population and draw randomly, *with replacement*, several *bootstrap samples* each still having n elements. This means that, for instance, initial value x_1 may be drawn several times in a bootstrap sample. In fact for samples of typical size (100–10 000) about 73% of the overall sample would be included at least once, and about 18% more than once, in each bootstrap sample. For each of these new samples, the same estimate (e.g. mean or proportion) as for the original sample is computed and the sampling variance among these replicated estimates is considered to be an approximation of variance of the original estimate. The number of bootstrap samples is usually in the range 25–200.

Again, this is suitable only for an intended simple random sample and there are several bootstrap modifications to apply for a practical survey. For stratification, for example, it would be more appropriate to select bootstrap samples in each stratum separately, the stratum sample sizes being the same as in the original sample. It is also possible to change the bootstrap sample size and have in each bootstrap sample, say, only half of the elements of the original sample. As in the case of the jackknife there are unanswered questions about how the technique is affected by weighting methods and the identification of the best bootstrap procedure for different types of surveys. There are even more questions: if we *reweight* each selected bootstrap sample separately, would it increase the efficiency of the procedure? In many cases, perhaps, the trial and error approach could be beneficial: experimenting with various bootstrap algorithms and comparison of the results with variance estimates of a traditional approach that is known to be reliable for the sample design in point may be beneficial.

The resampling techniques are therefore very attractive from a practical point of view – they require no knowledge of mathematical formulae and can be readily applied using various software packages. But we emphasise again that no single method can provide a universal solution and much more practical research is needed to establish the validity of different resampling methods for various surveys. Jackknife/bootstrap packages can be like 'black boxes' where a user does not know what the limitations of the algorithm are; sometimes even the algorithm itself is not explained. There are examples, in fact, when bootstrap and jackknife *fail* to produce an adequate replication (see, for instance, Efron and Tibshirani [17]), so that the limitations must be known *before* applying a particular procedure.

3.1.7 Variance for quota sampling

Quota sampling is, perhaps, the main non-probability sampling method in common use and a little should be said about the problems associated with variance calculations for this method.

The limitations and problems of quota sampling are well known. However, from the statistical point of view, the main problem with quota sampling (and the main reason why it tends to be rejected by academics) is that the respondents from a quota sample usually have *different probabilities of selection that are unknown* and therefore are not compensated for.

Remember that, in general, there is no great problem with respondents having different probabilities of selection if these probabilities are known (e.g. in stratified sampling); the sample can then be weighted to 'neutralise' the unequal probabilities. The most troublesome aspect of quota sampling is that the unequal and *unknown* probabilities mean that there is no way to compensate for these varying probabilities. And this is one of the main reasons why a quota sample may be biased. See the discussion of quota sampling in section 1.16 for more information on why the selection probabilities are variable and unknown.

However, one must not be totally negative about quota sampling. Sometimes, as we have previously noted, this kind of sampling may be the only sampling method acceptable in terms of time and cost or practicable in the circumstances. The regrettable fact is that there are no reliable statistical methods for calculating the variance of an estimate derived from a quota sample. Even the jackknife and bootstrap techniques will be unreliable in this case – the different probabilities of selection will not be taken into account when a jackknife/bootstrap subsample is drawn.

A quota sample data set may appear to contain no weighting. Someone, presumably the project organiser, has assumed that the quota controls provided all the sample balancing that is required. Conceptually, however, the sample has been weighted, by giving a weight of 1.0 to those persons interviewed and zero to those who might have been interviewed but were not. Theoretically then, any subgroup within the sample consists of a number of persons not less than the number of persons interviewed, with a mean weight greater than zero but not greater than 1.0. This is a largely philosophical concept, however, as the numbers of potential respondents are generally not recorded and zero-weighted respondents have no effect in variance calculations.

But some weighting may be applied to quota samples to counter imbalances not controlled through the setting of quotas, though this is likely to be less extensive than in the case of weighted probability samples. Quota samples, even where some weighting has been performed, therefore do not provide any evidence of the full extent of (implicit) weighting, and thus of the extent to which they are non-random. This is the implication of the 'unknown probability of selection'.

Simple common sense and caution are recommended when dealing with the problem of variance estimation for a quota sample. The conservative approach is to be recommended, that is, to assume that the variance is the maximum possible – it is safer to overestimate the variance than to underestimate it. There are some possible approaches to a purely empirical estimation of variance. If the survey is repeated a reasonable number of times the actual variation of estimates in the different surveys can be measured. Of course, items whose values are likely to fluctuate in the population should not be used. Due allowance must also be made for any trends over time revealed by the surveys and variation about the trend line should be used as the measure. Unless the number of repeats is reasonably large, naturally the variance estimate will be coarse, but if a reasonable number of estimates within the survey (that are not expected to be correlated) are taken together it may be possible to make a usable comparison with the amount of variation that would have been expected from simple random samples. If we have only two surveys it may be possible to examine a series of differences between surveys within multiple non-overlapping subsamples. Within a single survey it may be possible, under favourable conditions (particularly adequate scale) to treat the sample as multiple quota-matched replicates and to proceed in the same way. (See Stephan and McCarthy [56] for a discussion of this.) Alternatively, each group of respondents associated with one interviewer and/or sampling location can be assumed to be a 'cluster' and the corresponding cluster sampling formula can then be used. In most cases, this will already give a variance estimate greater than for a simple random sample. It is also recommended at least to consider some weighting in the final sample, to compensate for most obvious imbalances. The 'clustering' variance can then be further multiplied by the so-called weighting effect (this is defined and discussed in section 3.3) to give a 'conservative' estimate of the total variance. Of course, a jackknife or bootstrap method can also be applied to obtain another variance estimate. Choosing the maximum of the first and second estimates and accepting this as the final estimate would be playing safe. There could be other techniques depending on the particular survey. Thus, a 'conservative' approach will give us at least some degree of reliability in variance estimates.

There is a folklore rule of thumb that says that the variance of estimates from a quota sample should be regarded as being double those that would be obtained from simple random samples of equivalent size. There is no scientific basis whatever for this assertion, but it is not without merit. In the absence of any concrete evidence it is at least an acknowledgement of the existence of the problem, and is very much preferable to ignoring it by treating the sample as simple random.

3.2   Design effect and effective sample size

Design effect (notation DE) is defined as the ratio of the variance of an estimate derived from a survey to the variance of an estimate of the same measure based on a simple random sample of the same size. The actual variance is therefore the variance of a simple random sample estimate multiplied by the design effect. Hence, the *standard error* of an estimate is the standard error of a similar estimate from a simple random sample of the same size multiplied by the *square root* of the design effect. *Effective sample size* (notation n_e) is the original unweighted sample size n divided by the design effect. In other words, it is the size of a 'simple random' sample that would yield an estimate with equivalent variance.

These definitions may seem a trifle artificial but there is a simple and natural logic behind them. To illustrate this, denote by x a variable we measure and by $\bar{x}$ an estimate of the mean value of x. The letters V and V_{ran} denote the actual variance and variance for simple random sampling, respectively. It is well known that for a simple random sample there is the following relationship:

$$V_{\text{ran}}(\bar{x}) = \frac{V(x)}{n}.$$

Therefore, the idea for a general case is to replace n by something else so that the same formula could be applied. It is then natural to call this substitute for n an 'effective sample size'. It can easily be seen that the definitions above do agree with this idea. In fact, by definition $\text{DE} = V(\bar{x})/V_{\text{ran}}(\bar{x})$ so that

$$V(\bar{x}) = \frac{V(x)}{V(x)/V(\bar{x})} = \frac{V(x)}{n\,V_{\text{ran}}(\bar{x})/V(\bar{x})} = \frac{V(x)}{n/\text{DE}} = \frac{V(x)}{n_{\text{e}}}.$$

Summarised below are the most important general properties of the design effect.

- A design effect applies to a specific attribute among a specific subset of the sample, not to the survey, or even to a question within the survey, or to the sample, as a whole. It is customary to carry out design effect calculations for selected key indicators to provide a general indication of the general levels of design effect that should be factored into any interpretation of the results.
- If the design effect is less than one, the effective sample size will be *greater* than the initial sample size, which means that simple random sampling would require a *greater* sample size to achieve the same precision. This seldom happens in practice and typical values of the design effect for a complex survey are from 1.5 to 3.5.
- For an estimate of a proportion, the design effect is symmetric, that is, it will be the same as for the estimate's complement. If the proportion estimate is zero or one, neither the design effect nor the effective sample size is defined (because both variances in the design effect definition will then be zero).
- Clustering and weighting practically always result in an increase of the design effect while stratification, if used intelligently, may decrease the design effect.
- Design effect does not depend on the scale of the weighting factors so that it will stay the same when all weights are multiplied or divided by a constant.
- Design effect depends much more on the complexity of the sample design than on the complexity of an estimate.

When two population groups are combined, the combined design effect can be greater or less than those of the individual groups. When the two group estimates are *similar*, a disproportionate sampling will usually markedly increase the design effect for the combined group. If the estimates are *different*, an optimum sampling allocation (which minimises the overall variance) for the two groups will usually help to reduce the combined design effect. If the allocation is far from optimum, the combined effect again can go up. For instance, if we have two equal population groups within which the incidence of an attribute is 50% and 1%, respectively, then sampling 100 respondents out of 1000 from the first group and 900 from the second one will produce a high combined design effect. To minimise the combined effect, clearly more respondents should be allocated to the first group because the first group will produce a greater contribution to the combined variance than the second group, for that proportion. It must be remembered, however, that an allocation that is optimal for one estimate may be less beneficial or have adverse effects for other estimates in the same survey.

Notice that a small design effect does not necessarily mean that the standard error will be small. For instance, for an estimate that is a ratio of ratios the standard error may already be high for simple random sampling. Therefore, even a 'good' design effect, of say 1.1, will still increase the standard error.

3.2.1   Effects of stratification and clustering

Stratification normally has a beneficial influence on the design effect when it is used to ensure that the strata are sampled in proportion to their populations and there is a difference between strata in the incidence of the attribute being measured. Where strata differ in this way or in their (internal) variability or in the cost of fieldwork it is possible to optimise the allocation of interviews between strata, for instance to obtain the greatest overall precision within a given budget.

One example of an allocation with a minimum variance within a given budget is given by Cochran [9], theorem 5.6. The cost C is supposed to be a linear function: $C = c_0 + \sum c_s n_s$, where n_s is the sample size in stratum s, c_0 a fixed overhead cost and c_s the per interview marginal cost in stratum s. The result is that, in the case of simple random sampling in each stratum, the variance is a minimum for a specified cost (and the cost is a minimum for a specified variance) if n_s is proportional to $\lambda_s \sqrt{V_s/c_s}$, where λ_s is the population proportion of stratum s and V_s is the variance of the variable in stratum s. An analysis of the proof of this result in [9] shows, however, that the proof will remain the same even in the general case if we introduce the effective sample size and multiply the strata variances by the corresponding design effects. We summarise this in the following proposition.

Proposition 3.1   *Let $\bar{x}_s$ be a mean estimate in stratum s and $\bar{x} = \sum_s \lambda_s \bar{x}_s$ be the total mean estimate, where λ_s is the population proportion of stratum s. Let V_s be the variance of x in stratum s, DE_s the design effect for x_s and C a linear cost function: $C = c_0 + \sum c_s n_s$. Then, if the sample size n_s in stratum s is proportional to $\lambda_s \sqrt{V_s \mathrm{DE}_s/c_s}$, the variance is a minimum for a specified cost and the cost is a minimum for a specified variance.*

Dispropor-
tionate
stratification

The variance of x and the design effects are, of course, not known before a survey is conducted. Therefore, *expected* values must be used when trying to optimise the sample size at the planning stage.

Where sampling is not proportionate to population, and is not disproportionally allocated to maximise the benefits in terms of the known or anticipated distribution of the measured attributes across the strata, then it is likely to be disadvantageous in terms of the precision of total-sample estimates. This is not necessarily a bad thing: it depends on the priorities. Surveys are generally carried out with a range of objectives in view and some of these may benefit from a particular stratification plan while others may not. This can be illustrated by a simple and extreme hypothetical example.

Example 3.1   Suppose we conduct a survey to determine what proportion of the adult population in Australia has tertiary qualifications, and how different the Australian Capital Territory (ACT) is in this respect from the rest of the country. We take a pure and perfectly executed simple random sample of 1000 interviews spread across the nation, 16 (1.6%) of which are in the ACT (i.e. in due proportion to population). This gives us a reasonable estimate (say 29% incidence with a standard error of 1.4%) for total Australia, but our estimate for the ACT by itself, whatever it might reasonably be, is obviously very wobbly and for practical purposes virtually useless. The relative standard error of the estimated difference between the ACT and the rest is so high as to make the second objective unachievable.

If the dominant objective of the survey had been to measure the difference between the ACT and the rest of Australia (with the same budget) we might have taken two similar simple random samples of 500 interviews in the ACT and 500 in the rest of Australia. This would now give us two estimates of comparable precision for the ACT and the rest of Australia. Assume these to be 47.1% (s.e. 2.23%) for ACT and 28.7% (s.e. 2.02%) for the rest of Australia: because these are true (or more correctly fictitious!) simple random samples the design effect of each is 1.0. We can now be confident that we have a reasonably precise measure of the difference (18%) which has a standard error of $\sqrt{2.23^2 + 2.02^2} = 3.01\%$. Disproportionate sampling has helped us to maximise the sensitivity of the comparison. (If we had anticipated the higher incidence in ACT we could have optimised the division of the 1000 interviews between it and the rest of Australia by allocating the numbers such that we got two estimates with equal standard errors, but the extra precision of the 'standard error of the difference' would have been very small.)

However, a national estimate synthesised from the two samples must be dominated by the 'rest of Australia' component, which makes up 98.4% of the final weighted estimate, at the expense of the ACT component which makes up 1.6% of the estimate. This means that the precision of the national estimate is governed by the precision of the 'rest of Australia' estimate, with the 500 ACT interviews contributing little influence, much less than their raw proportion and their share of the overall cost. In fact, the national estimate is $0.016 \cdot 47.1\% + 0.984 \cdot 28.7\% = 29.0\%$ with standard error $\sqrt{0.016^2 \cdot 2.23^2 + 0.984^2 \cdot 2.02^2} = 1.99\%$, which is very little less than the standard error of the dominant 'rest of Australia' component. The standard error for a simple random sampling is

$$\sqrt{\frac{0.29 \cdot 0.71}{1000}} \cdot 100\% = 1.43\%.$$

Therefore, the design effect is $1.99^2/1.43^2 = 1.93$ so that the national estimate is equivalent in precision to that from a single simple random sample of

$1000/1.93 = 517$ respondents (the effective sample size). Combining strata has therefore increased the design effect for the combined estimate. The disproportionate number of interviews in the ACT contributes very little to the precision of the estimate, but in this case the precision of the national estimate was legitimately subordinated to the precision of the difference. In the end it all comes down to priorities.

An extreme case

As a demonstration of the lengths to which this can be taken, consider the extreme case where the attribute being measured is 'membership of stratum s'. The incidence of this attribute is, of course, 100% within stratum s and zero outside it. The variance of each of these components is zero and therefore the variance of the combined estimate is zero. As the estimate is entirely dependent on the estimate of the proportion of the population that is in stratum s, and as this is *fixed* by the sample design, any number of samples drawn using this design will yield exactly the same estimate. The design effect is therefore zero.

This is an example of an attribute that a survey is not designed to *measure* but that is nevertheless likely to be reported in the course of analysis and illustrates the extreme effect that stratification can have. It points to the frequently overlooked fact that any estimate of an attribute that is defined wholly in terms of strata, whether these are strata proper or post-stratification groupings, must have zero variance and hence, of course, zero standard error.

There is, in fact, a general formula that allows us to calculate the total design effect from strata design effects (see Appendix E). The formula can be applied not only for stratification but, more generally, when several independent estimates are combined into one estimate. For simplicity, we consider only proportion estimates.

Theorem 3.1 *Assume that $p_1, \ldots, p_m$ are several independent proportion estimates and $p = \sum_{s=1}^{m} \lambda_s p_s$ is the total estimate, where λ_s is the proportion of the population in stratum s and $\sum_{s=1}^{m} \lambda_s = 1$. Let n_s be the number of respondents in sample s, n be the size of the combined sample and $\mu_s = n_s/n$ be the sampling proportion of sample s in the combined sample. Then the total design effect can be computed as*

$$\text{DE} = \sum_{s=1}^{m} \frac{\lambda_s^2}{\mu_s} \frac{p_s(1 - p_s)}{p(1 - p)} \text{DE}_s, \tag{3.14}$$

where DE_s is the design effect for p_s, while the total effective sample size is

$$n_e = 1 \bigg/ \left[\sum_{s} \frac{\lambda_s^2}{(n_s)_e} \frac{p_s(1 - p_s)}{p(1 - p)} \right]. \tag{3.15}$$

The effect of clustering is completely separate. What effect clustering has depends on the degree of homogeneity found within the clusters, known as 'intra-class correlation', or conversely the degree of heterogeneity between the clusters.

For a two-stage sampling procedure, when the first-stage units (clusters) are chosen randomly or with probability proportional to size, there is an interesting relationship between the intra-class correlation and the design effect discussed in Kish [35] (formula (5.4.1)):

$$DE = 1 + (b - 1)\rho,$$

where ρ is the *intra-class correlation coefficient* and b is the number of elements in each cluster. When clusters have different sizes, the weighted average cluster size

$$b' = \frac{\sum_{i=1}^{m} b_i^2}{\sum_{j=1}^{m} b_i},$$

where b_i is the size of cluster i, is used instead of b providing a reasonable approximation in most cases. The difference between the coefficient ρ and the standard correlation coefficient is that ρ is computed across not all possible pairs of elements but only across pairs from *a cluster*; the pairs where elements are from different clusters are not considered.

The formula for ρ given by Kish [35] (formula (5.6.14)) covers only the case when all clusters have the same size. While this may sometimes be true for the sample as a whole it is unlikely to hold for any subset of the sample (unless it is defined in terms of whole clusters). If the attribute defining the subset is randomly distributed throughout the population the number of respondents per cluster with that attribute would be binomially distributed. Thus, for instance, if a sample consisted of 100 clusters of ten respondents and a subset of 300 was randomly selected we would only expect 27 of the clusters to yield exactly three respondents. About 70 would yield between two and four but the remainder would be more or less evenly split between yielding more or less than this. The following general formula which covers unequal clusters is given by Kendall and Stuart in [32], formula 26.25, and should be used for sample subsets.

Assume that there are m clusters in total, $x_{i,j}$ is the jth element in cluster i and k_i is the number of elements in cluster i. Then

$$\rho = \frac{\sum_{i=1}^{m} k_i^2(\bar{x}_i - \tilde{x})^2 - \sum_{i=1}^{m}\sum_{j=1}^{k_i}(x_{i,j} - \tilde{x})^2}{\sum_{i=1}^{m}(k_i - 1)\sum_{j=1}^{k_i}(x_{i,j} - \tilde{x})^2}, \tag{3.16}$$

where $\bar{x}_i = (\sum_{j=1}^{k_i} x_{i,j})/k_i$ is the mean value in cluster i and

$$\tilde{x} = \frac{\sum_{i=1}^{m}(k_i - 1)\sum_{j=1}^{k_i} x_{i,j}}{\sum_{i=1}^{m} k_i(k_i - 1)}$$

is the 'intra-class' mean. In practice, values $x_{i,j}$ should be weighted. Several practical examples of measurement of ρ are given by Harris [26].

If all clusters have the same size $k_i = k$, formula (3.16) simplifies to (see Kendall and Stuart [32], formula 26.57):

$$\rho = \frac{1}{k-1}\left(\frac{k\sigma_c^2}{\sigma^2} - 1\right), \tag{3.17}$$

where σ^2 is the total variance and σ_c^2 is the variance of cluster means:

$$\sigma^2 = \frac{1}{km}\sum_{i=1}^{m}\sum_{j=1}^{k}(x_{i,j} - \tilde{x})^2, \quad \sigma_c^2 = \frac{1}{m}\sum_{i=1}^{m}(\bar{x}_i - \tilde{x})^2.$$

Note that σ_c^2 cannot be greater than σ^2 so that the maximum value for ρ in (3.17) is 1. On the other hand, the minimum value for ρ is $-1/(k-1)$ when $\sigma_c^2 = 0$. Therefore, values of ρ are not symmetric.

Another consequence of formula (3.17) is that the intra-class correlation coefficient should generally be small for variables with a low incidence in the population because in that case the variance of cluster means will be small.

The question becomes: are the means of the clusters more spread out than would be expected from a purely random distribution? In the purely random case, with equal sized clusters, it is sensible to assume that cluster means have a binomial distribution so that their variance is proportional to $p(1 - p)$, for proportion estimates. Therefore, in the general case the expectation should be that the spread of cluster means and hence the design effect due to clustering should rise with $p(1 - p)$, being at its greatest for a 50% estimate. Another general fact is that, the bigger the mean cluster size, the bigger the potential effect of clustering.

Equation (3.16) implies that the effect of clustering is less when the clusters are smaller. Equally, when we are considering a subset of the sample (other than a subset of clusters) the mean number of elements per cluster *in that subset* will be less, and for very small subsets there may be little or no clustering effect.

Neither Kish nor Kendall and Stuart make any allowance for the effect of stratification. Kendall and Stuart's $\tilde{x}$ is calculated for the total sample whereas for a stratified sample it would be more appropriate to use the mean for the *stratum* in which the cluster occurs. Where a sample is clustered it is important not to fall into the trap of attributing to the clustering those effects that are properly the result of stratification, or of some other systematic variation within the population.

Consider a stratified and clustered sample, where the clusters are, as they preferably should be, each contained wholly within one stratum. If a measure varies widely between strata, then the cluster means (for the *total* sample) will have a higher than random variance even if there is no clustering effect within the individual strata. Assessment of the effect of clustering should therefore take into account any known systematic variations in the population (whether or not these are reflected in the stratification) that could reasonably be expected to affect the distribution of cluster means. The implications of this are illustrated in the example below.

Spurious
clustering
effect

Example 3.2   The Sunday Times is a newspaper published in Perth, Western Australia (WA). It is known to be widely read within WA, but because of the limitations of geography its circulation outside WA is negligible. A national survey of 1000 adults is carried out to measure readership of a range of newspapers including this. The sample is stratified with 10% of the sample being in WA, in line with the population. Within each geographical stratum (of which WA is one) the interviews are conducted in clusters of ten interviews each, ten clusters being in WA. Readership of the Sunday Times is estimated at 6% overall, but when it is analysed by cluster the following distribution of numbers of readers is found:

Readers in cluster	Number of clusters
0	90
1	0
2	0
3	1
4	1
5	1
6	3
7	3
8	0
9	1
10	0

A 6% estimate from a simple random sample of 1000 would have a standard error of 0.75% (the design effect being 1.0), and this is our reference point.

Consider first the result treated as an unstratified but clustered sample. Overall the mean number of readers per cluster is 0.6 and the variance of the number of readers per cluster is 3.5. If the number of readers per cluster had been binomially distributed with the same mean the variance would have been 0.56, so there is clearly some major effect. Equation (3.16) gives a value of ρ of $+0.58$, which in turn gives a design effect of 6.2. This very high design effect implies a very low level of precision, giving the estimate of 6% a standard error of 1.9%. If the *clusters* are selected randomly, the proportion of clusters in WA is itself subject to a wide margin of error – the same error as would be expected if we had taken a random national sample of 100 individuals. The standard error of a 10% estimate based on a random sample of 100 is 3%: in other words the relative standard error is 30%. The design effect of 6.2 based on the assumption of an unstratified sample is therefore real.

When the stratification is taken into account the picture is very different. It comes as no surprise to find that the 10 clusters with readers are all in the stratum (WA) that forms the paper's distribution area. Within the ten WA clusters the mean number of readers is 6.0 and the variance 2.6, or very similar to the variance of 2.4 which would have been seen had the distribution been purely binomial. Within WA there is therefore no clustering effect of any real consequence: outside there is similarly no clustering effect as all clusters have a mean of zero. The strong 'clustering effect' initially suggested by equation (3.16) is in fact spurious.

In this stratified design the variance is calculated using formulae (3.2) and (3.16) but using the *stratum* mean for the calculation of $\tilde{x}$ within each stratum. ρ is now 0.05. This small positive value is compatible with the observation that the variance of cluster means within the WA stratum is only slightly greater than that of a binomial distribution with the same mean. The standard error is now 0.51% and the design effect 0.46 (for this measure).

In this example stratification has in fact a marked *beneficial* effect on the precision of the estimate. This is an extreme example, but one that could happen in practice, designed to draw attention to the possibility that uncritical application of standard formulae can yield totally misleading results. A correct interpretation of the situation has reduced the design effect by a factor of 13. The same effect would be observed, if to a lesser degree, whenever there is variation in the means or proportions between strata.

This improvement can be explained in logical terms as follows. The proportion of adults reading the Sunday Times can be regarded as the product of two proportions: the proportion of adults living in WA and the proportion of WA adults reading the Sunday Times. In a (national) simple random sample, both elements would have been subject to a margin of error. As our sample has been deliberately stratified to reflect the *known* proportion of the adult population living in WA the only uncertainty in the estimate is the extent of readership within WA.

If we had been working with an unstratified sample, but we had found by inspection that this measure had been clearly associated with geography, it is possible that a better estimate of the variance of the measure would have been achieved through post-stratification – forcing the sample to reflect the known (in this case geographical) distribution of the population, typically by means of weighting. Whatever number of clusters we have in the circulation area we can weight the results so that these represent the correct proportion of the weighted sample. In this case, external evidence (availability of the paper) makes this a reasonable thing to do and the attribute common to the clusters showing high numbers of readers is completely aligned with that. However, there would be many cases where *ad hoc* post-stratification on the basis of some presumed or apparent causal differentiating factor, within or across strata, would be very difficult to substantiate beyond reasonable doubt. Unfortunately also there is no precise way to estimate the effects of such post-stratification.

Calculating the variance for each stratum separately and taking the weighted mean of the variances across strata (equation (3.2)) is equivalent to substituting the stratum mean for the overall mean in equation (3.16). The stratum mean rather than the population mean thus becomes the expected value against which each cluster mean is compared. It is tempting to speculate that a better result could be obtained by substituting an *expected* value of $\tilde{x}$ for each cluster in equation (3.16). However, there is no known statistical justification for this, and to do so would involve a considerable amount of work. It would, as a minimum, require an examination of other attributes of the *clusters* that might explain between-cluster variation, the selection of one or more and the re-division of the samples into cells that might be presumed to be homogeneous with respect to cluster behaviour and for which the mean of the cluster values might constitute a reasonable expected value for each cluster in the cell. The default, assuming that the expected value for all clusters would be the same (the overall 'intra-class' mean), is equivalent to equation (3.16) as it stands.

It must also be remembered that the effect of clustering is not consistent within a survey. Some attributes may be more subject to clustering than others. If the survey in the above example had also included questions on roofing materials we would expect to find strong clustering effects. If one interview is conducted at a house with a slate roof it is quite probable that most or all of the houses in the immediate neighbourhood have slate roofs: this is an attribute that for good historical reasons is quite tightly clustered geographically. However, had we asked the respondents in that survey whether they were left-handed it is likely that we would have found little or no clustering effect. Left-handedness may run in families but there is no obvious reason why it should congregate in neighbourhoods.

It is therefore dangerous to assume that a single measure of clustering effect can be applied to a whole survey. Being realistic, however, one cannot expect to undertake a full calculation of the design effect for every single figure extracted from a survey. Informed judgement and common sense should be applied to anticipate whether and how far any particular measure being examined is likely to be affected by clustering.

A further complication is that in some cases the clustering may not be totally linked to the stratification. Clustering is almost invariably a logistic expedient, designed to reduce the cost of fieldwork, and is therefore spatial. Stratification, while frequently spatial, is not necessarily so. Clusters may therefore occasionally cut across stratum boundaries. In a survey of staff of a large retailing company, for instance, the sample may be stratified by employee type (management, checkout operators, etc.) but clustered by retail outlet, so that each cluster may contain respondents from more than one stratum. In such a case there is no simple solution, other than to regard the cluster as being in fact multiple clusters, one per affected stratum. Just as when considering a subset of the sample that is not just a subset of clusters, the clustering effect will be reduced as the number of respondents considered in each cluster reduces.

3.2.2 Design effect in data analysis

When interpreting survey results, it is important to remember that a design effect is the net result of a number of factors affecting the purity of the sample. It is not sufficient to apply a single design effect figure to each and every analysis or interpretation of a data set. There are several techniques that are helpful in data analysis and in overall assessment of a sample design.

- It is useful to split the overall design effect into two components: the first component is due to stratification and the second is due to other factors used in the sampling design. The *stratification design effect* is computed as the ratio of the variance of an estimate of the stratified random sampling to the variance of an estimate of the same thing derived from a simple random sampling. In other words, it is simply the design effect for stratified random sampling. In the case of proportions, the actual formula for the stratification component can be obtained from Theorem 3.1 by letting design effects within strata be equal to 1.0:

$$\text{stratification component} = \sum_{s=1}^{m} \frac{\lambda_s^2}{\mu_s} \frac{p_s(1 - p_s)}{p(1 - p)}, \tag{3.18}$$

using the same notation. The second component is then the ratio of the total design effect to the stratification component.

- Another, more direct, measurement of the second component can be obtained if the *stratum* design effect is computed first, for all strata. The *average* stratum design effect will then give a reasonable measure of the overall design effect *without* stratification. This component may in turn be split into the separate effects of design and execution factors such as clustering and weighting, which will be discussed below.

- For many surveys, because of the often large number of variables to be analysed it is customary first to choose several key variables, and variables where a high design effect might be anticipated, and to compute their design effects. If these prove to be reasonably uniform, the average design effect among the key variables can be used as an 'average' or 'rule-of-thumb' measure for the total sample. This would allow a 'nominal' effective sample size to be estimated which, in turn, gives a very quick method of getting a rough estimate of the variance for *any* variable. For instance, the rough variance for a proportion estimate would be $p(1 - p)$ divided by the nominal effective sample size. If the design effects are not uniform, and there is an ample number of them, they should at least give some guidance about the likely magnitude of the design effect to be expected in any individual situation. Alternatively, there is a 'conservative' approach that uses the *maximum* design effect among key variables as the overall figure.

- A further approach is to split the original sample into key cells between which differences might reasonably be expected (including perhaps obvious demographic variables such as age, sex etc.) and to calculate design effects in each cell separately. Clearly, it can be combined with the 'average' approach producing an average figure for every cell. This analysis usually helps to reveal the most problematic population groups.

It is not practicable to assess the design effect of every possible measure among every possible subset of the sample. Looking at the way in which specimen design effects vary throughout the survey may, however, help the user to understand which parts of the survey data, or which subsets of the sample, are liable to show particularly large design effects. More particular analysis can therefore be undertaken selectively to check the design effects of specific estimates of particular interest where it is suspected that the design effect may be particularly high.

This approach is perhaps open to the criticism of lacking rigour. However, we are attempting to provide some practical guidance for researchers whose primary interest is in extracting meaning from the data before them and for whom a quick but realistic assessment is more valuable than a detailed but time consuming calculation. Those for whom the statistical niceties are of themselves the principal area of interest, and who have the necessary time and resources, will no doubt prefer to take a more formal and punctilious approach, and there is plenty of other material in the published literature to assist them.

In addition, it must always be borne in mind that any estimate of a design effect is just an estimate and subject to its own margin of error in any particular case as will be illustrated below. Any calculations based on a calculated design effect are therefore subject to an additional element of uncertainty.

3.2.3 Design effect examples

To demonstrate what values of design effects are likely to be encountered in real life, we have calculated design effects for several variables from the Roy Morgan Single Source survey database (Australia, October 2003–September 2004 with 56 344 respondents).

Respondents were sampled across eleven geographical strata while the total number of clusters was 8070 with an average cluster size of 6.98. There was a sophisticated weighting procedure to address unequal probabilities of selection as well as to make sure that the sample was representative with respect to age, sex, state and regional area. Though normally reported as a whole, the sample comprises twelve monthly replications. This gives us an opportunity to observe how much the estimates of design effects can vary between replications – intended to be matched samples.

Formula (3.11) was employed to compute the variance of estimates, which was then used to calculate design effects for the twelve-month period and for individual months.

Table 3.1 shows design effects for several demographic and other variables whose population distributions can be expected to vary very little over time. It presents design effects averaged across all categories of a variable. The last column shows the standard deviation of the twelve individual monthly design effects. There was some variation in mean design effects (between 1.53 and 2.18 apart from one prominent but unsurprising outlier). The sample was slightly disproportionately stratified, but this had little impact on the overall design effects, all the stratification components being close to 1.0 and the mean within-stratum design effects being very close to the overall estimate. When design effects were estimated for the twelve individual monthly replicates the mean for every variable was very close to the overall design effect for that variable. However, the individual months' estimates showed appreciable variation, as shown by the standard deviation of those estimates. The standard deviation is probably more appropriately compared with DE − 1 than with DE. It gives some indication of the likely margin of error in the estimate of any particular design effect.

Table 3.1. Design effect estimates – demographics

Variable	Number of categories	Total DE	DE due to stratification	Mean stratum DE	Mean monthly DE	SD of monthly DE
Sex	2	1.53	1.04	1.52	1.55	0.07
Age	6	1.76	1.04	1.75	1.77	0.17
Education	5	1.82	1.02	1.79	1.81	0.11
Work status	7	1.77	1.03	1.75	1.76	0.17
Occupation	6	1.85	1.02	1.81	1.78	0.26
Employer	4	1.77	1.03	1.81	1.76	0.14
Main income	7	1.65	1.03	1.68	1.64	0.12
Number of incomes	2	1.94	1.03	1.94	1.93	0.12
Household income	5	2.07	1.04	2.02	2.05	0.18
Marital status	2	1.91	1.04	1.86	1.92	0.10
Number of children	4	1.70	1.03	1.69	1.69	0.12
Household size	3	1.85	1.03	1.84	1.84	0.15
Dwelling type	2	4.67	1.03	3.96	4.68	0.32
Home ownership	4	2.18	1.04	2.11	2.17	0.23
Grocery buyer	3	2.12	1.04	2.03	2.11	0.12
Socio-economic quintile	5	1.78	1.03	1.76	1.77	0.11
Household life-cycle	6	1.83	1.04	1.77	1.82	0.15
Car make driven	5	1.63	1.03	1.59	1.62	0.12
Main financial institution	6	1.60	1.03	1.63	1.58	0.12
Buying a new car	2	1.67	1.05	1.63	1.66	0.10
American Express	2	1.68	1.06	1.53	1.67	0.13
Diners Club	2	1.53	1.06	1.43	1.52	0.20
Visa	2	1.93	1.03	1.89	1.92	0.11
MasterCard	2	1.54	1.04	1.52	1.52	0.10

The highest design effect is for the dwelling type. This is not surprising because the dwelling type is often the same for all respondents from the same cluster. In general, when clusters are close to homogeneous for a particular variable, the design effect for that variable will tend to approximate the average cluster size.[1]

Table 3.2 shows design effects for average-issue readership estimates for 48 Australian magazines. There is general consistency: only six lie outside the range 1.4–1.9, and the highest estimates are mostly for magazines which have distinct demographic profiles or, in the case of Foxtel Magazine, have readers with access to (terrestrial) pay-TV. Again the individual months' design effects show considerable variation, even though they are calculated from carefully matched and substantial

---

[1] This happens because in that case the precision of an estimate will be equivalent to the precision of a simple random sample estimate for which only one respondent is chosen from each cluster. For instance, in the case of a proportion estimate $\hat{p}$ its variance will be $\hat{p}(1 - \hat{p})/m$, where m is the number of clusters, according to the formula from section 3.1.2.

Table 3.2. Design effect estimates – magazines

Magazine	Proportion (%)	Total DE	DE due to stratification	Mean stratum DE	Mean monthly DE	SD of monthly DE
Australian Geographic	2.90	1.40	1.03	1.38	1.38	0.13
Australian Good Taste	4.69	1.54	1.04	1.52	1.51	0.12
Australian PC World	1.79	1.62	1.05	1.50	1.62	0.28
Australian Reader's Digest	5.85	1.55	1.03	1.49	1.54	0.16
Belle	1.32	1.60	1.06	1.59	1.53	0.25
Better Homes and Gardens	8.62	1.56	1.03	1.50	1.55	0.15
Bride To Be	0.69	1.72	1.06	1.38	1.64	0.52
BRW	1.60	1.77	1.08	1.49	1.72	0.33
Bulletin	1.86	1.68	1.05	1.60	1.63	0.28
Burke's Backyard	4.16	1.36	1.02	1.39	1.35	0.20
Cleo	4.34	1.77	1.05	1.73	1.73	0.17
Cosmopolitan	5.32	1.75	1.05	1.70	1.71	0.24
Dolly	3.09	1.61	1.03	1.66	1.59	0.13
English Woman's Weekly	1.20	1.33	1.03	1.28	1.32	0.22
Family Circle	3.10	1.47	1.03	1.46	1.45	0.13
Financial Review Magazine	1.74	1.89	1.09	1.60	1.83	0.44
Foxtel Magazine	8.09	2.08	1.07	2.11	2.05	0.22
Gardening Australia	2.12	1.27	1.02	1.28	1.26	0.14
Girlfriend	2.20	1.56	1.04	1.49	1.56	0.21
Good Medicine	2.44	1.44	1.03	1.45	1.42	0.16
Harper's Bazaar	1.32	1.78	1.08	1.54	1.75	0.28
Home Beautiful	2.14	1.41	1.04	1.47	1.40	0.13
House & Garden	3.98	1.57	1.04	1.56	1.55	0.28
InStyle	1.92	1.73	1.08	1.59	1.69	0.24
Marie Claire	3.70	1.67	1.06	1.60	1.63	0.20
Men's Health	1.81	1.80	1.06	1.64	1.77	0.30
Money Magazine	1.45	1.57	1.05	1.55	1.53	0.27
Motor	2.14	1.98	1.05	1.76	1.93	0.26
National Geographic	5.23	1.64	1.04	1.55	1.60	0.18
New Idea	11.18	1.51	1.03	1.52	1.50	0.09
New Scientist	1.29	1.93	1.04	1.82	1.88	0.36
New Woman	1.83	1.67	1.05	1.57	1.63	0.28
New Weekly	3.47	1.63	1.05	1.48	1.61	0.20
Personal Investor	0.95	1.54	1.07	1.42	1.52	0.17
Rolling Stone	2.07	1.89	1.05	1.81	1.85	0.28
Shares	1.14	1.53	1.07	1.42	1.50	0.23
Super Food Ideas	4.88	1.55	1.04	1.56	1.50	0.25
Take 5	4.25	1.50	0.99	1.53	1.50	0.18
That's Life	6.63	1.52	0.98	1.58	1.51	0.08
Time	2.41	1.68	1.06	1.57	1.66	0.22
TV Hits	1.76	1.76	1.04	1.75	1.74	0.26

Table 3.2. (*cont.*)

Magazine	Proportion (%)	Total DE	DE due to stratification	Mean stratum DE	Mean monthly DE	SD of monthly DE
TV Soap	3.23	1.74	1.05	1.66	1.69	0.22
TV Week	7.13	1.63	1.03	1.64	1.62	0.10
Vogue Australia	2.30	1.80	1.07	1.68	1.75	0.31
Vogue Living	1.59	1.49	1.05	1.36	1.47	0.17
Who	4.58	1.65	1.05	1.56	1.62	0.22
Woman's Day	14.44	1.49	1.03	1.45	1.47	0.11
Women's Weekly	17.41	1.62	1.03	1.55	1.55	0.07

Table 3.3. Design effect estimates – newspapers

Regional newspaper (Monday–Friday average)	Stratum	Proportion (%)	SD of monthly proportion (%)	Design effect	Mean monthly DE	SD of monthly DE
The Daily Telegraph	Sydney	23.83	1.83	1.79	1.74	0.30
The Daily Telegraph	other NSW	14.94	2.86	1.63	1.60	0.26
The Sydney Morning Herald	Sydney	20.39	2.32	2.34	2.28	0.29
The Sydney Morning Herald	other NSW	7.37	1.16	1.79	1.75	0.43
Herald Sun	Melbourne	38.41	1.93	1.56	1.55	0.20
Herald Sun	other VIC	36.33	3.05	1.71	1.69	0.30
The Age	Melbourne	21.03	1.71	2.52	2.51	0.30
The Age	other VIC	8.83	2.35	1.66	1.60	0.41
The Courier Mail	Brisbane	31.84	1.95	1.82	1.82	0.32
The Courier Mail	other QLD	9.75	1.17	1.77	1.73	0.34
The Adelaide Advertiser	Adelaide	46.71	2.35	1.86	1.86	0.37
The West Australian	Perth	39.18	2.52	1.78	1.78	0.26
The West Australian	other WA	32.68	3.36	1.58	1.63	0.62
The Hobart Mercury	Greater Hobart	66.53	6.17	1.60	1.52	0.55
Illawarra Mercury	Wollongong	35.44	7.12	1.58	1.49	0.78

samples. There is, however, also considerable variation here in the monthly readership estimates. These are not attributes that remain static over time in the population and they include the extreme case of a Danish royal wedding souvenir issue.

Table 3.3 shows similar figures for major Australian newspapers. All these are regional papers and the results are presented for their principal circulation areas only.

The standard deviation of monthly design effects can be considered as a rough estimate of the standard error of the design effect. A direct formula to compute the standard error of a design effect estimate would be very complicated and not practicable. Therefore, the standard deviation of monthly design effects provides a good alternative to assess the precision of the design effect. There is considerable variation here: even though newspaper readership is not static over time, the variation in monthly readership estimates relative to the mean tends to be considerably less than the corresponding variation in the monthly design effect estimates.

Tables 3.1–3.3 show that the standard deviation of monthly design effects is relatively low for the demographic and financial variables – only two of the 24 estimates have standard deviations greater than 0.25, or greater than a quarter of DE − 1. For magazines (measured on the full national sample) the variation in monthly estimates is much greater. Only for the largest magazines is the standard deviation *less than* a quarter of DE − 1. For the newspapers, where the proportion reading is considerably higher, the standard deviations are also high but here the sample sizes are also lower (particularly for the last three newspapers in the table. Where the number of interviews contributing to the readership estimate is lower, whether in the numerator or in the denominator, the variation in monthly design effects is greater.

3.3   Weighting effect and calibrated sample size

The problem of computing the design effect is equivalent to the problem of variance calculation and it may, as we have seen, require a great deal of computation. Furthermore, the design effect is different for different variables and even for different categories within a variable. It would be beneficial, therefore, to have a simpler, more practical, tool that would give us an overall assessment of statistical effects of sampling/weighting. Fortunately, there is such a tool and below we describe it and discuss its properties.

3.3.1   Calibrated sample size and its properties

Assume that we have a sample of n respondents and their final weights are $w_1, \ldots, w_n$. Then the *calibrated sample size* (notation n_c) is defined as

$$n_c = \frac{\left(\sum_{i=1}^{n} w_i \right)^2}{\sum_{i=1}^{n} w_i^2}. \tag{3.19}$$

The *weighting effect* (notation WE) is then defined as the original unweighted sample size n divided by the calibrated sample size n_c.

There are very few papers (see Conway [10] and Sharot [52]) where formula (3.19) is discussed. It is also unfortunate that there is a confusion in terminology. In the two cited papers, the term 'effective sample size' is applied to what the present authors would prefer to call the 'calibrated sample size'. We believe that the term 'effective sample size' should be associated only with the design effect (see, for instance, Harris [26] and Kish [36], 7.1D, page 204) and should reflect *all* sampling and weighting effects. On the other hand, the calibrated sample size reflects *only* the statistical effects of weighting and that is why it is associated with the weighting effect WE. The word 'calibrated' was also chosen to emphasise that what we get is the result of calibration of our sample against *known* values or more authoritative estimates to make it more representative. The original idea was, of course, to use the calibrated sample size as a simple *substitution* for the effective sample size but it is still better to distinguish between these quite different concepts. Formula (3.19) is also mentioned in [38].

The main advantage, therefore, of the calibrated sample size is its simplicity: among any given subset of the sample it is *the same number* for all survey variables (a kind of overall survey effect), though it must still be computed individually for each subset. Above all it is very easy to compute for any sample design.

Perhaps one of the first questions to ask is the following: does the weighting effect have any statistical relationship with the design effect at all? In other words, could we consider the weighting effect as a special form of the design effect? The next result does give a positive answer to that question.

Theorem 3.2   *Assume that n respondents have been chosen by simple random sampling and they have values $x_1, \ldots, x_n$ of a variable x. Also assume that there is a set of weights $w_1, \ldots, w_n$ which would remain the same when the sampling is repeated. Then for the weighted mean estimate*

$$\bar{x}_w = \frac{\sum_{i=1}^{n} w_i x_i}{\sum_{i=1}^{n} w_i}$$

the design effect is computed as $(n \sum_{i=1}^{n} w_i^2)/(\sum_{i=1}^{n} w_i)^2$, that is, it coincides with the weighting effect. (Hence, the effective sample size for $\bar{x}_w$ is equal to the calibrated sample size.)

The estimate in the theorem is obviously not the best possible (although still unbiased) in the case of simple random sampling. Therefore, it is intuitively clear that the weighting effect should not be less than 1.0. In fact, the intuition is correct: it is formally proved below in the first property of the calibrated sample size. Another conclusion from this theorem is that the calibrated sample size has a theoretical justification; it really is the design effect if the weighting alone is considered to have an effect and other sampling considerations can be ignored. The relationship between the weighting effect and overall design effect is discussed later, in section 3.3.4.

Properties
of the
'calibrated
sample size'
measure

Next, we consider several other useful properties of the calibrated sample size and the weighting effect (a proof of the first three properties is given in Appendix E).

- The calibrated sample size cannot be greater than the original unweighted sample size (and hence the weighting effect can never be less than 1.0). They are equal if and only if all weights are constant.
- If a sample is divided into several cells then the total calibrated sample size cannot be greater than the sum of the calibrated sample sizes of the cells.
- The absolute maximum value for the weighting effect is given by the formula

$$\text{WE}_{\max} = \frac{(\theta + 1)^2}{4\theta} = \frac{\theta}{4} + \frac{1}{2} + \frac{1}{4\theta},$$

where θ is the ratio of the maximum respondent's weight to the minimum respondent's weight across the whole sample. For instance, if the maximum weight is 3.0 and the minimum weight is 0.3 then $\theta = 10.0$ and we can be absolutely sure that the weighting effect will not exceed $11^2/40 = 3.025$. But the actual effect in most cases, of course, will be much smaller than this maximum number. This number can be achieved in practice only if there are two weight values and the number of respondents with the high value is $n/(\theta + 1)$, where n is the sample size.
- More weighting will usually result in an increased weighting effect and a reduced calibrated sample size. More precisely, if the variation in weights is increased relative to the mean weight, the calibrated sample size is decreased.
- As with effective sample size, scaling (multiplication of all weights by the same factor) does not change the calibrated sample size.
- It must be emphasised once again that the calibrated sample size and weighting effect are both *sample* characteristics and do not depend on survey variables or estimates. For the total sample, or within any subset, the weighting effect is the same for all categories of all variables.
- For simple (e.g. unclustered) probability samples, the weighting effect may be a 'conservative' estimate in the sense that it is usually higher than the average design effect across all survey variables. Therefore, the variance may be slightly overestimated for many variables when we use the calibrated sample size (that is, if we estimate the sampling variance as the variance of simple random sampling multiplied by the weighting effect). However, the more complex a survey, the greater is the likelihood that any variable may be strongly affected by the additional complexity and so may have a design effect significantly greater than the weighting effect.

Limitations
of the
weighting
effect

Notice also that the calibrated sample size is very easy to program into any software. Doing so would greatly improve those statistical packages that use the total sum of weights as a 'sample size' in statistical calculations.

Of course, there is a price to be paid for these useful properties. Perhaps the weakest point of the calibrated sample size is that it does not take into account *clustering*. As has been said, it may also underestimate variance for variables that are strongly affected by sample design. However, it *was designed* to be less precise and the loss of precision is more than adequately compensated for by simplicity of computation and other properties described above.

A further useful thing to know is how the calibrated sample size is affected when several independent estimates are combined into one estimate. For instance, we may know or expect weighting effects in several independent samples or in several strata and would like to estimate the overall weighting effect. Of course, we can simply compute the weights and then obtain the weighting effect. But there is also a direct formula that gives the overall weighting effect and calibrated sample size. It resembles the corresponding formula for design effect.

More precisely, suppose that m independent samples with sizes $n_1, \ldots, n_m$ are combined into one sample using proportions $\lambda_1, \ldots, \lambda_m$ where $\sum_{s=1}^{m} \lambda_s = 1$. (In other words, for estimates $\hat{x}_1, \ldots, \hat{x}_m$ the overall estimate would be $\lambda_1 \hat{x}_1 + \cdots + \lambda_m \hat{x}_m$.) Then the total calibrated sample size for this procedure can be computed as

$$ n_c = 1 \bigg/ \left[\frac{\lambda_1}{(n_1)_c} + \cdots + \frac{\lambda_m}{(n_m)_c} \right], \tag{3.20} $$

where $(n_s)_c$ is the calibrated sample size in sample s, while the total weighting effect is

$$ \text{WE} = \sum_s \frac{\lambda_s^2}{\mu_s} \text{WE}_s, \tag{3.21} $$

where $\mu_s = n_s/n$ ($n = n_1 + \cdots + n_m$). These formulae are proved in Appendix E.

In particular, in the case of proportional stratification, the total weighting effect is simply the convex combination of strata weighting effects: $\text{WE} = \sum_{s=1}^{m} \lambda_s \text{WE}_s$, so that it cannot exceed the *maximum* weighting effect across strata. If, on the other hand, sampling is very disproportional, it may greatly increase the combined weighting effect. For instance, if for the first stratum the population proportion is 50% while its sampling proportion is 10%, then the 'contribution' of this stratum into the combined effect is $0.5^2/0.1\text{WE}_1 = 2.5\text{WE}_1$ so that the *total* weighting effect will be at least 2.5 independently of what happens in other strata! This illustrates the particular danger of grossly *under-sampling* large segments of the population to be measured. Because the weighting effect is computed from the squared weights under-sampling is more damaging than over-sampling.

As in the case of the design effect, it is beneficial to separate the *stratification component* of the weighting effect. This component can be computed if we assume that sampling is simple random in each stratum. In this case, therefore, the weighting effect in each stratum is equal to 1.0, so that formula (3.21) can be applied:

$$ \text{stratification component} = \sum_s \frac{\lambda_s^2}{\mu_s}. \tag{3.22} $$

The second component is then the ratio of the total weighting effect to the stratification component. Alternatively, the second component can be measured as the average weighting effect across all strata. The key cell analysis of weighting effect (similarly to the design effect described in section 3.2.2) will also help to reveal which groups are most problematic.

3.3.2   Calibrated error

The design effect definition implies that, for a variable x, the standard error of an estimate $\bar{x}$ of the mean value is expressed by

$$\text{s.e.}(\bar{x}) = \sqrt{\text{DE}}\frac{S}{\sqrt{n}},\tag{3.23}$$

where S is the standard deviation of the original variable x. When design effect calculations are not practicable, using the weighting effect could be the best alternative (and certainly better than doing nothing). If we replace the design effect by the weighting effect in the standard error formula (3.23), we get a 'substitution' for the standard error that can be used in many practical situations. We call this substitute the *calibrated error* (notation c.e.) and it is computed by the formula

$$\text{c.e.}(\bar{x}) = \sqrt{\text{WE}}\frac{S}{\sqrt{n}},\tag{3.24}$$

where WE is the weighting effect. It can also be expressed in terms of the calibrated sample size n_c:

$$\text{c.e.}(\bar{x}) = \frac{S}{\sqrt{n/\text{WE}}} = \frac{S}{\sqrt{n_c}}.$$

As usual, the formulae are simpler for a proportion estimate $\hat{p}$:

$$\text{c.e.}(\hat{p}) = \sqrt{\text{WE}}\sqrt{\frac{\hat{p}(1-\hat{p})}{n}} = \sqrt{\frac{\hat{p}(1-\hat{p})}{n_c}}.$$

As with the calibrated sample size, the advantage of the calibrated error is its simplicity: it is easy to compute and to program into any software. The drawback is that the calibrated error could be slightly overestimated or underestimated compared with the standard error depending on how strongly variables are affected by clustering. Nevertheless, it still gives much more realistic results than the formula based on the unweighted (or weighted) sample size.

By definition, the calibrated error depends only on the final weighting and does not depend on other elements of the sample design, except for adjustments made for disproportionate stratification. However, it is still a measure of precision: if the sample is unclustered it gives an approximation (most often, an upper bound) of the average error that is made when a population parameter is estimated from sample data.

3.3.3   Weighting effect for stratified random sampling

We now consider how the weighting effect and the design effect are related in the case of stratified random sampling (where sampling is simple random within each stratum) and the only weights applied are those necessary to re-proportion the strata. For simplicity, we will deal only with proportion estimates. The formulae for weighting effect and design effect are then simply formulae (3.22) and (3.18):

$$\text{WE} = \sum_{s=1}^{m} \frac{\lambda_s^2}{\mu_s} \qquad (3.25)$$

and

$$\text{DE} = \sum_{s=1}^{m} \frac{\lambda_s^2}{\mu_s} \frac{p_s(1-p_s)}{p(1-p)}, \qquad (3.26)$$

where m is the number of population strata, $\lambda_1, \dots, \lambda_m$ are the proportions of the population occupied by each stratum, $p, p_1, \dots, p_m$ are the corresponding proportion estimates and $\mu_1, \dots, \mu_m$ are the proportions of the (unweighted) sample occupied by each stratum (that is, $\mu_s = n_s/n$, where n_s is the sample size in stratum s and n is the overall sample size).

Using these formulae, we obtain several interesting corollaries.

- If the proportion estimates are the same in all strata, the design effect coincides with the weighting effect.
- If the total estimate p is equal to 0.5, the design effect cannot exceed the weighting effect. They are equal if and only if all strata estimates are 0.5.
- If the sampling is proportional, the design effect again cannot exceed the weighting effect. They are equal if and only if all strata estimates are the same (and equal to p).

The corollaries confirm that the weighting effect can often be used as a 'conservative' substitute for the design effect, generally overstating the variance rather than under-stating it in the absence of any other major complications such as a strong clustering effect. It is not true, however, that the design effect is *always* less than or equal to the weighting effect as shown in the following simple example.

Example 3.3   Assume that a population is divided into two strata with population proportions 0.7 and 0.3, respectively. Suppose that the sampling proportions of the strata are 0.95 and 0.05, respectively, while the strata estimates are $p_1 = 0.01$ and $p_2 = 0.45$. Then the total estimate is $p = 0.7 \cdot 0.01 + 0.3 \cdot 0.45 = 0.142$ so that

$$\text{DE} = \frac{0.7^2/0.95 \cdot 0.01 \cdot 0.99 + 0.3^2/0.05 \cdot 0.45 \cdot 0.55}{0.142 \cdot 0.858} = 3.7$$

and

$$\text{WE} = \frac{0.7^2}{0.95} + \frac{0.3^2}{0.05} = 2.3.$$

In other words, the design effect is approximately 1.6 times as great as the weight-ing effect. This has arisen because the allocation of the sample to the strata was dysfunctional: the stratum with the higher variance was under-sampled.

In fact, there is no upper limit for the ratio DE/WE. This is shown in the next more general example.

Example 3.4   Let the population and sampling proportions be $\lambda_1 = 1 - \varepsilon$, $\lambda_2 = \varepsilon$, $\mu_1 = 1 - \varepsilon^3$ and $\mu_2 = \varepsilon^3$, where ε is a number from 0 to 1. Then, for a sufficiently small ε, the ratio DE/WE will be close to the ratio $[p_2(1 - p_2)]/[p_1(1 - p_1)]$ (the calculations are given in Appendix E). Consequently, if the estimates are such that p_2 is close to 0.5, p_1 is close to 0.0 and p_2 is, say, 100 times greater than p_1, the design effect will be approximately 50 times greater than the weighting effect. Therefore, potentially there is no upper limit for the ratio DE/WE.

Clearly, the situation in the example is very artificial because extreme population or sampling proportions are very seldom found in practice. In real surveys, most design effects are less than 5.0 even for the most complicated survey designs. If for many variables the design effect exceeds 5.0, it is advisable to find out what caused it.

3.3.4   Design effect versus weighting and clustering effect

Weighting usually has little effect on the contribution of individual clusters to the overall estimates. A whole cluster may be up-weighted or down-weighted according to whether the stratum it belongs to is under- or over-represented in the sample. There will also be some effect if members of a cluster are disproportionately of types that are particularly affected by weighting. However, in general weighting and clustering may be regarded as substantially independent in their effects. Kish [37] suggested that the overall design effect could be regarded as being the product of the effects of clustering and weighting. Gabler *et al.* [20] showed that, with certain assumptions, this product could be regarded as a conservative or upper-bound estimate for the design effect. This model has been adopted, for instance, in determining the sample sizes needed for a given precision in planning the European Social Survey.

   If this model holds, it is very convenient. The weighting effect can be calculated very easily, and is constant (for the whole sample or for any subset) across all variables. The clustering effect is less easy to measure and is different for each category of each variable (for any subset). Nevertheless it should not be difficult to anticipate which measures are liable to be particularly affected by sample clustering. Experience, and calculation of some specimen clustering effects for a data set, should enable a rough but realistic estimate of the likely value of ρ and thence, with the cluster size, of the clustering effect affecting any estimate. We have already seen that precisely calculated estimates of design effects are themselves subject to a margin of uncertainty. A realistic working estimate that can be obtained easily may be little less valid, and at least as useful as one requiring lengthy calculation.

   To illustrate the relationship between the design effect and the weighting and clustering effects, we have used the same database as in section 3.2.3. The weighting effect for the total survey sample was 1.45.

   To take into account the effect of clustering, we have calculated the intra-class correlation coefficient ρ according to formula (3.16) (the national mean $\bar{x}$ was used because for the chosen variables the stratification effect was very small). The coefficient can then be converted into a 'clustering effect' CE by formula (5.4.1) from Kish [35]:

$$CE = 1 + (b - 1)\rho,$$

where b is the average cluster size, in this survey 6.98. We use the notation CE to distinguish it from the total design effect DE.

Tables 3.4 and 3.5 examine the contention that the overall design effect can be estimated (conservatively) as the product of the weighting effect and the clustering effect. For substantially the same range of variables as in Tables 3.1 and 3.2, the design effect has been calculated in three ways:

- using formula (3.11), as before;
- as the product of the weighting and clustering effects (the weighting effect here is a constant 1.45); and
- as the ratio of the variance of the twelve individual monthly estimates to the 'simple-random-sample' variance $p(1 - p)$ of the annual (or mean) estimate.

Table 3.4. Design effect estimates – calculated and empirical

Category	Proportion (%)	ρ	CE	CE × WE	Design effect	'Monthly' DE
Education: Basic	22.98	0.078	1.47	2.13	1.82	2.51
Intermediate	20.03	0.037	1.22	1.77	1.60	0.95
Secondary	18.22	0.034	1.20	1.74	1.72	2.71
Some Tertiary	10.10	0.026	1.16	1.68	1.86	2.06
Diploma/Degree	28.68	0.119	1.71	2.48	2.12	2.54
Work status: Full Time	39.56	0.072	1.43	2.07	1.81	1.78
Part Time	18.27	0.033	1.20	1.74	1.68	1.13
Home Duties	8.25	0.031	1.18	1.71	1.54	1.15
Don't Work	3.72	0.032	1.19	1.73	1.78	2.24
Looking for work	4.97	0.026	1.15	1.67	2.01	3.89
Retired	18.16	0.085	1.51	2.19	1.60	1.01
Students	7.07	0.033	1.20	1.74	1.99	0.84
Occupation: Prof/Manager	15.55	0.070	1.42	2.06	1.92	3.12
White-Collar	20.68	0.033	1.20	1.74	1.63	2.93
Skilled Workers	7.22	0.012	1.07	1.55	1.64	1.35
Farm Owner	0.51	0.122	1.73	2.51	2.41	4.65
Others	13.87	0.022	1.13	1.64	1.71	1.81
Not Employed	42.17	0.067	1.40	2.03	1.80	1.86
Employer: Public Service	14.02	0.034	1.20	1.74	1.70	0.71
Private Industry	39.52	0.073	1.43	2.07	1.76	1.73
Self-Employed	4.29	0.040	1.24	1.80	1.80	0.56
Not Employed	42.17	0.067	1.40	2.03	1.80	1.86
Multi-Income H/h: No	49.46	0.094	1.56	2.26	1.94	3.70
Yes	50.53	0.099	1.59	2.31	1.94	3.70

Table 3.4. (*cont.*)

Category	Proportion (%)	ρ	CE	CE × WE	Design effect	'Monthly' DE
H/h Income: Under $25000	16.51	0.090	1.54	2.23	1.70	2.95
$25000 to $49999	18.23	0.045	1.27	1.84	1.62	2.44
$50000 to $99999	24.20	0.055	1.33	1.93	1.83	3.80
$100000 or More	14.78	0.097	1.58	2.29	2.37	4.63
No Answer	26.28	0.155	1.93	2.80	2.85	2.07
Married/De Facto: Yes	58.29	0.109	1.65	2.39	1.91	1.82
No	41.71	0.070	1.42	2.06	1.91	1.82
Children: None	63.28	0.099	1.59	2.31	1.88	1.74
1 Child	15.36	0.021	1.12	1.62	1.70	1.44
2 Children	13.87	0.028	1.17	1.70	1.61	0.93
3+ Children	7.49	0.019	1.11	1.61	1.60	1.58
H/h size: 1–2 People	40.86	0.107	1.64	2.38	1.85	1.00
3–4 People	42.20	0.061	1.37	1.99	1.69	1.71
5+ People	16.94	0.039	1.23	1.78	2.02	0.74
Dwelling: Detached House	83.71	0.286	2.71	3.93	4.67	2.27
Other	16.29	0.392	3.34	4.84	4.67	2.27
Home owning: Own Home	39.40	0.121	1.72	2.49	2.14	1.38
Paying Off	31.06	0.094	1.56	2.26	2.12	2.49
Renting	28.14	0.131	1.79	2.60	2.73	2.15
Other/Not Stated	1.39	0.023	1.14	1.65	1.74	1.60
Grocery buyer: Usually Buy	59.49	0.104	1.62	2.35	1.99	1.75
Sometimes Buy	26.56	0.074	1.44	2.09	2.16	4.42
Never Buy Groceries	13.94	0.060	1.36	1.97	2.22	2.99
Household: Young Singles	11.49	0.081	1.48	2.15	2.37	1.30
Young Couples	7.05	0.019	1.11	1.61	1.73	1.12
Young Parents	23.72	0.054	1.32	1.91	1.78	1.20
Mid-Life Families	12.59	0.022	1.13	1.64	1.81	1.03
Mid-Life Households	29.37	0.050	1.30	1.89	1.68	2.18
Older Households	15.80	0.080	1.48	2.15	1.58	0.86
Car Driven: Ford	14.86	0.027	1.16	1.68	1.68	2.41
Holden	16.08	0.025	1.15	1.67	1.59	0.80
Toyota	15.89	0.018	1.11	1.61	1.43	2.15
Other/No answer	34.33	0.048	1.28	1.86	1.60	2.08
Don't Drive	18.84	0.068	1.40	2.03	2.01	2.45
Main Bank: ANZ	10.01	0.022	1.13	1.64	1.50	0.76
Commonwealth	30.48	0.054	1.32	1.91	1.62	1.31
NAB	10.3	0.026	1.16	1.68	1.59	1.19
Westpac	12.06	0.031	1.18	1.71	1.56	2.20
Other	34.22	0.070	1.42	2.06	2.06	1.30
None/Can't say	2.94	0.034	1.20	1.74	1.74	2.99
Intend to buy new car	12.80	0.036	1.22	1.77	1.67	0.91
Card Held: AmEx	5.33	0.043	1.25	1.81	1.68	3.28
Diner's Club	1.47	0.019	1.11	1.61	1.53	1.39
Visa	40.97	0.104	1.62	2.35	1.93	4.21
MasterCard	19.24	0.033	1.20	1.74	1.54	2.67
Mean				1.99	1.87	1.86

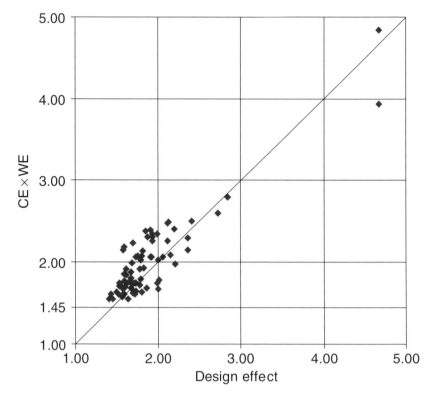

Figure 3.1   Demographics. The correlation between the design effect and the product of clustering and weighting effects is 0.88. The horizontal line shows the constant weighting effect of 1.45.

Age and sex have been excluded from Table 3.4 because their design effects are artificially low. Post-stratification is used to ensure that the sex proportions and broad age proportions correspond with population projections for each month.

The three sources show a similar pattern. In all of them dwelling type is a conspicuous outlier. We have previously seen that design effect estimates are subject to a degree of uncertainty, which would tend to reduce the degree of correlation between them. Nevertheless the correlations remain positive. The correlation between the overall effect and that produced by the product of clustering and weighting effects is 0.88 (see Figure 3.1). Even if the outlying values for dwelling types are removed the correlation is still 0.68. Given that every individual estimate is surrounded by a halo of uncertainty this is encouraging. The mean value for CE × WE is also higher than that of the overall design effects, which supports the assumption that CE × WE is in general a conservative estimate.

Here the fit is less good. Table 3.5 shows a similar set of calculations for a series of Australian magazines. The correlation between CE × WE and the overall design effect is only 0.40 but values of ρ, and thus of clustering effects, are smaller (see Figure 3.2). The estimate CE × WE relies more heavily on the constant weighting effect. Here we are dealing with respondent attributes with generally low incidence.

Table 3.5. Design effect estimates – actual and surrogate

Magazine	Proportion (%)	ρ	CE	CE $\times$ WE	DE
Australian Geographic	2.90	0.005	1.03	1.49	1.40
Australian Good Taste	4.69	0.013	1.08	1.57	1.54
Australian PC World	1.79	0.009	1.05	1.52	1.62
Australian Reader's Digest	5.85	0.023	1.14	1.65	1.55
Belle	1.32	0.012	1.07	1.55	1.60
Better Homes and Gardens	8.62	0.032	1.19	1.73	1.56
Bride To Be	0.69	0.011	1.07	1.55	1.72
BRW	1.60	0.024	1.14	1.65	1.77
Bulletin	1.86	0.017	1.10	1.60	1.68
Burke's Backyard	4.16	0.012	1.07	1.55	1.36
Cleo	4.34	0.014	1.08	1.57	1.77
Cosmopolitan	5.32	0.014	1.08	1.57	1.75
Dolly	3.09	0.011	1.07	1.55	1.61
English Woman's Weekly	1.20	0.006	1.04	1.51	1.33
Family Circle	3.10	0.016	1.10	1.60	1.47
Financial Review Magazine	1.74	0.047	1.28	1.86	1.89
Foxtel Magazine	8.09	0.069	1.42	2.06	2.08
Gardening Australia	2.12	0.010	1.06	1.54	1.27
Girlfriend	2.20	0.006	1.04	1.51	1.56
Good Medicine	2.44	0.004	1.02	1.48	1.44
Harper's Bazaar	1.32	0.010	1.06	1.54	1.78
Home Beautiful	2.14	0.003	1.02	1.48	1.41
House & Garden	3.98	0.020	1.12	1.62	1.57
InStyle	1.92	0.017	1.10	1.60	1.73
Marie Claire	3.70	0.016	1.09	1.58	1.67
Men's Health	1.81	0.009	1.05	1.52	1.80
Money Magazine	1.45	0.006	1.04	1.51	1.57
Motor	2.14	0.007	1.04	1.51	1.98
National Geographic	5.23	0.023	1.14	1.65	1.64
New Idea	11.18	0.018	1.11	1.61	1.51
New Scientist	1.29	0.007	1.04	1.51	1.93
New Woman	1.83	0.014	1.09	1.58	1.67
New Weekly	3.47	0.015	1.09	1.58	1.63
Personal Investor	0.95	0.011	1.06	1.54	1.54
Rolling Stone	2.07	0.011	1.07	1.55	1.89
Shares	1.14	0.004	1.02	1.48	1.53
Super Food Ideas	4.88	0.017	1.10	1.60	1.55
Take 5	4.25	0.020	1.12	1.62	1.50
That's Life	6.63	0.028	1.17	1.70	1.52
Time	2.41	0.027	1.16	1.68	1.68
TV Hits	1.76	0.018	1.11	1.61	1.76
TV Soap	3.23	0.022	1.13	1.64	1.74

(*cont.*)

Table 3.5. (*cont.*)

Magazine	Proportion (%)	ρ	CE	CE×WE	DE
TV Week	7.13	0.015	1.09	1.58	1.63
Vogue Australia	2.30	0.017	1.10	1.60	1.80
Vogue Living	1.59	0.008	1.05	1.52	1.49
Who	4.58	0.014	1.08	1.57	1.65
Woman's Day	14.44	0.019	1.11	1.61	1.49
Women's Weekly	17.41	0.043	1.25	1.81	1.62

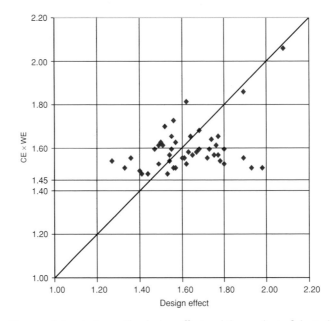

Figure 3.2   Magazines. The correlation between the design effect and the product of clustering and weighting effects is 0.40. The horizontal line shows the constant weighting effect of 1.45.

The nine magazines that achieve more then 5% readership do show a better relationship for these two measures. To some extent this may be because estimates of ρ are inevitably less precise for low incidence measures. With an average cluster size of seven, for a 3% incidence magazine there is on average only one-fifth of a reader per cluster.

3.3.5   Comparison of design effect and weighting effect in a drug survey

Here we consider a relationship between design effect and weighting effect in another, more complex 'real-life' survey, the 1998 National Drug Strategy Household Survey.

This was managed by the Australian Institute of Health and Welfare (on behalf of the Commonwealth Department of Health and Family Services), and was conducted by Roy Morgan Research.

A multi-stage stratified sample design (with seventeen geographic strata) was used. Three separately identified samples were used, being combined as appropriate at the analysis stage. The first sample consisted of 4012 respondents aged 14 and over. A total of 1983 sample-two interviews were completed in the same households as sample-one interviews. Finally, 4035 sample-three interviews were completed in eight of the strata only, with persons aged 14–39 in the same neighbourhoods as those asked to complete sample-one questionnaires. Some of the geographic strata were heavily over-sampled for specific reasons. The complex design evolved as a result of a variety of objectives being set by a variety of stakeholders with differing interests. Within each stratum, locations (clusters) were chosen by a systematic sampling method. Cluster sizes varied, principally from sample to sample but also to a lesser extent from stratum to stratum within each sample. A complex weighting system was applied using household size, sex, age and region.

Table 3.6 shows two sets of design effects for key variables in the survey (all three samples combined with 10 030 respondents), with the kind permission of the Australian Institute of Health and Welfare. The weighted stratified mean estimate (3.1) was used to estimate proportions while formula (3.10) (within each stratum separately) was employed to calculate the variance of estimates. The first set relates to respondents' claims of 'Drugs ever tried' while the second relates to 'Drugs tried in the last 12 months'; for convenience, we put these together. D_{tot} denotes the total design effect, D_{str} denotes the design effect due to stratification while D_{av} denotes the mean within-stratum design effect.

The overall weighting effect was 2.88 with the stratification component 1.75 and the average stratum weighting effect 1.80.

As can be seen, the total weighting effect of 2.88 is higher than the average national design effect of 2.73 (which just happens to be the same in both sets of data). If we investigate the variables for which the design effect is actually greater than 2.88, we find that across all thirty proportions in both sets of data, nine total design effects are greater than the total weighting effect. The biggest design effect is 4.54, which is about 1.6 times the weighting effect.

As we would expect from our analysis of the weighting effect in stratified random sampling (section 3.3.3), the *stratification component* of the weighting effect should be on the high side when we compare it with the stratification components of the design effects. In fact, this is true: the strata weighting component is 1.75 and only four stratification components of (thirty) design effects exceed this number, the biggest of them being 2.13. What is even more interesting is that for *only one* of the nine design effects that are greater than the weighting effect is the stratification component greater than 1.75. In other words, stratification is *not* the main reason why a design effect would exceed the weighting effect. The only other reason would be, of course, that the design effects within strata are high. This is again easily confirmed by the tables: for seven out of the nine variables, the mean stratum design effect is greater

Table 3.6. Design effect – drugs survey

Drugs	P (%)	Ever tried Design effect D_{tot}	D_{str}	D_{av}	P(%)	Tried in last 12 months Design effect D_{tot}	D_{str}	D_{av}
Tobacco	63.41	3.87	1.75	2.21	25.37	2.93	1.74	1.92
Alcohol	86.54	4.35	1.72	2.34	78.36	4.54	1.74	2.43
Pain killers/ analgesics	11.10	2.81	1.76	1.61	4.92	2.91	1.73	1.94
Tranquilisers/ sleeping pills	5.96	2.78	1.66	1.82	2.85	2.37	1.70	1.51
Steroids	0.75	3.51	2.00	1.59	0.22	2.44	2.13	0.86
Barbiturates	1.51	2.01	1.54	1.49	0.24	1.78	1.74	1.01
Amphetamines	8.44	2.66	1.69	1.69	3.55	2.75	1.75	1.56
Marijuana	37.64	3.50	1.72	2.43	17.05	3.21	1.67	1.92
Heroin	2.13	1.92	1.72	1.44	0.75	2.29	1.74	1.25
Methadone	0.46	1.47	1.47	1.11	0.16	1.95	1.35	1.02
Cocaine	4.14	2.54	1.77	1.36	1.33	2.93	1.71	1.22
Any hallucinogens	9.56	2.80	1.61	2.06	2.89	2.71	1.59	1.62
Ecstasy/ designer drugs	4.61	2.41	1.70	1.68	2.33	2.28	1.63	1.43
Inhalants	3.77	2.04	1.60	1.43	0.82	1.53	1.51	1.23
Injecting drugs	2.01	2.21	1.54	1.36	0.72	2.00	1.51	1.15
Average effect		2.73	1.68	1.71		2.73	1.68	1.47

than the mean stratum weighting effect of 1.80. Therefore, *clustering* is what really 'drives' the design effect 'beyond' the weighting effect.

There could be, of course, all kinds of reasons why clustering has different effects for different variables. However, we have observed earlier (see pages 82, 96) that the relative impact of clustering depends, among other things, on the product $p(1 - p)$. To see this relationship for the drug survey, we can plot the mean stratum design effect versus product $p(1 - p)$, for each variable.

Figure 3.3 shows that the design effect tends to increase as the proportion becomes closer to 50%. In fact, the correlation coefficient between products $p(1 - p)$ and mean stratum design effects of 0.844 also confirms the relationship. Six of the nine solid circles have the highest values of $p(1 - p)$ so that the distance from p to 50% is indeed a good 'detector' to identify variables with relatively high design effects.

Therefore, the analysis above demonstrates again that the weighting effect adjusted to take into account the clustering effect can be used as a good conservative substitute for the design effect.

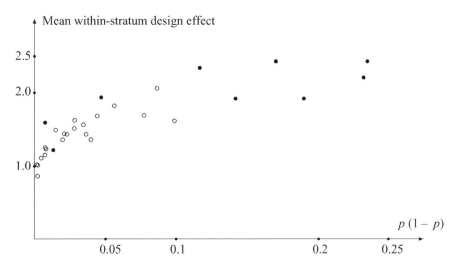

Figure 3.3   Mean stratum design effect plotted against $p(1-p)$ for each drug-use variable. Solid circles mark points that correspond to the nine total design effects greater than the weighting effect of 2.88; other points are indicated by open circles.

The value of an estimated design effect based on the weighting and clustering effects is that the estimation can be relatively straightforward. The weighting effect is readily calculated and is constant across all variables for any subset of the sample. With some preliminary exploration and experience, and knowledge of the subject matter of the survey, it should not be difficult to identify variables or categories likely to be subject to a clustering effect, and to make a rough but realistic estimate of the likely magnitude of this. To identify most strongly affected variables, factors such as variation of proportions between clusters as well as the magnitude of $p(1-p)$ should be considered. A design effect calculated in this way, even if discounted slightly for low incidence items, is likely to be a useful tool where nothing better is immediately available. It may not be accurate, but then the design effect estimate is also subject to a margin of error, and it is likely to be on the conservative side.

3.3.6   Statistical reasons for weighting

The first property of the calibrated sample size in section 3.3.1 is part of a more general fact: weighting increases not just the weighting effect but, in most cases, the design effect as well.[2] The result is that the standard error of a weighted estimate will generally be greater than the standard error of the unweighted estimate. This provokes the following naive question: if the standard error is increased, and our estimates are therefore less precise, why do we need weighting at all? Would it not be better from a statistical point of view to use the unweighted estimate? Of course, there are practical

---

[2] We exclude here the trivial cases where estimates have been determined solely by target sums of weights set in the weighting process and where the design effect is therefore zero, see page 94.

reasons that make weighting absolutely necessary but it is comforting to know that these are supported by good statistical arguments.

To answer these questions, one has to recall that the standard error, by definition, is the typical (strictly the 'root-mean-square') sampling error. In other words, if the sampling is done a large number of times then the standard error will be the *standard deviation* of the resulting estimates. But any *particular* sampling error can be greater or smaller than the average error, partly by chance and partly depending on how biased the sample is. In general, one cannot measure particular sampling errors. Usually we have only one estimate to work with and the standard error, *estimated* from the one measurement we have, is the only tool we can use in practice to estimate the likely precision of an estimate.

However, the statistical reason for weighting is that our unweighted sample is known to be biased in some way and so there is a good chance that the particular unweighted error (the difference between the particular estimate and the true value) is greater than the particular weighted error. Consider a case where the standard error of an unweighted mean is calculated as 0.5. The standard error is simply the (expected) standard deviation of the means of a large number of similarly drawn samples. This simply means that about 32% of a large number of similarly made estimates of that mean would be expected to lie outside a range of ±0.5 from the mean of those estimates. If the measurement is unbiased the mean of the estimates will coincide with the true mean and so the same proportion of estimates will be more than one standard error away from the true mean.

But if the measurement is biased, so that the mean of the estimates is not the same as the true value, it can be shown that the root-mean-square difference between the individual means and the *true* mean is greater than the root-mean-square difference between the individual means and the mean of the sample means. So any particular difference between the particular estimate and the true mean is likely to be greater than the difference between the particular estimate and the mean of all the sample means.

Now of course we do not (generally) know the true mean. And we have only one sample so that we do not know what the mean of a large number of sample means would be. But if we believe that the weighting process that counteracts an obvious bias will also tend to reduce other unseen biases, then we can assume that the same process will tend to reduce the difference between any particular (unweighted) estimate and the true estimate (the particular error).

However, the picture is complicated by the fact that, as we have seen, the standard error of the weighted estimate of the mean is likely to be greater than the standard error of the unweighted estimate (provided that the distribution of individual values around the mean is not materially changed by the weighting process). This brings us to examine the question of the circumstances under which weighting may not be wholly beneficial.

3.3.7   Utility of weighting

Having chosen and implemented a weighting procedure for a given survey, it is reasonable to ask whether the weighting is 'useful' or not. In other words, is there any 'gain' for survey estimates when the weighting is introduced? Furthermore, it would be even more beneficial to have not just a simple 'yes/no' answer but a mathematical tool that would *measure* how useful the weighting is, a measure of the *utility of weighting*. It is clear that the utility should be measured for each estimate individually, similarly to the design effect, because different estimates are affected by weighting in different ways. In this subsection, we introduce one such measure of utility which is easy to compute and which could be used in practice.

There are two main factors that should, in our opinion, be reflected in the definition of any measure of weighting utility. The first factor is the difference between an unweighted survey estimate and the same estimate after weighting. The utility should then increase or decrease with this difference: the bigger the difference, the greater the utility of weighting is presumed to be. It may happen, of course, that the difference is high simply because the weighting is 'wrong' for this estimate. However, the assumption here is that the weighting was done in the best possible way so that weighted estimates are assumed to be more accurate than unweighted ones. In fact they represent our *best* estimates, based on the sample data.

These arguments can be illustrated by a simple example. Assume, for instance, that we have a disproportionately stratified random sample. In this sample, the stratification weights will have a big impact on estimates that are widely varied between strata. For these estimates, therefore, weighting is very beneficial because unweighted estimates could be very wrong. If, however, a variable is constant or almost constant across all strata, its estimates will not be strongly affected by weighting and so the corresponding weighting utility ought to be low.

The second factor to be included into any measure of weighting utility is related to the difference between the final confidence limits and the confidence limits from an unweighted sample. In other words, one should assess how much 'wider' a confidence interval of an estimate becomes once weighting has been taken into account. The most natural thing to consider would be, perhaps, the difference between the standard errors (the final error less the unweighted-sample error). However, a standard error reflects *all* sampling and weighting effects, not just the effects of weighting. Therefore, if we are interested solely in weighting, it is more appropriate to talk in terms of calibrated errors (see section 3.3.2 for details) rather than standard errors (although for a simple random sample, the calibrated error is in fact the same as the standard error). In other words, we consider the difference between the final calibrated error and the calibrated error that would come from an unweighted sample. This factor, therefore, works in the opposite direction: if the difference between calibrated errors is increasing, the utility of weighting should go down and if the difference is decreasing, the utility should go up.

Based on these arguments, the authors propose the following measure of utility of weighting. Let $x_1, \ldots, x_n$ be observations of variable x in a sample with n respondents. Denote by $\bar{x}$ the final, weighted estimate of the mean value of x:

$$\bar{x} = \frac{\sum_{i=1}^{n} w_i x_i}{\sum_{i=1}^{n} w_i},$$

where w_i is the weight of respondent i. On the other hand, denote by $\bar{x}_{\text{unw}}$ the original unweighted estimate of the mean value:

$$\bar{x}_{\text{unw}} = \frac{1}{n}\sum_{i=1}^{n} x_i.$$

Utility defined

Then the utility of weighting for estimate $\bar{x}$ (notation $U(\bar{x})$) is defined as the ratio of the difference between estimates to the difference between calibrated errors

$$U(\bar{x}) = \frac{|\bar{x} - \bar{x}_{\text{unw}}|}{|\text{c.e.}(\bar{x}) - \text{c.e.}(\bar{x}_{\text{unw}})|}. \qquad (3.27)$$

Recall that the calibrated error is the simple random sample error times the square root of the weighting effect. Therefore, the calibrated error of the unweighted sample estimate $\bar{x}_{\text{unw}}$ is simply the standard error $S/\sqrt{n}$ (because the weighting effect is 1.0), where S is the standard deviation of variable x. On the other hand, the final calibrated error of $\bar{x}$ is defined by formula (3.24) so that the utility can be expressed as

$$U(\bar{x}) = \frac{\sqrt{n}|\bar{x} - \bar{x}_{\text{unw}}|}{S(\sqrt{\text{WE}} - 1)},$$

where WE is the weighting effect.

In the case of proportion estimates, the standard deviation S is computed as $\sqrt{\hat{p}(1 - \hat{p})}$ so that in this case we obtain

$$U(\hat{p}) = \frac{|\hat{p} - \hat{p}_{\text{unw}}|}{|\text{c.e.}(\hat{p}) - \text{c.e.}(\hat{p}_{\text{unw}})|} = \frac{\sqrt{n}|\hat{p} - \hat{p}_{\text{unw}}|}{\sqrt{\hat{p}(1 - \hat{p})}(\sqrt{\text{WE}} - 1)}. \qquad (3.28)$$

The utility of weighting depends, like the standard error, on the square root of the sample size: the higher n, the higher the utility (which makes sense because in this case the confidence interval becomes narrower).

It is also clear that if utilities of weighting for several estimates from the same sample and over the same subset are to be compared, the sample size n and weighting effect WE will be constant. Therefore, the relative difference between utilities in this case will depend only on the term $|\bar{x} - \bar{x}_{\text{unw}}|/S$ (or $|\hat{p} - \hat{p}_{\text{unw}}|/\sqrt{\hat{p}(1 - \hat{p})}$ for proportions).

What are 'high' and 'low' values for the utility? There is no 'mathematical' answer to this question, and an interpretation of utility values depends on the particular sample design. One fairly obvious criterion would be that the change in calibrated errors (see section 3.3.2) should not exceed the change in estimates so that utility values less than 1.0 should be considered as very 'low'. In other words, the conclusion in the case of a utility value less than 1.0 would be that the weighting produces more loss than gain, and if it happens for many estimates, the whole weighting procedure should perhaps be revised.

To illustrate this, consider, for example, the case when the weighting effect is 2.0 and the sample contains 100 respondents. Table 3.7 gives utility values for several selected values of a proportion estimate $\hat{p}$ and the difference $|\hat{p} - \hat{p}_{\text{unw}}|$.

Table 3.7. Utility of weighting for $n = 100$ and WE $= 2.0$

$\hat{p}$	$|\hat{p} - \hat{p}_{unw}|$									
	0.01	0.02	0.03	0.04	0.05	0.06	0.07	0.08	0.09	0.10
0.01	2.426	4.853	7.279	9.706	12.132	14.558	16.985	19.411	21.837	24.264
0.02	1.724	3.449	5.173	6.898	8.622	10.347	12.071	13.796	15.520	17.244
0.03	1.415	2.830	4.246	5.661	7.076	8.491	9.907	11.322	12.737	14.152
0.04	1.232	2.464	3.696	4.928	6.160	7.392	8.624	9.856	11.088	12.320
0.05	1.108	2.215	3.323	4.431	5.539	6.646	7.754	8.862	9.969	11.077
0.06	1.017	2.033	3.050	4.066	5.083	6.099	7.116	8.133	9.149	10.166
0.07	0.946	1.892	2.839	3.785	4.731	5.677	6.623	7.570	8.516	9.462
0.08	0.890	1.780	2.670	3.560	4.449	5.339	6.229	7.119	8.009	8.899
0.09	0.844	1.687	2.531	3.374	4.218	5.062	5.905	6.749	7.592	8.436
0.10	0.805	1.609	2.414	3.219	4.024	4.828	5.633	6.438	7.243	8.047
0.11	0.772	1.543	2.315	3.086	3.858	4.630	5.401	6.173	6.944	7.716
0.12	0.743	1.486	2.229	2.972	3.715	4.458	5.200	5.943	6.686	7.429
0.13	0.718	1.436	2.154	2.871	3.589	4.307	5.025	5.743	6.461	7.179
0.14	0.696	1.392	2.087	2.783	3.479	4.175	4.870	5.566	6.262	6.958
0.15	0.676	1.352	2.028	2.704	3.381	4.057	4.733	5.409	6.085	6.761
0.20	0.604	1.207	1.811	2.414	3.018	3.621	4.225	4.828	5.432	6.036
0.25	0.558	1.115	1.673	2.230	2.788	3.345	3.903	4.460	5.018	5.575
0.30	0.527	1.054	1.580	2.107	2.634	3.161	3.688	4.215	4.741	5.268
0.35	0.506	1.012	1.518	2.025	2.531	3.037	3.543	4.049	4.555	5.062
0.40	0.493	0.986	1.478	1.971	2.464	2.957	3.450	3.942	4.435	4.928
0.45	0.485	0.971	1.456	1.941	2.426	2.912	3.397	3.882	4.367	4.853
0.50	0.483	0.966	1.449	1.931	2.414	2.897	3.380	3.863	4.346	4.828

For other values of n and WE multiply the figures in Table 3.7 by

$$\frac{0.0414\sqrt{n}}{\sqrt{WE - 1}}.$$

Thus if the sample size were 1000 and the weighting effect the same, all the above utility figures would be increased by a factor of over three ($\sqrt{10}$). It must be borne in mind, of course, that where the weighting effect is close to 1.0 the changes in estimates induced by the weighting will probably be small. It turns out that there is a close relationship between utility of weighting and calibrated confidence limits. The word 'calibrated' in this context means that the standard error is replaced by the calibrated error. For example, the 95% calibrated confidence limits for $\bar{x}$ are defined as $\bar{x} \pm 1.96$ c.e.$(\bar{x})$. These calibrated limits can be compared with the original 'unweighted sample' confidence limits $\bar{x}_{unw} \pm 1.96$ c.e.$(\bar{x}_{unw})$, and this comparison is related to the utility of weighting. More precisely, denote, for simplicity, by e the calibrated error of $\bar{x}$ and by e_{unw} the calibrated error of $\bar{x}_{unw}$ (so that

$U(\bar{x}) = |\bar{x} - \bar{x}_{\text{unw}}|/(e - e_{\text{unw}}))$. Then we have the following result (see Appendix E for a proof).

Proposition 3.2   *Let k be a positive real number. Using the notations above, the statement $U(\bar{x}) \leq k$ is equivalent to the statement that the interval $[\bar{x} - ke, \bar{x} + ke]$ contains the interval $[\bar{x}_{\text{unw}} - ke_{\text{unw}}, \bar{x}_{\text{unw}} + ke_{\text{unw}}]$.*

In particular, the equality $U(\bar{x}) = k$ implies that either the left ends or the right ends of the two intervals are the same.

This result allows us to say, for example, that utility values less than 1.96 can still be considered as too low: a value less than 1.96 means that the 95% 'calibrated' confidence limits for $\bar{x}$ will contain the 'original' 95% confidence limits for $\bar{x}_{\text{unw}}$. This means in fact that our 'confidence' in the estimate has decreased so that the weighting for this estimate was not 'useful'.

But even 1.96 is only a lower bound for 'low' values and it is up to the user to decide which utility values are 'low' for a particular sample. The critical utility value is equal to the z-score associated with the confidence interval the user has in mind. Besides, the utility function is only an estimate and subject to its own sampling error.

Finally, we indicate several situations where calculation of utility of weighting could be beneficial.

- As was discussed earlier, the utility of weighting can be used to identify variables for which weighting does not have any gain. If the sample size is small, there could be many estimates with a low utility of weighting (because standard errors are relatively high). If this is the case, it would be worthwhile to revise the weighting procedure to improve the overall utility of weighting.
- Formulae (3.27) and (3.28) can be applied to find out which estimates are most affected by weighting. This could produce a useful insight into the sample design and perhaps even indicate how the weighting procedure could be improved.
- 'Weighting performance' can be compared for various groups of variables by computing the average utility of weighting for each group. For instance, the overall average weighting utility can be compared with the average utility *among key variables*. If the latter figure is much lower than the overall average utility of weighting, it is a good reason for concern about sample design. If there are expectations that one group of variables should be affected by weighting more than another group, this kind of analysis could be especially beneficial.
- Average weighting utility figures (either across all variables or across groups of variables) can be compared with similar figures from *another sample* of a similar size and design.

An example of low utility of weighting is given by Ward *et al.* [59] in their examination of the Politz–Simmons 'not-at-home' correction method (see [45]), where they found a severe erosion of precision through the use of weights with high variance was accompanied by only small changes in most estimates.

3.3.8   Treatment of weighted data by statistical software

Several specialised variance estimation programs exist, specifically designed for evaluating the effect of sample design and execution on the precision of estimates. A number of these have been developed in academic circles or in government departments or agencies, often originally for use with specific large-scale quantitative surveys. They vary somewhat in what they can do, but all are designed to treat data that have been gathered from samples using probability methods of different kinds. Stratification, multi-stage selection of sampling units, selection with and without replacement, clustering, post-stratification and weighting are generally recognised. Some of this software has general purpose tabulation and analysis capabilities but it is, in general, probably more appropriate for the assessment of the effects of sample design and execution as a background for more extensive analysis and exploration, or for the checking of specific estimates identified as interesting in other analysis. The 'ultimate cluster sampling model' as described by Kalton [30] is generally used. Taylor series approximation and repeated replication (random groups, jackknife, bootstrap, balanced half-samples, etc.) are the main tools used for estimating variance. Generally the variance and design effect are computed for means, totals and proportions but some also estimate variances for regression and more complex statistics.

Such software is clearly of great benefit for the serious and specific study of the effects of sampling and weighting in a project. However, our concern here is with the performance of the 'bread-and-butter' software widely used to provide essentially descriptive statistics from survey data sets. This can be generally classified in two types: general purpose statistical packages and specialised survey processing systems. Both types are designed to accept data from a wide range of projects. The input required normally consists of both the data set itself and a description of the data (metadata) identifying to the software the content, layout and format of the data set.

We do not propose to review or discuss specific packages of either type here. There are many of them, doubtless including many unknown to us, and they may change over time. We confine ourselves to offering some general advice and warnings on their use with sample survey data. One reason for advising caution with these software packages is that they vary in their ability to handle weighted data correctly and may treat the data in different ways when doing anything but the most basic accumulations.

It is of the greatest importance that anyone contemplating using such a software package with weighted data should understand how the weights are treated, especially if intending to use it to calculate standard errors or to perform significance tests.

General purpose statistical packages

General purpose statistical packages will be familiar to most readers. They may offer either a fully functional system, operated through menu selection or by 'scripts' or command files, or a library of routines that can be easily incorporated in the user's own software, allowing rapid and reliable development of *ad hoc* analysis programs. Facilities available range from simple descriptive statistics, through significance tests, to advanced analytical, modelling and forecasting techniques. In this 'general purpose' category we would also include rudimentary statistical programs offering basic functionality, many of them available free or at little cost. If weighted data are to be used it is important to check the documentation to find a statement of how the weights are handled. For the more sophisticated and extensively documented packages, this may be hard to track down; for the simplest it may not exist.

Specialist survey software

Most large-scale survey practitioners prefer to use one of the numerous software systems developed specifically for sample surveys. These typically offer less statistical sophistication but more practical assistance. Many consist of closely linked modules that cover the entire survey process from questionnaire formulation, through the capture, validation, editing and management of data to the final generation of large quantities of fully labelled tabulations. They have usually been developed by people closely involved with practical survey research and thus generally have the facility to handle efficiently things that, while not peculiar to sample surveys, are regularly used in them while being less frequently encountered in other statistical applications (for instance, multiple-response questions and the rotation of the order of questions or response categories). Some allow interactive analysis with individual customised tabulations being generated on demand by end users of the data with minimal training.

The first thing to establish is whether the software recognises the concept of weights. Some, especially among the low-cost or free packages, do not, and if this is the case then they will make no sense of weighted data. Attempts to press them into service by multiplying all the other data by the respective weighting factors or duplicating each case a number of times corresponding to the integer value nearest the weight value may provide satisfactory aggregate values but will produce hopelessly incorrect estimates of standard errors, confidence limits, etc. Such software is therefore not considered further.

We also assume to start with that the software distinguishes between 'weights' and 'quantities' (see page 46). Any software that does not obviously do this should be rejected out of hand: it may produce correct totals but it will not produce correct means of quantities.

Replication weights

The most essential thing to establish is what the term 'weight' means in the context of any particular software package. It is used in this book, as stated at the beginning of Chapter 2, in the sense of a multiplier applied to vary the contribution a case makes to the total. However, some software packages treat what is *termed* a 'weight' differently. There, a weight is meant to refer to a number of *identical* cases or observations in the 'logical' data set represented by a single case in the physical data set. The weight therefore indicates the number of replications of a case to be used and we shall refer to 'weights' used in this way as *replication weights*. This usage is very different from the usage of 'weight' current in survey research. It is not a practice to be recommended and may be responsible for much confusion and error. It is sometimes resorted to in order to save space in the storage of very large data sets with many identical records, but the likelihood of this being of practical value in survey research projects seems remote. With a 'typical' questionnaire and sample size the chance of identical results from two or more interviews is small. On the other hand the use of weighting to balance samples is widespread.

The use of 'replication weights' also implies that weights should have integer values. Part of the confusion may also arise from the readiness of some software to accept fractional replication weights. If the weights are intended to indicate replications of actual sample cases it is not clear what the fractional parts are supposed to represent. The combination of the usage of the name and the fact that for many purposes (including conventional frequency counts and cross-tabulations) replication weights behave in the same way as conventional weights may induce users to assume that they may be treated as conventional weights for all purposes, but this is not the case.

Replication weights, if used strictly to represent replicated cases, must by their nature be intended to have integer values equal to or greater than one, and thus in any data set a mean value greater than 1.0 and a sum of weights greater than the number of cases physically present. If they truly represent replicated cases in the data set, then (assuming that the data set represents an unweighted simple random sample) the calculation of standard errors and the execution of significance tests will be done correctly.

If, however, the weights were intended to be adjustments to the sample composition, for any of the purposes already discussed, or if the weights incorporate a scaling factor for convenience of representation, then software that treats the weights as replication weights is liable to produce results capable of misleading anyone not fully aware of how the weights are being used and of the level of correction necessary in any individual case. If the sum of weights is treated as the sample size in the calculation of standard errors, then if the mean weight is greater than 1.0, naturally the standard error is understated. If the weights have been scaled to represent population projections, for instance, the standard error shown could be wildly inaccurate.

It may not be immediately obvious how weights are handled by any piece of software in the calculation of standard errors, confidence limits or significance tests. Differences in treatment of elements of the calculation will affect the nature and extent of the correction that must be made to the results to allow for the design effect.

Software may not always be consistent in its behaviour. For instance weighted results may be presented when frequency counts or cross-tabulations are required but an automated significance test may be performed using *unweighted* data. The authors have seen such a case where a survey design involved heavy weighting and an automated chi-square test (on unweighted data) reported a certain estimate as being significantly above the overall mean, whereas in fact the weighted estimate was slightly *below* the weighted mean.

It would not be realistic to expect general purpose analysis software to be able to evaluate or take into account design effects arising out of sampling or sample design issues. The range of sample designs means that a great deal of thought and effort needs to go into the calculation of design effects in any one case. In evaluating survey results, the factoring in of design effects will probably often be done mentally at the interpretation stage. However, it is important to know that such a

Table 3.8. Test data set

Category k	Value v	Weight w_1	Weight w_2
1	1	1.0	2.0
1	3	1.5	3.0
1	5	2.0	4.0
1	2	2.0	4.0
1	2	1.5	3.0
1	4	2.0	4.0
1	2	1.0	2.0
1	1	1.5	3.0
2	3	2.0	4.0
2	3	1.0	2.0
2	5	2.5	5.0
2	2	2.0	4.0
2	4	2.0	4.0
2	4	2.5	5.0
2	1	1.0	2.0
2	3	2.0	4.0
2	3	1.5	3.0
2	1	1.5	3.0
2	4	2.0	4.0
2	3	2.0	4.0

correction is done from a sound base; hence the need to know how the weights are used.

It is worth stressing at this stage the need to avoid an exclusive preoccupation with measures of precision or statistical significance. Interpretation of survey results is concerned primarily with the magnitude of estimates and with the strength of relationships between measures, and the meaning and implications of these, rather than with questions of purely statistical significance. This will be explored more fully in the next chapter. For the moment it suffices to say that software that uses 'weights' in a way that does not correctly calculate standard errors and similar measures, but that does correctly report weighted totals, can normally still be used satisfactorily for most purposes in exploring a survey data set. It is simply necessary to know what kinds of output can be taken at face value.

Testing the software
The sample data set presented in Table 3.8 may be used as a test. If this is used with a software package under consideration, the treatment of weights can be inferred from the results of a small number of straightforward calculations and we indicate the probable causes of different results that may be produced.

This data set is designed to identify the ways in which the software handles the weighting process and the subsequent calculations. Software packages normally include the quick generation of basic descriptive statistics for individual variables and these can be used. They generally include the range of values, the mean, the variance and/or standard deviation and a standard error.

There are 20 cases. They are divided into two categories with eight and twelve members. The 'value' is the quantity to be examined. w_1 is the weight of main interest and w_2 is a second weight used for checking, its values being double those of w_1. All software should agree on the sums of the (unweighted) values $\sum v = 56$ and of the weights $\sum w_1 = 34.5$, $\sum w_2 = 69.0$ and on the sums of the weighted values $\sum vw_1 = 104.5$, $\sum vw_2 = 209.0$.

The mean of the weighted values

$$\frac{\sum vw_1}{\sum w_1}$$

should be given as 3.0290 (104.5/34.5). If a result of 5.2250 (104.5/20) is given the weights are obviously not being used as weights. If some other value is shown then possibly something has been done with the values of the weights. At least one low-cost software package rounds weights to the nearest integer. This would produce a mean of 2.9167 (105.0/36.0) if the rounding of exact halves is done according to the IEEE method (rounding to the nearest *even* integer) or 3.0 (114.0/38.0) if halves are always rounded up. If such rounding is encountered it probably means that the 'weights' are being used as replication weights.

The sum of the weights may be displayed in integer form and it may not always be immediately clear whether the rounded or unrounded number has been used in further calculations. If the sum of the weights is sufficiently large, of course, the difference may be of no practical consequence, but it is worth knowing what the software is doing.

The next statistics to consider are the variance and the related standard deviation. The correct estimate of the weighted *sample* variance of v is 1.5354 and the standard deviation is 1.2391. Note that these figures are the same whichever set of weights is used, because the only difference between the two sets is one of scaling.

If a value of 1.6162 (standard deviation 1.2713) is given, then an attempt has been made to represent the population variance by multiplying by $n/(n-1)$. This (Bessel's correction) would be a correct thing to do with an unweighted simple random sample, provided it is made clear that the estimated population variance is being displayed. If the variance is shown as 1.5812 (standard deviation 1.2575) then the correction used has been based on the sum of weights

$$\frac{\sum w_1}{\sum w_1 - 1}.$$

There is no theoretical basis for applying this kind of correction where the data are weighted, though intuitively it seems more appropriate to use the actual number of cases rather than the (arbitrary) sum of weights. n in this case could be regarded

as the sum of weights re-scaled to a mean weight of 1.0. But for practical purposes, where n is large the ratio $n/(n-1)$ is so close to 1.0 as to be negligible
and the population variance estimate is virtually the same as the sample variance: it
is certainly of far less concern than any other element of the calculations. As long
as sample sizes are reasonably large, there is no need to worry about such small
differences.

The standard error is perhaps the most critical statistic for determining the usability
of the software with weighted data. In this case we know that we have a sample that
has appreciable variation in the weights. We can reasonably conclude that it is not
a simple random sample, but we know nothing else about it. The safest expedient
is therefore to calculate the standard error of the mean using the 'calibrated sample
size'. This is 18.6706 ($= (\sum w_1)^2 / \sum w_1^2$), and dividing the standard deviation by
the square root of this gives a standard error of 0.2868. A standard error of 0.2771
indicates that the standard deviation has been divided by the square root of the raw
sample size (20). Here the difference is small because the calibrated sample size is
close to the raw sample size, but this is not always the case.

However, if the standard error is shown as 0.2110 (or thereabouts) this means
that the standard deviation has been divided by the *square root of the sum of the
weights*. This is the most potentially dangerous condition, as the resultant standard
error is determined by the scaling of the weights. If for instance the weights are
scaled for convenience to indicate the population size, then two similarly drawn samples with very different sample sizes but equivalent sums of weights could appear
to yield the same standard error. A quick test for this is simply to generate (as we
have done in the test data set) a second set of weights of a constant multiple of the
value of the original weights and to use these to calculate the standard error. The
standard error should remain the same (except where a population-variance correction has been based on the sum of the weights, when there should be a very small
difference).

The value of the standard error is, of course, determined in part by the method
used to calculate the variance. Given below are the standard errors resulting from the
possible combinations of variance estimation and standard error calculation described
above.

	Variance correction		
	uncorrected	$\sum w / \left(\sum w - 1 \right)$	$n/(n-1)$
$\sqrt{n_c}$	0.2868	0.2910	0.2942
$\sqrt{n}$	0.2771	0.2812	0.2843
$\sqrt{\sum w}$	0.2110	0.2141	0.2164

If standard errors are not calculated correctly for weighted data then it may reasonably
be assumed that any significance testing is also performed incorrectly on such data.

If sums of weights are used in place of the calibrated (or unweighted) sample size the effect will depend on the size of the mean weight. If the mean weight is high, any significance test will overstate the level of significance. Where the weights are low tests will understate.

If the sum of the weights has been used in calculating the standard error, and no software is available that does the job properly, then it may be possible to obtain at least more realistic estimates of the standard error by re-scaling all the weights so that they sum to the calibrated sample size

$$w' = w \frac{\sum w}{\sum w^2}.$$

This may be adequate when the whole sample is being used, but will not necessarily be adequate for any subset of the sample. It is at best an emergency work-around, not a solution.

If weights are not correctly treated in the software, it may still be usable for general cross-tabulation work. If any form of variance estimation or significance test is required it may still be possible to use it provided that appropriate adjustments are made in interpreting the output, for instance by factoring in a known or presumed design effect.

Earlier the effect of rounding the weights was mentioned. It would also be as well to emphasise that undesirable rounding may be found in the output from some systems. Consider the result of cross-tabulating 'category' by 'value' in the example data set given. The totals (weighted) should be as follows.

Category	$v = 1$	$v = 2$	$v = 3$	$v = 4$	$v = 5$	total
1	2.5	4.5	1.5	2.0	2.0	12.5
2	2.5	2.0	8.5	6.5	2.5	22.0
total	5.0	6.5	10.0	8.5	4.5	34.5

One popular statistical package produced the following interesting result.

Category	$v = 1$	$v = 2$	$v = 3$	$v = 4$	$v = 5$	total
1	3	5	2	2	2	14
2	3	2	9	7	3	24
total	6	7	11	9	5	38

Notice that not only have the cell totals been rounded, but the row, column and overall totals are the sums of the *rounded* cell totals. Percentages (not shown here) were based on the rounded numbers. The marginal distributions of the cross-tabulation were different from the weighted frequency counts for the individual variables, produced separately by the same package, though here the percentages were correctly calculated on the unrounded numbers, the rounding to integers being done only in displaying the sums of weights.

Furthermore, when asked to perform a chi-square test, the same package used the rounded cell and total figures, producing a chi-square value of 6.54. Had the unrounded figures been used, the value would have been 6.15, though both results would have been incorrect: if weighted figures are being used the test should be carried out as described in the next chapter.

3.4   Missing data

It often happens in practice that certain respondents do not answer some questions in a survey. This is most prevalent in self-completion surveys although it may happen in face-to-face interviewing as well. Even with modern computer-assisted interviewing systems that automatically guarantee that data are *technically* complete (in the sense that all fields that should contain data will contain something) a respondent may *refuse* or be unable to answer some questions. Furthermore, even the most careful and conscientious respondents are inclined to miss the occasional question or to give incomplete or ambiguous answers. This is well known especially in the social sciences. The problem, therefore, is important and below we discuss possible approaches as well as statistical effects.

3.4.1   Imputation techniques

There is an extensive literature on techniques for dealing with the 'missing data problem'. The more sophisticated statistical packages have at least some method of handling missing observations when performing statistical analysis. We give a very brief overview of possible alternative approaches to dealing with the situation where answers to a question are missing.

- The conservative approach is to leave answers as they are and to accept that the estimates reported add to less than their correct total.
- The proportions reported can simply be scaled to the correct total.
- Respondents with missing answers can be *randomly* allocated in equal proportions across all possible answer categories.
- Respondents with missing answers can be randomly allocated to answer categories in proportion to the numbers of respondents already in those categories. This has the same effect as the scaling proportions to the correct total, but by creating a complete set of data, internal consistency is preserved.
- Respondents with missing values can either be assigned an average value, for continuous variables (with a natural ordering, like age or income) or be assigned to the category with the greatest frequency, for categorical variables.
- Respondents with missing values can be assigned a value held by a similar respondent.
- Evidence from other questions answered by respondents with partial missing data can be used to predict the missing answers.

Random
allocation

The first two approaches obviously leave data incomplete and may generate inconsistent answers when data are tabulated. Assuming that something has to be done to make the data complete and internally consistent, the proportional random allocation as well as the average approach are frequently used. But these and similar approaches that implicitly do the same thing have the disadvantage of, in effect, assuming that those who *failed* to give a response are *typical* and representative of the sample as a whole.

The term 'missing at random' is usually used to describe the assumption underlying these approaches. Frequently it can be seen that the missing respondents are atypical and unrepresentative in obvious aspects. However, the unrepresentativeness of the missing responses for individual questions may be no greater than the unrepresentativeness of the respondents missing from the sample when the response rate is low.

There are two further principal practical concerns about the 'proportional random' and 'average' allocation approaches. Firstly, both methods dilute the strength of relationships between variables. It is reasonable to assume that the value that would have been given had a respondent answered a question (the 'true' value) is related to the respondent's answers to other questions, so that there is some degree of internal consistency. A response inserted in either of these ways cannot have that association. Where two variables are correlated or otherwise associated, the introduction of such values into one or both variables must necessarily cause the strength of association between them to be understated when they are cross-analysed. Since one of the principal purposes of surveys is to examine the strength of relationships between variables, this may be a concern.

Secondly, a distribution of responses 'proportionately at random' or the insertion of a mean should allow for the fact that the distribution of responses or the mean value is not necessarily the same throughout the sample. All subsets are potentially different. Some attempt can reasonably be made to minimise the effect by partitioning the sample into two or more subsets and dealing with the missing responses separately within each. Overall, however, the effect will be to make each subset resemble the overall sample, to reduce diversity. Although this problem is not confined to 'missing-at-random' approaches, it is likely to be most severe and to have the greatest effect with them.

Inserting a mean value for a missing numerical quantity also has the effect of reducing the estimate of the variance, unless these inserted values can be identified and excluded from the calculation.

'Hot-deck'
transfer

Copying a value from a 'similar' respondent involves a judgement about what is an appropriate measure of similarity in any case. The most primitive form of this is the 'hot-deck' technique. For each incomplete variable a 'predictor variable' is selected. This is a variable that correlates (or otherwise corresponds) well with the incomplete variable. Respondents are then sorted (perhaps within stratum or post-stratum) in ascending or descending order of values of the predictor variable. Each respondent with a missing value is then assigned the value of that incomplete variable held by the immediately preceding respondent whose value was not missing. Apart from biases introduced by the choice of ascending or descending sort sequence, the 'hot-deck' method depends on the predictive power of the single variable selected for comparison or prediction. In the days of electro-mechanical data handling, where it originated, its advantage was that it offered a simple, consistent procedure that preserved at least some of the variation and inter-relationships of the 'complete' data. More sophisticated variants of this method could use multiple predictor variables to generate a composite measure of similarity.

'Customised' The most consistent (and most complicated) is therefore the last approach that includes
imputation   identification of predictor variables, analysis of respondents' answers to predictor variables and imputation, on the basis of this analysis, of the most probable answers for respondents with missing responses. There is a wide range of possible imputation techniques, from linear regression to neural networks. In most cases, they produce better results than random allocation or the average value approach.

It is beyond the scope of this book to compare the performance of various imputation techniques and to discuss their suitability for different situations. However, one very important measure of performance that is often overlooked is obtained by applying a method of imputation to respondents who already *have data*. This involves taking a value that exists, treating it as missing, imputing a value on the basis of other available evidence, and then comparing the imputed value with the actual value. This can be done for a number of respondents and the average prediction error calculated. After all, the accuracy of imputation for missing-data respondents is our principal concern and the only way to assess it is to see what happens among respondents with data. It has to be said, however, that respondents with responses present may have better quality data from which the missing responses can be imputed than people who are inclined to fail to answer.

Where missing values are replaced by imputed values it must be possible to identify which values have been imputed. This is not just a matter of good practice: it is, we suggest, ethically indefensible not to do so, particularly where the data set may be passed on in unit record form to other parties for subsequent or independent analysis. There is also the good practical reason of being able to reconstruct the original data set either to examine the effects of imputation or to experiment with alternative methods of imputation. Each field in which an imputed value may occur should be associated with another field that contains an indicator showing whether the value in any case is actual or imputed.

3.4.2   Effect on variance estimates

Having done the imputation, the next question is: how will it affect variance formulae for mean or proportion estimates? The question is important because some sort of imputation is done for many surveys due to the fact that missing values occur very frequently, even when the greatest effort is made to ensure high quality of both sampling and data recording. It is also clear that one cannot simply ignore that question, saying that there is no effect. Nevertheless, statistical literature does not pay much attention to this problem, with most discussions being limited, as usual, to simple random sampling.

Here we briefly consider the imputation effects, concentrating our efforts on getting a workable formula rather than on general theory. Notice that imputation, like sample design, will have different effects for different variables. This means that it is not very useful to talk about an 'average' effect and we should really deduce a new variance formula.

One particular problem with data imputation is that there are so many different imputation techniques, and even more situations where these techniques can be applied. Hence, when a variance formula is presented, the danger is that it could be too specific and not suitable for many surveys. On the other hand, a general formula may also not be very beneficial if it does not give a practical algorithm for calculating variance. The approach we have chosen is first to present a general tool to derive a variance formula that could be employed for almost any survey. Next, we choose our path, making several reasonable assumptions, and obtain a specific formula that, we believe, can still be applied in many cases. Any reader can, of course, use the same tool and choose another path by making different assumptions. One assumption that has to be made, of course, is that imputed values can be readily identified in the data set.

Let x be a variable of interest for a survey with n respondents. Assume that the first m respondents have data (i.e. we know values $x_1, \ldots, x_m$) while data for respondents $x_{m+1}, \ldots, x_n$ are 'missing'. Denote by f the variable of imputed values so that for missing respondents we will use imputed values $f_{m+1}, \ldots, f_n$ instead of the actual ones. Let $\tilde{x}$ be the weighted mean estimate with imputed values:

$$\tilde{x} = \frac{\sum_{i=1}^{m} w_i x_i + \sum_{i=m+1}^{n} w_i f_i}{\sum_{i=1}^{n} w_i}, \tag{3.29}$$

where w_i is the weight of respondent i. This is the estimate (in general, biased) for which we will actually derive a variance formula. Notice that the estimate includes proportions as well: both x and f would be binary variables (with values 0 or 1) in this case. We deliberately distinguish the estimate above from $\bar{x}$ which is still reserved for the mean without imputed values:

$$\bar{x} = \frac{\sum_{i=1}^{n} w_i x_i}{\sum_{i=1}^{n} w_i}.$$

One more variable we need is the *imputation error* $\epsilon_i = f_i - x_i$ for each respondent i. It is now simple to express $\tilde{x}$ in terms of $\bar{x}$ and an error term (see calculations in Appendix E):

$$\tilde{x} = \bar{x} + \alpha \tilde{\epsilon}, \tag{3.30}$$

where

$$\tilde{\epsilon} = \frac{\sum_{i=m+1}^{n} w_i \epsilon_i}{\sum_{i=m+1}^{n} w_i}$$

is the average error among missing respondents and

$$\alpha = \frac{\sum_{i=m+1}^{n} w_i}{\sum_{i=1}^{n} w_i}$$

is the *item non-response* rate.

This equation is our main tool for computing the variance. To start, we make the first assumption:

- for a given variable, the non-response rate α is presumed to be constant if the survey is repeated.

If the survey is conducted only once, this assumption is perhaps unavoidable (unless there is an alternative to equation (3.30) to derive a variance formula). But for many surveys it is also justified by practice. It is assumed that non-response to individual questions resulting from poor questionnaire design has been minimised by testing. Most changes in non-response rate occur when the sampling procedure is changed, or the questionnaire is changed, but the assumption above is, of course, conditional on there being no changes in sampling methodology. However, for readers who do have a chance to measure the variation of α and are not happy with the assumption above, we will give an alternative expression for variance (see Remark 3.1 at the end of this subsection).

Now the standard formula for the variance of the sum of two variables can be expressed as:

$$\text{var}(\tilde{x}) = \text{var}(\bar{x}) + \alpha^2 \text{var}(\tilde{\epsilon}) + 2\alpha \text{cov}(\bar{x}, \tilde{\epsilon}). \tag{3.31}$$

This is a very general formula that can in fact be used for most surveys. However, it is perhaps too general and we must now state the second assumption:

- the average imputation error does not depend on the sampling estimate $\bar{x}$.

This assumption, we believe, is very reasonable because the imputation procedure is usually independent of the sampling procedure. Notice that we *do not* assume that the error has any particular distribution. The independence of summands in equation (3.30) allows us, therefore, to get rid of the covariance and to state that

$$\text{var}(\tilde{x}) = \text{var}(\bar{x}) + \alpha^2 \text{var}(\tilde{\epsilon}). \tag{3.32}$$

If a reader feels that the independence assumption is not true in a particular survey then, of course, the covariance should still be calculated. However, it is not obvious how to compute it in general and any estimate of the covariance would have to rest on a number of explicit assumptions.

The next step is to calculate the two summands in equation (3.32). The variance of $\bar{x}$ is estimated by the usual methods as discussed previously, the only difference being that now imputed values should be used for the missing ones. The second summand is obviously more difficult to compute. In principle, $\tilde{\epsilon}$ is itself a ratio estimate and so its variance ought to be estimated by the same formula as the variance of $\bar{x}$. However, we do not actually know the error values for missing respondents (otherwise they would not be missing) so that it is extremely difficult, if not impossible, to calculate, in general, the effective sample size for them. This is where we make the last assumption:

- suppose that, for missing respondents, the *calibrated* sample size can replace the *effective* sample size, to calculate the variance of the average error $\tilde{\epsilon}$.

This assumption is clearly more restrictive than the first two but, on the other hand, we are attempting to solve a more difficult problem. If the sample is clustered, it is also recommended to take into account the clustering effect, to get a conservative variance estimate. In this situation that can be a good thing because we do not really know how big the error is among missing respondents; we can only estimate it using respondents with data. However, the clustering effect should not be large in this case because missing respondents usually constitute a relatively small subsample.[3]

Of course, a reader can make any other assumption that might be more appropriate for a particular survey and that would lead to a calculation of the effective sample size. However, even strong assumptions are not always very useful. For instance, it is commonly assumed in many research papers (but not here) that the error is normally distributed. But that still does not allow us to obtain the variance of $\tilde{\epsilon}$ because weights interact with errors (it is not a simple random sample) and they are not constant from survey to survey, so that one would need more assumptions anyway to obtain a practical formula.

To summarise our discussion, we obtain the following final formula for the variance.

Proposition 3.3   *Under the three assumptions above, the variance of $\tilde{x}$ can be estimated as*

$$\mathrm{var}(\tilde{x}) = \frac{\mathrm{var}(x)}{n_e} + \frac{\alpha^2 \mathrm{var}(\epsilon)}{(n-m)_c}, \tag{3.33}$$

where n_e is the total effective sample size and $(n-m)_c$ is the calibrated sample size for missing respondents. The variance of x can be estimated by the usual formula

$$\mathrm{var}(x) = \frac{\sum_{i=1}^{m} w_i x_i^2 + \sum_{i=m+1}^{n} w_i f_i^2}{\sum_{i=1}^{n} w_i} - \left[\frac{\sum_{i=1}^{m} w_i x_i + \sum_{i=1}^{m} w_i f_i}{\sum_{i=1}^{n} w_i} \right]^2 \tag{3.34}$$

---

[3] For a subsample, the average cluster size b is not greater than the total average cluster size because each cluster will have fewer respondents. Thus, the clustering effect formula $1 + (b-1)\rho$ implies that the clustering effect should, in general, become smaller for a subsample.

*(alternatively, it can be estimated using only respondents with data) while the variance
of ε must be based on respondents with data:*

$$\text{var}(\epsilon) = \frac{\sum_{i=1}^{m} w_i \epsilon_i^2}{\sum_{i=1}^{m} w_i} - \left[\frac{\sum_{i=1}^{m} w_i \epsilon_i}{\sum_{i=1}^{m} w_i} \right]^2. \qquad (3.35)$$

It must be emphasised once again that in the formula used to calculate the effective sample size n_e (or design effect) the imputed values should be used for missing
respondents. In the cases where design effect calculations are not possible, the alternative is, as we know, to replace n_e by the calibrated sample size n_c which is much
easier to compute.

As we see, the final variance for the imputed estimate is actually greater than
the variance of $\bar{x}$, which is what one would expect. The increase will vanish when
$\alpha = 0.0$, that is when there are no missing respondents. On the other hand, if
$\alpha = 1.0$, *all* respondents in the sample are missing. But it is impossible, of course,
to impute data for the whole sample – and dangerous to impute a substantial
proportion.

It is also worthwhile to give a separate formula for proportion estimates.

Corollary 3.1   *Let $\tilde{p}$ be the proportion estimate with imputed values (i.e. it is simply
$\tilde{x}$ where x and f are binary variables). Denote by R the proportion of 'correct
prediction', i.e. the proportion of respondents with data for which imputed values f_i
coincide with actual values x_i, as described on page 134. Then the variance of $\tilde{p}$ can
be estimated by the formula*

$$\text{var}(\tilde{p}) = \frac{\tilde{p}(1 - \tilde{p})}{n_e} + \frac{\alpha^2}{(n - m)_c}(1 - R - \bar{\epsilon}^2), \qquad (3.36)$$

*where $\bar{\epsilon} = (\sum_{i=1}^{m} w_i \epsilon_i)/(\sum_{i=1}^{m} w_i)$ is the average imputation error among respon-
dents with data.*

R is calculated here as a measure of the power of the imputation method in use.
Notice that in this case $\epsilon_i = f_i - x_i$ can have only values -1, 0 and $+1$ due to the
fact that both x and f are binary variables. Therefore, $|\bar{\epsilon}|$ cannot be greater than
$1 - R$ because some values of -1 and 1 will be cancelled out when $\bar{\epsilon}$ is calculated.
If the summand $\bar{\epsilon}^2$ is too difficult to compute, it can as a last resort be ignored. If
we can assume that the error is symmetrically distributed, we can in fact legitimately
ignore this summand because then it should be very small. In the case when the
error is not symmetric, the trade-off would be that we get an upper-bound estimate
for the variance. The percentage of correct predictions is therefore a crucial piece
of information for computing the variance of proportion estimates. To compute this
percentage, some respondents with data should be excluded and their data should be
imputed and then compared with their original data. It may not be practicable to store
all 'simulated' data for all respondents and all variables. The solution is usually to
compute the percentage once, for each variable, during the imputation procedure and
then use it in variance calculations assuming that, for a given variable, it is the same
number for any subsample.

Remark 3.1   If the item non-response rate cannot be assumed to be constant, there is still an alternative way to compute the variance. We need to estimate the variance of $\alpha\tilde{\epsilon}$, where α is now a random variable. But we still assume that α is independent of $\bar{x}$ so that the covariance term in (3.31) (which is now $2\text{cov}(\bar{x}, \alpha\tilde{\epsilon})$) can still be regarded as zero. To compute the variance of $\alpha\tilde{\epsilon}$, we represent it as a ratio $\tilde{\epsilon}/(1/\alpha)$ and then apply the ratio formula (3.4):

$$\text{var}(\alpha\tilde{\epsilon}) = \alpha^2[\text{var}(\tilde{\epsilon}) + (\alpha\tilde{\epsilon})^2\text{var}(1/\alpha) - 2\alpha\tilde{\epsilon}\text{cov}(\tilde{\epsilon}, 1/\alpha)].$$

To get rid of the covariance, we further assume that the average error is independent of the non-response rate. Consequently,

$$\text{var}(\alpha\tilde{\epsilon}) = \alpha^2\text{var}(\tilde{\epsilon}) + \alpha^4\tilde{\epsilon}^2\text{var}(1/\alpha).$$

The average error among missing respondents $\tilde{\epsilon}$ should be approximated, of course, by the average error among respondents with data $\bar{\epsilon}$. Observe that the first summand is exactly the expression we have used before. Therefore, the only difference in variance calculations will be that we get an extra summand, namely,

$$\alpha^4\tilde{\epsilon}^2\text{var}(1/\alpha).$$

Clearly, the variance of $1/\alpha$ can be computed only if there are several measurements of α for the same survey conducted several times.

4 Significance testing

4.1 The purpose and philosophy of significance testing

Possibly no other subject within the broad area of statistics has given rise to so much misunderstanding as 'significance testing'. This may be in part because non-statistical meanings of the words tend to get in the way, but also because statisticians have not been able to reach a consensus on how significance tests should be used or interpreted. Since significance tests were developed, effectively in the first half of the twentieth century, there has been a lively debate over the philosophy of significance tests and what they mean. Statisticians working within a variety of other disciplines have differed in their views. The controversies have sometimes been almost theological in their approaches and in their semantic subtlety, and occasionally in their acrimoniousness (see Morrison and Henkel [43]).

Not much has changed in this respect in the last fifty years. What has changed is that significance testing has become more accessible to the general researcher. No longer is a good grounding in statistics necessary to perform a 'significance test': anyone with access to one of the more popular statistical software packages can carry out a significance test procedure at the click of a mouse, without having to know anything about it at all. But this is a danger. Researchers may not now need to be taught the mechanics of the calculation in the same way or in the same detail. But this does not absolve us from the responsibility of knowing, and passing on to others, the thinking that underlies them. Without the appropriate knowledge one may be able to carry out the procedure. But carrying out the procedure is not the same as performing a test, and the researcher may need to provide something more than what the data set contains as input and to exercise an informed judgement in interpreting the output.

We use the broad term 'significance test' to designate the process of classifying a result or estimate by the probability of its having occurred by chance. The term may not be entirely accurate and it may not fit comfortably with all uses to which the related techniques are put, but it is the accepted term. The term itself may be in part a reason for the confusion in many minds. 'Significance' suggests meaningfulness; a 'significant' result must be given credence and attention, and should perhaps be acted upon. A 'test' can suggest something to be passed or failed. There are situations in which such interpretations of the term are wholly appropriate. In our present context of sample surveys very often they are not, and therein lies perhaps the root of much of the confusion.

4.1.1   Why test for significance?

Agriculture and process control

In the early days of 'significance testing' much of the work was done in experimental agriculture and industrial process control. In the agricultural field, a researcher might want to know whether a new seed variety, a new method of sowing or a new fertiliser produces a different yield, either better or worse than what it was being compared with. A carefully balanced unbiased experiment would be set up that gives both the new treatment and the existing 'control' an equal chance. As seeds and soils vary, the experiment would be repeated (replicated) many times with small plots randomly allocated between new treatment and control. The experiment would be evaluated with the amount of variation occurring *within* the new-treatment and control groups being taken into account in assessing the overall performance. The researchers need to know how probable it is that any difference in the overall or average performance between the two would have been due to chance, given the scale of the experiment. The test may determine whether a new treatment is persevered with or set aside.

In industrial control a production line machine filling bottles of sauce may be set to put slightly more than the declared weight of sauce in each bottle. The manufacturer knows that there will inevitably be some variation in the amount going into the bottles and does not want customers (or Weights and Measures inspectors) complaining that they have been given short weight. Equally he does not want to give away more excess sauce than is necessary. The amount of bottle-to-bottle variation in weight filled has been determined by experiment. The machine is adjusted so that it will fill the bottles such that no more than a predetermined (very small) proportion of them is likely to be below the accepted minimum. But the process must be monitored to ensure that it performs consistently. Both the average fill weight and the variation in fill weight should remain constant over time. Deviation from this is detected by means of samples of filled bottles. Results from the examination of samples are used to determine whether the machine is performing within accepted limits or whether it should be stopped and recalibrated.

There are many more fields in which the existence of a genuine 'effect' has to be detected within a background of random fluctuations. An estimate of the magnitude of an effect is made in the knowledge that repeating the experiment would almost certainly not give exactly the same result. An experiment that gives us an estimate of the effect should also give us, or allow us to infer, an indication of the likely range of chance variation around that estimate. This applies to sample surveys just as much as it does to experimental agriculture.

This is the kind of information that significance testing procedures are designed to provide. A significance test does not make (or even imply) a decision: it provides, in a probabilistic form, a piece of information that contributes to a decision.

All statistics can do is to provide an estimate with a 'margin of error' relative to our sample estimate. The margin of error is not absolute: it is expressed in terms of probability, as in 'an estimated 32% with 95% probability that results would fall within a range of $\pm 2\%$'. It is up to the researcher to determine the implications of the figure of 32%. It is also up to the researcher to determine the implications of a figure of 30% or 34%, or any other value.

In a survey we may be presented with an estimate and we need to determine whether its value is worthy of further attention. In popular but unscientific parlance, is it 'significant'? To answer this question we need to set it in context, knowing not only how it was obtained but something of what it is to be compared against. Crucially, what we need to know is the margin of error for each of these. Our typical unit of measurement for 'margins of error' is the *standard error*. The standard error of an estimate is in fact the standard deviation of repeated estimates, that is, the dispersion around the 'true' value of a series of observations made independently in the same way. It is calculated from the variance of the variable itself and the effective sample size, covered in the previous chapter.

The Central Limit Theorem

The foundation stone of much of statistical theory, the Central Limit Theorem, tells us that (for practical purposes) the means of samples follow a normal distribution, so that about two-thirds of them will lie within one standard deviation of the mean of all samples, and about 95% will lie within two standard deviations of it. For an unbiased estimate, the mean of sample means is the population mean. We can therefore say that the 95% confidence interval for an estimate is about two standard errors either side of it. (This does not hold exactly for very small samples or proportions very near zero or one, but is for most purposes a reasonable working rule.)

The comparison we make for this estimate may be one of several kinds. We may compare the estimate with:

- a known value for the population (i.e. a value not subject to sampling error) including, for instance, the basic demographic information routinely collected in most surveys for analysis purposes;
- a hypothesised value or some 'critical' value necessary to the interpretation of the test;
- an estimate from another source that is also subject to sampling error; or
- one or more other estimates from the same sample also subject to its own sampling error.

Comparison with a fixed value

In the first case, where we are starting from a fixed value, we need to consider how samples drawn from a population with this value would vary. For this we need to know the distribution of this value. If this is a proportion there is no problem. If it is a mean we need to know how the variable itself is distributed. In the absence of other reliable information we may have to take the variance within the sample as our best estimate of the variance in the population. What we are seeking to find is whether the sample-based estimate is within the reasonable range of expectation; to be more precise, what is the probability that the estimate from one such sample would differ from the population value by as much as or more than what is observed?

In the second case we are starting from the sample estimate and working back to an inference about the population. If this is the value we observe from our one sample, how probable is it that the 'true' value is at least as different from the observed value as the 'critical' value is?

Comparison with other estimates

The third case requires us to take into account the fact that both estimates have their own margin of error and that we need to use the variance of each estimate to calculate the variance and thus the standard error of the *difference* between the estimates. If we had large numbers of pairs of estimates, how would the differences vary?

The fourth case is similar, but requires us to take into account that the two estimates may be in part or in whole derived from the same individuals within the sample and that their contributions to the two estimates may be correlated.

The result of all these calculations is a probability estimate. It gives us an idea of how likely the difference we are considering is to have arisen by chance, as a result of the natural variation in samples. But there is a temptation to translate this from a probability figure to a crude black-and-white condition. A difference is adjudged to be either 'significant' or 'non-significant'. The danger is that this may lead us to an automatic identification of 'significance' with 'importance'. There may be a tendency to disregard anything that is 'not significant' and to attach an excessive importance to anything that is.

Tests and decisions

This association of significance tests with decision making would have been appropriate in the case of experimental agriculture and industrial process control. If a sufficiently improbable result is encountered, a certain action is to be taken. The reduction of the process of evaluation to a simple rule is designed to ensure consistency of treatment or that the procedures can be controlled by non-statisticians. In tightly defined and controlled situations, where a decision is *required* on each occasion, some form of criterion or action standard has to be set and adhered to. Human judgement should not be allowed to interfere. In survey research this is not often the case. True, we may need to make a decision on the strength of survey results but it is rare in practice for the decision to hinge on a single number exclusively. Usually, an individual estimate contributes to the building up of a broader structure of knowledge. Our decision is then taken based on the sum of the evidence before us. Certain estimates may weigh more heavily in our judgement than others but that is part of the judgement process.

An over-rigid interpretation of significance testing is something to avoid. It is not enough to know whether the result of a test is that a value is determined to be inside or outside whatever confidence interval criterion we have in mind. If we have decided, for instance, that we require '$P < 0.05$' to be satisfied, what are we to do with a result of '$P = 0.06$'? To divide results uncritically into those which are above a fixed significance criterion and therefore to be accepted as real and those which are below and can be ignored is to fail to understand the purpose and nature of significance testing. Significance tests are an aid to the researcher's judgement, not a substitute for it.

We have already seen that the design effect estimate in any case is subject to a margin of error. There are other elements in the calculation too that are not exact. The sample variance is only an estimate of the population variance (and has its own standard error). The P-value is therefore itself only an estimate and subject to error. Although it never seems to be done, it would perhaps be more appropriate to be less categorical and to express it as such and to write, for example, '$P = 0.05 \pm 0.02$'.

The magic '95%'

How confident do we have to be that a difference is 'real' before we can accept it? What probability of being wrong are we prepared to tolerate? The figure of 95% (or 5%) is perhaps the most frequently encountered. We may wish to say 'there is a better than 95% chance' that a result will not differ from some reference value by more than a stated amount, or that there is 'less than 0.05 probability' that an observed difference could have arisen by chance. But use of this figure of 95% is simply a convention which through frequent use seems to have acquired a certain authoritative status. It is not a figure which has to be used automatically and indiscriminately in all cases. It seems to have arisen with R. A. Fisher and his agricultural experiments. The conjunction of nice round numbers (one chance in twenty, plus-or-minus two standard errors) resulted in a number that he felt comfortable with for his particular decision making purposes. There is no reason why this figure should be automatically applied in each and every context.

So how great do the odds have to be against a difference arising by chance before we accept it as 'real'? Is a one in ten chance adequate, or does it have to be one in a thousand? There is no firm rule which can be applied here. If a decision has to be made it comes down to balancing the *risk* of taking a wrong decision against the *consequences* of that decision. This is a matter for judgement and, above all, knowledge of the situation on which the research is intended to shed light.

Legal systems that derive from English law require the jury in a criminal trial to be satisfied 'beyond reasonable doubt' of the guilt of the accused before returning a verdict of 'guilty'. The law, wisely, does not specify what 'reasonable doubt' is, but it is generally held that juries require more certainty of guilt for offences with more severe penalties. The probability of error is weighed against the consequences of that error. On a more mundane level we may decide to go ahead with an excursion if we are satisfied that there is no more than a 25% chance of rain, but be unwilling to build a house where there is a 0.1% chance of flooding in any year.

Hypothesis testing

Another reason for the over-rigid association of significance tests with decision making is the use of hypotheses. A hypothesis is a proposition which is to be tested for its conformity with the evidence, and either rejected because it is incompatible or accepted (at least for the time being) because it is compatible with the evidence. The logician and philosopher will say that it is not possible to prove a hypothesis. All that can be said of a hypothesis (as of a theory) is that it is compatible with, and is supported by, the known evidence. As Einstein put it: 'No amount of experimentation can prove me right; a single experiment can prove me wrong.'

Because of this, the statistician resorts to the subterfuge of trying to support one hypothesis by setting up and knocking down the contrary hypothesis. To demonstrate that we should accept one hypothesis we argue that it is impossible, or at least unreasonable, to accept the opposite. To accept that a difference is real we set up a dummy hypothesis (called the 'null hypothesis'), often that there is no difference, and then demonstrate that this null hypothesis is not tenable. The strict logical division of the outcomes into acceptance or rejection forces on the test the character of a decision, which in many cases is unwarranted.

Significance tests simply report the probability that a difference between a result and some reference value may have occurred by chance. They do not say anything about how big the real difference is. The estimate we have is our best estimate but it is of course subject to error. The 'true' value may be bigger or smaller than what we have observed, and the difference between our observation and the 'expected' or reference value may also be bigger or smaller. Let us illustrate the implications of this with an example. Suppose that we want to know whether a majority of a population has a particular attribute. We have a true unbiased simple random sample of 400, and we find that 54% of the sample have that attribute. We want to know whether this represents a genuine change from some well established (e.g. census based) estimate of 50%. If we assume that 50% is the 'true' population value, a simple calculation gives us a standard error for this estimate of 2.5% so that 54% falls at the upper bound of the 90% confidence interval of $\pm 4\%$. There is therefore only a 5% chance that the estimate of 54% (or greater) could be observed under this assumption. Hence, we can 'safely' reject the assumption and be reasonably confident that there has been a real increase. However, calculations of confidence intervals for 54% show that there is also a 16% chance that the real change is in the range from zero to $+2\%$, such that we might say that it is no great cause for concern. On the other hand there is also a 20% chance that the real value is now 56% or more and the implied increase of 6% might be of great consequence. It is far more enlightening to have an estimate, with an indication of the range of possible variation ('difference $+4\% \pm 4\%$'), than a black-and-white statement 'significant at the 95% confidence level'. This allows us to consider how we would view a result if it were at various points within the likely range.

Significance tests do not tell us anything about the absolute strength of the relationship. The fact that one relationship may be assessed as 'significant with $P < 0.001$' and a second 'with $P < 0.05$' does not make the first result more important: it simply means that we can be that much more confident that such a relationship does in fact exist. The confidence interval around the estimate is largely a function of sample size. The bigger the sample, the more precise the estimate, and for any given difference the greater our confidence in its reality. This should be a further warning against an over-rigid interpretation of significance tests: exactly the same difference reported in two separate surveys could be regarded as 'significant' in the larger one and as 'not significant' in the smaller.

Nor does a significance test tell us how important a result is. Statistical significance is not the same as practical significance. If we find that a result is statistically significant, does it add to our knowledge, or allow us to draw conclusions which will lead to the formulation of a course of action? If we accept that this difference genuinely exists within the whole population, does it matter? Can we do anything with it, or about it? Is it 'actionable'? The difference between *statistical* significance, which can be evaluated according to a set of rules and procedures, and *practical* significance, which is totally dependent on circumstances, is fundamental. The practical significance of a result is a matter for interpretation, judgement and knowledge of the context but this is what the survey is really about. In particular, the question of causality is outside the bounds of significance testing and is a matter for knowledge and common sense. Researchers should always have in mind the principle that results should be examined first for their practical significance, and only then for their statistical significance.

Where significance testing has to be done it is better to treat the result as a way of estimating the likely range of uncertainty around a result, or the probability of a possible explanation being correct where possible. It should be regarded as a decision indicator only where necessary.

It is all too easy to concentrate on the results of tests at the expense of what should be the real priority, the estimation of the magnitude of effects. It is so comforting to think that, once the threshold for significance has been established and the necessary calculations have been done, the result of the test will not require further interpretation. The result will either meet the criterion or it will not. We shall be spared having to think about it!

4.1.2   Significantly different from . . . what?

A further problem, potentially a more serious one, is the question of what a survey estimate should be compared with. Often when we wish to apply a significance test we are testing a difference between two (or more) values. The 'null hypothesis' approach is often taken to mean that we can test the observed result against the hypothesis that both (or all) groups could be expected to be equal and that any differences which are seen, and which are greater than could reasonably be explained by sampling fluctuation, are worthy of note. But very often such a null hypothesis is unreasonable. Two examples will illustrate this.

- If we have a large and well conducted survey of the general population which finds that men are on average 60 mm taller than women, should we test this difference against a null hypothesis that they should be the same height on average? Common sense says not. If, in a survey of employees of a company, we find that the average height of men is only 10 mm greater than that of women and that this difference is in itself 'not statistically significant', should we dismiss it as of no further interest? If we do we are missing the point, because common sense should tell us that there is something odd here. What is truly significant is the very *absence* of statistical significance. The problem has arisen because we were using only internal evidence, that is, evidence from within the survey data itself, whereas to conduct a proper test we should have brought in information from outside. We should have tested the observed difference for compatibility with an *expected* difference based on the 60 mm estimate for the general population. However, to do this we should have had to supply additional evidence and input this explicitly into the significance test.

Alternatively in a similar survey we might find that in the company as a whole the mean height difference was 60 mm, but when analysing one section of the company in isolation a difference of 10 mm was found, again not in itself a statistically significant difference, judging it against a null hypothesis of 'no difference'. However, this difference should obviously have been compared with the company-wide difference (or with the mean for all other employees). The additional evidence required, though drawn from within the same survey, was outside the scope of the initial analysis, and might not have been considered.

- If in a controlled agricultural experiment (and the sampling issues of experimental agriculture are not fundamentally different from those of surveys of the human population) we find that a new fertiliser produces a mean increased cabbage yield of 5% with a standard error of 2% we might call this a clear (i.e. very low risk) success: only about 1% of cases should yield a result worse than 'no change'. If, however, we also know that a typical farmer would need to grow 3% more cabbages just to cover the increased cost of the new fertiliser, then the calculation is radically changed. With a more realistic null hypothesis of '3% increase' there is now a very real risk (about 16% chance) that a farmer could be out of pocket by changing, and a high probability that the net benefit would be small.

These examples show the need to consider well the formulation of the hypothesis to be tested to ensure that it is relevant and appropriate. In particular they demonstrate the dangers of automated significance testing. Many tabulation systems offer the user the option of testing every number in a table for 'significance'. But normally this test is applied relative to a neutral null hypothesis (under which the subset of the sample being tested is either regarded in isolation or assumed to be typical of the sample as a whole). There is no opportunity to direct the system to take other internal information into account in formulating a more realistic null hypothesis. There is therefore a risk that if the test is done on the strictly limited information immediately available to the system, many such tests will be done against inappropriate hypotheses and will produce misleading results. Reliance on such tests as a means of screening data is potentially extremely dangerous. There is no such thing as a context-free significance test.

In 1996 the American Psychological Association commissioned a major inquiry into the use of null hypothesis significance testing in experimental psychology. It concluded that failure to understand the pitfalls of null hypothesis tests was widespread. There were claims that as many as 60% of research psychologists were using null hypothesis tests wrongly, most particularly in the formulation of inappropriate null hypotheses. Although resisting pressure for a total ban on the use of null hypothesis tests in the publication of experimental work in serious journals, it called for much greater awareness among researchers of the principles and problems involved.

All this is not to deny the validity or usefulness of significance testing. Our purpose is to sound a warning to users that there is more to significance testing than selection of the appropriate test and its correct implementation. The formulation of the correct hypothesis is a topic often neglected in the literature and in teaching courses, but one which is vital to the correct and effective use of significance testing.

4.1.3   Use (and abuse) of the null hypothesis

The results of a survey consist of many frequencies, means, percentages and other numbers. The ultimate objective is to draw conclusions about the population using these data. It must never be forgotten that all inferences and conclusions based on sample data are *subject to various sources of error*. Hence, instead of precise statements one can formulate hypotheses about population parameters and check whether the sample data support them or not.

It is an established practice to choose between two hypotheses, one of them being called the *null hypothesis* H_0 and the other the *alternative hypothesis* H_A. In many texts, the null hypothesis is described as 'no difference' or 'no effect'. This may be appropriate in many artificial and controlled experimental situations but, in the authors' opinion, automatic use of this restricted definition is potentially very misleading. For example, it may be well known from a previous large-scale study that there is a difference in the level of readership of a magazine between two age groups but the difference from the present survey appears to be larger than in the past. The hypothesis of 'no difference' is obviously not appropriate in this case and the correct null hypothesis should be that the difference is 'within our expectations from the past'.

In fact, the null hypothesis can have many formulations but the key difference between H_0 and H_A is that H_A is the original *hypothesis of practical interest* (the one we are really trying to examine) and H_0 is simply the *opposite hypothesis*. It is the null hypothesis which is actually tested and the data are intended to provide evidence about H_0.

Notice that, whatever hypotheses we formulate, there are in formal terms always only *two* possibilities – either H_0 is true (and H_A is false) or H_0 is false (and H_A is true), and we are attempting to assign probabilities to these two outcomes. In some texts, it is possible to find a formulation of H_0 and H_A where there is a third possibility – for instance, H_0 is 'there is no difference' while H_A is 'the difference is positive', leaving the possibility that the difference is negative. In our opinion, this kind of formulation is not just unhelpful but simply wrong and the correct formulation of H_A in this case should be 'the difference is positive or negative'.

From a practical point of view, the testing procedure is quite simple: take the sample data, calculate certain numbers using a specified formula and find the significance level in a table. To understand the calculations, it is useful to know the main ingredients of a significance test from a conceptual point of view. We begin by stating the procedure in formal mathematical terms.

- Identify the hypotheses H_0 and H_A. Define the population parameter of interest and identify the ranges of parameter values corresponding to H_0 and to H_A. Among the possible values under H_0, identify the limit value, that is, the 'closest' to the range under H_A.
- Take a test variable (called a *statistic*), its distribution being in a certain known family of distributions under H_0 (each such distribution is called a *null distribution*) and in a different family under H_A. Among null distributions, take only the 'limit' distribution, the distribution corresponding to the limit value of the parameter.
- Using the sample data, compute the value of the 'limit' statistic.
- Specify values of the statistic which are 'extreme' under H_0, that is, values which would suggest that H_A better explains the data. If the 'extreme' values form one 'tail' (they are either all above or all below the observed value) H_A is called *one-tailed*, and if they form two 'tails' (some being above and some below the observed value) H_A is called *two-tailed*.
- Find the probability of 'extreme' values of the statistic beginning from the computed value. This probability is called the *P-value* (or *significance level*).

The following example reproduces this process step by step. A survey carried out among 200 cricketers (assume a simple random sample for convenience) finds that 25% of them bat left-handed. The most reliable estimate of the incidence of left-handedness in the population is 12%. Even given the relatively small size of the sample, can we still conclude that cricketers are more likely than the population in general to have this characteristic, or could such a difference reasonably be expected to occur by chance in a sample of this size?

- The null hypothesis (H_0). The 'population parameter of interest' is the proportion of the population (of cricketers) that is left handed. The null hypothesis could be framed in two ways. Either the incidence of left-handedness among cricketers really is 12%, or it is not greater than 12%. As our sample proportion is greater than our general-population estimate it makes sense to choose the second of these. The corresponding alternative hypothesis H_A is that incidence is greater than 12%. Whichever way the null hypothesis is expressed, the relevant limit value is 12%.
- The test statistic. Our test statistic here is a proportion (the incidence of left-handedness in the sample). Across many samples of size n drawn from a population where the incidence is 12% we would expect this proportion $\hat{p}$ to be approximately normally distributed with a mean of 0.12 and a standard deviation of $\sqrt{p(1-p)/n}$ or 0.023. As we are dealing with a proportion we can use a standard deviation based on the population proportion. We do not need to assume that the population variance is the same as the sample variance. In this case they are clearly different. We are arguing from a 'known' population value to determine whether the observed value lies within the range of reasonable expectation based on the population value.
- The limit statistic. The value of the limit statistic in this case is 0.12 (12%).
- Extreme values. The values we would consider extreme under H_0 are all greater than the limit statistic, so we can use a one-tailed test. We decide that we require a high level of confidence in our verdict and therefore determine that extreme values

are those that we would expect to occur by chance with a probability of less than 0.01 (less than once per 100 trials).

- Probability of extreme values. In fact the observed value (25%) lies some 5.6 standard deviations above the limit value. This is well beyond the range of values we have provided in Table H1 in Appendix H ($P < 0.0001$). Clearly the probability of such a result arising by chance is very small indeed. We can reject the null hypothesis with confidence and conclude that cricketers are considerably more likely than the population at large to be left handed.

An alternative way of approaching this is to choose a suitable P-value and then determine the value of the test statistic above which we should reject the null hypothesis. Table H1 in Appendix H shows that to achieve $P < 0.01$ we need a result that is 2.33 standard deviations above the limit statistic. Taking the limit statistic (0.12) and its standard deviation (0.023), the critical value for this is therefore $0.12 + 2.33 \times 0.023$ or 0.174. That is, if the limit value of the null hypothesis (12%) is the true incidence for cricketers we would expect a result of 17.4% or more to occur in only 1% of all trials.

If the estimate were not from a simple random sample and had a design effect of 1.5, then we should make allowance for this in calculating the standard deviation of the limit value, multiplying it by the square root of this number. This would have given a standard deviation of 0.028 and the critical value would be $0.12 + 2.33 \times 0.028$ or 0.186 (which does not materially affect our conclusion).

A large P-value should not be interpreted as 'H_0 is true' (lack of evidence against H_0 could be, for instance, because the sample size is too small). If a decision has to be made on the basis of test results, it is a subjective matter, depending on the risks and consequences of making a wrong decision, to decide which P-values are in favour of H_A and which in favour of H_0. But it is worth remembering that such a decision is always subject to error.

A common mistake is to interpret a P-value as the 'probability of the null hypothesis being true'. In fact, there is no practical sense in the latter 'probability' since the null hypothesis is true or not true independently of what we think of it. The right interpretation of, say, $P = 5\%$ is that if we do the same sampling a hundred times and compute a hundred values of the test statistic then only about five of them should be in the same 'extreme' tail as our original value.

It is perhaps appropriate at this point to look at the terms in which statistical significance is expressed. Strictly speaking, we are considering the probability of an observed difference of some sort being due to chance. For a result that is 'significant' we might say that there is less than 5% or 1% probability that the observed difference is a chance variation which might be seen in a different sample. In academic and scientific circles it is standard practice in the publication of results to express this by annotating the results with '$P < 0.05$' or '$P < 0.01$', at least when communicating to other academics and scientists. A low P-value, usually expressed as a proportion, is the standard form of expression for scientists and specialist statisticians. It represents the estimate of the probability of making a correct choice by accepting the null hypothesis.

However, there is also a convention of expressing the result in terms of the complement of this figure, and as a percentage. A result may be described as 'significant at the 95% confidence level'. This presumably arises from familiarity with the concept of 95% confidence limits for estimates. Although this form of expression may be deprecated by some it can be argued that it is a legitimate mode of expression. Certainly it is so well entrenched that there is little point in objecting to it or in expecting to convert all its users to the perceived orthodoxy. As the figures involved are normally close to zero or to 100% there is rarely any possibility of confusion.

What may be objected to with greater justification is the slipshod extension of this in pronouncements such as: 'This result is 95% significant' or 'We can be 95% confident that . . .' Such statements should be avoided if only because they raise the suspicion that the speaker does not adequately understand the process and reasoning by which the conclusion was reached. But in all cases the main requirement is to ensure that the language used conveys unambiguously to the intended audience the intended meaning, and is compatible with the test and its results.

At this point it is appropriate to mention in passing some terms that will be encountered from time to time in discussion of the possibility of inferential error in the interpretation of significance tests. The unhelpfully named 'type I error' and 'type II error' are the mistakes of rejecting the null hypothesis when it is true and of accepting it when it is false, respectively. They are also (equally unhelpfully) sometimes called α and β errors and the probabilities of making them are called the α-risk and the β-risk.

With a sufficiently large sample, almost any difference will be significant. The reason for this is simple: if we compare, for example, proportions from two population groups, it is very unlikely that the 'true' population proportions for these groups are exactly the same. Therefore, there will be a difference (however small) between the proportions in the population and hence this difference will be detected with a large enough sample size. It again shows how inappropriate the 'no difference' null hypothesis is – with a large enough sample it should be rejected in practically all situations. What is obviously much more important from a practical point of view is the *magnitude* of the difference, and whether the difference is 'within our expectations' or not.

The result of a test should not make us feel obliged in all cases to decide whether we accept or reject either the null or the alternative hypothesis. We can also suspend or defer judgement and look for supporting evidence before reaching any conclusion. Improbable events occur from time to time, and differences that are not obviously 'statistically significant' may yet be very important if they are real. Other evidence within the same data set may bolster or weaken our confidence in the reality of the apparent effect.

4.2   Principles of significance testing

Formulation of an appropriate null hypothesis and the selection of the right test can sometimes be difficult. We would recommend several guiding principles which could be useful when choosing a test. We shall illustrate these principles with a specific example. Assume that we have information from 2000 respondents from a population of registered voters in the Australian State of Victoria (1000 males and 1000 females) and that 400 males and 450 females vote for the Australian Labor party (ALP). We also know that the overall Australian percentage among male voters is 46% and among female voters 41%.

- Always formulate the null hypothesis *first*, then select a test. Clearly, any particular choice of H_0 depends on the purpose of the data analysis. It is essential to *identify the right expectations* in each case. Clearly, we could test whether there is a difference between the proportions of men and women voting ALP in Victoria. However, it is a relatively 'poor' hypothesis and it would be much more useful to test whether the difference between proportions is what we expect. We could assume that Victorian men and women would behave the same way as Australians in general, so that the expected frequencies would be 460 and 410 respectively. Hence, the test should compare observed frequencies (400, 450) and expected frequencies (460, 410). This example shows that automatic testing of the hypothesis 'no difference', without expectations, is not a good idea. The most we can learn without using expected values is that 'there is a difference'. We cannot tell from the test alone whether that difference is contributing to our knowledge.

  Above all, the null hypothesis must be realistic and defensible. If it is set up to be knocked down, then there is no value in formulating a null hypothesis that was not tenable in the first place.
- Choice of a test is also affected by the sampling procedure even after formulation of the null hypothesis. For instance, in the previous example there could be three different ways of sampling leading to different tests (H_0 is that the observed and expected frequencies are the same).
  1. The 2000 respondents are from one sample and the marginal frequencies for the population (the balance between the sexes and between ALP voters and others in the population) are not known. Then there are four observed frequencies (400, 600, 450, 550) and four expected ones (460, 540, 410, 590) and so the chi-square test with three degrees of freedom is appropriate.
  2. There are two independent samples of 1000 males and 1000 females. Hence, in both samples we have observed and expected frequencies, so that H_0 becomes 'the difference between proportions is what we expect' and the Z-test can be used.
  3. We may have a sample of 850 ALP voters from Victoria with 400 males and 450 females. In this case, two expected frequencies can be computed using the percentage of males and females among ALP voters in the whole of Australia. Then the chi-square test with one degree of freedom is the best one.
  All three tests will give essentially the same conclusion.
- The choice of test as illustrated in the example above may also be determined or conditioned by the internal comparison most relevant to the viewpoint from which the researcher approaches the question.

One-tailed
and
two-tailed
tests

- It is not always easy to choose between a 'one-tailed' or 'two-tailed' version of H_A. This refers to whether one or both 'tails' of the probability distribution have to be regarded as possible values. In general, if something can be said about the *direction* of a difference in a hypothesis (for instance that 'the true value is not more than 5% *greater* than the estimate, but we are not concerned if it is less') then a one-tailed test is appropriate. We are concerned with the probability that a result as far or further *in the observed direction* could happen by chance, under our null hypothesis. A one-tailed test only has to consider one end of the distribution and is therefore more sensitive and will show a lower P-value.

  A 'point' null hypothesis, whether or not it is based on a known population value, is almost invariably 'wrong' in the sense that it is most unlikely to be exactly the same as the true population value. But we are not seeking to determine whether the null hypothesis is true, only whether or not it is compatible with the result we have. We are in effect saying, 'If this hypothesis is correct, then in only $x\%$ of trials would we expect to see a number outside the range $y \pm z$.' In some cases there may be no 'true' value for the population, or the value is unknown and unknowable. We may be speculating about the way it would behave if it were subject to some event to which a sample has been exposed. If, for instance, two alternative formulations of a product are tested to see which is preferred by consumers, it may be appropriate to begin with the expectation that the two are equally likely to be preferred and that 'zero difference' is the only rational null hypothesis. Similarly, when monitoring changes over time in attitudes or opinions through a series of samples it may be valid to assume a null hypothesis of 'no change' and to be prepared to consider a difference in either direction.

4.2.1 Significance testing with non-simple-random samples

The preceding chapters have covered a number of variations from simple random sampling and the effects these can have on the variance, and thus the precision, of estimates derived from samples. The overall effect of these is summed up in the term 'design effect'. Just as it is incorporated into the assessment of confidence limits, so also the design effect must be built into, or at least taken account of in, the testing of statistical significance.

Where the probability of selection of respondents is unknown and no formal calculation of design effects for individual estimates is possible, for instance with quota samples, it is strictly speaking not possible to conduct a significance test. The reality, however, is that such samples are widely used and that at least some indication of statistical significance is often required for the interpretation of results. In practice a design effect of 2.0 is often used as a rough rule of thumb for quota samples. It cannot be justified mathematically, and it should not be assumed to be the same for all kinds of quota samples. Quotas which are more tightly set, with smaller individual quota cells, so that more potential respondents are 'out of quota', should probably have a higher design effect than those which have looser quotas. Similarly, sampling in circumstances which are more difficult to reproduce should carry a higher design effect. The use of such an estimated or assumed design effect can be justified only on the grounds that, if a significance test has to be done, it is better at least to recognise that the design effect is liable to be appreciably greater than 1.0 than to shut our eyes to the problem and just stick to the standard textbook formulae for simple random samples.

Even for probability samples and where the necessary information and facilities exist to calculate design effects, it may not always be practicable to perform the detailed calculations required without delaying the whole process of data analysis and interpretation. The ability to provide a reasonable, realistic and simple approximation may be very valuable at the stage of screening the results of a survey. Researchers who have learned and not forgotten the apparently dying art of mental arithmetic may find it useful to be able to make mental allowance for the design effect while scanning the results.

It must not be forgotten that the appropriate value of the design effect is only one of a number of factors which must be considered in assessing the practical significance of any individual result. The possible biasing effects of non-sampling errors, the level of confidence required in individual cases, the formulation of the correct hypothesis to apply to any difference – all these may, individually and collectively, be far more important than variations in estimates of the design effect.

It is often possible to use the design effect or its square root as an additional element in the conventional simple random sample formulae. This is generally true when proportions or percentages are used in the calculation. But for some tests (or for some formulae) the frequencies themselves are generally required and the calculation becomes more complex. The chi-square test of goodness of fit is a case in point.

4.2.2   Significance tests with weighted data

In practice, if the weighting is used simply to correct minor imbalances in the sample, the effect is likely to be small and may often be ignored for practical purposes without great loss. However, when a wide range of weights has to be applied within the sample great care must be exercised in significance testing, particularly when this is automated.

The weighting effect is often a large component of the design effect. The presence of weighting is itself an indication that the sample cannot be treated as a simple random one. This applies whether the weighting is used only to counter designed-in imbalances such as differential selection probabilities or also includes an element of non-response weighting.

If the data have been weighted (which is frequently the case), this should be taken into account where possible when significance tests are conducted. Some authorities recommend using unweighted data for significance testing but we disagree with this approach as being both normally unnecessary and open to serious error. The unweighted estimate of the difference to be tested may be different from the weighted estimate. Weighted and unweighted estimates should always be compared first if this is contemplated. Since the weighting was (presumably) introduced to improve accuracy, the weighted difference is preferred as the better estimate: indeed, if the sample has been heavily stratified and the strata have been differentially sampled, it may be the only realistic estimate.

The use of weighting to redress imbalances in the sample (other than stratification) will cause significance tests to be less sensitive than they appear to be. In general, the more variation in weights, or the greater the range of weights used within the sample, the greater will be the overstatement of the significance of the results by any test on weighted data unless the appropriate correction is applied. This can often be remedied by replacing the actual sample size by the effective sample size in calculations. But for some tests such as the chi-square test this replacement is not sufficient and a special modification is needed (discussed later) if weighting is used.

Problems with many popular statistical software packages were discussed in Chapter 3. Some packages do not make any allowance for the effect of weighting if weights are present, treating the weighted sample size as though it were the unweighted sample size. These will generally tend to be more conservative if the mean weight is less than 1.0, and will normally overstate the significance of results if the mean weight is greater than 1.0. Even if the mean weight is 1.0, if there is a wide range of weights within the sample, the significance will almost always be overstated. At least one analysis package even presents weighted results but performs the significance test on unweighted figures. This can result in apparently inconsistent or absurd output if the weighted results are very different from the unweighted results.

For only one of the tests described is there no known way of using weighted data. There are, however, other less frequently used tests for which weighting cannot be accommodated. So what should be done in such a situation? We offer two suggestions, if such tests are essential.

- Perform the tests on unweighted data after carefully comparing the weighted results (proportions, means, distributions) against comparable unweighted figures. Use common sense to gauge the effect of weighting on the results and envisage how the unweighted test results might apply within the weighted data.
- If the variance of the weights is not too great, re-scale the weights so that they sum to the effective sample size, or at least to the calibrated sample size. Then run the test using the sums of weights as though they were unweighted counts.

These suggestions have no basis in theory and should not be regarded as a definitive solution, but they are both an improvement on simply stripping the weights off and blindly performing the test without them. As you will have gathered by reading this far, significance tests are intended to be an *aid* to judgement and should be used (only) for what they can contribute to the evaluation process.

4.3 Choosing a test

Table 4.1 summarises how to find an appropriate test. The second column gives conditions which, in conjunction with the null hypothesis, define the test to be used.

Table 4.1. Choosing a test

Null hypothesis	Condition	Test
mean value is a specified number	(i) a large sample or (ii) a small sample from a normal population	test 4.4.1
proportion is a specified number	a large sample	test 4.4.2

difference between means is
    what we expect
	two independent samples:
	(i) two large samples or
	(ii) two small samples from
	    normal populations
		test 4.5.1

difference between proportions
    is what we expect
	two independent large
	    samples
		test 4.5.2

difference between correlated
    proportions is what we expect
	either two categories from
	    the same sample or two
	    overlapping samples
		test 4.5.3

no difference in ratings	two separate items or the
	    same item on two separate
	    occasions
		test 4.5.4

population proportions are what we expect	discrete population	test 4.6
two variables are independent		test 4.7.1

no difference in rating *or*
    there is a difference in rating
    in a particular direction
	two large independent
	    samples
		test 4.7.2

If a condition is not met, the test is not recommended. A sample is 'large' if it contains at least 50 respondents. (This does not mean that a sample of size 50 is to be considered adequate or appropriate for any purpose, simply that if the sample size is much below 50 it does not behave strictly in accordance with the formulae given for 'large' samples.) For any chosen test, the computational procedure is the same: take the desired hypotheses H_0 and H_A (among proposed versions), compute the value of the required statistic and use this value to determine the P-value from the indicated table in Appendix H.

The following notation will be common for all tests:

	population	sample
proportion	p	$\hat{p}$
mean	μ	$\bar{x}$
standard deviation of a variable of interest	σ	S

The testing formulae will also require the standard error of an estimate of μ or p; for simplicity, it will be denoted s.e. Recall that the standard error of an estimate is computed as the square root of the variance of this estimate (notice that it is *not* the same as the variance σ^2 of the variable of interest). Letters n and n_e will denote the sample size and the effective sample size, respectively. The null hypothesis mean and proportion values will be denoted by μ_0 and p_0, respectively. Where applicable, the 'expected' difference between two estimates will be denoted by e.

4.4 Testing particular values of a mean or proportion

4.4.1 Z-test and t-test for mean

The test checks whether the sampling mean $\bar{x}$ is consistent with an 'expected' number μ_0 which is specified in advance. The standard deviation S is assumed to be known. The standard error of $\bar{x}$ is then computed as

$$\text{s.e.} = \frac{S}{\sqrt{n_e}}.$$

If the population variance σ^2 is known (which is very seldom), a better formula for s.e. is $\sigma/\sqrt{n_e}$.

We also need the 'discrepancy' between the observed and expected means:

$$d = \bar{x} - \mu_0.$$

If the sample is large, the Z-test is used while the t-test is recommended for a small sample size if the population is (approximately) normal. t is calculated in the same way as Z but Table H3 is used instead of Table H1, with the number of 'degrees of freedom' $(n - 1)$ being taken into account. The test details are given in the following table:

null hypothesis	$\mu = \mu_0$	$\mu \leq \mu_0$	$\mu \geq \mu_0$
alternative hypothesis	$\mu \neq \mu_0$	$\mu > \mu_0$	$\mu < \mu_0$
	(two-tailed)	(one-tailed)	(one-tailed)
statistic to compute	$Z = \lvert d \rvert/\text{s.e.}$	$Z = d/\text{s.e.}$	$Z = -d/\text{s.e.}$
table to find P-value	large sample: Table H1		
	small sample, normal population: Table H3 with		
	$n - 1$ degrees of freedom		

Notice that if the sample is small and the population distribution is far from normal, the test is not applicable. The reason is that the distribution of $\bar{x}$ in this case cannot be assumed to be normal (and this assumption is the basis of the test). When the sample is large, the distribution of $\bar{x}$ is approximately normal by the Central Limit Theorem. On the other hand, when the population is normal, the distribution of $\bar{x}$ is also normal by the standard properties of normal distributions. When both conditions have failed, there is no reason why $\bar{x}$ should have a normal distribution which means that alternative methods must be sought. If it is possible to determine the shape of the distribution of $\bar{x}$, the statistic value can still be converted into a P-value using a different table. If, however, there is no way to identify the distribution of $\bar{x}$, the only recommendation is then to skip significance testing (and increase the sample size next time).

With this test, it may be sometimes better simply to report confidence limits.

Example 4.1   In a survey with a sample of adult men the mean height of respondents was found to be 1.80 m, with a standard deviation of 0.08 m. The population mean is known to be 1.77 m. The effective sample size is 120. Is the sample significantly taller than could reasonably be expected if it is drawn randomly from the population?

Sample mean $\bar{x} = 1.80$.
Expected mean $\mu_0 = 1.77$.
Difference $d = 0.03$.
Expected standard error s.e. $= S/\sqrt{n_e} = 0.08/\sqrt{120} = 0.0073$.
The statistic $Z = 0.03/0.0073 = 4.1$.

As the hypothesis contains an indication of direction, a one-tailed test is appropriate. The Z-value indicates a very high level of significance ($> 99\%$) and so it can be reasonably assumed that the sample was not drawn randomly from the overall population.

4.4.2   Z-test for proportion

As in the previous test, the intention is to determine how much the sampling proportion $\hat{p}$ differs from an 'expected' value p_0 specified in advance. For proportions, the population variance is computed as $p_0(1 - p_0)$ (assuming that the 'true' proportion is p_0) so that the standard error of $\hat{p}$ is

$$\text{s.e.} = \sqrt{\frac{p_0(1 - p_0)}{n_e}}.$$

The difference between the observed and expected values is again denoted by d:

$$d = \hat{p} - p_0.$$

The test is then very similar to the corresponding test for means:

null hypothesis	$p = p_0$	$p \leq p_0$	$p \geq p_0$
alternative hypothesis	$p \neq p_0$	$p > p_0$	$p < p_0$
	(two-tailed)	(one-tailed)	(one-tailed)
statistic to compute	$Z = |d|/\text{s.e.}$	$Z = d/\text{s.e.}$	$Z = -d/\text{s.e.}$
table to find P-value	large sample: Table H1		

Similarly, computation of confidence intervals can be an alternative to this test.

Example 4.2   In a survey with a sample of individuals (effective sample size 800) it was found that 35% claimed to own a dog. However, in one region (effective sample size 200) the proportion was 40%. Is this reasonable grounds for concluding that dog ownership is actually more widespread in that region?

> Sampling proportion $\hat{p} = 0.40$.
> Expected value $p_0 = 0.35$.
> Difference $d = 0.05$.
> Standard error of estimate $= \sqrt{0.35(1 - 0.35)/200} = 0.034$.
> $Z = 0.05/0.034 = 1.47$.

As the hypothesis contains an indication of direction, a one-tailed test is appropriate. The Z-value from Table H1 indicates a reasonable level of significance ($P = 0.072$) and so it can be assumed that the region concerned does indeed have a higher than average level of dog ownership. However, the 95% confidence limits of the estimate are $\pm 6.8\%$ so it would be imprudent to make any categorical statement about the size of the difference.

4.5   Testing the difference between means or proportions

In this section, sample estimates are indexed by 1 or 2 if there are two samples (e.g. n_1 and n_2 are the sizes of the first and second samples respectively).

4.5.1   Difference between two independent means

The test compares the difference between mean values $\bar{x}_1$ and $\bar{x}_2$ of two independent samples with an 'expected' difference e. The number e is not supplied by the test and should come from an 'outside' source of information. If there is no evidence about what could be expected, it may be reasonable to take $e = 0$ but the user should consider carefully whether the 'no difference' hypothesis is *really* what needs to be tested.

The sampling standard deviations S_1 and S_2 are assumed to be known. The standard error s.e. of the difference $\bar{x}_1 - \bar{x}_2$ is then estimated as

$$\text{s.e.} = \sqrt{\frac{S_1^2}{n_{1,e}} + \frac{S_2^2}{n_{2,e}}},$$

where $n_{1,e}$ and $n_{2,e}$ are the effective sample sizes in the first and second samples, respectively.

As with the test for single values, the Z-test is recommended for large samples.

If the null hypothesis is the 'no difference' one, it is reasonable sometimes to assume that the two populations have the same variance. In this case, it may be better to compute the standard deviation as the square root of the *pooled* variance estimate. However, in pooling the estimates they must not be weighted in proportion to their respective sums of weights. The weighting schemes, and the mean weights applied, may be arbitrarily different between two different samples, and even between two subsamples. The effective sample sizes $n_{1,e}$, $n_{2,e}$ of the two (sub)samples, should be used instead:

$$S = \sqrt{\frac{n_{1,e}S_1^2 + n_{2,e}S_2^2}{n_{1,e} + n_{2,e}}}.$$

Then the standard error s.e. can be computed as $S\sqrt{1/n_{1,e} + 1/n_{2,e}}$. But the pooled variance cannot be used if the expected difference e is non-zero.

Let

$$d = \bar{x}_1 - \bar{x}_2 - e$$

be the 'discrepancy' between the 'observed' and the 'expected' difference. Then the test is the following:

null hypothesis	$\mu_1 - \mu_2 = e$	$\mu_1 - \mu_2 \leq e$	$\mu_1 - \mu_2 \geq e$
alternative hypothesis	$\mu_1 - \mu_2 \neq e$	$\mu_1 - \mu_2 > e$	$\mu_1 - \mu_2 < e$
	(two-tailed)	(one-tailed)	(one-tailed)
statistic to compute	$Z = \lvert d\rvert/\text{s.e.}$	$Z = d/\text{s.e.}$	$Z = -d/\text{s.e.}$
table to find P-value	large sample: Table H1		
	small sample, normal population: Table H3 with		
	$n_1 + n_2 - 2$ degrees of freedom		

Example 4.3   Because of the result of the test in Example 4.1 a second sample was selected, supposedly in the same way, with a calibrated sample size of 150. This yielded a mean height of 1.785 m with a standard deviation of 0.05 m. Is it reasonable to conclude that these two estimates are compatible? What is the likelihood that the difference between the two means arose by chance?

The null hypothesis is that the population from which these samples were drawn is the same and that therefore there should be no difference between the means. The standard deviations of the two samples are markedly different so that we should not pool the variances in this case.

s.e.$_1$ = 0.0073 m (from Example 4.1).
s.e.$_2$ = $\sqrt{0.05/150}$ = 0.0041 m.
Difference d = 0.015 m.
Standard error of the difference s.e. = $\sqrt{0.08^2/120 + 0.05^2/150}$ = 0.0084 m.
$Z = d/\text{s.e.} = 1.79$.

As we have no prior expectation of the direction of any difference between the two samples a two-tailed test is appropriate. From Table H1, with $Z = 1.79$, $P = 0.073$, so the odds are about 13:1 against this happening by chance and we can be reasonably confident that some other influence is at work. Whether this level of confidence is *sufficient* is of course a matter for judgement in the individual circumstances.

4.5.2   Difference between two independent proportions

An initial word of warning is necessary. 'Independent proportions' refers to two estimates of the incidence of some attribute within two samples (or two subsets of one sample) which do not overlap. There is thus no possible correlation between the estimates. However, if we want to examine the proportions with two attributes within the *same* sample or subsample these are 'correlated attributes' even if no two sample members can possess both attributes. Correlated proportions are dealt with in section 4.5.3.

The test is very similar to the previous one, the number e being now the 'expected' difference between two proportions. The standard error of the difference $\hat{p}_1 - \hat{p}_2$ is given by the formula

$$\text{s.e.} = \sqrt{\frac{\hat{p}_1(1 - \hat{p}_1)}{n_{1,e}} + \frac{\hat{p}_2(1 - \hat{p}_2)}{n_{2,e}}}. \tag{4.1}$$

As with the difference between means, it is possible to use the pooled estimate when the null hypothesis is $p_1 = p_2$. The common proportion $\hat{p}$ is then estimated as the weighted average of $\hat{p}_1$ and $\hat{p}_2$ As in section 4.5.1, this weighted average must use the respective effective sample sizes, not the (arbitrary) sums of weights, of the (sub)samples within which $\hat{p}_1$ and $\hat{p}_2$ are calculated, so that

$$\hat{p} = \frac{n_{1,e}\hat{p}_1 + n_{2,e}\hat{p}_2}{n_{1,e} + n_{2,e}}.$$

The standard error will then be

$$\text{s.e.} = \sqrt{\hat{p}(1 - \hat{p})\left(\frac{1}{n_{1,e}} + \frac{1}{n_{2,e}}\right)}.$$

But remember that this is not applicable when the expected difference between proportions is non-zero.

Again, denote by d the difference between observed and expected figures:

$$d = \hat{p}_1 - \hat{p}_2 - e.$$

Then the test details are the following:

null hypothesis	$p_1 - p_2 = e$	$p_1 - p_2 \leq e$	$p_1 - p_2 \geq e$
alternative hypothesis	$p_1 - p_2 \neq e$	$p_1 - p_2 > e$	$p_1 - p_2 < e$
	(two-tailed)	(one-tailed)	(one-tailed)
statistic to compute	$Z = |d|/\text{s.e.}$	$Z = d/\text{s.e.}$	$Z = -d/\text{s.e.}$
table to find P-value	large sample: Table H1		

Example 4.4   In Example 4.2 we had one region where dog ownership was estimated at 40%. In an adjoining region the corresponding estimate was only 30%, though the sample size was smaller (effective sample size 100). Is this difference likely to have occurred by chance or can we reasonably conclude that there is a real difference between these two regions?

s.e.$_1$ (from Example 4.2) = 0.035 (3.5%).
s.e.$_2$ = $\sqrt{0.3(1 - 0.3)/100}$ = 0.046.
Difference $d = 0.1$.
Standard error of the difference s.e. = 0.057 (5.7%) from Example 4.1.
$Z = d/\text{s.e.} = 1.75$.

From Table H1, assuming a two-tailed test, we find that there is only an 8% probability of a difference of that magnitude or greater arising by chance.

4.5.3   Difference between correlated proportions

It is necessary sometimes to test the difference between two proportions which do not come from independent samples. For simplicity, assume that we deal with 'large' samples. The main difficulty in this case is the fact that the two proportion estimates $\hat{p}_1$ and $\hat{p}_2$ are not independent so that the standard error of their difference cannot be computed by formula (4.1) any more. The formula should now incorporate the *covariance* between $\hat{p}_1$ and $\hat{p}_2$:

$$\text{var}(\hat{p}_1 - \hat{p}_2) = \text{var}(\hat{p}_1) + \text{var}(\hat{p}_2) - 2\text{cov}(\hat{p}_1, \hat{p}_2).$$

In general, it is a very difficult problem to calculate the covariance especially if the sampling is not simple random – it is definitely not easier than to compute the variance.

The approach we take, although not strictly mathematical, is nevertheless practical, and it does give a good approximation in most cases. The covariance is first computed for simple random sampling and then, when sampling is not simple random, all estimates in the formula become weighted with the number of respondents being replaced by the effective sample size.

We consider only two very common situations where there is a relatively simple formula for the standard error.

Case 1: The two proportions are related to different categories of the same question and are derived from the same sample   If the question can have only a single response (e.g. sex: male or female) the proportions are clearly mutually exclusive – it is impossible for a respondent to be in more than one category and the categories are negatively correlated. If, however, we have a multiple response question ('Which of these illnesses have you suffered?'), it is possible to have respondents who answer 'yes' for *both* of any pair of categories, and the proportions may be positively correlated, negatively correlated or uncorrelated. The categories are uncorrelated only if being a member of one category is independent of membership of the other. If the proportion of sample members that is in both categories is equal to the product of the proportions that are in each, then the two are uncorrelated. But bear in mind that two attributes could be positively correlated in one part of a sample and negatively correlated in another but still appear to be uncorrelated in the overall sample.

To consider all possible situations, denote by $\hat{p}_{1,2}$ the 'overlapping' proportion, i.e. the proportion of respondents which are in both categories. Note that this may be zero in any case and *must* be zero in the case of a single-response question.

For a simple random sample, the covariance between $\hat{p}_1$ and $\hat{p}_2$ is given by (see Appendix F)

$$\text{cov}(\hat{p}_1, \hat{p}_2) = \frac{\hat{p}_{1,2} - \hat{p}_1 \hat{p}_2}{n}. \tag{4.2}$$

Hence, an estimate of the standard error s.e. of the difference $\hat{p}_1 - \hat{p}_2$ can now be obtained in the general case by using weighted estimates and incorporating the effective sample size:

$$\text{s.e.} = \sqrt{\frac{\hat{p}_1(1 - \hat{p}_1) + \hat{p}_2(1 - \hat{p}_2) - 2(\hat{p}_{1,2} - \hat{p}_1 \hat{p}_2)}{n_e}}.$$

Where the two proportions are mutually exclusive $p_{1,2}$ is zero so that the equation can be written:

$$\text{s.e.} = \sqrt{\frac{\hat{p}_1(1 - \hat{p}_1) + \hat{p}_2(1 - \hat{p}_2) + 2\hat{p}_1 \hat{p}_2}{n_e}}.$$

Case 2: The proportions measure the incidence of the same attribute but are derived from two partially overlapping (or disjoint) samples or groups of a sample   An obvious example of this case is, for instance, comparison of proportions from the same sample between two overlapping (or disjoint) demographic groups. This situation may also arise if a survey is conducted on a regular basis (say, monthly) and we are interested to test the difference between proportions from overlapping time intervals, say, one proportion (p_1) is from January–June and the other (p_2) is from April–September. n_1 and n_2 are the respective sample sizes.

To calculate the standard error of the difference $\hat{p}_1 - \hat{p}_2$, we need more notation for the 'overlapping' subsample: n_b ('b' stands for 'both') will be the number of respondents in this subsample and $\hat{p}_b$ will be its proportion. Then the covariance between $\hat{p}_1$ and $\hat{p}_2$ in the case of simple random sampling is computed by the formula

$$\text{cov}(\hat{p}_1, \hat{p}_2) = \frac{n_b \hat{p}_b(1 - \hat{p}_b)}{n_1 n_2} = \alpha \beta \frac{\hat{p}_b(1 - \hat{p}_b)}{n_b}, \tag{4.3}$$

where $\alpha = n_b/n_1$ and $\beta = n_b/n_2$ are the proportions of the first and second samples, respectively, which are also in the 'overlapping' subsample. Assuming now that all estimates (including α and β) are weighted, the general formula for the standard error is obtained:

$$\text{s.e.} = \sqrt{\frac{\hat{p}_1(1 - \hat{p}_1)}{n_{1,e}} + \frac{\hat{p}_2(1 - \hat{p}_2)}{n_{2,e}} - 2\alpha\beta\frac{\hat{p}_b(1 - \hat{p}_b)}{n_{b,e}}}.$$

In both cases, once there is an estimate for s.e., the test table is the same as for two independent proportions (similarly to the previous test, $d = \hat{p}_1 - \hat{p}_2 - e$ is the 'discrepancy' between the observed and the expected difference):

null hypothesis	$p_1 - p_2 = e$	$p_1 - p_2 \le e$	$p_1 - p_2 \ge e$
alternative hypothesis	$p_1 - p_2 \neq e$	$p_1 - p_2 > e$	$p_1 - p_2 < e$
	(two-tailed)	(one-tailed)	(one-tailed)
statistic to compute	$Z = |d|/\text{s.e.}$	$Z = d/\text{s.e.}$	$Z = (-d)/\text{s.e.}$
table to find P-value	Table H1		

Example 4.5   In Example 4.2 we had a case where 40% of the sample in one region (effective sample size 200) owned a dog. It was also found that 34% owned a cat. Can we be confident that in the population there are more dog-owners than cat-owners? To establish this we also need to know the proportion owning both, and in this case that is 20%.

Thus we have $p_1 = 0.4$, $p_2 = 0.34$ and $p_b = 0.2$. Substituting these in the immediately preceding equation gives a standard error of the difference of 0.041, or 4.1%. With a difference of 0.06 this yields a Z of 1.46 (0.06/0.041). If our null hypothesis is that we expect no difference between the two proportions and we thus use a two-tailed test the P-value (from Table H1) is about 0.036 and so we can be very confident that the difference is real. If our null hypothesis is that we expect more cat-owners than dog-owners, a one-tailed test gives an even lower P-value of 0.018.

4.5.4   Difference between repeated or multiple measurements from the same sample

It commonly occurs that the same people use a numerical measure either to rate two separate items or to rate the same item on two separate occasions and one wants to test the difference between the two ratings. The test described in section 4.5.1 is clearly not applicable because in this case there is in fact only one sample. The correct test is the following: for each respondent take the difference between the two ratings and then calculate the average sampling difference across all respondents. The test in section 4.4.1 for single values of mean is then appropriate, with the null hypothesis being either $\mu = 0$ or $\mu \le 0$ or $\mu \ge 0$. As with any rating scale the assumption is that the scale gradations can be regarded as linear and that the numerical values assigned can be taken at face value.

Example 4.6   A biscuit manufacturer is considering altering the recipe for a variety of biscuit by raising the sugar content. Two batches of biscuits ('A' and the slightly less sweet 'B') are prepared, differing only in sugar content. A sample of people (effective size 100) is asked to taste the two biscuits and to rate each on a series of semantic scales, each describing an attribute of the biscuits. The null hypothesis is that the extra sweetness of 'A' will be imperceptible. On the 'sweetness' scale, a five-point scale whose categories are given integer scores of 1 to 5, biscuit 'A' receives a mean score of 3.25 with a standard deviation of 0.7 and 'B' a mean of 3.1 with a standard deviation of 0.8.

To analyse the data the scales are converted into a single variable by subtracting each person's 'B' score from the corresponding 'A' score. This gives a nine-point scale, from -4 to $+4$, representing the amount by which the sample members rated A 'higher' or 'lower' than B. The mean was 0.15 (which is of course the same as the difference between the two original means) and the standard deviation is 0.75. The standard error of the mean is therefore $0.75/\sqrt{100}$ or 0.075. The difference of 0.15 therefore gives a Z-value of 2.0. A one-tailed test indicated that this would be likely to occur by chance in less than one case in 40, so we can conclude that the difference is in fact perceptible. Even if the null hypothesis had been that no difference in sweetness would be perceived, a two-tailed test would have yielded a P-value of 0.05.

Notice that if the two scores had been treated (incorrectly) as being independent, the standard error would have been calculated as 0.11 and the Z value as 1.4. The covariance has played a considerable role here. Participants in the test have tended to rate *both* biscuits high or *both* low on the scale (reflecting the fact that people's preferences vary in the matter of sweetness). Transforming the two ratings in this way largely removes this effect. In this case it has increased the sensitivity of the test, but that is not its purpose, which is to make proper allowance for the covariance. (Whether or not the perceived difference in sweetness matters in determining the decision to be made about the formulation is, of course, quite another question.)

4.6   The chi-square test of fit

Suppose that there is a discrete population with k categories. The popular chi-square test of fit checks how sample data agree with the hypothesis that the population, or some attribute of that population, is distributed across these categories in certain proportions. A statistic (χ^2) is calculated and the computed value, in conjunction with the number of categories in the distribution, is used to determine the probability of differences between the observed and expected distributions occurring by chance. The most frequently encountered formula uses the observed frequencies $(o_1, \ldots, o_k)$

and the corresponding *expected* frequencies $(e_1, \ldots, e_k)$. The expected frequencies are those which would be seen if the sample were distributed in accordance with the population hypothesis:

$$\chi^2 = \sum_{i=1}^{k} \frac{(o_i - e_i)^2}{e_i}. \tag{4.4}$$

χ^2 may also, and more usefully, be defined in terms of proportions. Let n be the number of respondents over which the distribution is calculated, $p_1, \ldots, p_k$ the expected proportions falling into each of the k categories and $\hat{p}_1, \ldots, \hat{p}_k$ the respective sampling proportions. The formula then becomes:

$$\chi^2 = n \sum_{i=1}^{k} \frac{(\hat{p}_i - p_i)^2}{p_i}. \tag{4.5}$$

Percentages can be used in place of proportions if $n/100$ is substituted for n in this equation. Note that n here is not necessarily the sample size. It is the number of cases in which we are interested. This will generally be the members of the sample that possess a certain attribute (that attribute could simply be membership of the sample). The *incidence* of the attribute is of no relevance. We are only interested in how these cases are distributed across the k categories, and the proportions p_i and $\hat{p}_i$ are the proportions of those with the attributes who are in each of the k categories $(\sum_{i=1}^{k} p_i = \sum_{i=1}^{k} \hat{p}_i = 1.0)$.

The statistic χ^2 is then assumed to have the chi-square distribution with $k - 1$ degrees of freedom, and this is the basis of the chi-square test. Unfortunately, χ^2 will have this distribution *only* in the case of simple random sampling. If sampling is not simple random and includes, for example, clustering or stratification, or if any weights have been applied, the distribution of χ^2 (as calculated) may be far from the true chi-square distribution so that the values produced by the classical statistic can lead to very misleading P-values (both overestimated and underestimated). It is *not* recommended, therefore, to use the classical statistic for non-simple-random sampling. The problem of generalising the statistic is not trivial and a simple adjustment, such as the replacement of n by the corresponding *effective* sample number, would not solve the problem (the distribution could still be far from the chi-square distribution).

The only exception to this would be the case where in a stratified simple random sample, with proportionate or disproportionate sampling of the strata, the test is made on the distribution of an attribute across the strata themselves. In this case only, equation (4.4) can still be used.

There is an extensive research literature on the subject but many publications are concerned only with a specific sample design. In general, there are several formulae available for non-simple-random sampling and the more information there is about the sample the more precise a formula is available. Our approach will be based on the assumption that the information about *design effects* is available. From a theoretical point of view, this is usually the minimum requirement and, in fact, many generalised formulae need more information than just design effects. However, from a practical point of view, this is probably the maximum of what a user 'can afford' and calculations of a design effect can be, as we have seen, very complex. An alternative is to replace design effects by weighting effects which are much easier to compute. If even weighting effect calculations are not possible, for instance with unweighted quota samples, the only option is then to estimate design effects from previous experience. This is not a full answer, but it is infinitely preferable to ignoring the problem.

A general formula for the chi-square test of fit, which requires only design effect information, is given in the paper of Rao and Scott [47], formula 3.2. First, a coefficient λ is computed by the following formula:

$$\lambda = \sum_{i=1}^{k} \frac{(1 - \hat{p}_i)\mathrm{DE}_i}{k - 1}, \tag{4.6}$$

where DE_i is the design effect for the proportion estimate $\hat{p}_i$. It is easy to see that if all design effects are equal to 1.0, λ is equal to 1.0. If, on the other hand, all design effects DE_i are the same, say, $\mathrm{DE}_i = \mathrm{DE}$, then λ is also equal to DE.

The final statistic is then simply χ^2/λ, where χ^2 is calculated according to formula (4.5) with all proportions being weighted. This modified statistic will approximately have the chi-square distribution with $k - 1$ degrees of freedom. Thus, we obtain the following test:

null hypothesis	proportions of the k categories are $p_1, \ldots, p_k$
alternative hypothesis	at least one of the proportions is not what we expect
statistic to compute	χ^2/λ, where χ^2 and λ are computed by (4.5) and (4.6)
table to find P-value	Table H2 with $k - 1$ degrees of freedom

It may be necessary to estimate some population parameters to compute $\hat{p}_1, \ldots, \hat{p}_k$ or the design effects. In this case, similar to simple random sampling, the number of degrees of freedom will be *less* than $k - 1$. More precisely, the number of degrees of freedom will be $k - 1 - s$, where s is the number of population parameters one needs to estimate.

If the design effect calculations are not possible and the weighting effect is used instead, the coefficient λ is then simply equal to the weighting effect (because the weighting effect is the same for all estimates). The formula for the test statistic will then be (4.5), with n replaced by the corresponding calibrated number of cases.

Note that for a comparison of two proportions the two-tailed Z-test in section 4.4.2 is equivalent to this test (with one degree of freedom).

Example 4.7   In a non-simple-random sample an attribute is possessed by 50 sample members (unweighted). The incidence varies across five mutually exclusive categories, and the (weighted) distribution across those categories is given by $\hat{p}_i$, but a reasonable null hypothesis is that it should be distributed across the five categories in accord with the proportions of the population (and the weighted sample) that these categories represent (p_i).

Category	Observed $\hat{p}_i$	Expected p_i	DE_i	$(\hat{p}_i - p_i)^2/p_i$	$(1 - p_i)DE_i$
1	0.116	0.1	1.5	0.0027	1.32
2	0.186	0.2	1.6	0.0010	1.30
3	0.279	0.4	1.4	0.0366	1.00
4	0.186	0.1	1.7	0.0740	1.38
5	0.233	0.2	1.5	0.0053	1.15
sum	1.0	1.0	n/a	0.1195	6.17

The unadjusted chi-square value is 0.1195 multiplied by 50 (the *unweighted* number of respondents involved) or 5.9. The adjustment factor λ is 6.172/4 or 1.543, giving an adjusted chi-square of 3.9. With four degrees of freedom this gives a P-value (Table H2) of somewhere around 0.45, certainly not enough to convince us that there is anything abnormal about this distribution. The same distribution shown across 150 respondents would have produced a chi-square value of 11.6, yielding a more convincing P-value of about 0.025. Note that in this calculation we did not need to know the overall sample size nor the incidence of the attribute in each category.

4.7 Testing homogeneity and independence

Each variable with k categories defines k subpopulations in the obvious way. Two variables are called independent if each variable has the same distribution in all subpopulations defined by the other variable. It is a common problem to decide whether variables are related or not. The hypothesis of homogeneity can be formulated as 'no difference among populations', i.e. the distribution of a given variable is the same in all populations. Homogeneity and independence are in fact equivalent and for categorical variables they are tested in exactly the same way – using the chi-square test. When rating scales are used, the Kolmogorov–Smirnov test for homogeneity is more sensitive. There are also special tests for ranked data but they are not discussed here.

4.7.1 The chi-square test of independence

This is one of the most common tests and it is intended to give evidence whether two given variables are independent or not. The contingency table for the two variables should have at least two rows and at least two columns. (In the case of one row or column one gets in fact a goodness-of-fit test.) The cells in the table must be disjoint, i.e. each respondent should belong to one cell only. The 'rule of thumb' is that each cell should have at least twenty respondents in the sample, to make the results relatively reliable.

Suppose the first variable has k categories with marginal sample proportions $\hat{p}_1, \ldots, \hat{p}_k$ and the second variable has l categories with marginal sample proportions $\hat{q}_1, \ldots, \hat{q}_l$. Denote by $\hat{r}_{i,j}$ the cell proportion estimate, i.e. the proportion of respondents in the sample for whom the first variable has value i and the second has value j. The expected cell proportions are then $\hat{p}_i \hat{q}_j$ and the standard chi-square statistic to test independence is the following:

$$\chi^2 = n \sum_{i=1}^{k} \sum_{j=1}^{l} \frac{(\hat{r}_{i,j} - \hat{p}_i \hat{q}_j)^2}{\hat{p}_i \hat{q}_j}, \tag{4.7}$$

where n is the unweighted sample size.

As with the chi-square test of fit, this formula is not suitable for non-simple-random sampling and a generalised formula is required. Again we assume that the design effect information is known. A general formula for a non-simple-random sample has been published independently in two papers [48] and [4]. To this end, let $DE(\hat{r}_{i,j})$, $DE(\hat{p}_i)$, $DE(\hat{q}_j)$ be the design effects for estimates $\hat{r}_{i,j}$, $\hat{p}_i$, $\hat{q}_j$, respectively. The formula requires the following coefficient

$$\delta = \frac{1}{(k-1)(l-1)} \left[A - \sum_{i=1}^{k} (1 - \hat{p}_i) DE(\hat{p}_i) - \sum_{j=1}^{l} (1 - \hat{q}_j) DE(\hat{q}_j) \right], \tag{4.8}$$

where $A = \sum_{i=1}^{k} \sum_{j=1}^{l} (1 - \hat{p}_i \hat{q}_j) DE(\hat{r}_{i,j})$. If all design effects are the same and equal, for instance, to DE then δ is also equal to DE. In particular, when all design effects are equal to one, the coefficient is also equal to one.

The generalised statistic from the cited papers is then simply χ^2/δ, and it has approximately the chi-square distribution with $(k-1)(l-1)$ degrees of freedom. Hence, we obtain the summary of the test:

null hypothesis	two variables are independent
alternative hypothesis	two variables are not independent
statistic to compute	χ^2/δ, where χ^2 and δ are computed by (4.7) and (4.8)
table to find P-value	Table H2 with $(k-1)(l-1)$ degrees of freedom

The trade-off of the generalised formula is that if the test has to be repeated for a subsample, the design effects should be recalculated – the same cell may have a different design effect in a different subsample.

As with the test of fit, if the weighting effect is to replace the design effects, the statistic will be computed by formula (4.7), where n is replaced by the calibrated sample size.

If the sample is clustered and clustering has an appreciable effect on one or both of the variables, the value of δ may sometimes appear surprisingly low. This is because the individual cells will have relatively low numbers of respondents per cluster and thus the clustering effect will be weakened and the design effect reduced.

Note also that the test is two-dimensional, i.e. for two variables only. It is possible sometimes that the contingency table is produced from three or more variables. In this case, the test is not appropriate even if the table appears to be two-dimensional. (In a three-dimensional case, the null hypothesis would be that the three variables are independent, and the chi-square statistic would be different.)

4.7.2   Kolmogorov–Smirnov test (ordered categories)

This is another (unweighted) test for homogeneity, when data come from two large independent samples and are from variables with ordered categories. The test is based on the Kolmogorov–Smirnov statistic derived from two samples:

$$D = \max_x |F_1(x) - F_2(x)|,$$

where F_1 and F_2 are the cumulative empirical distributions for the first and second samples.

To compute this statistic, denote by n_1 and n_2 the sample sizes in the first and second samples and suppose that the rating scale has k categories given in natural order, say from very low to very high. For each category i, denote by $\hat{p}_i$ and $\hat{q}_i$ the corresponding sample proportions of this category in the first and second samples, respectively. Put

$$\hat{r}_1 = \hat{p}_1 - \hat{q}_1, \qquad \hat{r}_2 = (\hat{p}_1 - \hat{q}_1) + (\hat{p}_2 - \hat{q}_2), \qquad \hat{r}_{k-1} = \sum_{i=1}^{k-1}(\hat{p}_i - \hat{q}_i).$$

Hence, the statistic D is computed as the maximum among all absolute values of r_i:

$$D = \max(|\hat{r}_1|, \ldots, |\hat{r}_{k-1}|).$$

Note that the last term $\hat{r}_k = \sum_{i=1}^{k}(\hat{p}_i - \hat{q}_i)$ is not used because it is zero (due to the fact that $\hat{p}_1 + \cdots + \hat{p}_k = \hat{q}_1 + \cdots + \hat{q}_k = 1$).

For large sample sizes, there is a direct formula which gives approximate P-values for this statistic. More precisely, Smirnov has obtained the following asymptotic distribution of statistic D:

$$P\left(D > z\sqrt{\frac{1}{n_1} + \frac{1}{n_2}}\right) \approx 2\sum_{j=1}^{\infty}(-1)^{j-1}\exp(-2j^2z^2).$$

The first term in this sum still gives a good approximation

$$P\left(D > z\sqrt{\frac{1}{n_1} + \frac{1}{n_2}}\right) \approx 2\exp(-2z^2)$$

and if $z\sqrt{1/n_1 + 1/n_2}$ is replaced by a, the formula becomes

$$P(D > a) \approx 2\exp[-2a^2n_1n_2/(n_1 + n_2)].$$

In other words, for a given value of D the right-hand side of this formula evaluated at that value gives the corresponding (right-tailed) P-value. Hence, the test table is the following:

null hypothesis	no difference in rating between populations
alternative hypothesis	there is a difference in rating between populations (two-tailed)
statistic to compute	$D = \max(|r_1|, \ldots, |r_{k-1}|)$
formula for left-tailed P-value	$1 - 2\exp[-2D^2 n_1 n_2/(n_1 + n_2)]$

5 Measuring relationships between variables

5.1 Analysis of contingency tables

One of the goals of any survey is to study relationships between variables and it is important to be able to measure how strongly two variables are associated. In many (if not most) cases, it is actually more useful to know the strength of association between variables rather than to test a hypothesis and conclude that a difference is 'significant' or not. It might be, for example, that for two given pairs of variables, significance testing will result in the conclusion that variables in both pairs are not independent. However, these two pairs may still have very different degrees of association for variables within each of them. Therefore, it is important to know not just the 'yes/no' answer but the magnitude or strength of the association between variables. The level of statistical significance is, of course, in part a function of the sample size, whereas the strength of the association is independent of sample size.

5.1.1 Numerical and categorical variables

Let us begin by discriminating between two major types of variables, those that are inherently numerical and those that are not.

Numerical variables sometimes have an absolute numerical value (height, age, income, etc.), and although different units of measurement may be used (height in inches, centimetres or metres) the relative values for different respondents are preserved and the nature of the results will not be affected by the choice.

But frequently in surveys variables are represented numerically for convenience where the numbers, or their ratios, cannot necessarily be taken at face value, but do meet the principal requirement of discriminating consistently and meaningfully between groups of respondents. For instance in measuring the level of education of a respondent it is common to ask the age at which the respondent (first) finished full-time education. This yields a clearly numerical value, but not one that is necessarily proportional to the degree of 'educatedness'; someone who graduated from a university at 21 is not necessarily 1.5 times as 'educated' as someone who left school at 14. An alternative measure of education may be to establish how far up the education ladder the respondent progressed, from basic primary school to post-graduate study, using an ordered list of verbally described categories, to which numerical values may be assigned. By and large these two measures would yield similar results and should fulfil their basic function of discriminating. The strictly numerical value (age) has the advantages of minimising the possibility of confusion between categories and the incidence of awkward cases that do not fit neatly into any of the categories in the list. It also lends itself much more readily to cross-cultural comparisons, there being some difficulty in equating the lists of types of education or institutions in use in different countries.

Assigned numeric values

The use of a verbal list also raises the problem of how numerical values are to be assigned to the items on that list. Often it is not difficult to *order* the items logically, so that they form an agreed spectrum. Simply assigning a value equivalent to the position of the item in the list (frequently done) makes the tacit assumption that the intervals between all pairs of adjacent items are equal in size. In the case of our education example, two different types of course or institution may be different in nature, but equal in status. In such cases it may be of value to be able to discriminate between respondents who passed through each type, and therefore important to keep the numerical value assigned to each separate from the identifying code (a subject we shall return to later).

Verbal lists may also be used in preference to overtly numerical measures simply because respondents find it easier to relate verbal categories to their own experience and modes of thought than to some quasi-abstract numerical values. We may for example in a political poll ask, 'How likely are you to vote at the coming election?' and ask the respondent to choose from the following list:

I shall definitely vote
I shall probably vote
I am undecided
I shall probably not vote
I shall definitely not vote

We might then assign values of 1.0, 0.75, 0.5, 0.25, 0.0 to the five response categories. Or we might decide that there is some element of uncertainty in the responses and that we should use values of 0.9, 0.7, 0.5, 0.3 and 0.1; or we may, with the benefit of experience and other knowledge, decide to use some other set of values. But using our judgement in assigning values is still likely to provide better quality information than asking members of the public, 'What is the probability of your voting at the next election?' and expecting a numerical response. People in general prove to be more comfortable with placing themselves in verbal categories than with assigning themselves numerical values, so ordered verbal lists, or semantic scales, are a frequently used means of eliciting pieces of information that can then be assigned numeric values by the researcher. Typically, semantic scale categories are given integer values, though there is no intrinsic reason why this should be done. Real values could be assigned such that the distribution of values has convenient statistical characteristics (such as an even or normal-looking distribution, or zero mean and unit variance), or the wording of the verbal categories could be fine tuned with practice to achieve the same effect.

Ordered verbal lists are thus a way of providing numerical values which, while not exact, are realistic and useful. The inexactness is only one of the problems associated with many numeric measures in surveys. Some measures may be reasonably firm: respondents are likely to know within a small margin of error how tall they are and, within perhaps a slightly larger margin of error, what they weigh. They can usually be expected to be exact about how many children they have. Other measures are 'softer'. Respondents may not be able to give a precise answer to a question of 'fact' because they do not consciously record the factual information on which it would have to be based. A question such as 'How much did you spend on meals on your last holiday trip?' will probably produce many heavily rounded estimates (as well as a large 'don't know' group) if the respondent is expected to provide an unprompted numerical response. Providing a prompt list of a series of ranges may focus the thoughts of respondents better and enable them to provide a more realistic guess. More importantly it would probably reduce the number of those unwilling to provide any estimate at all.

The use of categories, and the (possible) assignment of a nominal value to each category is a legitimate information gathering technique where it can be shown, or reasonably inferred, that the information it yields is of better quality (more realistic and reliable) than an exact numerical measure. Although this approach forces respondents into categories, such variables remain numerical and should be treated as such. Any numerical variable may, of course, be converted into a series of categories (typically ranges of values) for analysis purposes. This is frequently done for the purpose of identifying or comparing other attributes of subsets of the sample of particular interest.

Attempts to get 'average' or 'typical' values for something that is inherently variable may have a similar problem. The estimates respondents give may also be biased because of psychological pressures. It is well known that in many cultures people understate the number of cigarettes they smoke and the amount of alcohol they drink. People often overstate the frequency with which they do things, as may be seen from comparisons of public and industry statistics with the responses to questions such as 'How often do you . . . ?' and 'When did you last . . . ?' It is also clear that people often overstate (probably unconsciously) the consistency or regularity of their behaviour. They may be generalising from their most recent behaviour without allowing for shifts in behaviour over time, but in many cases they may simply be responding to the implication of the question wording and the stimulus material. Asked how often they do something and to choose between 'once a week', 'once a fortnight', 'once a month' and other similar response categories, most respondents feel sufficiently comfortable with the way the alternatives are presented to make a choice, so that 'don't know' responses and refusals or omissions are minimised.

Such apparent measures of 'hard fact' are often measures of respondents' estimates of them, with their attendant margins of error and biases. They may be suspect as quantitative measures in isolation, but they may still be extremely useful in revealing the ways in which, and the extent to which, levels of one variable are related to or explained by differences in other variables. The absolute values may be open to question, but the relative values are helpful in placing respondents in an appropriate position within the spectrum of variation occurring within the population.

'Soft' measures may also be subject to variation within the respondent. The answer given may vary depending on the context or on the current mood of the respondent. There is also the risk that they may mean different things to different respondents. Numerical estimates of 'satisfaction', for instance, may be related to levels of expectation, and some kinds of respondents may have consistently higher or lower expectations than others.

However, such categories may still be the best means of getting usable estimates. We must simply be aware of the ways and the extent to which the responses from individual respondents, and the numerical values assigned to them, are subject to error. It is always dangerous to apply mathematical analysis techniques that are more sophisticated than the data to which they are applied.

Measuring association

An obvious measure of degree of association between two numerical variables is the product-moment correlation coefficient. It has the disadvantage that it can be computed only for variables that are truly numeric in character. In sample surveys particularly, many variables cannot be treated as numeric values and it is essential to discriminate between those that can and those that cannot, and also to understand the possible implications and shortcomings of ways in which values are assigned. Even if the original variable is inherently continuous, the numerical values are often recorded in the form of ranges of values, to each of which a single value is assigned (which might be either the mean of the items in that range, or more likely an arbitrary value intended to represent that range, for instance the mid-point). The effect of such grouping is to reduce slightly the variance of the variable and to reduce the correlation coefficient of any pair of variables of which one or both is treated in this way.

There is also a variety of regression methods that are often used to assess relationships, usually with a view to being able to predict, or rather to explain, the value of one dependent variable in terms of the values of one or more independent variables, either in their original state or after some kind of transformation. Logistic regression may be used to explain the membership of a defined subset. Regression methods assume that at least the independent or explanatory variables are numerical in character and capable of being manipulated arithmetically.

As in any data set it is necessary to be aware of the possibility of non-linear relationships. 'Age' and 'income' do not generally correlate well for the general population, because income tends to be highest for people in the middle of the age range and lowest at the ends of the range. Diligent inspection of contingency tables and/or scatter plots beforehand should reveal this and less obvious relationships and indicate transformation or other appropriate action.

More problematic is the matter of skewed distributions or outlying values that can influence calculations. In sample surveys distributions are often encountered that contain a small number of exceptional (usually high) values. In a survey on travel, for instance, a question on 'number of trips made by air in the last year' may throw up one or more people who are very frequent fliers and who have very high incomes, who would probably form a very small minority of the survey population. The precise number captured in any sample might be subject to wide fluctuation, but would have a considerable influence on the value of the correlation between these two variables. Both these measures might also be expected to yield distinctly non-normal distributions, and a normal distribution is an assumption for the assessment of the product-moment correlation coefficient. Non-normal distributions will still often yield reasonable looking values, but these may be inflated or deflated by the shape of the underlying distributions. Transforming the values in some way, to approximate normality more closely, may be beneficial. Logarithms or powers of the observed values can often be useful in this. Including in the calculation only a relevant subset of the sample (for instance in this example perhaps excluding non-fliers) may also help.

A sinister hidden danger lies in the inadvertent inclusion of values assigned for operational convenience. A case where two variables predominantly have values in the range 0–10, but where one researcher has applied a value such as 99 to indicate 'no information' (a far from uncommon practice) is liable to produce a spurious positive correlation if (as often happens) the people who fail to answer one question are disproportionately likely to fail to answer the other, but fails to exclude these people from the calculation. This is not a matter of mathematics, but of a simple practical pitfall for which researchers must be on the lookout.

Non-numerical variables

Many variables, however, do not have any intrinsic numerical quality, even though responses may be assigned numerical values for convenience. If we ask respondents which State of the USA they live in there is no *logical* reason why Alabama should be assigned the value 1 and Wyoming the value 50, except possibly the convenience of being able to find any desired State from a list quickly. But this is only a convention: the States could have been ordered and numbered in ascending or descending order of area or population or purely arbitrarily. In fact they need not have been given numbers at all: they could be referred to by their two-character postal abbreviation. But both of these methods derive from the conventions in use in general computing of using either numbers or text to identify data items. In other systems of recording, the States could be identified with colours or geometric shapes. All that is required is a convenient and unambiguous 'tag' of some kind to act as an identifier. Whether or not this tag is present in the data associated with a respondent is taken to be an indicator of whether or not that respondent possesses that attribute. The practice of using numbers as identifiers must not seduce us into applying numerical methods to data that are not themselves numerical.

Of course such variables can be formed into others that may have a numerical or quasi-numerical form. In the States example this could be some numerical attribute of the States themselves, such as the population density or the percentage of population of Hispanic extraction. However, it must be remembered that, in the context of a survey sample, these attributes remain attributes of the sample members, that is to say, a *respondent* is classified as 'living in a State that has a $x\%$ Hispanic population'. Extreme care should be exercised in any attempt to use these numerical values in any cross-analysis to ensure that their use is both logically and arithmetically valid in the context.

Categorical variables

It is with such variables as these that we are principally concerned here. They are usually called *categorical* variables. They consist of a number of categories, normally with logical or Boolean rather than arithmetic definitions. In our 'States' example, the categories could be individual States or they could be convenient groupings of States (New England, Pacific Coast, etc.). The same list of States could be grouped in different ways (regions, Republican/Democrat government, maritime/inland, etc.) yielding several different variables, none of whose groupings would necessarily be obvious from the values identifying the individual States.

Of course, any numerical variable can be turned into what is functionally a categorical variable. Generally this is done by dividing the spectrum of values into a series of ranges, either using convenient or conventional break-points or by choosing values that yield roughly equal sized subsets (e.g. quintiles). While these can be treated like true categorical variables, they nevertheless retain some numerical qualities, in that they are ordered.

Multiple-response variables

In survey work it is often convenient to present questions to respondents in a form that permits multiple responses. We may, for instance, show respondents a list of illnesses and ask them which they have ever suffered from. Respondents can nominate any number of categories, including none. One way of handling such information is to record the responses as a series of binary or logical variables. There would be one of these per response-category, and probably, for convenience, an additional 'any-of-these/none-of-these' variable. This is the approach used, indeed required, by much numerically oriented statistical software. It has the disadvantage that treating a long list of such variables together for analysis purposes may result in laborious input and inconvenient output. Many specialist survey processing software packages permit the use of 'multiple-response variables', which allow the set of response categories, along with summary categories, 'none-of-these' and 'no-answer' categories to be treated together, and present the output similarly to the way in which the question was presented to the respondent. The physical recording of the data may, however, still take the form of logical values, one per response category.

It often happens that the nature of the question is such that, although the researcher intends that only one response should be given by each respondent, some respondents may legitimately insist that two or more responses are equally appropriate. Questions like 'What was the main purpose of your journey?' often yield such replies. Attempts to force the respondent to reduce the reply to a single response may be counter-productive if they jeopardise further cooperation. In some situations, particularly with self-completion questionnaires, there may be no opportunity to pick up the problem until the data are in the processing stage. If multiple responses cannot be tolerated by the data entry or analysis software the researcher may be left with no options except deleting all but one response, deleting all responses and moving the respondent to an 'invalid answer' category, or selecting one 'primary' response and creating additional variables for 'secondary', 'tertiary' and subsequent responses. In such cases the researcher is unnecessarily and unjustifiably altering the information provided by the respondent, by forcing the respondent's view of the situation to conform with the researcher's.

Multiple-response variables are very convenient for creating conventional contingency tables for visual inspection, but they do present certain practical problems for statistical purposes, because of the overlap between categories. This will be alluded to further in this chapter.

The contingency table or cross-tabulation is the backbone of survey analysis. At a minimum it consists of a two-dimensional matrix of numbers, the rows representing the categories of one variable and the columns those of another. Each cell of the matrix contains a count of the number (weighted if appropriate) of cases that fall into both the row category *and* the column category (the intersection of the two categories). Marginal totals are usually also presented and the figures may be in addition expressed as percentages of the column totals and/or the row totals. Sometimes they are also presented in index form.[1] Three-dimensional tables with three variables are not uncommon (the third dimension often represented as separate sheets of paper) and higher-dimension tables are possible, though not very tractable.

The contingency table is thus purely descriptive in its function, but may be used as the material for tests that use aggregate data such as the chi-square test. For this purpose the column and row categories must be mutually exclusive. However, purely descriptive tabulations often contain multiple variables in columns and/or rows, overlapping categories, as in multiple-response variables, and summary (e.g. subtotal) categories.

5.1.2 Measuring a difference between two distributions

Another topic very seldom discussed in statistical literature is the measurement of how close two *distributions* are to each other; in other words, how we are to measure the strength of 'fit' between two distributions. Of course, the distributions are required to have the same number of categories.

We shall discuss in section 5.1.3 how to measure the strength of association between variables. However, the strength of fit is quite different – variables with the same number of categories may have a perfect association but still have very different probabilities for the same categories. Conversely, variables may have exactly the

[1] The 'index' is a convenient way of expressing a value in terms of its relationship to a base value, as in a government Consumer Price Index, or (as here) to an expected value. The observed value is divided by the base or expected value and (conventionally) multiplied by 100, the 'expected value' here being the size the cell would have been if the row and column categories were independent (index $= 100 p_{xy}/p_x p_y$).

same marginal distributions but still have a very 'poor' relationship. The problem is appropriate only for variables with more than two categories – for binary variables, we can simply take the difference between proportions.

Perhaps the first reaction to this problem is – can we not use the chi-square statistic of 'fit'? Unfortunately, this statistic has two problems that make it unsuitable for this measurement.

- The 'expected' frequencies/proportions used in the chi-square statistic could be zero so that the statistic value cannot be computed in this case. An example of how this might occur is given below.
- In many cases it does not make sense to say that one of the two distributions is 'expected' and the other one is 'observed'. For example, if we have two distributions from two independent samples, both of them are 'observed' and neither is 'expected'. Any measure of the strength of fit should be symmetric.

However it can be used in a modified form (see below).

The P-value would not be very useful either – it usually depends on the sample size. The measure should really depend on the distribution probabilities and not on the sample size; the sample size should only tell us *how reliable* the measurement of strength of fit is. As we shall see in section 5.1.3, the measures of association between variables do not depend on the sample size.

There are at least three kinds of situations where it would be useful to be able to measure the strength of fit.

- As we have mentioned, it might be necessary to compare two distributions, either from two samples or a distribution from a sample versus an 'expected' distribution.
- The currently fashionable market research technique called *data fusion* is another example where such measurements would be useful to assess one aspect of the quality of the data set. Data fusion involves taking data sets from two (or more) surveys and combining them to form a data set that appears to be from one survey. An individual respondent from one sample (the 'recipient') is 'married' with an individual from another (the 'donor') and 'acquires' all the information provided by both. Preservation of the marginal distributions of responses thus transferred to the final fused sample is an obvious requirement. For a further discussion of data fusion see section 5.6.

    This is in fact the situation where 'expected' distributions may have zero proportions while the same proportions for a 'fused' distribution may be non-zero. For instance, in a household expenditure survey we might expect to find no dog-owners with zero expenditure on dog food. If, however, the information about dog ownership had come from a 'donor' survey, data fusion can easily produce a non-zero number of such respondents: a dog owning donor could be 'married' with a recipient who does not buy dog food.

- More generally, strength of fit could be measured for any model that 'predicts' distributions. Therefore, predicted distributions are compared with 'actual' distributions and the strength of fit will indicate how good the model is.

The following three formulae can be used to measure the strength of fit between two distributions expressed as proportions $(p_i)_{i=1}^n$ and $(q_i)_{i=1}^n$. All formulae are 'canonical' in the sense that the minimum value is always zero, when the distributions are identical, and the maximum value is always 1.

1. 'Euclidean' distance

This is, perhaps, the simplest formula for computing the distance:

$$d_1 = \sqrt{\frac{1}{2} \sum_{i=1}^{n} (p_i - q_i)^2}.$$

See Appendix G for a proof that the maximum value of this distance is 1. The maximum value will be achieved if in both distributions there is a category with the probability of one (then, of course, other categories will have zero probabilities) and this category should be *different* for these distributions (e.g. the first distribution is $(1, 0, 0)$ and the second $(0, 1, 0)$).

We have called it a 'Euclidean' distance because it closely resembles the usual Euclidean distance between vectors.

2. 'Symmetric' chi-square distance

It is also possible to 'adjust' the chi-square statistic and make it symmetric by dividing by the *sum* of 'expected' and 'observed' probabilities:

$$d_2 = \frac{1}{2} \sum_{i=1}^{n} \frac{(p_i - q_i)^2}{p_i + q_i}.$$

For this coefficient, therefore, there is no need to distinguish between 'expected' and 'observed' distributions and it is also logical to assume that the sum $p_i + q_i$ is positive for any i (otherwise the corresponding category can simply be excluded from both distributions).

See Appendix G again for a proof that the maximum value is 1. The maximum value is achieved when for any category i at least one of the two probabilities (p_i or q_i) is zero.

3. 'Geometric' distance

Finally, a geometric measure with a simple and natural interpretation can be introduced if we treat the distributions as vectors in a finite dimensional space. Consider the following points in $\mathbb{R}^n$:

$$\bar{a} = (\sqrt{p_1}, \ldots, \sqrt{p_n}) \qquad \text{and} \qquad \bar{b} = (\sqrt{q_1}, \ldots, \sqrt{q_n}).$$

The proposed distance is simply the sine of the angle between these two vectors and is given by the following formula:

$$d_3 = \sqrt{1 - \left(\sum_{i=1}^{n} \sqrt{p_i q_i} \right)^2}.$$

Similarly to the 'symmetric' chi-square distance, the maximum value of 1 is achieved when the product of the two probabilities p_i and q_i is zero for all categories. The minimum value of zero is achieved when the two distributions are the same. See Appendix G for a proof of these statements.

5.1.3 Strength of association between categorical variables

There is an extensive research literature on measures of association for contingency tables of which we mention just the books of Kendall and Stuart [32] and Everitt [18]. Many different measures have been proposed and it is not easy to choose between them. There is no 'universal' measure suitable for all situations so that different formulae may have to be used in different cases. It seems obvious, however, that any useful measure of association should satisfy at least three conditions.

- The measure should be 'canonical' in the sense that it should have a minimum and a maximum value (usually 0 and 1) and both values should be 'achievable' in certain extreme situations that are clearly defined.
- There should be a 'natural' generalisation that will work for weighted data and non-simple-random sampling. This means that the measure should depend on proportions rather than on frequencies.
- The measure should have an 'intuitive' meaning to assist in interpretation of actual results.

We consider only the general case, that is, that the measure should be suitable for any pair of categorical variables where the categories within each variable are mutually exclusive. There could be more requirements in some special cases, for example, if values of the variables are *ordered*, but that will not be discussed here. Where a multiple-choice variable is involved it must normally be converted into a series of binary variables, which is inconvenient and makes the general relationship more difficult to envisage. However, where the degree of overlap between categories is slight it may be acceptable to ignore it and to treat the categories of the variable(s) as though they were mutually exclusive (and to treat the variable as a single-response variable), the number of cases being taken as the sum of the numbers in each cell (weighted if appropriate).

Measures of association

We will consider three measures of association that satisfy these conditions and are in common use. For all formulae, $(r_{i,j})$ will denote the cell proportions (in a contingency table with k rows and l columns) while $(p_i)_{i=1}^k$ and $(q_j)_{j=1}^l$ will denote the marginal proportions. The marginal probabilities are assumed to be non-zero.

1. Cramer's coefficient

This coefficient was defined by Cramer in 1946 and is calculated according to the following formula:

$$C = \sqrt{\frac{1}{\min(k-1, l-1)} \sum_{i=1}^{k} \sum_{j=1}^{l} \frac{(r_{i,j} - p_i q_j)^2}{p_i q_j}}. \tag{5.1}$$

The formula is closely related to the chi-square statistic – the sum under the square root is simply the chi-square statistic (for a simple random sample) divided by the unweighted sample size. In the case of weighted data, all proportions must be weighted.

The coefficient has values from 0 to 1 and it is obvious that the value will be zero only when $r_{i,j} = p_i q_j$ for all i and j, which is equivalent to the independence of the variables. To see when the maximum value of 1 is achieved, assume, for example, that the number of columns l is less than the number of rows k. Then the maximum value will occur for any table for which every cell proportion $r_{i,j}$ is either zero or equal to one of the row proportions p_i (see Appendix G for details). The value cannot be negative. There is no question of the 'direction' of any association between truly categorical variables.

An interpretation of C is given by Kendall and Stuart [32], section 33.51: Cramer's coefficient is the *mean squared canonical correlation*. The canonical correlation is defined as follows: for two categorical variables, *scores* are allocated to each category of each variable in such a way that the correlation between variables (based on the scores) is maximised. To solve the problem, the Lagrange multipliers method is used and there will be $m = \min(k, l)$ equations that will result in m different correlations. One of these correlations will be 1 and the other $m - 1$ are called the canonical correlations.

It is possible, therefore, to interpret C as some sort of a generalised 'correlation' between variables in a contingency table. Among coefficients for which the minimum value corresponds to the independence of the variables, Cramer's coefficient is probably one of the best and is commonly used in practice.

2. Goodman and Kruskal measures

Another approach to contingency tables is based on the *predictive* association between variables and is described by Goodman and Kruskal [21]. Its purpose is to measure how much one variable helps to 'predict' values of the other variable, in relative terms.

Assume, for instance, that we want to predict a 'row' value, that is a category from 1 to k. If there is no information available about this variable, the best 'guess' would be to take the category with the largest probability $\max_i(p_i)$. The error in judgement is then

$$\text{'prior' error} = E_1 = 1 - \max_i(p_i).$$

On the other hand, if now the 'column' information is available, the prediction will be within each column separately and again the row with the largest probability is chosen. For column j, the probability of correct prediction will then be $\max_i(r_{i,j})/q_j$ (it is, in fact, a conditional probability). Because column j will occur with probability q_j, the total 'posterior' probability is computed by the formula

$$\text{'posterior' probability} = \sum_{j=1}^{l} q_j \frac{\max_i(r_{i,j})}{q_j} = \sum_{j=1}^{l} \max_i(r_{i,j})$$

so that the error of prediction is

$$\text{`posterior' error} = E_2 = 1 - \sum_{j=1}^{l} \max_i(r_{i,j}).$$

The coefficient that measures how much columns 'help' to predict rows is given by

$$\lambda_1 = \frac{E_1 - E_2}{E_1} = \frac{\sum_{j=1}^{l} \max_i(r_{i,j}) - \max_i(p_i)}{1 - \max_i(p_i)}.$$

In other words, if, for instance, $\lambda_1 = 0.2$, it means that the 'column' information will reduce the prediction error for rows by 20%.

The coefficient is again between 0 and 1. The maximum value will be achieved when the numerator and denominator in the fraction above are the same, i.e. $\sum_{j=1}^{l} \max_i(r_{i,j}) = 1$. This will happen only if each $r_{i,j}$ is either zero or coincides with the column probability q_j.

It is interesting to see when this coefficient will be equal to its minimum value, zero. The formula for λ_1 shows that a value of zero will be achieved if

$$\sum_{j=1}^{l} \max_i(r_{i,j}) = \max_i(p_i).$$

Assume, for simplicity, that the first row marginal probability is the maximum one among (p_i). Therefore,

$$\sum_{j=1}^{l} \max_i(r_{i,j}) = p_1.$$

We know that the marginal probability p_1 is the sum of the corresponding cell probabilities $r_{1,1}, \ldots, r_{1,l}$. The formula above shows that even if each of these cell probabilities is replaced by the largest probability in the corresponding column, the final sum is still p_1. Consequently, this means that each cell probability in the first row $r_{1,1}, \ldots, r_{1,l}$ should be the largest one in the corresponding column (e.g. $r_{1,3}$ is largest in column 3).

It is clear why the coefficient λ_1 ought to be zero in this case – whatever column value we have, we will always 'predict' the first row because the first probability in each column is the largest one. Thus, the 'column' information does not change our 'prior' prediction and so does not reduce the prediction error. Notice that this situation is more general than the independence of the variables – variables may be dependent but λ_1 may still be equal to zero. But *if* the variables are independent, the coefficient is equal to zero because in this case the first row probabilities will be $p_1 q_1, \ldots, p_1 q_l$ so that each of them is largest in the corresponding column (assuming that $p_1 = \max_i(p_i)$).

Similarly, if we want to predict column values using the 'row' information, the corresponding 'predictive' coefficient is computed in the same way

$$\lambda_2 = \frac{\sum_{i=1}^{k} \max_j(r_{i,j}) - \max_j(q_j)}{1 - \max_j(q_j)}.$$

The coefficients λ_1 and λ_2 were designed for asymmetric situations when one variable is explanatory and the other one is dependent. It is also possible to define a symmetric coefficient when both variables can be explanatory and dependent. The coefficient is an average of λ_1 and λ_2:

$$\lambda = \frac{\sum_{j=1}^{l} \max_i(r_{i,j}) + \sum_{i=1}^{k} \max_j(r_{i,j}) - \max_i(p_i) - \max_j(q_j)}{2 - \max_i(p_i) - \max_j(q_j)}.$$

The tables for which this coefficient achieves its minimum and maximum values (which are still 0 and 1) are even more 'extreme'. The zero value will occur when both λ_1 and λ_2 are zero. Assume again, for simplicity, that p_1 is the maximum among (p_i) and q_1 is the maximum among (q_j). Therefore, the cell probabilities from the first row $r_{1,1}, \ldots, r_{1,l}$ should be the largest ones in the corresponding columns and now also the cell probabilities from the first column $r_{1,1}, \ldots, r_{k,1}$ should be the largest ones in the corresponding rows. In particular, $r_{1,1}$ should be the largest probability among all cells.

The value of 1 for λ will be achieved, according to the arguments above, when each $r_{i,j}$ is either zero or should *simultaneously* be equal to p_i and q_j. This means, in particular, that the table is 'quadratic', i.e. $k = l$ and marginal row probabilities should be the same as column marginal probabilities (perhaps, in a different order). An example of this kind of table is given below:

0	0	p_1	p_1
p_2	0	0	p_2
0	p_3	0	p_3
p_2	p_3	p_1	

The above analysis of the zero value situation shows what kind of problems will be encountered with coefficients λ_1 and λ_2. As we have seen, if the first row probabilities are the largest ones in the corresponding columns, the first coefficient is zero *whatever the probabilities are in the other rows*. This may include many tables where one value 'dominates' other values and the variables are far from being independent. Hence, even a zero value of λ_1 or λ_2 does not really allow us to draw definite conclusions about the cell distribution $(r_{i,j})$. In general, values of λ_1 and λ_2 may be very low if the cell/marginal distributions in the table are skewed.

3. Entropy coefficients

A third approach to studying relationships between variables comes from information theory and is based on the concept of *entropy*. For an event with probability p, the *amount of uncertainty* is defined as $-\ln(p)$. If we have a distribution, it is possible then to define the average amount of uncertainty across all events and this average uncertainty is called entropy. In mathematical terms, for a distribution with probabilities $z_1, \ldots, z_n$ the formula for entropy is

$$E = -z_1 \ln(z_1) - \cdots - z_n \ln(z_n).$$

It is clear that any entropy is a non-negative number, with zero value being achieved if each probability is either 0 or 1; in this case there is no uncertainty. The maximal value for entropy is, in fact, $\ln(n)$ and is achieved when all probabilities z_i are the same (see for instance [14], section 3.5).

Therefore, we can define entropies for the row and column variables:

$$E(P) = -\sum_{i=1}^{k} p_i \ln(p_i), \quad E(Q) = -\sum_{j=1}^{l} q_j \ln(q_j).$$

This is the 'prior' amount of uncertainty, without any additional information. One natural thing to do is then to measure how much *reduction* in uncertainty of one variable we get when the other variable is introduced. Suppose, for example, that we initially had the 'row' entropy $E(P)$ and now the 'column' information will be used to reduce it. For any cell (i, j), we now have to use the conditional probability $r_{i,j}/q_j$ from column j, as in the Goodman and Kruskal approach. The uncertainty for this cell is then $-\ln(r_{i,j}/q_j)$ and the 'posterior' entropy is computed as the average uncertainty:

$$E(P|Q) = -\sum_{i,j} r_{i,j} \ln(r_{i,j}/q_j).$$

This number is still non-negative because $r_{i,j}/q_j \leq 1$. Now the coefficient used to measure association between variables can be defined:

$$\theta_1 = \frac{E(P) - E(P|Q)}{E(P)}.$$

The interpretation of this coefficient is straightforward – it shows the reduction in the amount of uncertainty for 'rows' when 'column' information is introduced.

Similarly, if the 'row' information is used to predict column values, the corresponding coefficient can be defined in the same way:

$$E(Q|P) = -\sum_{i,j} r_{i,j} \ln(r_{i,j}/p_i)$$

and

$$\theta_2 = \frac{E(Q) - E(Q|P)}{E(Q)}.$$

It is also possible to express these coefficients in terms of the *joint entropy* that corresponds to the cell distribution and is defined by

$$E(P, Q) = -\sum_{i=1}^{k} \sum_{j=1}^{l} r_{i,j} \ln(r_{i,j}).$$

We then have (see Appendix G for details)

$$E(P|Q) = E(P, Q) - E(Q) \quad \text{and} \quad E(Q|P) = E(P, Q) - E(P). \quad (5.2)$$

These formulae imply, in particular, that $E(P, Q) \geq E(P)$ and $E(P, Q) \geq E(Q)$, so that the cell distribution has a greater (or equal) average amount of uncertainty than each of the marginal distributions.

Hence, the coefficients can be expressed as

$$\theta_1 = \frac{E(P) - (E(P, Q) - E(Q))}{E(P)} = \frac{E(P) + E(Q) - E(P, Q)}{E(P)}$$

and

$$\theta_2 = \frac{E(Q) - (E(P, Q) - E(P))}{E(Q)} = \frac{E(P) + E(Q) - E(P, Q)}{E(Q)}.$$

Now we are ready to consider maximum and minimum values of the coefficients. The maximum value, for instance, for θ_1 will be when $E(P|Q)$ achieves its own minimum value which is zero. Hence, the maximum value for θ_1 (and similarly for θ_2) is 1 and it will happen when

$$E(Q|P) = -\sum_{i,j} r_{i,j} \ln(r_{i,j}/p_i) = 0.$$

This can be only if $r_{i,j} \ln(r_{i,j}/p_i) = 0$ for any i, j so that any cell proportion should be either zero or equal to the row total p_i. This result is the same as for the corresponding Goodman and Kruskal measure.

To obtain the minimum value of θ_1 and θ_2, we need to know the maximum value of $E(P, Q)$. It is proved in Appendix G that $E(P, Q) \le E(P) + E(Q)$ (so that the average amount of uncertainty for the cell distribution cannot exceed the sum of average uncertainty amounts for the marginal distributions), with the equality being achieved if and only if the variables are independent. Consequently, the minimum value for both coefficients is zero and is achieved only when the variables are totally independent, as with Cramer's coefficient.

Finally, a symmetric coefficient can be obtained if we take an average of θ_1 and θ_2. It could be a 'simple' arithmetic average $(\theta_1 + \theta_2)/2$, or the average could use different weights for θ_1 and θ_2 depending on what is more appropriate for a particular situation.

It is sometimes recommended to use the following formula for a symmetric coefficient:

$$\frac{E(P) + E(Q) - E(P, Q)}{E(P) + E(Q)}.$$

However, the problem with this coefficient is that it does not have a 'canonical' maximum value in the sense that it is not clear for which tables the maximum value is achieved. Indeed, the 'absolute' maximum value would obviously be when $E(P, Q) = 0$, which means that $r_{i,j} \ln(r_{i,j}) = 0$ for any pair (i, j). Therefore, any cell probability would have to be either 0 or 1 which is impossible if we assume that all marginal probabilities are non-zero. Hence, the maximum value must be less than 1 and there is no clear definition of tables for which it will be achieved. Notice also that this coefficient is *not* an average of θ_1 and θ_2, it is smaller than both of them.

5.1.4 Correspondence analysis

This is a potentially useful multivariate technique that analyses the 'geometric structure' of the relationship between rows and columns in a contingency table in which two categorical variables are cross-tabulated.

A simple direct measure of the relationship between a row category and a column category is the degree to which the intersection, the proportion of the sample with both the row and the column attribute, is greater or less than the product of the column and row marginal proportions. This is often expressed by indexing the actual size of the intersection cell on the product of the two marginal proportions. However, correspondence analysis takes into account information about how the row category interacts with the other column categories and how the column category interacts with the other row categories, and how these interact with each other. These other interactions may reinforce the effect seen in the intersection cell or weaken it.

Correspondence analysis uses aggregated data, in the form of a two-way contingency table, not the individual data items. This works because we are dealing with categorical data where for each cell the row attribute is either present or absent for each sample member, as is the column attribute. The size of the intersection cell and the two marginal totals thus allow a full distribution of the incidence of all four possible combinations of row and column attribute presence or absence to be determined.

From the contingency table aggregate figures a new set of unnamed variables (one less than the lower of the numbers of rows and columns) is postulated such that the first k of these variables will 'explain' the original variables in the best possible way, for any k. The first variable postulated explains the greatest amount of the variation and subsequent variables explain decreasing amounts. Each variable category becomes a point on this set of dimensions that can be graphed.

It is beyond the scope of this book to discuss the mathematics of correspondence analysis (which requires a certain level of mathematical knowledge). Instead, this technique will be illustrated with an example. For technical details and theory see Greenacre [22, 23] and Hoffman and Franke [29].

Correspondence analysis provides a graphic summary in the form of plots that show the relationships between categories of the original variables. The plot shows a selected pair of the *postulated* variables. In practice the first two are normally used as they generally exhibit far more explanatory power than the remainder. The position of each row category and each column category is plotted on the x and y axes of the graph.

The interpretation of the plot is outwardly simple. The origin represents the 'centre of gravity' of the data. Categories plotted further away from the origin are individually more distinctive than those close to it. A category at the origin appears to have no net interaction with other categories.

Items plotted away from the centre in the same direction are taken to show some affinity. Items away from the centre in opposite directions have negative affinities. Items away from the centre in directions at right-angles are taken to have no affinity. As many items, from row and column categories, may be plotted in the single two-dimensional space some distortion is inevitable. Correspondence analysis purports only to give the best possible two-dimensional representation of a more complex multi-dimensional pattern.

Table 5.1. Input for correspondence analysis

Federal vote, first preference	Total	Bank where respondent has a transaction account					
		ANZ	Bank of Melbourne	Common-wealth	National Australia	St. George	Westpac Bank
(unweighted)	40172	5963	2105	16397	6859	3866	5457
(population '000)	11940	1742	689	4993	2130	1165	1578
Australian	40.0%	35.7%	39.4%	44.1%	34.6%	40.0%	37.7%
Labor Party	100	89	98	110	86	100	94
Liberal	31.3%	35.6%	39.7%	28.0%	36.1%	32.2%	33.3%
	100	114	127	90	115	103	106
Australian	5.0%	5.1%	4.7%	4.7%	4.6%	6.2%	4.9%
Democrats	100	100	93	93	91	123	98
Independent/	4.5%	4.9%	3.8%	4.1%	4.6%	4.8%	4.5%
Other	100	107	85	89	101	106	99
National Party	3.3%	3.7%	1.6%	2.8%	5.2%	2.1%	4.3%
	100	113	50	85	159	64	132
Greens	3.1%	3.0%	3.0%	3.2%	2.8%	2.9%	2.4%
	100	97	97	102	89	93	77
One Nation	2.9%	3.0%	0.8%	2.5%	3.2%	3.0%	2.8%
	100	103	27	86	112	102	98

Roy Morgan Single Source Australia, October 1999–September 2000. Filter: electors with a bank account.

The example chosen is taken from a real survey with a large sample. It illustrates the transition from contingency table to correspondence analysis. Table 5.1 shows the voting intention of registered electors who bank with each of Australia's major banks. The figures shown are percentaged on the column totals, and the index figure is a simple measure of how the percentage in any column relates to the row-total percentage. Notice that it is not a *requirement* of correspondence analysis that the data be 'complete'.

Table 5.1 is expressed graphically in correspondence analysis as shown in Figure 5.1.

The associations make immediate sense to anyone familiar with the Australian political scene. The traditionally working-class Labor Party is associated with the traditionally working-class Commonwealth Bank: the stereotype works. The Bank of Melbourne has a negative relationship with One Nation. This is not surprising. Most Bank of Melbourne customers live in Melbourne where support for One Nation is minimal. Other relationships can be explained in part by reference to geography. The National Party's power base is Queensland, which is also National Australia Bank's strongest State. One Nation, also Queensland based, has affinities with National Australia Bank and with Westpac, both of which are relatively strong in that State.

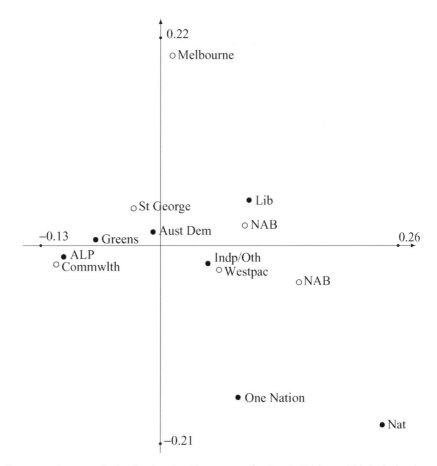

Figure 5.1   Correspondence analysis of voting–banking pattern for data in Table 5.1. This includes the largest banks only.

Having seen this, there are a number of things we must be careful of in using correspondence analysis. It takes into account all the information it is given. This included the indirect relationships between (here) the various banks and between the various parties. This may appear either to strengthen or to weaken the direct relationship.

The axes are unnamed and artificial and the scaling does not represent familiar units. Typically the graphical output is scaled to spread the plotted observations to fit a display space and the scale is adjusted to suit. It is always essential to refer back to the contingency table from which the correspondence analysis derives to see how strong the relationships illustrated really are. In this case Australian Labor Party supporters form 44% of Commonwealth Bank customers where 40% would be considered the norm – hardly a major difference.

In the graphic output the points are plotted with equal weight, and this may draw undue attention to small differences. National Party supporters are only some 5% of National Australia Bank customers (3% norm) and 28% of National Party supporters

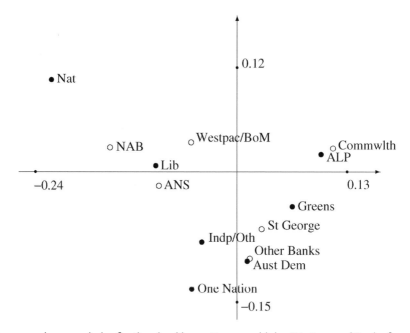

Figure 5.2   Correspondence analysis of voting–banking pattern, combining Westpac and Bank of Melbourne (a Westpac trading name) and combining minor banks into an 'all other banks' category.

use National Australia Bank (18% norm), so the relationship, however statistically significant, is not in practice anywhere near exclusive.

Effect of changing the variables

The selection of data to be included in the analysis can affect the appearance of the plotted results. In the original analysis we used only the largest banks and split off the Bank of Melbourne from Westpac. Bank of Melbourne is in fact a name under which Westpac traded (at the time of this survey) in the State of Victoria, for historical and marketing reasons. If we repeat the analysis, combining Bank of Melbourne with Westpac and including an 'all other banks' category, we obtain a strikingly different visual result, illustrated in Figure 5.2.

Apart from the very obvious reversal of the *x* axis there are some other notable changes. The previous alignment of One Nation with the National Party has been lost, because the influence of the previously separate Bank of Melbourne is no longer felt. The Democrats and the St. George Bank are now appreciably further from the centre. The Democrats and One Nation are now relatively closely aligned. This suggests that however different their political views might be in most respects these two groups may choose their banks in similar ways.

However, instead of combining all the minor banks we could have included them separately in the analysis, and this is illustrated in Figure 5.3. One Nation now loses its distinct position on the edge of the plot and moves into the centre, close to the Liberals and to the combined Westpac/Bank of Melbourne, probably because of the

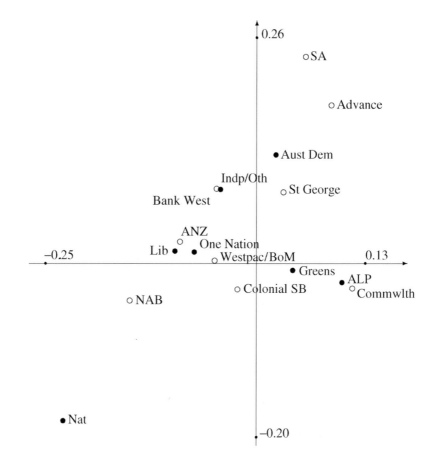

Figure 5.3   Correspondence analysis of voting–banking pattern, combining Westpac and Bank of Melbourne (a Westpac trading name) and plotting minor banks individually.

very varied nature of the relationships between that party and those minor banks clouding the issue.

The selection of the figures to be put into correspondence analysis thus has considerable bearing on the outcome. Although the numbers linking the major banks with the parties were the same all the way through this example, the resulting graphic representation was clearly influenced by the selection of other information included. It would be difficult to say that one selection or arrangement of banks was more appropriate than any other for this example or that one representation was more correct or realistic than any other. 'What you get out of it depends on what you put into it' is a criticism that can be levelled at many types of multivariate analysis and is certainly as true here as anywhere. Where judgement has to be used to select the entities to be represented in the analysis, the result will only be as good as that judgement was appropriate. For this reason caution is required at all times when using correspondence analysis, and particularly so when choices must be made about whether and how the categories of a variable are to be combined for analysis purposes. Where the relationships are weak to start with, the results correspondence analysis delivers will in any case be more liable to fluctuate with minor changes in the input. The only invariable rule is: always refer back to the contingency table from which the correspondence analysis was derived and see whether the pattern displayed makes sense. If it does not, then correspondence analysis is doing you a disservice.

5.2   Multivariate techniques

So far we have considered mainly measures of the relationship between two variables. There are a number of methods of examining the interactions between many variables and using those relationships to reduce the complex picture of inter-relationships to a simpler one. This can (generally) be more readily interpreted and can in turn be used as a means of producing classifications of sample members that may be used in further analysis. It is not the authors' intention to cover multivariate analysis methods: these are already well documented. But it is appropriate to point out that some of the points already made about the simpler univariate and bivariate analyses also apply to multivariate techniques. The availability of low-cost computing facilities and powerful but easily driven software has made multivariate methods readily accessible and their application a relatively trivial exercise, but it becomes all the more important that users should continue to give close attention to the nature of the task they are undertaking and the materials they use.

Multivariate methods fall broadly into two main classes. Those concerned with dependence are generally directed to providing a concise explanation or definition of a specific group of sample members. The aim is to provide as much discriminating power as possible with as few explanatory variables as possible: the concept of 'parsimony' is frequently invoked. Other methods are concerned with interdependence of attributes and aim to provide a more broadly applicable segmentation of sample members or sample-member attributes that can be used to facilitate further analysis. Again the reduction of a large unwieldy number of attributes to a simplified and more readily comprehended set is generally the objective.

Two examples of frequently used multivariate techniques are factor analysis (a term we shall use loosely here to cover a number of closely related methods including principal component analysis) and cluster analysis. The term 'cluster analysis' is potentially confusing in that it is sometimes used to mean the clustering or grouping of attributes or properties of objects though more often to mean the clustering (grouping or classification) of the objects themselves. The term here is used in the latter sense only; grouping of attributes is dealt with under 'factor analysis'.

The remarks about these two families of techniques apply in general also to other multivariate methods, such as canonical analysis, multiple regression, discriminant analysis and even the AID technique described in section 5.4.

Factor
analysis

Factor analysis and similar methods start with a (possibly large) number of input variables forming part of a data set and aim to replace these with a smaller number of variables (factors) collectively accounting for as much as possible of the variation in the input variables. Strictly speaking we actually end up with the same number of factors as we had variables and between them they account for the entire variation, but they are normally presented in descending order of the proportion of the overall variation for which they account and a cut-off point is selected, below which the 'minor' factors are discarded. The proportion of variance explained by the factors retained should ideally be considerably greater than the proportion of factors retained. If we start with 50 variables and retain ten 'major' factors we expect these to explain considerably more than 20% of the variation. If they do not, the value of the factor analysis is questionable.

These techniques generally start off with a correlation matrix. A factor is identified from the presence of a number of variables that show high correlations with each other and low correlations with the remaining variables. They are taken to represent collectively an underlying 'factor' of which the input variables are different expressions. They can therefore for practical purposes be replaced by that single factor.

The use of a correlation matrix means that the variables used have to be numeric. Categorical variables cannot be used except by treating their individual categories as separate (and usually negatively correlated) logical or binary variables.

The data set may be envisaged graphically or geometrically as a multi-dimensional space with each variable representing an axis or dimension. These dimensions are not at right angles and some dimensions are very closely aligned. A factor replaces a 'bundle' of closely aligned dimensions. Strictly speaking all the variables or dimensions contribute to every factor, but the amount of any variable's contribution is determined by its correlation with that factor.

Conversely a variable that does not correlate with anything else will not form a major factor. This brings us to the first question that any researcher should ask on looking at the results of a factor analysis: 'Why does this factor form?' The dimensions forming the data set for such kinds of analysis may have been selected in a number of ways. There may in some cases be objective criteria for determining what kinds of measures are to be used. This is particularly the case with behavioural data, where it may be possible to identify substantially the whole set of possible alternative behaviours, especially where these can be restricted experimentally.

Often, particularly in studies of human populations and those dealing with attitudes and perceptions, measures are semantic and preliminary studies are undertaken to elicit an exhaustive vocabulary used by people to verbalise their perceptions of the subject of the study. A danger of this lies in the very richness of language itself. Often there are many words or expressions that, though conveying subtle differences of meaning, are expressing substantially the same idea. A taste may be described as 'strong', ' full-bodied', 'robust' or 'full-flavoured'. If these are all used as measures in a survey they may exhibit a positive correlation. Respondents are often asked to select from a list those words that apply to the object they are considering, or to position that object on a series of scales or spectra each characterised by two opposing statements or descriptions (semantic differential scales). The verbal stimuli thus presented may not all be terms that would occur spontaneously to each respondent but they will probably be sufficiently familiar and comprehensible to allow all respondents to provide a sensible and considered response. So a respondent may well give very similar responses to the same object on a number of measures.

However, the repetition of the stimulus adds to its importance in forming the factors. A factor built around several such highly correlated measures will rank higher in terms of the percentage of variation explained than one that is largely determined by a single measure. The temptation is, naturally, to judge the importance of factors in proportion to percentage of variation explained, to set great store by factors that appear at the top of the list and to ignore those at the bottom.

It is tempting to argue that, in reducing multiple measures to the backbone of a single factor, the factor analysis method may simply be removing duplication that the researcher has put in. If measures are correlated, are they failing to give a balanced view of the object of the research? In the case of emotive or descriptive dimensions, does correlation indicate a bias on the part of the researcher in the selection of measures? Has the researcher in fact determined the outcome by determining the inputs ('You only get out of it what you put into it')? It is of course very difficult to judge whether the selection of descriptors is either comprehensive or balanced, because we do this within a cultural and linguistic framework that is generally common to researcher and respondents. Languages themselves vary in their treatment of some areas: relative to German, for instance, English is rich in words to describe colours and poor in words to describe sounds. Some languages make distinctions that are not made in others. It is open to question whether the problem is worst when researcher and respondents come from different cultures, or from the same culture, or from two superficially similar cultures, such as English and American.

It must also be remembered that, where respondents are assessing several different objects, their response to each one (as recorded numerically) may be influenced not only by the nature of their perception of it but also by the *strength* of their perception of it, or by their familiarity with it. This may also introduce spurious correlation.

This is not to deny the usefulness of factor analysis as a potential analysis tool. It must simply never be forgotten that it is a technique for dealing with a data set, and that the results it produces can only be as good as the data used. Even if the overall outcome of a factor analysis is suspect at face value, it may well be valuable to look at the differences between factor analysis solutions obtained from different subsets of a sample, or in respect of different objects.

Cluster analysis

Cluster analysis developed principally in the scientific field of numerical taxonomy where it is used to determine, for instance, whether the nature of the diversity within what is treated as a single species is such as to warrant its being treated as two or more species. It involves partitioning a data set into two or more subsets, using two or more variables, so as to maximise the homogeneity of each and the differences between them. While factor analysis seeks to group the measures, cluster analysis seeks to group objects associated with the measures (in surveys usually the respondents, but sometimes the objects being measured). The resulting clusters, often defined using a purposively selected subset of the available variables, are then treated as representing segments of the population to be examined separately and compared.

There are several approaches, with variations: 'bottom-up' or agglomerative clustering, which starts with each object in a 'cluster' of its own and gradually joins them together to form larger clusters; 'top-down' or divisive clustering, which starts typically with a single best splitting of the sample into two groups and then attempts similarly to split one of these, and so on; and non-hierarchical methods which may start with a random or purposive initial allocation of objects to a pre-set number of clusters and then seek to optimise the split by moving objects from one cluster to another.

Measures of similarity or distance

All methods rely on the definition of a means of calculating either the similarity of two objects or the distance between them. Distance or dissimilarity is often viewed as a function of the differences between two objects on individual dimensions in a multi-dimensional hyperspace. A great number of different possible ways of calculating this distance have been put forward, and the choice may be influenced by the nature of the individual measures. Some of these may be able to take any real value, some may be small integers, some may be binary, and of course there may be a mixture of these in any individual exercise. It is customary to standardise at least numerical values, re-expressing each value in terms of the relevant mean and standard deviation, to ensure comparability of scale.

Determining the distance between cases remains the most serious single problem. It is further complicated by the question of what to do when the measures are correlated and the dimensions of the hyperspace are thus not orthogonal. It is worth trying to remove the effect of correlation if possible. One of the tasks of cluster analysis is to find relationships within data that are *not* correlated overall. Perhaps a more insidious problem is that generally each variable is treated as having equal importance. Frequently experience and other knowledge of the subject matter will indicate that certain variables should be given additional weight. The choice of these and the relative weights to be assigned remain almost entirely matters of judgement, though preliminary analyses may give guidance. Practical usefulness of the variables themselves may also give guidance.

If a choice is available it may well be worth trying several likely looking definitions of distance to see whether they produce comparable solutions or configurations of clusters. While any method is likely to produce a division of the data set into clusters it is always advisable to check the robustness of the solution. Primitive methods should not be disdained. Calculating the means or distributions of the original variables for each cluster and visual inspection of these is a simple way of throwing up the salient points of distinction and may also reveal variables that are not contributing to the clustering process. Output from the clustering process should also include some measure of the proportion of the variation explained by the clusters. Hierarchical methods often do this progressively so that the user can gauge which configuration of clusters forms the most useful or usable classification.

With cluster analysis in particular the selection of an appropriate solution depends on the user's judgement and knowledge of the subject matter. Which configuration of clusters is most appropriate may also depend on the purpose for which it is sought. In short there is not necessarily one 'correct' solution. Bottom-up clustering methods usually provide a graphic depiction of at least the latter stages of the clustering process, showing how and at what stage the initial clusters merge, so that (as with classification and regression tree methods) judgement can be used to guide the selection of useful and usable clusters. The more commonly used top-down method usually requires the user to prespecify *how many* clusters are to be identified and then allocates cases to clusters, with the result that several attempts, with differing numbers of clusters, may be required. As the computing resources required for top-down cluster analysis are not great this is not usually a problem.

'Bottom-up' and 'top-down' methods

In bottom-up agglomerative methods, typically at each stage the two existing clusters that are 'closest' are merged to form one cluster. The other clusters remain as they were. The process of merging, or at least its final stages, can thus be mapped so that the relationships can be displayed graphically, usually in the form of a dendrogram. The individual sample members (if space permits) or the last clusters are (usually) shown on the vertical axis and some measure of the variation explained by the clustering is shown on the other axis. It is thus possible to see how and at what point individual clusters merge. This also means that consideration can be given to a very judgemental selection of which groupings, perhaps chosen at different points in the process, rather than just going for the 'last six' clusters. Top-down methods, by contrast, generally require a prespecified number of clusters and optimise the allocation of cases between that number of subsets.

Cluster analysis methods, like those in factor analysis, often require that the data used should be numerical (and preferably normally distributed). In much survey work researchers frequently want to include all kinds of non-numeric data. This presents special problems which are dealt with in section 5.5.

A more general warning is also appropriate here. Data that are likely to be used for any complex multivariate analysis should be scrutinised and considered carefully before use. We must always consider whether the whole data set or any individual variable to be used is suitable for the analysis we have in mind. The same problems of data quality arise as in the case of simple correlation calculations as discussed in section 5.1.1. As multivariate techniques often rely heavily on correlation coefficients we must be mindful of the effects on correlation of the grouping of data values, especially if they are grouped to the point of being binary.

Above all, the fact that in general so much of the data in surveys of human populations is of a non-factual and non-verifiable nature should make any researcher cautious about interpreting it at its face value. In assessing the results of simple, conventional 'head-counting' analysis we naturally make allowance for factors that may influence the ways in which respondents react to questions, from those of an outwardly factual nature to those 'softer' measures where familiarity with the subject matter, social pressure and 'political correctness', or aspects of the interview process may be expected to produce varying forms of distortion. It is much more important to be aware of these possible distortions in multivariate work. There is an ever-present danger that the use of sophisticated techniques with less sophisticated data may lead to an uncritical acceptance of results that may have been strongly, but not obviously, influenced by artefacts of the data collection process. Advanced statistical techniques require data of high or at least consistent 'mechanical' quality, and because of its nature much sample survey data cannot live up to this standard.

Multivariate techniques certainly have their place in the analysis of sample survey data, but their use requires an awareness of the limitations imposed by the data being analysed. We should first examine carefully any data to be used in a multivariate analysis using simple techniques. Only when we are satisfied that we understand and can allow for any effect that the nature of the data is likely to impose on the outcome should we proceed with the more complex analyses.

5.3   Regression analysis for weighted data

Regression analysis attempts to establish a relationship between a numerical variable (called the *dependent* variable) and one or more *explanatory* numerical variables (also called *independent* or *predictor* variables). The relationship is presumed to be of a known functional type (e.g. linear) and the corresponding function is called the *regression function*. The function parameters are chosen to minimise the 'prediction error', i.e. the discrepancy between predicted values of the dependent variable given by the regression function and actual values. Regression analysis is one of the most widely used statistical techniques and is covered in almost all statistical textbooks.

We assume that the reader is familiar with standard regression methods and our intention here is to discuss the appropriate use of regression for weighted data. It is unfortunate that this topic is generally ignored (like weighting itself) in statistical literature given that weighted and unweighted data may produce noticeably different regression functions.

Suppose that there is a sample of n respondents with k predictor variables $x^{(1)}, \ldots, x^{(k)}$ and also with a dependent variable y. A general regression model can be written as

$$y = g\left(x^{(1)}, \ldots, x^{(k)}\right) + \epsilon,$$

where g is a regression function and ϵ is an *error* term. It is usually assumed that the error is symmetric and follows a normal distribution. Regression functions typically belong to a specified class of functions (e.g. all linear functions or all quadratic functions).

The standard approach to choosing the 'best' regression function (from the specified class of functions) is to minimise the sum of squared errors computed across all respondents in the sample. For an unweighted sample, the sum of squared errors is

$$D = \sum_{i=1}^{n} \left(y_i - g\left(x_i^{(1)}, \ldots, x_i^{(k)}\right)\right)^2, \tag{5.3}$$

where y_i is the value of dependent variable for respondent i and $x_i^{(l)}$ is the value of lth predictor variable for respondent i ($l = 1, \ldots, k$).

The main point of this section is that in the case of a weighted sample the sum of squared errors should be computed as

$$D = \sum_{i=1}^{n} w_i \left(y_i - g\left(x_i^{(1)}, \ldots, x_i^{(k)}\right)\right)^2, \tag{5.4}$$

where w_i is the weight of respondent i. In other words, respondents' 'errors' are weighted in the same way as any other estimate from a weighted sample.

The suggested formula may seem obvious and not worth paying attention to but unfortunately the inappropriate formula (5.3) is often applied in practice for weighted samples. Some existing statistical software packages are not helpful either, with no 'weighted regression' option being available. Given the simplicity of implementation this is regrettable. Researchers, ignorant of the weighting process, have been known simply to multiply all the values of the dependent and independent variables by the respective weights to try to fudge their way round it!

It is worthwhile to illustrate the general formula (5.4) with an example. Consider, for instance, a very simple situation when there is only one predictor variable x and the regression model is linear. The regression function g can then be written as $g(x) = ax + b$, where a and b are two parameters. Therefore, the sum of squared errors D_{lin} which has to be minimised is simply

$$D_{\text{lin}} = \sum_{i=1}^{n} w_i(y_i - (ax_i + b))^2.$$

To find out which values of parameters a and b minimise this function, the same mathematical techniques as in the unweighted case can be used: function D_{lin} should be differentiated by a and b separately and the partial derivatives should be equated to zero. These calculations will result in the following formulae for parameters a and b:

$$a = \frac{\overline{xy} - \bar{x} \cdot \bar{y}}{\overline{x^2} - \bar{x}^2}, \qquad b = \bar{y} - a \cdot \bar{x},$$

where

$$\bar{x} = \frac{\sum_{i=1}^{n} w_i x_i}{\sum_{i=1}^{n} w_i}, \quad \bar{y} = \frac{\sum_{i=1}^{n} w_i y_i}{\sum_{i=1}^{n} w_i}, \quad \overline{x^2} = \frac{\sum_{i=1}^{n} w_i x_i^2}{\sum_{i=1}^{n} w_i}, \quad \overline{xy} = \frac{\sum_{i=1}^{n} w_i x_i y_i}{\sum_{i=1}^{n} w_i}.$$

Therefore, in this example the formulae obtained are similar to the corresponding formulae for the unweighted case with the only difference being that all averages are weighted.

Notice that the scaling of the weights has no effect. In equation (5.4) the value of D is affected by the mean weight but this does not affect the *relative* values from different regression functions g. In the formulae above, the weights appear in both numerator and denominator.

Quality of
regression

It is also customary to assess the quality of a regression model by computing the *coefficient of determination R* as well as the *adjusted* coefficient of determination R_{adjusted}. Both coefficients are in the range from 0 to 1 and can be interpreted as a percentage of variation of the dependent variable explained by the regression model. The higher the value, the greater is the percentage of variation explained.

Again, both coefficients are affected by weighting and their 'correct' formulae for a weighted sample are the following:

$$R^2 = 1 - \frac{\sum_{i=1}^{n} w_i \left(y_i - g\left(x_i^{(1)}, \ldots, x_i^{(k)}\right)\right)^2}{\sum_{i=1}^{n} w_i (y_i - \bar{y})^2}$$

and

$$R_{\text{adjusted}}^2 = 1 - \frac{n-1}{n-p} \frac{\sum_{i=1}^{n} w_i \left(y_i - g\left(x_i^{(1)}, \ldots, x_i^{(k)}\right)\right)^2}{\sum_{i=1}^{n} w_i (y_i - \bar{y})^2},$$

where p is the number of parameters in the regression model.

The coefficient R measures the 'absolute quality' of the model and will always increase when the number of regression parameters is increased. The adjusted coefficient R_{adjusted}, however, can also decrease if more parameters are added to the model without any improvement in quality. Where the sample size n is very large relative to p, of course the difference between the unadjusted and adjusted coefficients will be small anyway.

The main weakness of regression models is the assumption that the relationship between the dependent variable and predictor variables has a fixed type. In particular, the error term may not be symmetric or may not have a normal distribution. It is therefore crucial to investigate first whether the model assumptions are reasonable and what are the reasons that a particular relationship type should be good enough to approximate the dependent variable.

If the matter being investigated were relevant to only a subset of the population we would not hesitate to perform the regression analysis only among the corresponding subset of the sample to avoid dilution or contamination from data from outside the area of interest. We should therefore also consider carefully the question of whether we are right to treat the sample as representing a single population or whether we should consider partitioning the sample into two or more disjoint subsamples to see if there are any significant differences in the relationships between the dependent and predictor variables. Running separate regressions for each may yield different solutions which both draw attention to differences between the subsamples and give a clearer picture of the relationships within each.

Choice of the variable(s) for partitioning is probably a matter of background knowledge and common sense, though some trial-and-error experimentation may be in order. For instance in a survey of perceptions of different kinds of car, different patterns of regression might be found for groups who are: drivers of cars bought new or used; low-mileage or high-mileage drivers; those who use cars for work or only for family and recreational activities; or the segments identified by a cluster analysis.

5.4   Classification and regression trees

Classification and regression tree (C&RT) analysis is a term used to describe a family of closely related techniques for exploring and analysing the way in which multiple variables interact and contribute to the explanation of a nominated 'outcome' or dependent variable. The distinction between 'classification' and 'regression' trees hinges on whether the dependent variable is categorical and binary (e.g. membership or otherwise of some defined category) or can assume any value or one of a number of discrete values.

C&RT techniques are applied to construct a 'predictive' model for a dependent variable and a set of predictor variables. In the commonly used 'classification tree' techniques, the dependent variable is assumed to be binary (although it is possible to generalise the procedure for real-valued variables) while predictor variables can be either numerical or categorical. The use of a binary dependent variable may also be expressed as choosing a 'target group' and its complement. The method is somewhat similar to the regression technique but the main difference is that there are no prior assumptions about the distributions of the predictor variables or the form of relationship between them, and it can be much easier to incorporate unordered categorical variables. The principles and theory of classification and regression trees were developed largely by Breiman *et al.* [7]. The term 'tree' refers to the process by which an original single mass of data divides progressively into smaller and smaller 'branches' ending in indivisible 'leaves'.

In survey research C&RT techniques appear to be used primarily for the purpose of obtaining the most efficient and useful definition or description of a specified subset of the sample (and of the population it represents). Other uses include the formulation of decision rules in areas such as taxonomy or clinical diagnosis.

We shall illustrate the use of such techniques through the simple and long-established technique known as automatic interaction detection (AID) or chi-square automatic interaction detection (CHAID). Other, more elaborate, C&RT methods provide more sophisticated features and other refinements, but we are concerned here with illustrating the basic principles.

The actual AID algorithm is the following: assume that there is a 'dependent' binary variable and a set of 'independent' or 'predictor' or 'candidate' variables. The cases in the data set are progressively divided into smaller and smaller subsets using a criterion based on the predictor variables, most usually chi-square. The total sample is first split into two subsamples that are as different as possible in terms of the incidence of the 'target group'. All possible partitionings are considered, across all values of all independent variables, but using only one variable at a time. The partitioning that yields the highest value of chi-square is selected. Each of these two subsamples is again split according to the highest chi-square value. The procedure is continued so that at each stage we have a partitioning of the original sample into 'cells', or subsamples, with each respondent belonging to one and only one cell. The procedure will stop when certain predetermined conditions are satisfied ('stopping rules'), for instance, when cells become too small or the chi-square value becomes too small. The user generally has at least some control over when to stop splitting, generally by prespecifying the minimum acceptable value of chi-square, though the rule of thumb of a minimum of five cases per cell in chi-square tests is often applied automatically in addition.

Visual presentation

The result is typically presented as a tree diagram (dendrogram) showing the evolution of the splitting process, with the cells resulting from each split being ordered so that the one with the higher incidence of one of the categories of the dependent variable (or the 'target group') is consistently on the right or the left, or above. The points at which the sample or subsample is divided are called 'nodes' and (to continue the arboreal analogy) the final cells that are not to be further split are sometimes called 'leaves'. One of the attractions of this method of presentation, and indeed of the whole C&RT family of techniques, is its transparency and the ease with which its results can be understood by the non-technical user. Where excessive detail is given, the tree can be pruned judgementally to remove unfruitful detail.

Selection of stopping rules can affect the final output considerably, and they should be judiciously selected. Relatively lax rules with a large data set can produce a large volume of output including much detail that appears contradictory, counter-intuitive or meaningless. In particular, as cell sizes become small there is the danger of 'over-fitting' the model, incorporating relationships that occur by chance only in the data set under consideration but that would not appear in any other. On the other hand, too rigid a set of rules may prevent useful detail from emerging. It may be worth running an AID analysis several times with different stopping rules to see how these affect the output. As so often in survey work, the usability, the applicability of the result is what matters (given adequate assurance of validity).

When used in place of a regression, the proportions of the dependent variable in the final cell distribution can then be used as predicted values for all respondents. Therefore, all respondents from the same cell will get the same predicted value – the incidence proportion of the target group in that cell. The final cells can also be analysed by the values of independent variables to see which population groups they define.

Ordered and unordered variables

When considering all possible splittings, different approaches are recommended for unordered categorical variables on the one hand and ordered categorical and numerical variables on the other. A numeric or ordered variable that has only two values or categories (or is reduced to two by the definition of the analysis subsample) should be treated as an unordered categorical variable.

If this is an unordered categorical variable, there are two alternative approaches. The first is to take whichever partitioning into one category and the rest produces the highest chi-square value. For a variable with k categories there are thus k possible partitionings. As there is nothing to stop a variable being re-used at a later stage, the process may be repeated later to identify the one category among those not yet split off that produces the highest chi-square value at that stage. The other method selects whatever partitioning into two subsets of categories will produce the highest chi-square value, irrespective of the number of categories in each. A variable with k categories would thus have $2^{k-1} - 1$ possible partitionings.

The first method has the advantage that it will allow a multiple-choice variable to be treated properly, as a series of binary variables, with each being considered independently of the others. It is therefore preferable for the AID algorithm to be able to recognise and distinguish between variables that are to be treated as ordered and non-ordered.

Consideration should also be given to whether judgemental groupings of categories of unordered variables should also be included as independent variables. If 'make of car driven' is an independent variable it may be valuable also to include in the analysis such summary groupings as 'locally made/imported', 'American/European/Asian', 'luxury/average/cheap'. Such groupings will in no way hinder consideration of individual makes but may allow the real distinguishing attributes to emerge more clearly in the final picture.

However, if this variable is numerical or the categorical values are naturally ordered, with, say, four values $\{1, 2, 3, 4\}$, the following splittings are recommended: value $\{1\}$ versus values $\{2, 3, 4\}$, values $\{1, 2\}$ versus values $\{3, 4\}$ and values $\{1, 2, 3\}$ versus value $\{4\}$. This is done to keep the maximum 'similarity' of respondents in each subcell. All these groupings involve *one* division so that the two extreme categories always remain in different subcells. However, it may be legitimate to allow a partitioning into two cells but with two division points such that one cell consists of one or more adjacent values *not* including an extreme value and the other cell contains all the values outside this 'central' range, such as value $\{2\}$ versus values $\{1, 3, 4\}$, or values $\{2, 3\}$ versus values $\{1, 4\}$. This could occur in a case such as the use of 'age' as a predictor of income, where the middle age categories may contain the highest incidence of high-income respondents, and where limiting the partitioning to a single division could fail to reveal the nature and predictive power of the age variable.

An alternative approach where a non-linear relationship is found is to allow a partitioning into three cells, with two division points.

The approach also copes well with missing respondents (with respect to the dependent variable): they are distributed into the same cells though the splitting 'decisions' are made only on the basis of respondents with data. Therefore, the same value (the incidence proportion of the target group in that cell) will be allocated to the missing respondents within the corresponding cell, in the final cell distribution. Alternatively, proportions for respondents with data could be 'adjusted' to satisfy certain conditions, before being allocated to missing respondents. In practice we are frequently interested in one or other of the binary categories (the 'target group') and in membership or non-membership of that group rather than comparing the two binary categories with each other, so that the inclusion of any missing-data respondents in one of the groups may cause no problems. For independent variables, however, there should ideally not be any missing respondents (or they should be assigned values prior to the procedure). Some systems allow surrogate variables to be used in such cases, these possibly being identified using AID itself.

If the number of independent variables is large and the splitting is done many times with many cells being small, it may be preferable to use unweighted rather than weighted data. The reason is that weighting is usually done for the original sample as a whole (and maybe for a few subsamples) and, of course, the sum of weights could vary considerably about the 'true' value for many small subsamples. Therefore it may introduce more randomness in small subsamples.

The prediction results from this method are often better than regression results and the real advantage of AID is that there are no prior assumptions (whether linear or log-linear or any other) whatsoever about the relationship between the dependent and independent variables.

The problems with the AID procedure will start when the chi-square values become small so that there will be a much greater random element in the splittings. If the splitting process still has to be continued (e.g. if we have not revealed a required level of information content), it might be better to use another criterion for splittings rather than the chi-square test.

Figure 5.4 shows an Australian example of the AID procedure. The 'target group' in this case is 'holders of American Express cards', 2.7% of the adult population. Sex, age, socio-economic quintile, education and marital status have been used as independent variables. Marital status and sex are unordered categorical variables, the others are ordered. A relatively strict test for splitting a cell is applied, with a chi-square value of at least 10.83 (equivalent to $p < 0.001$ with 1 d.f.) required. Such a strict test can be applied here because of the large sample size (over 50 000). The 'persons' column shows in fact the weighted estimate of the number of persons in the population in thousands. The '% targ' column shows the incidence of the target group within this.

The first split uses socio-economic status. Of all possible valid partitions using any *one* of the candidate variables, separating the top socio-economic quintile from the rest gives the highest value of chi-square. 9.18% of the top group are AmEx holders compared with 1.1% in the remaining groups. This group, 20% of the population, contains 68% of AmEx card-holders.

This group can be further split to find a higher incidence of AmEx holders. Removing respondents aged under 25 gives us a slightly smaller group with 9.98% incidence. The best partitioning of this smaller group is by sex: 12.03% of the men have an AmEx card, but only 7.02% of the women do. And further partitioning the men by excluding the under-35 age group pushes the incidence up to 13.26% (notice that a variable can be used at more than one level). We have now identified a group (top-quintile men aged 35+) who are 8% of the population but 40% of AmEx holders.

It is possible to split this once more to find a very small subgroup within this (the less well educated) who have a higher incidence, but this group is very small and only emerges here because of the possibilities created by the very large sample size. This group, which appears to be out of line with the emerging stereotype, may be a result of 'over-fitting', but it could also be a small but valid niche segment of this market. The same could be said for the even smaller group of affluent young men planning to

```
ROY MORGAN SINGLE SOURCE AUSTRALIA: A.I.D. OCT 1999 - SEP 2000
Significance level: p<0.001
Variables: SEX, AGE (summary), SOCIO-ECONOMIC SCALE, EDUCATION, MARITAL STATUS

              SECTION OR SUB-SECTION OF POPULATION      PERSONS    % TARG
                 (PRIMARY...INTERMED) [education]          29      27.91%
                 |
              NOT(AGE-14-17...AGE-25-34) [age]           1249      13.26%
              | |
              |  NOT(PRIMARY...INTERMED) [education]     1220      12.91%
              |
           NOT(WOMEN) [sex]                              1653      12.03%
           | |
           | |  (PLAN-MARRY) [marriage]                     9      29.02%
           | | |
           |  (AGE-14-17...AGE-25-34) [age]               404       8.25%
           |    |
           |   NOT(PLAN-MARRY) [marriage]                 395       7.76%
           |
         (AGE-25-34...AGE-50-PLUS) [age]                 2800       9.98%
         | |
         |  (WOMEN) [sex]                                1147       7.02%
         |
      NOT(C-QUINTILE...FG-QUINTILE) [quintile]           3078       9.18%
      | |
      |  NOT(AGE-25-34...AGE-50-PLUS) [age]               278       1.09%
      |
   TOTAL POPULATION                                     15382       2.71%
      |
      |    (AGE-50-PLUS...AGE-65-PLUS) [age]              773       5.07%
      |      |
      |   (AB-QUINTILE + C-QUINTILE) [quintile]          3077       2.79%
      | | |
      | | |  (AGE-25-34 + AGE-35-49) [age]               1684       2.68%
      | | | |
      | |  NOT(AGE-50-PLUS...AGE-65-PLUS) [age]          2304       2.02%
      | |    |
      | |   NOT(AGE-25-34 + AGE-35-49) [age]              620       0.23%
      | |
      (C-QUINTILE...FG-QUINTILE) [quintile]             12304       1.10%
         |
         |      NOT(AGE-50-PLUS...AGE-65-PLUS) [age]     2372       1.04%
         |        |
         |     NOT(SINGLE) [marriage]                    4362       0.92%
         |     | |
         |     |  (AGE-50-PLUS...AGE-65-PLUS) [age]      1990       0.78%
         |     |
         |   (AB-QUINTILE...E-QUINTILE) [quintile]       6152       0.70%
         |   | |
         |   | |  (AGE-50-PLUS + AGE-50-64) [age]          68       0.76%
         |   | | |
         |   |  (SINGLE) [marriage]                      1790       0.15%
         |   |    |
         |   |   NOT(AGE-50-PLUS + AGE-50-64) [age]      1722       0.13%
         |   |
         NOT(AB-QUINTILE + C-QUINTILE) [quintile]        9227       0.53%
            |
            |  (AGE-18-24) [age]                          204       0.96%
            | |
            NOT(AB-QUINTILE...E-QUINTILE) [quintile]     3075       0.20%
               |
               NOT(AGE-18-24) [age]                      2870       0.14%
```

Figure 5.4   Automatic interaction detection (AID) procedure. The target group is 'holders of American Express cards'.

get married. Knowledge of the market and common sense are at least as important as statistical expertise in interpreting such groupings.

If we had relaxed the splitting criterion for chi-square to, say, $p < 0.05$ ($\chi^2 = 3.84$), the tree would have been more complex with many more branchings, though it is doubtful whether it would have yielded much more information in this case. In any sample it is possible that there may be many small subsets with a high incidence of the target group, but whether these are sufficiently large in the real world to warrant attention is another matter.

If our sample had been relatively small, however, it would probably have been necessary to use a less stringent criterion to produce a reasonable number of final nodes. In any AID analysis it may be helpful to run with two or more alternative splitting criteria to see which provides the most helpful and usable result.

In the present simple example a single subset stood out in terms of a single combination of attributes. It is also possible that AID could have revealed one or more secondary subsets with different combinations of attributes, and also with a high incidence of the target group. It is always worth checking all the branches of the tree for nodes where the incidence of the target group may be worthy of further consideration.

Information content

It can be useful to have a measure of the 'power' of AID in a specific case. It may help to know how much more information we have obtained by breaking down the sample into its multiple final nodes. This is often described as 'the proportion (or percentage) of uncertainty explained'. There are a number of measures that could be used for this, of which we shall consider two. In each case we shall use p to denote the overall incidence of the target group, m for the number of final nodes, p_i for the incidence of the target group in node i and f_i the proportion of the sample in node i ($\sum f_i = 1.0$). All proportions are weighted if appropriate.

The increased information content can be assessed by using a measure of the reduction in entropy, the amount of disorder or randomness in a system, as the tree branches up to the point where it cannot branch further. Comparing the total entropy at this point with the entropy as calculated originally for the undifferentiated sample is a way of doing this. Using Shannon's measure of information content $-p \ln p$ the entropy of the undifferentiated system is given by this simple formula. The entropy of the distribution of the sample across m final nodes is given by

$$-\sum_{i=1}^{m} f_i [p_i \ln p_i + (1 - p_i) \ln(1 - p_i)].$$

The reduction in entropy compared with the undifferentiated state is the measure of improvement.

The variance of the target group proportion may be calculated for the total sample ($p(1 - p)$) and then after the split into the final nodes.

$$\sum_{i=1}^{m} f_i p_i (1 - p_i)$$

is the variance of the proportion p around the node values and the reduction in variance may be regarded as the measure of improvement.

This can be thought of in another more graphic way. If we were to try to 'identify' members and non-members of the target group by selecting a proportion p of respondents at random from the undifferentiated sample we would correctly classify p^2 of them as members. We would similarly correctly classify $(1-p)^2$ of them as non-members. We would then have $p(1-p)$ of the sample incorrectly classified as members of the target group. If we do the same within each of the final nodes the total proportion incorrectly assigned to the target group will now be

$$\sum_{i=1}^{m} f_i p_i (1-p_i)$$

(as above) and the reduction in misallocations indicates the degree of improvement.

Of course, the real value of an AID analysis will lie in whether the nodes it identifies as containing the highest incidence of the target group are big enough to be usable (readily identifiable in the general population) and whether the incidence of the target group within these nodes is sufficiently higher than the overall average to make them worth pursuing. Again it comes back to the need to consider the actionability of the results before the statistical niceties.

5.5 Cluster analysis for categorical variables

The problem of cluster analysis (or segmentation) arises in many practical situations. For a given sample of respondents and a given set of variables of interest, the problem is to group respondents into clusters (or segments) in such a way that respondents in the same cluster have a similar profile (with respect to the variables of interest) while there is a significant difference between profiles of different clusters.

The standard statistical techniques of cluster analysis are based on the assumption that the variables of interest are numerical, i.e. values of each variable can be directly represented by numbers. For instance, analysis of variance is often used, the object being to minimise the variance within clusters and maximise the variance between clusters. Another well known method is distance analysis where the distance is defined simply as the absolute difference between values.

However, 'real-life' variables are very often categorical, that is, their values cannot be represented by numbers. For instance, if a respondent is asked to choose which of five brands of coffee he or she prefers, it would be a mistake to treat the five brands simply as numbers from 1 to 5 because the 'difference' between brands 1 and 2 is not smaller than the 'difference' between brands 1 and 5. The standard recommendation for categorical variables is to split them into several binary variables and consider these binary variables as numerical. The problem with that recommendation is that binary variables from different categorical variables may not be directly compatible with each other. It can also create a large number of binary variables which can make the description of cluster profiles overly complex whatever technique is used. Making them separate variables may at the same time inflate their collective importance relative to other variables in forming the clusters. These binary variables will also be negatively correlated which may have some adverse effect.

Conventional cluster analysis methods or software often require or assume numerical variables and more-or-less normal distribution of values. To accommodate the rag-bag of different question types and data forms that researchers regularly want to use as input, a different approach is necessary.

Below we suggest two methods of cluster analysis which can deal directly with categorical variables without 'converting' them into binary variables.

The first method (which we developed in conjunction with He Zhisong, our colleague at Roy Morgan Research) is based on the Euclidean distance for categorical variables. Instead of dealing with individual values it deals with distributions of frequencies of values.

Assume that there is a categorical variable with k categories. The new distance can be defined between any two subsets of respondents. Suppose that the variable's distribution is $p_1, \ldots, p_k$ in the first subset and $q_1, \ldots, q_k$ in the second subset. In other words, p_i and q_i are the proportions of respondents from the first and second subsets who have value i of the given variable. The distance d between the two subsets is defined as

$$d^2 = \sum_{i=1}^{k} (p_i - q_i)^2. \tag{5.5}$$

In particular, when one of the subsets has just one respondent (which will be the case for the cluster analysis algorithm because it requires either a distance between two respondents or a distance between a respondent and a cluster), one of the probabilities for that subset will be 1.0 while all others will be zero. Assume, for instance, that the second subset consists of one respondent with value l for the variable of interest. Then obviously $q_l = 1$ and $q_i = 0$ for $i \neq l$ so that the distance becomes

$$d^2 = \sum_{i \neq l} p_i^2 + (p_l - 1)^2 = \sum_{i=1}^{k} p_i^2 - 2p_l + 1. \tag{5.6}$$

If there are several variables the distances should be calculated for all of them and then added together. It is also possible to take into account relative importance of the variables by assigning weights to the variables (not to be confused with the weights assigned to respondents). If, for instance, the first variable is deemed to be twice as important as other variables it may have a weight of 2.0 while all other variables would have a weight of 1.0. In general, if there are m variables with weights $s_1, \ldots, s_m$, the total distance d between the two subsets is computed as

$$d = s_1 d_1 + \cdots + s_m d_m, \tag{5.7}$$

where d_j is the distance with respect to variable j. Note that the distances d_j from equation (5.5) are themselves sums of squares, so that d here is the conventional Euclidean distance and not the Manhattan distance.

The algorithm itself is similar to the well known K-means algorithm with the 'standard' distance replaced by the distance from equations (5.5)–(5.7). Denote by n

the required number of clusters – this number should be specified in advance. The algorithm has two steps.

- Step 1: n initial clusters are generated.
- Step 2: clusters are 'improved' using iteration.

Generating
the clusters

There are several possible ways to generate initial clusters. Below we suggest three approaches which we have actually tested.

The standard K-means approach to generating initial clusters is to find n respondents in the sample such that the shortest distance (according to equations (5.5)–(5.7)) between any two of these n respondents is the maximum possible. In other words, those n respondents are as far 'apart' from each other as is possible. An alternative approach could be to maximise the sum of distances between the n respondents. Once the n respondents have been identified, the initial clusters are constructed by 'attaching' *each* other respondent in the sample to the closest of these initial n respondents.

Another approach would be to run the AID procedure (see section 5.4) until n 'cells' are obtained – that is, the sample should be split $n - 1$ times according to the AID algorithm. The n cells could then be used as very reasonable initial clusters, defined by simple decision rules.

The main step of the algorithm (Step 2) is implemented iteratively. At the beginning of each iteration, the distance is calculated between each respondent and each current cluster using formula (5.6). This is done for each variable separately. Next, for each variable the distances are normalised – we have found that it improves the results – by calculating the current maximum and minimum distances d_{max} and d_{min} and replacing each distance d by the normalised distance $(d - d_{min})/(d_{max} - d_{min})$. The normalised distances for all variables are then added together according to formula (5.7).

Therefore, for each respondent there will be n distances between the respondent and each of the n clusters. The closest cluster is then chosen based on those distances and the respondent is moved to that cluster (if not already a member of it). Once each respondent has been placed in the closest cluster, the current iteration is completed. The cluster distributions are then updated and the procedure is repeated again.

The iterations will continue until there are no changes in cluster memberships or changes are 'trivial' (e.g very few respondents are moved or the change in cluster distributions is very small etc.). The clusters after the last iteration will be taken as the final ones.

The proposed distance method has been tested for several 'real-life' projects and has produced distinctive clusters. It is also an interesting observation that the method seems to be stable in the sense that very often the final clusters are the same independently of how the initial clusters are constructed. The method does not take much time to run and is therefore good to program.

A further question to consider for the distance method is how to take into account that some variables may be 'continuous', i.e. their values may have a 'natural' order and may represent a division of a numeric quantity into segments or ranges. For a continuous variable, even though values are still grouped into categories, the difference between two categories would not be constant but would depend on how 'far apart' the two categories are in the order of values. Therefore, it may be desirable to adjust the distance formula for continuous variables so that it takes into account the relationship between values.

Mixing categorical and 'continuous' variables	The main problem is how to mix categorical and continuous variables together because the distance for categorical variables should still be computed according to formulae (5.5)–(5.6). In other words, the total distance will be added across all variables and some of them may be categorical while some may be continuous. Hence, any modification of the distance should not create a bias toward categorical or continuous variables.

One way to modify the distance for continuous variables is to introduce coefficients in front of proportions in formula (5.6). (Formula (5.5) is not really needed because one of the subsets always consists of one respondent in the cluster analysis algorithm.) The coefficients could be proportional, for instance, to $|i - l|$ (in the same notation as in (5.6)) so that proportions p_i which are 'far' from l would get a greater coefficient than proportions which are 'close' to l. However, to preserve a balance with the unadjusted formula the average coefficient should be equal to 1. To achieve this, we need to calculate the mean among $k - 1$ numbers $|i - l|, i = 1, \ldots, k, i \neq l$. Denote this mean by $a_{k,l}$ (it will depend on k and l). Therefore, the modified distance for a continuous variable will be the following

$$d^2 = \sum_{i \neq l} \frac{|i - l|}{a_{k,l}} p_i^2 + (p_l - 1)^2, \tag{5.8}$$

where all notation is the same as in equation (5.6) (and the ps are weighted if appropriate).

Entropy and disorder	The second method of cluster analysis does not use distance but is based on the concept of entropy (see section 5.1.3 for the definition of entropy). Given that entropy is a measure of disorder, the idea is to reduce it as much as possible. This method could be helpful if the goal is to obtain 'extreme' clusters, i.e. to identify clusters as 'different' from each other as possible: the minimum value of entropy is obviously zero and this would happen if the distribution of each variable in each cluster consisted of only 0s and 1s.

As in the distance method, n initial clusters are first constructed and then 'improved' iteratively. For each iteration, the objective is to produce the biggest possible decrease in entropy that can be achieved by moving one respondent from his or her present cluster to another one. This respondent is then reassigned to the new cluster which completes the iteration. Cluster distributions are recalculated and the procedure is repeated until there is no decrease in entropy or the decrease is below some predetermined level.

The following formula is helpful to calculate the change in entropy when a respondent is moved from one cluster to another. Assume for simplicity that there is just one variable with k values and that a respondent with a weight of w has a value of

l of that variable and is moved from one cluster to another. Denote by $(U_1, \ldots, U_k)$ and $(V_1, \ldots, V_k)$ the weighted frequency distributions of the variable in the first and second clusters, respectively, before the chosen respondent is moved. In other words, U_j and V_j are the sums of weights of respondents in the first and second clusters with value j of the variable. Let $U = U_1 + \cdots + U_k$ and $V = V_1 + \cdots + V_k$ be the total sums of weights of respondents in the first and second clusters respectively. Also denote by E_{old} and E_{new} the total entropy (across all clusters) before and after the respondent is moved from the first cluster to the second. Then the change in entropy can be calculated as

$$W_0(E_{\text{old}} - E_{\text{new}}) = f_w(U) - f_w(U_l) - [f_w(V + w) - f_w(V_l + w)], \qquad (5.9)$$

where W_0 is the total sum of weights of respondents in the sample and the function f_w is defined as

$$f_w(x) = x \ln(x) - (x - w) \ln(x - w).$$

See Appendix G for a proof of this formula.

The entropy method can be slow where large sample sizes are used because entropy is updated each time a respondent is moved. But it may well be possible to speed up calculations if necessary, for instance by recalculating the entropy only after a number of respondents have been moved. As mentioned above, this entropy method tends to produce more 'extreme' clusters with some variable proportions being close to 0 or 1 and this may be preferable in some situations. It may for instance allow the clusters to be approximated by decision rules based on the responses to a limited number of questions, thus allowing the segmentation to be applied in later surveys.

In general, final clusters from the entropy method, whether 'extreme' or not, tend to be quite different from final clusters produced by the distance method (the assumption here is that the same variables are used).

Assessing the 'goodness' of a solution

How are we to assess the 'goodness' of clusters? Is there some single indicator that can tell us when we have achieved the best possible outcome? Unfortunately, there is no simple answer to this question. The main criterion is the practical 'utility' of clusters. Do they make sense and confirm or support what we already know? Do they suggest a new but cogent view of the population? Do they increase or extend our knowledge? Can they be applied to throw increased light on the rest of the survey information? These are obviously matters of judgement, based on prior knowledge, but judgement that we as researchers are expected to exercise and knowledge that as researchers we ought to have. The judgement used in interpreting the solutions is as important as the judgement exercised over what variables to include.

Nor is there any reliable criterion for determining the optimum number of clusters. The general guidance we can give is that they should be useful. A larger number may mean that no segment of adequate size emerges; alternatively it may identify a specific niche opportunity. A small number may mean that none of them is adequately distinct. The only reliable plan is to try a range of different numbers of clusters. The sample size may of course set an upper limit to what can be used in practice.

The relationships between solutions of different numbers of clusters should be examined where possible. For instance, examination of a six-cluster and then a five-cluster allocation using the same algorithm and the same data could reveal that one or two clusters had remained substantially stable but that some had fragmented and their members spread across several of the new clusters. Cross-tabulating cluster memberships between several solutions with different numbers of clusters may reveal which configurations of attributes yield the more stable clusters.

Another thing that must be considered is the cluster sizes. The algorithms presented above do not guarantee by themselves that each cluster will have a 'reasonable' size. It may happen that respondents do not adhere readily to a particular cluster and 'move away' from it so that the cluster will be too small at the final iteration. (This may also result in some other clusters having too many respondents.) Some clusters may even become empty especially if the requested number of clusters is too large relative to the number of variables and their values. An obvious way to constrain cluster sizes is to force respondents out of large clusters or into small clusters until each cluster satisfies predefined size restrictions. The movement should be done in the gentlest possible way, i.e. with the minimum 'deterioration' in distance or entropy. But this procedure clearly disturbs the balance between clusters achieved after the final iteration and should be used only when really necessary. The fact that some clusters may be too small or too large should serve as a warning that perhaps too many clusters were requested or that some variables should be omitted, modified or replaced.

However, there are mathematical measures that could also be helpful in cluster evaluation. One measure is again based on entropy and it is the 'percentage of uncertainty explained'. First, the 'initial' entropy is calculated in the original sample before cluster analysis and then the 'final' entropy is computed as the average entropy across final clusters. The 'final' entropy should be less than the 'initial' entropy because clusters should reduce the disorder and provide 'new information'. The 'percentage of uncertainty explained' is then calculated as the proportional reduction in entropy, or the difference between 'initial' and 'final' entropy expressed as a proportion of the 'initial' entropy.

Another possible measure is the Cramer coefficient discussed in section 5.1.3. Each variable has a distribution in each cluster and so these distributions will form a matrix for which the Cramer coefficient can be computed. Therefore, it will be a measure of how different the distributions of variables are in different clusters.

Consequently, the average measure (percentage of uncertainty explained or Cramer coefficient) across all variables can be used to assess the overall 'quality' of clusters. Both measures are 'canonical' in the sense that their values are always from 0 to 1. However, there are no firm rules about what constitutes a 'good' number – it depends on which variables are chosen as well as on the number of clusters.

For each variable, the percentage of uncertainty explained or Cramer coefficient can be viewed as a kind of 'contribution' of that variable to cluster analysis. Hence, another way to use those measures would be to experiment with different sets of variables by retaining variables with 'high contributions' and discarding or replacing variables with 'low' contributions, to improve final clusters.

How many
variables?

There is a common misconception that using more variables leads to a better outcome. This is not necessarily true. Adding variables that do not contribute may be making things worse for the others by increasing the amount of noise in the data. Also the clustering process may be affected by the kinds of spurious correlation (or association) encountered in factor analysis (see page 194). Care and thought are needed. The temptation to use too many variables should be resisted.

In general, cluster analysis is an exploratory tool to discover new relationships in data. Whatever technique is employed, it is unlikely that the best and most useful solution will be obtained at the first attempt. As many alternative configurations of relevant variables and numbers of clusters as can be managed should be tried and examined before selecting one or a small number for further use.

Below we present one example where cluster analysis has been performed.

The purpose of the project was to cluster respondents according to their wine consumption habits. The Roy Morgan Single Source survey database (September 2003–August 2004) was used and only wine drinkers aged 18 or over were used in the cluster analysis, with an unweighted sample size of 12 747.

In total, seventeen variables were chosen covering wine consumption questions, demographic variables and attitudes to wine.

In this example, the distance algorithm (with formula (5.6)) has been applied. Several runs with different numbers of clusters have been performed and it has been decided that the set of six clusters seems to give 'optimal' results. For those six clusters, the percentage of uncertainty explained is 23.2% and the clusters have the following sizes:

Cluster	1	2	3	4	5	6
Proportion (%)	16.7	18.3	10.9	15.9	19.6	18.6

In Table 5.2 we show the distribution of all variables within the six clusters produced by the distance algorithm. The last column also shows the total distribution of each variable in the sample. All numbers are percentages.

The first nine variables are related to the volume as well as the amount spent on wine (in the last four weeks). Column 'W' shows the weight assigned to each variable. The weights are arbitrarily scaled: it is their relative sizes that matter. The remaining eight variables, shown in Table 5.3, were attitudinal.

It is also interesting to see distributions across a few demographic variables, even though they were not used in the cluster analysis (Table 5.4).

Below we summarise the most important features of the six clusters.

- Cluster 1: 'Occasional Consumers'. They drink wine only occasionally, and are more likely to be women than men.

Table 5.2. Cluster profiles (1)

Variable	W	Value	1	2	3	4	5	6	Total
Bottled red	4	0 glasses	36.9	11.7	60.7	14.0	43.7	18.0	29.1
wine volume		1–7 glasses	40.1	57.2	21.2	45.2	41.1	38.8	41.9
		8–28 glasses	20.8	27.5	16.1	36.5	14.8	36.2	25.7
		29+ glasses	2.2	3.7	1.9	4.3	0.4	7.0	3.3
Cask red	4	0 glasses	90.6	91.4	48.1	31.4	86.5	90.7	75.9
wine volume		1–7 glasses	3.9	5.6	14.2	25.1	6.7	4.9	9.4
		8–28 glasses	5.3	2.7	32.2	37.7	6.7	4.2	13.0
		29+ glasses	0.1	0.2	5.5	5.8	0.1	0.2	1.7
Bottled white	4	0 glasses	31.6	28.3	57.6	20.9	48.5	18.1	32.9
wine volume		1–7 glasses	46.2	51.7	23.3	44.9	38.1	40.1	41.8
		8–28 glasses	19.8	18.3	17.8	31.5	12.8	36.4	22.9
		29+ glasses	2.4	1.7	1.3	2.7	0.6	5.4	2.4
Cask white	4	0 glasses	89.2	92.9	36.2	34.7	84.8	89.5	74.6
wine volume		1–7 glasses	6.1	4.9	22.2	27.0	10.3	5.7	11.7
		8–28 glasses	4.6	2.2	32.0	30.7	4.3	4.4	11.2
		29+ glasses	0.0	0.0	9.6	7.6	0.6	0.4	2.5
Sparkling wine	4	0 glasses	60.9	60.4	81.2	51.1	71.1	47.3	61.0
volume		1–7 glasses	32.6	35.2	15.9	40.1	27.1	44.4	33.6
		8–28 glasses	5.4	4.2	2.6	8.0	1.6	7.2	4.9
		29+ glasses	1.0	0.2	0.3	0.8	0.2	1.1	0.6
Fortified wine	4	0 glasses	81.7	69.3	81.0	64.7	76.1	74.8	74.3
volume		1–7 glasses	15.8	28.8	14.4	30.7	21.6	23.2	22.9
		8–28 glasses	2.1	1.8	3.9	4.2	2.2	1.8	2.5
		29+ glasses	0.4	0.1	0.6	0.4	0.1	0.1	0.3
Wine volume as	6	0%	29.7	50.8	24.4	14.8	34.4	3.6	26.7
a proportion of		1–24%	21.7	26.1	15.8	23.6	14.4	16.6	19.8
total alcohol		25–49%	17.7	13.4	13.5	21.3	10.5	20.7	16.2
volume		50–74%	30.9	9.7	46.4	40.3	40.7	59.1	37.4
		75+%	0.0	0.0	0.0	0.0	0.0	0.0	0.0
Dollars spent on	10	none	0.0	16.6	51.1	7.1	97.7	16.9	32.1
last bottle of		$1–$15	92.3	47.4	39.8	76.6	0.0	57.3	51.2
wine purchased		$16–$30	7.1	30.4	7.0	14.0	1.8	21.8	14.1
in last 4 weeks		$31–$69	0.5	4.9	1.6	2.0	0.4	3.3	2.2
		$70+	0.1	0.6	0.5	0.3	0.1	0.8	0.4
Dollars spent on	10	none	98.7	99.0	0.1	0.0	99.5	99.6	72.7
last cask of		$1–$9	0.1	0.4	98.5	97.8	0.0	0.0	26.4
wine purchased		$10–$19	1.0	0.6	1.4	2.1	0.5	0.4	0.9
in last 4 weeks		$20+	0.2	0.0	0.0	0.1	0.0	0.0	0.1

Table 5.3. Cluster profiles (2)

Variable	W	Value	1	2	3	4	5	6	Total
I like to buy brands	6	Disagree	62.9	20.2	72.7	24.4	65.2	20.0	42.5
I haven't tried		Can't Say	2.4	1.9	7.5	3.9	6.2	4.2	4.2
before		Agree	34.7	78.0	19.8	71.7	28.6	75.8	53.3
I will buy wines based	3	Disagree	66.6	25.8	71.2	40.9	63.8	32.0	48.6
on a good review		Can't Say	2.9	1.8	9.5	4.9	8.5	4.0	5.1
		Agree	30.5	72.3	19.3	54.2	27.7	64.0	46.4
One of the things I	3	Disagree	74.7	29.6	70.3	37.5	70.3	36.1	52.0
love about wine is		Can't Say	3.5	2.2	9.6	4.3	8.0	4.5	5.1
that there is so		Agree	21.8	68.2	20.2	58.2	21.6	59.4	42.8
much to learn									
I would be more likely	3	Disagree	66.2	41.1	68.6	46.8	62.1	42.3	53.5
to choose a wine if		Can't Say	3.5	1.9	8.9	4.1	7.5	3.8	4.7
I knew it had won		Agree	30.3	57.1	22.5	49.1	30.4	53.9	41.7
some medals									
The wine region is an	3	Disagree	67.4	27.9	64.8	37.3	57.9	32.5	46.8
important factor when		Can't Say	3.5	1.8	8.9	3.1	8.3	3.4	4.6
choosing a wine		Agree	29.0	70.3	26.3	59.7	33.8	64.1	48.6
For my first drink of	6	Disagree	73.5	90.6	48.7	41.4	74.0	3.2	55.8
the evening I prefer		Can't Say	3.3	2.3	7.4	2.8	8.8	3.4	4.6
a glass of wine		Agree	23.3	7.2	44.0	55.8	17.3	93.4	39.6
I often order the wine	6	Disagree	74.0	25.7	67.5	29.2	71.0	23.3	47.3
in restaurants when		Can't Say	2.9	2.0	8.9	3.2	8.0	3.7	4.6
I am in the company		Agree	23.1	72.3	23.6	67.6	21.0	73.0	48.1
of others									
I take my time when	6	Disagree	66.2	8.0	66.4	18.7	61.9	15.3	37.7
choosing wine		Can't Say	4.3	2.4	9.9	5.0	9.9	4.2	5.8
		Agree	29.5	89.6	23.6	76.3	28.2	80.5	56.5

- Cluster 2: 'Dedicated Discoverers'. Mainly men, regular but not 'heavy' wine drinkers, they like to try out new brands of wine but wine in general is not their preferred type of alcohol. However, they do spend much more than average on bottled wine while spending very little on cask wine. They tend to be in the middle age groups with a relatively high proportion from the AB quintile. They love to learn more about wine and like to buy wine based on a good review. Almost 90% of them take their time when choosing wine.
- Cluster 3: 'Fixed Habituals'. Generally, they drink more than the average but do not like sparkling wine. They have a limited repertoire and are reluctant to experiment. Almost all spend at least some money on cask wine. They are more likely to be middle aged and older.

Table 5.4. Cluster profiles (3)

Variable	Value	1	2	3	4	5	6	Total
Sex	men	44.6	69.5	48.9	53.0	45.9	31.0	48.7
	women	55.4	30.5	51.1	47.0	54.1	69.0	51.3
Age	18−24	11.5	10.3	5.5	5.0	16.4	6.9	9.7
	25−34	17.0	27.2	8.5	12.8	17.2	19.6	17.8
	35−49	33.3	33.9	29.0	30.2	28.4	30.5	31.0
	50+	38.2	28.6	57.1	52.0	38.1	43.0	41.6
Socio-economic	AB	27.0	41.1	14.3	28.5	23.6	41.8	30.5
quintiles	C	22.7	26.3	19.8	25.2	24.4	24.8	24.2
	D	23.4	16.8	20.3	20.6	20.1	15.4	19.3
	E	16.8	9.6	24.2	15.7	17.3	11.8	15.3
	FG	10.0	6.3	21.5	10.0	14.6	6.1	10.8

- Cluster 4: 'Definite Drinkers'. These have the highest consumption of wine, being more than twice as likely to drink 29+ glasses per month than the average. All of them spend some money on cask wine but the money spent on bottled wine is only slightly above average. They tend to be middle aged and older. They are also more likely to prefer a glass of wine as the first drink of the evening.
- Cluster 5: 'Indifferents'. They do not drink (or spend much money on) wine and they are very likely to stay with the brands they have tried. They are more likely to be younger.
- Cluster 6: 'Smart & Sassy'. These are mainly women with a relatively high proportion from the AB quintile, mainly above average wine drinkers for whom wine tends to be the main alcohol drink, with sparkling wine being especially popular. They spend more than average on expensive bottled wine. They like to buy brands they have not tried before and in general love to learn more about wine. Almost all of them prefer a glass of wine as the first drink of the evening.

5.6   Data fusion

Surveys are carried out to estimate the incidence or distribution of attributes of a population in isolation but also, as we have seen, to examine the strengths of relationships between two or more of them. In the richness of these relationships lies much of the value of survey data. The ability to cross-analyse variables is central to the evaluation process.

But of course, two variables can be cross-analysed only when they come from the same set of respondents. The two variables form a series of pairs of values, one pair per respondent, and it is the joint distribution of the combinations of the values in these pairs that form the contingency table. We look for differences between this joint distribution and a putative distribution that would be expected if the relationship

between the variables were random (or in accordance with some particular expectation). The differences provide the information that adds to our understanding of the
issues.

But often we come up against cases where we have two pieces of information, from
different sources, that look as though they might have an interesting relationship. How
useful it would be if we could examine their joint distribution.

History of
data fusion

What has become known as data fusion has been with us in at least a primitive form
since mankind began to reason, or at least since the Greeks invented the syllogism.
If two known relationships have a common element it *can* be reasonable to assume
a relationship of some kind between the two non-common elements. If we know
from one survey that BMW drivers tend to be younger, high-income men and, from a
separate survey, that certain magazines are read disproportionately by younger, high-
income men, then it is not unreasonable to suspect that those publications might be
read disproportionately by BMW drivers. This kind of inference has been part and
parcel of survey research, and particularly of media research and planning, since its
inception.

At least as long ago as the 1960s there was speculation that the emerging computer
technology might make it possible to simulate the cross-analysis of a variable from
one data set with a variable from another, by linking respondents in pairs, one from
each set. In the days of electro-mechanical punch-card equipment crude methods were
devised to match a respondent from one data set with a respondent from another on
the basis of the shared values of one or two variables. Naturally, with two data sets of
any size one respondent could be matched with any one of a possibly large number of
possible respondents in the other data set, who may have shown considerable variation.
Any linkage was likely to be tenuous. The technique was used mainly as a way of
imputing missing individual data items (see page 134). From the 1980s, with the
advent of low-cost computers and then powerful desktop machines, resources ceased
to be an obstacle and interest in the possibilities of simulated merging increased. The
term 'fusion' came to be applied to the linking or merging of data in this way. Fused
data sets started to become a commercial reality.

Donors and
recipients

Modern data fusion replaces the collective inference with a comparatively sophisticated physical linking of respondents from different surveys. If a certain respondent
from one survey is considered to be sufficiently similar to a specific respondent from
the other, all the responses from those two respondents can be pooled and treated
as though they came from one person. In practice, typically the information from
one (the 'donor') is appended to information from the other (the 'recipient') and the
inference is made that the recipient would have provided the same answers as the
donor did, had he or she been asked the same questions.

For the purpose of matching, or 'marrying', pairs of respondents, similarity can
be measured in terms of the information we have about *both* respondents, that is,
from the responses they gave to those questions that are common to both surveys
(the 'common' variables, sometimes known as 'hooks'). This information will vary,

but most surveys include some more-or-less standard demographic questions. Other questions may be included specifically to assist with matching if this is part of the original intent.

Applications
of fusion

Data sets to be fused can conveniently be placed into several categories.

- Independently conducted surveys may offer an opportunity for added value if they can be combined.
- Surveys may be conducted with fusion in mind and designed to provide assistance with the process.
- Surveys requiring a very long questionnaire may use replicated samples, each of which is asked a basic core set of questions and one or more of a number of question modules, thus reducing the total length (and burden) of the individual interview.
- A two-stage survey (interviewing the same sample twice) may have attrition between the stages and fusion may be a way of reconstructing the missing second-stage data, preserving the first-stage results intact.

In the second and third cases care will be taken to minimise the practical problems of matching respondents. Sample composition will be controlled and common variables will be consistent. In addition, the common variables will contain specific items that help to match respondents on issues that are related to the subject matter of the individual surveys. A survey on media usage may for instance be intended to be merged with one on holiday travel. Both surveys would include comparable basic questions on media and holiday travel, the intent being to maximise the collective discriminatory or predictive power of the common variables (a subject we shall return to later).

Principles of
matching

Matching algorithms vary but generally seek to strike a balance between two con-flicting aims – of matching each respondent from one sample to *one* and only one respondent from the other, and of matching each respondent from one sample to the *most similar* respondent from the other. There is usually a compromise, with some matches better than others. The varying quality of pairings has spawned a fanciful marriage-related terminology from 'love at first sight' for respondents with a very high degree of similarity, 'shotgun wedding' for two who are ill suited but are married for want of a better alternative, via 'childhood sweethearts', 'adultery' or 'bigamy', and 'marriage of convenience'. Some donors or recipients may not be matchable at all: they may be left 'on the shelf' and discarded.

There is no single established technique or method for the matching process. We do not propose to review methods in use but to confine ourselves to general principles. The requirements for matching will depend on the surveys concerned and their subject matter. Different variables will be important in different circumstances. However, the number of variables available for matching is usually sufficient for there to be a question of determining the priorities. The number of possible combinations of values in the common variables is the product of the numbers of values or categories in each, and this can easily be greater than the number of respondents in either sample.

The number of exact matches of donors and recipients, on all common variables, may therefore be very small.

It is customary to discriminate between variables where the donor and recipient *must* match and those where a match is *desirable*. In many cases it will be an absolute requirement that donor and recipient be of the same sex (so much for the marriage analogy) but geographic location could be essential in one case and irrelevant in another. Common variables can be designated as 'critical' or 'preferred' for matching purposes, and not all common variables need be used.

The definition of 'match' may itself be flexible, even for critical variables. We could, for instance say that a donor and recipient must be in the same geographical region, or we could allow them to be in adjoining regions. To require an exact match in age would be unrealistic, so we could set a limit to the difference that would be acceptable, say ten or perhaps twenty years. These are matters of judgement depending on the circumstances, and also on the degree of sophistication the sample sizes permit.

The definition of a match on a preferred variable may be similarly flexible, and in addition each individual variable may be assigned a weight to indicate its relative importance. In the case of numerical variables the degree of difference may also be used. If 'age' is seen as virtually critical it would be possible to use a measure of difference in combination with a weight to make a close match virtually critical without the problems of designating an arbitrary cut-off point for determining a match.

The degree of similarity between any potential recipient and donor may be calculated according to some kind of distance formula, due allowance being made for differences in the units of measurement for different variables. Alternative approaches may or may not make much difference to the end result, and trials of different methods may be needed to determine which produces the most usable result. For a brief review of some possible approaches see Soong and de Montigny [55].

To perform the matching the samples are normally divided into 'cells', potential donors and recipients within each cell all having the same combination of critical attributes, and we attempt to find matches for donors and recipients within each cell. This procedure has the practical advantage of reducing the number of potential pairings. Donors are then matched with recipients to optimise the overall quality of matching. The measure of goodness of matching will of course depend on the distance measure. For each matching pair the donor's information is then appended to that of the recipient.

Ideally, every recipient is matched with a donor and every donor with a recipient. This supposes that there are equal numbers of donors and recipients and, of course, that the numbers are equal within each cell. In reality of course this is most unlikely to be the case. We have to consider the problem of what to do when the numbers are unequal.

Which sample is the donor?

First however, we have to consider the most fundamental question: which of the samples is to be the recipient and which the donor? The recipient sample is normally characterised by undergoing the least change, ideally none. The fused sample will use the values of the common variables and the weighting factors taken from the recipient sample. The non-common data from the donor are simply grafted onto each recipient. When analysed, the sample should yield estimates for all 'recipient variables' that match exactly the values that would be obtained from the original 'recipient' sample. Some considerations that apply in making the choice include: whether one of the surveys is a recognised 'industry standard' survey so that the results already made public should still be reproduced after any fusion with another source; whether one of the samples is of better quality and thus more reliable than the other; and whether one sample is larger, and thus more stable.

Samples of different size

This last consideration leads on to the question of what we are to do if the samples are of very different sizes. We cannot get a straightforward one-to-one match without discarding a large number of respondents from the larger sample.

Consider first the case where the recipient sample is larger. This is probably more common anyway; industry-standard surveys tend to have large and good quality samples and so are well fitted to act as recipients. A solution, of course, is to allow multiple recipients to share the same donor. A donor's data can be duplicated and attached to each of several recipients to which he or she is most similar. Of course, if this is done it is desirable that there should be as little variation as possible in the number of donors per recipient. Variation in the number of times a donor's information is used is a form of weighting of the donor results, but one that is not immediately visible in the fused data. Where multiple recipients share a donor, the fused data of a recipient should preferably contain an indication of the number of (other) recipients served by its donor. The duplication of donors does not mean an increase in sample size for the donor information in the fused data set. It still came from the same number of respondents. In fact the effective sample size has probably gone down as a further source of variance has been added by the variation in the number of times it is used. Its original weight (in the donor sample) has been replaced (in the fused sample) by the sum of the weights of the recipients to which it has been matched so the weighting effect alone is very likely to increase.

It is immediately obvious that this is going to cause severe practical difficulties in calculating the variance of any estimate from the donor portion of such a fused data set – especially if standard statistical software is used.

The opposite case, where it is considered more important to use the smaller sample as the recipient, can be approached in a similar way. Each individual recipient can be split, or duplicated, the required number of times to provide the best pattern of matching with the donors. The weight of each replicate must be reduced so that the sum of the replicate weights remains the same as that of the original individual recipient, and of course the sum of weights for the fused sample remains the same in aggregate. But the number of respondents has not increased, despite appearances, so that similar statistical difficulties arise in calculating the variance of estimates, this time with the emphasis on the recipient based estimates.

Even where the two samples are of very similar size overall there will inevitably be variation in the matching cells. Some cells may have an excess of donors, others of recipients. Three possible approaches suggest themselves.

- We can be consistent in always taking the larger (or the smaller) sample (within the cell) to be the recipient. This will cause further statistical complications in variance estimation, though as we shall see by the end of this section, this may be the least of our worries.
- We can consistently treat one of the sources as donors for all cells and duplicate donors or split recipients to use all respondents from both sources.
- Still consistently treating one source as donors we can discard individual donors or recipients who cannot be matched.

If the problem of inconsistent sample sizes in the cells is causing an uncomfortable level of loss or complication, the cell sizes may be too small and thought should be given to reducing or simplifying the critical variables to reduce the number of cells.

In each case, the weights of the individual donors will change as they acquire the weights of their recipients, so that donor based estimates cannot be expected to be preserved exactly in the fused sample. If the fusion has gone well what can be hoped for, and tested, is that as little violence as possible has been done to the donor data in the transition. Ideally the donor data will look very similar in the fused data set. Furthermore, the relationships between different variables *within* the donor data should also be substantially preserved.

Assessing the quality of fusion

The achievement of these two aims is sometimes cited as evidence of successful fusion. It is not. It is a mere prerequisite for successful fusion. The success or otherwise of fusion lies in the degree to which it reveals the relationship between a donor item and a recipient item as it would appear had both been collected from the same sample.

The methods of matching described here are fairly crude. It is likely that more elegant and sophisticated methods may exist or be developed, but this does not affect the general principle.

The mechanism of fusion thus outlined combines the data from the two sources in a way that permits the cross-analysis of attributes recorded by different individuals to reproduce what would have been seen had the whole amount of data been collected from the one sample. That is the theory and the hope.

When two different data sets are fused, of course, there is generally little or no evidence for how well the fusion has reproduced such relationships. We normally have no benchmark: that is why we need the fusion process. Only by controlled experiment can we gain some idea of how well it works.

The classic experiment is to take a single large sample, split it into two matching halves and then fuse the halves. The resulting sample thus contains both donor and recipient data. A set of variables (such as would be expected to occur in most surveys) is designated as the 'common variables', and used for matching. Analysis of the way in which donor data and recipient data are related gives us an idea of how well the fusion has worked. In particular we can observe the relationship between two variables, one from the donor and the other from the recipient, and compare that with the 'true' relationship when both are taken from the same sample. How well does the strength of relationship 'across the fusion line' hold up in the fused data set? We shall use the term 'fused estimate' to represent an estimate derived from a combination of donor and recipient variables.

The short answer is that it depends largely on the power of the common variables used in matching to predict or explain the two variables concerned. If the matching variables are totally unrelated to both, then no relationship will appear to exist between the two variables. If they are cross-tabulated the sizes of individual cells of the table will be approximately the product of the column and row proportions.

An experiment of precisely this type was sponsored by the (UK) Market Research Development Fund and we quote this because the results were published in some detail. Baker *et al.* [2] took two halves of a 12 000 interview sample of (UK) TGI respondents and tried several methods of fusing them. The resulting samples were analysed to determine how well the fusion process delivered what was present in the 'real' data. We also quote from our own experiments along similar lines with an initial sample of 24 508 respondents from the (Australian) Roy Morgan Single Source survey, also illustrated in Levine *et al.* [40a]. In both studies what emerged was the phenomenon of 'regression to the mean'. We will illustrate this with an example.

Regression to the mean

Drivers of cars bought new are more likely than drivers of used cars to read the Sydney Morning Herald. If we take the recipient information alone we find that 16% of all people were Sydney Morning Herald readers. But 24% of new-car drivers read it. This gives an index value of 148 (48% more likely than average). However, if we replace the 'real' new-car drivers with donors only 20% of new-car drivers did (index 129). The fused (donor) result is more average than the 'real' (recipient) result. The estimate has 'regressed' towards the mean of 16%. The same holds for drivers of used cars and non-drivers. In both cases the fused result is closer to the overall mean (the index values are closer to 100).

Filter: New South Wales, n = 3663

	Total %	Type of car driven		
		New	Used	Non-drivers
		% index	% index	% index
SMH readers (R)				
Source: Recipients	16	24 (148)	12 (77)	12 (76)
Source: Donors		20 (129)	13 (86)	13 (86)

If we had to rely on the fused data the general conclusion would still be valid. People with cars bought new are more likely to be readers. But they are not *as much* more likely as they should be; the relationship has been diluted. In this case the common variables we used (including sex, age, education, occupation, income and frequency of newspaper reading) were collectively reasonable predictors of both new-car drivers and Sydney Morning Herald readers.

When we looked at how well the donors had been matched to recipients in respect of these attributes the results were not perfect but noticeably better than random. 42%

of new-car driving donors had been matched with similar recipients. If the matching had been random we would have expected 32% to be correctly matched. 55% of used-car donors matched with used-car recipients (49% expected). Non-drivers were better matched (46% versus 19% expected) as they are better predicted by the common variables. Sydney Morning Herald readers fared better: 42% of donor readers were matched with a recipient reader (16% expected, geography being a critical variable).

This was an example where the relationship was preserved fairly well by the common variables. Here is a case where it is not. Grocery buyers in our recipient sample told us what type of washing machine they had (10% of machines were front-loaders) and what brand of washing powder they used. So did our donors. Omomatic is a detergent formulated for use in front-loading washing machines. Within the recipient data we duly find that users of Omomatic (3% of this group) tend to have front-loading washing machines. Those with front-loaders are about thirty times as likely to use Omomatic as those with top-loaders. However, if we had been using a fused data set and relying on the donors for the type of washing machine the picture would have been far less clear. There is still some positive relationship, but it is very weak. This is regression almost back to the mean.

Filter: grocery buyers with a washing machine; Recipients, n = 8327

	All	Omomatic users	(R)
Machine type:			
Recipients			
Front-load	10%	75%	(807)
Top-load	90%	25%	(27)
Donors			
Front-load	10%	17%	(184)
Top-load	91%*	84% *	(93)

*A small number had both.

This example was chosen because it would have been spotted by anyone with a knowledge of the product category looking at results from a fused data set. But in the absence of such prior knowledge it might have gone unremarked. Here is a clear case where fusion has lost a very strong relationship, simply because neither of the respondent attributes was strongly related to the common variables. In fact when the samples were fused, only 12% of the donors with front-loading machines were matched with corresponding recipients – a little better than random, but not much.

Now when we included 'type of washing machine' among the critical variables and re-did the fusion the problem disappeared. However, this was an exceptional case and the improvement was very localised. This survey covered a very wide range of topics and the change helped the Omomatic situation but did nothing to improve another problem area, mobile phones. Nor did it provide any improvement on the two-thirds of disposable nappy (diaper) buyers who apparently had no infant children. Inserting very specialised critical variables can plug obvious holes but does not necessarily provide an overall benefit. As more special critical variables are inserted the matching process gets more and more cumbersome as the number of 'must-match' combinations increases. As Baker *et al.* pointed out, increasing the number of common variables can make the fusion worse, not better. The selection of critical and preferred matching variables is likely to be made without advance knowledge of the detailed effect.

Regression to the mean should be a general phenomenon. The reasoning is simple. If the matching variables cannot (other than in exceptional and trivial cases) predict perfectly the sample members with and without particular attributes, they cannot be used as an exact surrogate for that attribute. This can be demonstrated, even where we do not have the luxury of a split sample with duplicated variables. If an AID analysis of the recipient sample using the designated common variables as predictors and a (non-common) attribute as target shows that the matching variables cannot predict accurately the people with the required attribute in either the donor or the recipient samples, it is clear that they will not predict who should be matched to whom to preserve the full detail. The process is based on probabilities. All we can do is maximise the probability of a suitable match, but inevitably many people will be mismatched. The number of attributes we wish to transfer from donor to recipient is usually fairly large. The large number of possible combinations of possession/non-possession of those attributes means that the best possible match would produce incorrect transfer of some attributes at least. An additional element of randomness is therefore introduced. So in theory, fusion should cause regression to the mean in all cases where the incidence of a recipient-attribute/donor-attribute combination is measured. Only the degree of regression should vary, depending on the predictive power of the matching variables. It should not, in theory, be possible for the incidence to be higher in a fused data set than in a 'single-source' data set. This implies that 'false negatives' (failure to show a true difference) will be more common than 'false positives', which is probably the right way round.

But Baker *et al.* in their split-sample experiment demonstrated that it is possible for a fused data set to show a stronger relationship between two attributes from different samples than would have come from a single sample. Their main fusion involved three critical and eleven other matching variables. In one table they present results comparing the indexed incidences of 154 combinations of attributes when both were obtained from a single sample with the incidence obtained from the fused sample with one of the attributes transferred in the fusion process. Reading of fourteen national newspapers was crossed with eleven 'target group' definitions ranging from 'have dark hair' to 'own stocks and shares'. Within the 'real' (non-fused) data owners of stocks and shares were almost twice as likely as the average to read the Daily Telegraph (index 195) and about half as likely as average (index 52) to read the Star. In the fused data the same tendencies appeared but with the indices closer to 100 (162, 61). The expected pattern of regression to the mean was found in general, but not consistently.

If we take only the 97 cases where the 'real' result was an index of 110 or more or 90 or less (to allow a reasonable chance of a substantial regression being observed) regression towards the mean occurred in 80 cases, to varying degrees. However, in 17 cases the fused data showed a *stronger* association than the 'real' data, albeit in

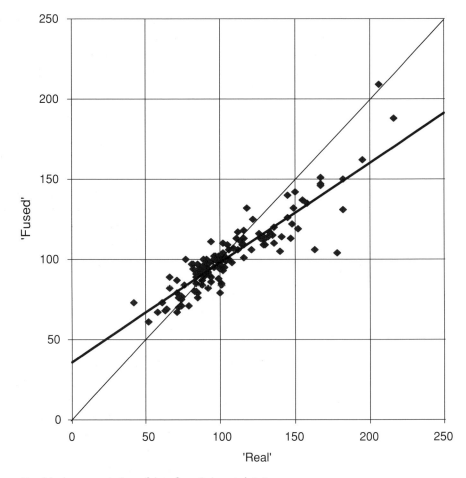

Figure 5.5   Graphical representation of data from Baker *et al.* [2].

most cases only slightly stronger. Now we have seen that this should not happen, so if it does we have to presume that this is evidence of the randomising element introduced by the fusion process. This is perhaps not surprising, given some of the marginal decisions that must be made during the fusion process itself. When presented graphically (Figure 5.5) the pattern is clear. There is a strong positive association between the 'real' and fused results (because of the nature of the figures we have not calculated correlation or regression coefficients) and a clear general pattern of regression to the mean. But there is also evidence of a consistent fuzziness around the regression trend. Sample size has something to do with this, of course, but Baker *et al.* were dealing with fairly substantial samples (some 6000 each).

For the three least 'successful' target groups they then repeated the exercise using a fusion process that included eleven additional non-critical matching attributes, of which two in fact comprised two of the 'under-performing' target groups. The 42 results showed a general but somewhat erratic improvement. Most of the regressions to the mean were reduced but some increased.

Commercial
implications
of regression
to the mean

So fusion evidently 'works', to the extent that if a relationship 'across the fusion line' would show up in a 'single-source' data set it should also show up in a fused data set, if to a lesser extent. It thus provides evidence for things that we could otherwise only have presumed. Why, then, does it matter if the strength of association is not exactly reproduced? Within a fused data set we can distinguish three kinds of data combinations.

- Recipient variable with recipient variable. These should preserve the strength of the original relationships as they are subject only to any discarding and re-weighting of original respondents.
- Donor variable with donor variable. These should similarly reproduce much of the strength of relationship that they had in their original survey though the donor data are probably subject to more variation in the transfer.
- Recipient variable with donor variable (fused estimate). This is where the problems will tend to occur, with uncertainty about the degree of regression to the mean.

In many cases fusion may be used precisely because measuring relationships is the important issue. Major media surveys are used as a currency for buying and selling media, with large amounts of money changing hands on the strength of the results taken at their face value. An advertising medium is sold not only on its overall audience delivery, but on its ability to reach specific target groups within the population more selectively and/or more cost effectively than other media. Because of their complexity, media surveys often do not contain a wide range of information apart from the audience measurements and demographic classifiers. Fusion presents an opportunity to merge such surveys with other surveys that contain the desired range of extended information. The worry is that if, for instance, a newspaper from the recipient survey is examined against a target group from the donor survey, regression to the mean may make it appear to have less of a competitive advantage in reaching that group, especially by comparison with a medium also from the donor survey. It could thus be commercially disadvantaged. Inconsistencies in the degree of regression to the mean could also work to the advantage or disadvantage of an individual donor medium relative to other donor media. And as Rothman [49] pointed out, a niche publication will suffer because the blurring effect of fusion will weaken the link with its target market.

It is the very uncertainty of the results that is the problem. It is all very well to know that the general degree of regression to the mean is such-and-such, but the typical researcher is probably interested in a specific estimate, with decisions possibly hanging on the outcome.

Statistical
implications

We have so far said nothing about the statistical implications of fusion, and for good reason. Statistical theory gives very little guidance in this area. All we can say in general is that it is almost certain that the variance of a fused estimate (the combination of a donor variable and a recipient variable) will be greater, and often probably considerably greater, than would have been the case had the estimate been derived from information collected in the conventional way from a single sample.

The increased variance is in part the result of additional weighting applied to donor data as a result of the varying levels of multiple use of donors and/or recipients. But there is also the inescapable element of randomness in the matching process referred to on page 223. This element of chance is what accounts for the phenomenon of occurrences where the regression to the mean is negative and the relationship appears stronger than it should.

A further general point that can be made is that the effective sample size for a fused estimate is almost certainly smaller than the *lesser* of the donor and recipient effective sample sizes.

The two fusion experiments referred to above were performed under ideal but artificial conditions. The two samples being fused were of almost equal size, they were drawn in the same way and the questions used were identical. And of course we had the luxury of being able to verify the results. In reality, fusion will often be undertaken between samples that are materially different in one or more of these respects. This adds further to the uncertainty.

In the present state of knowledge, estimating the variance, and thus the standard error, of any fused estimate is highly problematical. Design effects for such estimates are not readily estimated and the weighting effect is no longer a reliable surrogate, even if applied specifically to the smaller sample with duplications allowed for. We therefore particularly caution against any attempt to apply significance testing to a fused estimate.

We do not wish to condemn data fusion. It clearly has a considerable degree of validity. Done well, it can give us valuable guidance on relationships that would otherwise have to be inferred. The crucial thing to bear in mind is that a fused estimate is not the same as, and not as valid as, an estimate derived from a single sample, and that it must be treated with circumspection and caution.

Appendix A
Review of general terminology

For convenience, we present a short list of elementary statistical terms and formulae.

Statistics as a science deals with mathematical methods of collecting, summarising and analysing data and presenting results of analysis in a mathematical form.

A *population* (sometimes called a *universe*) is a set of objects to be studied. The purpose of a statistical analysis is to draw conclusions about a population. In most cases, statistics is concerned with a particular population characteristic called a *parameter* of the population.

Statistical methods can be applied (only) in situations when it is impracticable or impossible to collect information about *all* objects in the population but the information is available for a *subset* of the population called a *sample*. The process of estimating or predicting population parameters using sample data is called *statistical inference*.

A sample is described as *representative* if it is believed that it fairly and comprehensively represents the population from which it is drawn. A sample is *biased* if it over-represents or under-represents a particular population group. The words 'unbiased' and 'representative' are usually interchangeable. Both are relative terms, not absolute. Except in highly artificial situations no sample will be representative in every respect. The terms are sometimes used to describe the intentions of the sampler or the design of the sample rather than the outcome. If a sample is known to be biased, and the nature and magnitude of the bias are known, very often *weighting* is used to 'fix' the most obvious imbalances.

Two samples of the same population are *independent* if the selection of respondents for one sample does not depend on or affect the selection of respondents for the other. Samples are not independent if membership of one sample precludes membership of the other (e.g. people in one wave of a survey are not interviewed in a subsequent wave), but if such samples are very small relative to the population they may for practical purposes generally be treated as independent.

A sample is *random* when all objects in the population have an equal chance of selection. A random sample is called *simple* if each member of the sample is selected independently of all other members. The standard statistical formulae are related to a simple random sample, which is ideal from a theoretical point of view but relatively rare in practice.

A function of sample observations is called a *statistic*.

Significance testing can be defined as the testing of hypotheses about a population based on sample data from that population.

Statistics is closely related to *probability theory*. The reason is that any conclusion about a population based on sample data cannot be categorical because the sample does not have complete information about the population. Therefore, all statistical statements about population parameters are *probabilistic*, that is, population parameters are *estimated* and a probabilistic statement is made about how close an estimate is to the 'true' value.

Another relationship between statistics and probability theory is that statistics, strictly speaking, deals only with samples chosen by a *probabilistic method*, that is, samples where the probability of selection for each respondent *is known*. If the probabilities of selection are not known, statistical methods of analysis are not strictly applicable.

The mathematical definition of *probability* is quite abstract but from a practical point of view the probability of an outcome can be considered as 'the proportion of success in many trials' (for instance the proportion of times on which a tossed coin will show 'heads'). The probability of an occurrence can often only be measured empirically by observing how many times it occurs relative to the number of possible occurrences. Therefore, the words 'probability' and 'proportion' are often used interchangeably. The *value of probability* can range from zero (absolute certainty that something will not happen) to 1.0 (absolute certainty that it will). It is also customary to express probability in percentages; for instance, the statements 'probability $= 0.12$' and 'probability $= 12\%$' are considered to be the same.

A *random variable* is the probability theory synonym for a population parameter which is measured in a sample; it is more 'strict' and has a formal mathematical definition but we do not go into details here. In sample survey research language, variables are either numerical or categorical. In its simplest terms, a numerical variable can be used in arithmetic combination with others, a categorical variable cannot. Some variables, where the number of categories is very limited, may be usable as either numerical or categorical. For a fuller discussion see section 5.1.1.

A *distribution* of a variable is given by values of the variable together with the probability of each value occurring, or the proportions of all occurrences taken by each possible value. Clearly, the sum of all probabilities should be equal to one. In practice, variables are usually *discrete*, i.e. take a finite number of values, either because there are only a limited number of values in practice (number of children in families), or because the measurement used has limited precision (heights of children measured in whole centimetres or inches). For such variables, the distribution is given simply by the finite number of probabilities.

The behaviour of random variables can be studied via a *histogram* – a graphical representation of sample data, typically with the x axis being values of the variable and the y axis being the incidence, or the proportion of a value among all values.

If a variable can potentially take any value within a defined range (e.g. any positive number, any real number) then each value could be unique, and so sample values are generally grouped in convenient small intervals and the number of observations in each group plotted. For such variables, as the sample size and/or the number of groups increases, the histogram generally becomes closer and closer to a curve. The function whose graph is this curve is called the *density function*.

There are a number of common forms of distribution encountered in survey research, of which the 'normal' (or Gaussian) distribution is the most common. The density function for a normal distribution has the familiar 'bell-curve' symmetrical shape (see Table C2 in Appendix C). When the mean value is zero and variance is equal to one, this is called a *standard normal distribution*. Distributions are often converted to this form (standardised) for ease of display, further computation or comparison. A population with a normal variable is said to be a *normal population*. In a normal distribution most of the values are clustered about the mean and extreme values (in the 'tails' of the distribution) are rare. The more extreme they are the rarer they are.

The condition that the population is normal is sometimes required in significance tests or in other statistical techniques. In practice, this condition is seldom checked and the assumption is that the population is automatically normal. It is strongly recommended to check this condition before applying a technique where it is required, simply because sometimes the population is *not* normal. For instance, if the variable in question is *binary*, it has only two values (zero and one) and therefore cannot have a normal distribution. In other words, significance tests or other techniques requiring normality of the population *cannot be used for binary variables*. A *skewed* distribution can sometimes be turned arithmetically into an approximately normal distribution by applying a transformation function to all values. For instance, in the case of a variable where the values form a skewed 'bell-shaped' distribution with most values below the mean, the logarithms of the values may be more or less normally distributed.

Population mean (or *expected value*) is the average value (with respect to the whole population) of a variable x and is often denoted by μ or $E(x)$. Unless explicitly stated to the contrary, the mean is normally the arithmetic mean, that is, the sum of all observed values divided by the number of observations. Other types of mean (the geometric and harmonic means) may occasionally be encountered. If the data are weighted the arithmetic mean is calculated by multiplying each observed value by its weight, summing these products and dividing by the sum of the weights.

The *population variance* of variable x is the mean value of the variable $(x - \mu)^2$, where μ is the mean of x, and is the mean squared difference of the individual values from the overall mean. Variance measures how the values of x are scattered around the mean value. The population variance is usually denoted by σ^2. Notice that this is distinctly different from the usage of the term 'variance' by accountants who use it for the arithmetic difference between two values, often a planned one and an actual one.

The *population deviation* is the square root of the population variance (common notation σ_x, for variable x), and is perhaps the most commonly encountered measure of the 'scatter' of values around the mean. It is equivalent to the 'root-mean-squared deviation' measure used in other disciplines such as electrical engineering.

The *population median* of variable x is a number m such that $x \leq m$ with probability 50% (then of course $x > m$ also with probability 50%). There may be more than one number satisfying this property (e.g. if a variable has a finite number of values) and so the median is not uniquely defined. The median is sometimes used in preference to the mean where a population is small, the values irregularly distributed or the mean subject to distortion because of a few extreme values. However, it is of limited use computationally.

The *sample mean* (or *expected value*) is the arithmetic average value of sample observations $x_1, \ldots, x_n$ and is usually denoted by $\bar{x}$. For a simple random sample, it is computed by the formula

$$\bar{x} = \frac{1}{n} \sum_{i=1}^{n} x_i$$

while for a *weighted* sample the weighted average is used

$$\bar{x} = \frac{\sum_{i=1}^{n} w_i x_i}{\sum_{i=1}^{n} w_i},$$

where w_i is the weight for respondent i. Notice that $\bar{x}$ is *not the same* as the population mean and that different samples generally produce different mean values. The sample mean $\bar{x}$ is an *estimate* of μ.

The *sample variance* is the mean squared difference of the sample values from the sample mean. It is usually denoted by S^2 and is calculated by the formulae

$$\text{simple random sample} \quad S^2 = \frac{1}{n-1} \left[\sum_{i=1}^{n} x_i^2 - \frac{1}{n} \left(\sum_{i=1}^{n} x_i \right)^2 \right],$$

$$\text{weighted sample} \quad S^2 = \frac{\sum_{i=1}^{n} w_i x_i^2}{\sum_{i=1}^{n} w_i} - \left(\frac{\sum_{i=1}^{n} w_i x_i}{\sum_{i=1}^{n} w_i} \right)^2,$$

where n is the unweighted sample size. Again notice that S^2 is not the same as the population variance σ^2: S^2 is an estimate of σ^2 and is itself subject to sampling error.

The reader may note that the variance formula for simple random sampling has $n-1$ in the denominator and not n as might be expected. The division by $n-1$ rather than n is customary and the (mathematical) reason for this is that the variance estimate with $n-1$ in the denominator is unbiased – its average value coincides with the population variance σ^2 (a proof of this fact is standard and can be found in many statistical textbooks). On the other hand, the estimate with n in the denominator is biased – it slightly underestimates the true variance. The difference between the two estimates is negligible when the sample size is large.

However, when the sample has been weighted, the sum of weights, rather than the sample size, must be used to derive a variance estimate. If sampling is not simple random and requires weighting, most variance estimates are generally biased and a simple substitution, for instance, of the sum of weights by the sum of weights minus one would not remove the bias. Furthermore, there is no single variance formula suitable for all situations – the correct formula depends on sample design and the weighting procedure. See Chapter 3 for particular formulae and techniques for estimating variance.

The *standard deviation* is the square root of the sample variance and is usually denoted by S.

The *sample median*, as for the population median, is the number such that 50% of sample values $x_1, \ldots, x_n$ are less than or equal to this number and 50% of the values are greater than this number. If n is odd, it is simply the 'middle' value $x_{(n+1)/2}$. If n is even, there are two 'middle' values, $x_{n/2}$ and $x_{n/2+1}$, and the median value should be between them so that in this case it is not uniquely defined; to avoid multiple choices, the average $(x_{n/2} + x_{n/2+1})/2$ is usually taken as the sample median. For a weighted sample, the median is 'weighted': it is the number such that sample values on the left side of this number have the same sum of weights as values on the right side. Geometrically, the sample median is the x-value such that the vertical line at this value divides the histogram into two parts with equal areas. The median is sometimes used in preference to the mean where the sample size is small or the distribution is non-normal and a few extreme values could seriously affect the mean. Where a distribution has only a small number of possible values the median may be of little or no use: a large number of the observations may have the 'median' value and the proportions above and below this value may not be evenly balanced.

Now we can define statistical concepts which measure how different sample estimates are from 'true' values. It is important here to remember the fundamental distinction between the variance of a variable (that is, the extent to which individual values vary about their mean) and the variance of the estimate of the mean of that variable. Confusion between these two measures is far from uncommon and is the cause of much needless misunderstanding. The two are related, however; the larger the variance of a variable, the larger will be the estimate of the variance of its mean, other things being equal.

The sample mean $\bar{x}$ is an estimate and it will take different values when sampling is repeated. Therefore, it can also be considered as a *random variable* which takes certain values with certain probabilities. For simple random sampling, it can be shown that the *mean value* of this variable coincides with the 'true' mean value μ of the *original variable* x. In other words, if the sampling is repeated many times, the overall average value of sample means will be approximately equal to μ. (Any estimate of μ with this property is called *unbiased*.)

The *standard error* of an estimate is the most frequently used measure of the precision of that estimate. It may be regarded as the standard deviation of repeated estimates of the mean. The standard error of the sample mean $\bar{x}$ is the square root of the variance of variable $\bar{x}$. Note that here we are dealing with how the means are distributed, not with how variable x is distributed about its mean. Whatever the shape of the distribution of a variable, when a large number of samples of equal size are drawn in the same manner, the *means* of those samples have an approximately normal distribution. In other words, variable $\bar{x}$ is approximately normal when the sample size is large. This is known as the *Central Limit Theorem*.

Now we may want to estimate how the means of small samples would vary around the population mean, but we generally have only one sample to work with, so we have to infer this from what we know of the sample we have, using the sample variance of the variable and the sample size. Ideally we should base the estimate on the population variance. However, generally we do not know this and we are thrown back on the assumption that the (known) sample variance can be used as an estimate of the (unknown) population variance. In most cases this can safely be done, but there are some exceptions.

For a simple random sample with n respondents, the formula for the standard error is

$$\text{s.e.}(\bar{x}) = \frac{S}{\sqrt{n}},$$

where S is the standard deviation of the original variable x.

For a non-simple-random sample, this formula *is not valid* and there is no universal formula suitable for all situations. The correct formula depends on the sampling and weighting procedure and various formulae and methods for estimating the variance of $\bar{x}$ are discussed in Chapter 3. Once the variance of the estimate is known, the standard error is then the square root of that variance and it is customary, in the general case, to express the standard error of $\bar{x}$ in terms of *effective sample size* and/or *design effect*.

Denote by V_{ran} the variance of $\bar{x}$ for simple random sampling (in other words, $V_{\text{ran}} = S^2/n$). Let V be the 'correct' variance of $\bar{x}$ calculated according to the chosen sampling and weighting procedure. Then the design effect DE is computed as

$$\text{DE} = \frac{V}{V_{\text{ran}}}$$

while the effective sample size n_e is given by

$$n_e = \frac{n}{\text{DE}} = \frac{n V_{\text{ran}}}{V}.$$

Then the standard error of $\bar{x}$ can be expressed either in terms of the effective sample size

$$\text{s.e.}(\bar{x}) = \frac{S}{\sqrt{n_e}}$$

or in terms of the design effect

$$\text{s.e.}(\bar{x}) = \sqrt{\text{DE}}\frac{S}{\sqrt{n}}.$$

Notice that, strictly speaking, any formula for the standard error gives only an *estimate* of the standard error based on the sample data. Every different sample will produce a (slightly) different estimate of the standard error.

The standard error can be interpreted as the typical ('root-mean-square' average) error we make when a population parameter, say μ, is measured. In other words, if we repeat the sampling many times (in fact, infinitely many times), obtain each time an estimate $\bar{x}$ and calculate the average of differences $(\bar{x} - \mu)^2$, then the square root of the latter average gives us the standard error of the estimate of the mean. Of course, as with any variable, it is impossible to take an infinite number of samples and calculate their means so that the standard error can generally only be estimated using one sample's data.

When the population parameter to be measured is a *proportion* (i.e. the corresponding variable is binary and has only two values – zero and one), the variance formulae become simpler. Let p be the 'true' proportion value and $\hat{p}$ its sample estimate. Then the population variance σ^2 and sample variance S^2 are computed by the formulae:

$$\sigma^2 = p(1 - p), \quad S^2 = \hat{p}(1 - \hat{p}).$$

The respective standard deviations are the square roots of these while the standard error of $\hat{p}$ is estimated by

$$\text{s.e.}(\hat{p}) = \sqrt{\text{DE}}\sqrt{\frac{\hat{p}(1 - \hat{p})}{n}}.$$

The *confidence limits* of a population parameter (e.g. the mean) form an interval (called *confidence interval*) such that there is a (stated) probability that the interval contains the 'true' value. More precisely, the statement '[2.4, 2.8] is a 95% confidence interval for a proportion estimate' means that if we repeat the sampling which led to the interval a hundred times and make the same measurements and calculations under the same conditions (so that we get a hundred different intervals) then approximately ninety-five times the true value of the proportion will fall within that interval. It is exactly in this sense we can say that 'the chances are 95 out of 100 that the interval [2.4, 2.8] contains the true proportion value', with the further implicit expectation that the probability that the range is wholly above the true value is the same as the probability that it is wholly below the true value.

If the distribution is symmetrical (or nearly so) it is common to quote the estimated mean or proportion and the confidence limits as a 'plus-or-minus' figure (2.6 ± 0.2). Where a variable is normally distributed, or can be regarded as such for practical purposes, the confidence limits can be estimated from the standard error. (If the sample size is large, this can still be done in most practical situations using the Central Limit Theorem.) They are often expressed as so many standard errors above and below the estimate: $\bar{x} \pm k\,\text{s.e.}(\bar{x})$. The most common values of k are the following:

confidence level	90%	95%	99%
k	1.645	1.96	2.58

(values of k for other percentiles can be found in Table H1). The 95% confidence limits are, for convenience of mental calculation, often taken as twice the standard error above and below the mean.

However, when the estimated proportion is small (or very large), and particularly where the sample size is not very large, the confidence limits may not be at all symmetrical. An estimate of a proportion of 0.1% with a sample size of 2000 can obviously not be regarded as having 95% confidence limits of $[-0.04\%, 0.24\%]$. The use of the sample variance as an estimate of the population variance is inappropriate here. Cochran [9] suggests that the normal approximation should be used only when the smaller of the numbers of observations making up the proportion has a value ranging from 40 for a 20% estimate (i.e. a sample size of 200), through 60 for a 10% estimate ($n = 600$) and 70 for 5% ($n = 1400$) to 80 when the proportion is very small. The numbers should be divided by the design effect where the sample is not simple random.

To obtain a truer estimate when the normal approximation cannot be used we must work back from the population to the sample. We can estimate the upper confidence limit by asking: what incidence in the population would have a 2.5% chance of yielding an estimate of 0.1% or less in a sample of 2000? This works in *all* cases because the upper confidence limit has a convenient property: if it is the true population proportion, then there is a 2.5% chance that any sample will yield the original sample estimate or less. Similarly we estimate the lower confidence limit by asking: what incidence in the population would yield that estimate or more on only 2.5% of occasions?

For a simple random sample the number of successes k in n trials is distributed as the binomial expansion of $(p + q)^n$ where p is the proportion in the population and $q = 1 - p$. If k is the number of successes in a sample of size n, then the upper confidence limit is the lowest value p for which the value

$$\sum_{s=0}^{k}\left[\binom{n}{s} p^s (1 - p)^{n-s}\right]$$

is not greater than 0.025. A corresponding calculation can be made for the lower confidence limit. This calculation is not very convenient, and look-up tables are generally used. The published look-up tables are intended for use with simple random samples, so again the design effect or effective sample size should be included in the estimation process.

We must also consider the extreme case, where the sample yields an estimate of zero for a proportion. This is a perfectly possible outcome when the proportion in the population is very small and the sample is not extremely large. Clearly the simple formula

$$\text{s.e.}(\hat{p}) = \sqrt{\frac{\hat{p}(1 - \hat{p})}{n}}$$

will yield zero for the estimate of the standard error and is of no help to us. In this case, the same principle applies: we must work back from assumed population values. However, because only the extreme term of the binomial distribution is required in this case, the upper 95% confidence limit is simply given by $p_{\text{upper}} = 1 - 0.025^{1/n_e}$.

The lower limit may be assumed to be zero for all practical purposes. In some cases we may know that the true value is greater than zero, in which case it can be assumed to be 'very small' and the fact that the sample estimate lies outside the confidence interval is of no consequence.

Finally, there are several terms related to a *pair of variables* x and y.

The *population covariance* between x and y is defined as

$$\sigma_{x,y} = E((x - E(x))(y - E(y))),$$

where E denotes the (population) mean value of the corresponding variable. There is also a simpler expression for the covariance – it is the mean value of the product of two variables minus the product of their mean values:

$$\sigma_{x,y} = E(xy) - E(x)E(y).$$

The *population correlation coefficient* between variables x and y (common notation $\rho_{x,y}$) is given by

$$\rho_{x,y} = \frac{\sigma_{x,y}}{\sigma_x \sigma_y}$$

(symbols σ_x and σ_y denote the population deviation of x and y, see the corresponding definition above).

The *sample covariance* between x and y is computed by the following formula

$$\text{cov}(x, y) = \frac{1}{n}\sum_{i=1}^{n}(x_i - \bar{x})(y_i - \bar{y}) = \frac{1}{n}\sum_{i=1}^{n}x_i y_i - \bar{x}\bar{y},$$

where n is the sample size and (x_i), (y_i) are sample values for variables x, y. For a weighted sample, the formula becomes

$$\text{cov}(x, y) = \frac{\sum_{i=1}^{n} w_i x_i y_i}{\sum_{i=1}^{n} w_i} - \bar{x}\bar{y},$$

where $\bar{x}$ and $\bar{y}$ are weighted.

The *sample correlation coefficient* r between x and y is simply the covariance divided by the product of sample deviations of x and y. (The deviations are *not* the standard deviations – the corresponding formula uses sample size n rather than $n - 1$.) An equivalent formula for r is the following:

$$r = \frac{\sum_{i=1}^{n} x_i y_i - \left(\sum_{i=1}^{n} x_i\right)\left(\sum_{i=1}^{n} y_i\right)/n}{\sqrt{\sum_{i=1}^{n} x_i^2 - \left(\sum_{i=1}^{n} x_i\right)^2/n}\sqrt{\sum_{i=1}^{n} x_i^2 - \left(\sum_{i=1}^{n} y_i\right)^2/n}}$$

for a simple random sample and

$$r = \frac{\sum_{i=1}^{n} w_i x_i y_i - \left(\sum_{i=1}^{n} w_i x_i\right)\left(\sum_{i=1}^{n} w_i y_i\right)/W}{\sqrt{\sum_{i=1}^{n} w_i x_i^2 - \left(\sum_{i=1}^{n} w_i x_i\right)^2/W}\sqrt{\sum_{i=1}^{n} w_i y_i^2 - \left(\sum_{i=1}^{n} w_i y_i\right)^2/W}}$$

for a weighted sample (where $W = \sum_{i=1}^{n} w_i$ is the total sum of weights).

This has the convenience from a computational point of view that it can be calculated in one pass of the data, without prior knowledge of the means.

The sample correlation coefficient is itself only an estimate. For small or moderate values of r and reasonably large samples its standard error $(1 - r^2)/\sqrt{n}$ can be used to determine confidence limits.

If $r = 0$, variables x and y are said to be *uncorrelated*. A value greater than zero (up to the maximum possible value of 1.0) indicates that above-average values of x tend to be associated with above average values of y. A value of 1.0 or -1.0 indicates that all values of x can be predicted from the corresponding values of y (and *vice versa*) if the means and variances of both x and y are known. Correlation does not, however, as has been said many times, imply any causal relationship between the two variables.

Appendix B
Further reading

For those who want to read further we offer below some suggestions. We have not attempted to be comprehensive, but to put forward a few texts that we feel may be of use to the reader in search of further insight.

Many textbooks on the survey research process cover the mechanics of a range of different sampling methods, even though they may gloss over the consequences. Of the more specialised books, overall perhaps the most approachable but wide-ranging coverage of sampling issues is in Cochran *Sampling Techniques* [9]. Kish's *Survey Sampling* [35], in spite of its age, remains the sampler's 'Bible'. Both take a very 'correct' approach to the subject so do not expect to find too many concessions to expediency in either. The readable and not too mathematical *Survey Methods in Social Investigation* by Moser and Kalton [44] looks at sampling in the broader context of survey planning and design. To appreciate the practicalities of the interviewer's task in carrying out the sampling plan an understanding of the conduct of fieldwork on the ground is helpful and a good introduction to this is Macfarlane Smith's [41] *Interviewing in Market and Social Research*. A range of useful views on the question of non-response can be found in *Survey Nonresponse* by Groves *et al*. [25], a collection of papers from a major conference on the subject.

A useful review of survey practice is *Household Sample Surveys in Developing and Transitional Countries* [58] from the United Nations, which includes a wide range of topics covering most aspects of the survey design and execution process, including weighting. Although as the name implies it covers the countries where survey research is less well developed, the need to design surveys in the absence of established infrastructure provides good illustrations of the basic principles that underlie all survey work.

For those who want to delve into the detail of variance estimation for complex samples there are three texts that will provide a wealth of material. They are written for readers with a strong mathematical bent. The most challenging mathematically is Lehtonen and Pahkinen *Practical Methods for Design and Analysis of Complex Surveys* [40]. More compact is Lee *et al. Analyzing Complex Surveys* [39] while Skinner *et al.*'s *Analysis of Complex Surveys* [54] covers similar ground.

The mechanics of significance testing, and tests beyond the limited range we have covered are covered in a wide range of statistics texts and we do not feel able to single out any in particular. However, it is rare to find any allusion to the problems of non-simple-random samples or weighted data sets so any reading in these areas needs to be done with due regard for these.

For the philosophy of significance testing we recommend Chow *Statistical Significance: Rationale, Validity and Utility* [8] as an in-depth review of the thinking behind the subject, at the same time requiring little or no mathematical ability. An interesting collection of material illustrating the diversity of opinion among researchers, particularly in the behavioural sciences, is *The Significance Test Controversy*, edited by Morrison and Henkel [43].

A good survey of existing regression methods is given by Ryan in *Modern Regression Methods* [50].

Much of the material on correspondence analysis is in French and the main English language source is Greenacre's *Theory and Applications of Correspondence Analysis* [22] and the later follow-up *Correspondence Analysis in Practice* [23]. An article by Hoffman and Franke, Correspondence analysis: graphical representation of categorical data in marketing research [29], may serve as a gentler introduction.

Although much has developed in detail since it was published (1977) Sheth's *Multivariate Methods for Market and Survey Research* [53] provides a useful wide-ranging review, from a variety of viewpoints, of the various multivariate analysis techniques used in market and social surveys. Their use in surveys of non-human populations in the natural sciences is described by Digby and Kempton in *Multivariate Analysis of Ecological Communities* [15].

Appendix C
Summary tables for several common distributions

Table C1. Discrete random variables

Distribution	Probability function	Mean	Variance
Binomial	$\binom{n}{i} p^i (1-p)^{n-i}$, $0 \le p \le 1$, $i = 0, \ldots, n$	np	$np(1-p)$
Negative binomial	$\binom{i-1}{r-1} p^i (1-p)^{i-r}$, $i = r, r+1, \ldots$, $r = 1, 2, \ldots, 0 < p < 1$	$\dfrac{r}{p}$	$\dfrac{r(1-p)}{p^2}$
Geometric	$p(1-p)^{i-1}, 0 < p < 1$, $i = 1, 2, 3, \ldots$	$\dfrac{1}{p}$	$\dfrac{1-p}{p^2}$
Hypergeometric	$\dfrac{\binom{M}{i}\binom{N-M}{n-i}}{\binom{N}{n}}$, $M = 1, \ldots, N$ $i = 0, 1, \ldots, \min(n, M)$	$\dfrac{nM}{N}$	$\dfrac{N-n}{N-1}\dfrac{nM}{N}\left(1 - \dfrac{M}{N}\right)$
Poisson	$\dfrac{\lambda^i \exp(-\lambda)}{i!}$, $i = 0, 1, 2, \ldots, \lambda > 0$,	λ	λ
Beta-binomial	$\binom{n}{i} \dfrac{B(\alpha+i, n+\beta-i)}{B(\alpha, \beta)}$ $\alpha, \beta > 0, \ i = 0, 1, \ldots, n$ (B is the beta-function)	$\dfrac{n\alpha}{\alpha+\beta}$	$\dfrac{n\alpha\beta(n+\alpha+\beta)}{(\alpha+\beta)^2(1+\alpha+\beta)}$

Table C2. Continuous random variables

Distribution	Density function	Mean	Variance
Normal	$y = \dfrac{1}{\sigma\sqrt{2\pi}}\exp\left[-\dfrac{(x-\mu)^2}{2\sigma^2}\right],$ $\mu, \sigma \in \mathbb{R}$	μ	σ^2
Uniform	$y = \frac{1}{b-a},$ $a \le x \le b, a < b$	$\dfrac{b+a}{2}$	$\dfrac{(b-a)^2}{12}$
Gamma	$y = \frac{\lambda^\alpha}{\Gamma(\alpha)}x^{\alpha-1}\exp(-\lambda x),$ $x > 0, \alpha > 0, \lambda > 0$ (Γ is the gamma-function: $\Gamma(a) = \int_0^\infty x^{a-1}\exp(-x)\,\mathrm{d}x$)	$\dfrac{\alpha}{\lambda}$	$\dfrac{\alpha}{\lambda^2}$
Beta	$y = \frac{\Gamma(\alpha+\beta)}{\Gamma(\alpha)\Gamma(\beta)}x^{\alpha-1}(1-x)^{\beta-1},$ $0 < x < 1, \alpha, \beta > 0$	$\dfrac{\alpha}{\alpha+\beta}$	$\dfrac{\alpha\beta}{(\alpha+\beta)^2(\alpha+\beta+1)}$
Chi-square	$y = \dfrac{x^{k/2-1}\exp(-x/2)}{2^{k/2}\Gamma(k/2)}$ $x, k > 0$	k	$2k$
Exponential	$y = \lambda\exp(-\lambda x), x, \lambda > 0$	$\dfrac{1}{\lambda}$	$\dfrac{1}{\lambda^2}$
Double exponential	$y = \frac{1}{2\sigma}\exp(-|x-\theta|/\sigma)$ $x, \theta \in \mathbb{R}, \sigma > 0$	θ	$2\sigma^2$
Logistic	$y = \dfrac{\exp(-(x-\theta)/\sigma)}{\sigma[1+\exp(-(x-\theta)/\sigma)]^2}$ $x, \theta \in \mathbb{R}, \sigma > 0$	θ	$\dfrac{\sigma^2\pi^2}{3}$

Appendix D
Chapter 2: mathematical proofs

D1 Marginal weighting

Minimisation of variance

With the Lagrange multipliers method, the new function is introduced

$$
F = \sum_{i,j,k} w_{i,j,k}^2 n_{i,j,k} - \sum_{i=1}^{n} \lambda_i \left(\sum_{j,k} w_{i,j,k} n_{i,j,k} - P_i \right)
$$
$$
- \sum_{j=1}^{m} \mu_j \left(\sum_{i,k} w_{i,j,k} n_{i,j,k} - Q_j \right) - \sum_{k=1}^{l} \nu_k \left(\sum_{i,j} w_{i,j,k} n_{i,j,k} - R_k \right).
$$

The partial derivatives of F with respect to all $w_{i,j,k}$ are then computed and equated to zero:

$$
2w_{i,j,k} n_{i,j,k} - \lambda_i n_{i,j,k} - \mu_j n_{i,j,k} - \nu_k n_{i,j,k} = 0,
$$

so that we obtain formula (2.3). The expression $w_{i,j,k} n_{i,j,k}$ is then substituted in formula (2.1) by the expression $0.5(\lambda_i + \mu_j + \nu_k) n_{i,j,k}$ which will give us the system (2.2).

The last question to discuss is whether we get a point of maximum or a point of minimum.

There is a well known general method for deciding whether we get an extreme point and, if so, whether it is a point of maximum or a point of minimum. The method is to analyse the matrix of second derivatives of F at the 'suspected' point and to decide whether the matrix is so-called positive definite or negative definite. However, in all our examples where we need to apply this method, the matrix of second derivatives is actually diagonal and there is a simpler way to check a 'suspected' point.

Assume that we are given a multi-dimensional function $F : \mathbb{R}^d \to \mathbb{R}$ and we have to decide whether a vector $\bar{z} = (z_1, \ldots, z_d) \in \mathbb{R}^d$ is an extreme point or not. Clearly, one has to investigate then the difference between the value at this point and the value $F(\bar{x})$ at other points $\bar{x} \in \mathbb{R}^d$ in a vicinity of $\bar{z}$. The difference $F(\bar{x}) - F(\bar{z})$ is approximated, under certain conditions of 'smoothness', by the quadratic form from the Taylor series expansion

$$F(\bar{x}) - F(\bar{z}) \approx \frac{1}{2} \sum_{i,j=1}^{d} a_{i,j}(x_i - z_i)(x_j - z_j),$$

where

$$\bar{x} = (x_1, \ldots, x_d) \in \mathbb{R}^d \quad \text{and} \quad a_{i,j} = \frac{\partial^2 F}{\partial x_i \partial x_j}(\bar{z}).$$

The difference between $F(\bar{x}) - F(\bar{z})$ and the quadratic form can be considered negligible in the vicinity of $\bar{z}$ so that the sign of the expression in the right-hand side is crucial for the sign of the difference $F(\bar{x}) - F(\bar{z})$.

If the matrix $A = (a_{i,j})$ is diagonal, $a_{i,j} = 0$ for $i \neq j$ and so

$$F(\bar{x}) - F(\bar{z}) \approx \frac{1}{2} \sum_{i=1}^{d} a_{i,i}(x_i - z_i)^2.$$

The expression $(x_i - z_i)^2$ is obviously non-negative so that the sign of the difference $F(\bar{x}) - F(\bar{z})$ entirely depends on the diagonal elements of A. If all $a_{i,i}$ are non-negative, the difference $F(\bar{x}) - F(\bar{z})$ is always non-negative (in the vicinity of $\bar{z}$) so that $\bar{z}$ is a point of minimum. On the other hand, if all $a_{i,i}$ are less than or equal to zero, the difference $F(\bar{x}) - F(\bar{z})$ is also less than or equal to zero in the vicinity of $\bar{z}$ and hence $\bar{z}$ is a point of maximum.

This simple 'recipe' is good enough for all our examples.

In our particular case, the 'suspected' point is the solution obtained by the Lagrange multipliers method. The second derivative of F with respect to $w_{i,j,k}$ will be $2n_{i,j,k}$ which is non-negative and the matrix of second derivatives is diagonal (because the expression for the first derivative of F depends only on the variable $w_{i,j,k}$). Therefore, we get a point of minimum.

D2   Aggregate weighting

Rim weighting

To prove formula (2.6), we will again use the Lagrange multipliers method. The function to minimise is

$$f = \sum_{i=1}^{n} \left(w_i' - w_i\right)^2$$

and the new function is

$$F = \sum_{i=1}^{n} \left(w_i' - w_i\right)^2 - \lambda \left(\sum_{i=1}^{n} w_i' - W\right) - \mu \left(\sum_{i=1}^{n} w_i' x_i - tW\right).$$

Taking the derivative with respect to w_i' and equating it to zero, we obtain

$$2\left(w_i' - w_i\right) - \lambda - \mu x_i = 0$$

or

$$w_i' = w_i + \frac{1}{2}(\lambda + \mu x_i). \tag{D1}$$

Replacing w_i' by this expression in the equation $\sum_{i=1}^n w_i' = W$, we get $\sum_{i=1}^n (\lambda + \mu x_i) = 0$ or $\lambda = -\mu \bar{x}_0$. Hence, if λ is replaced by $-\mu \bar{x}_0$ in equation (D1), the formula for w_i' becomes

$$w_i' = w_i + \frac{1}{2}\mu(x_i - \bar{x}_0). \tag{D2}$$

Now w_i' can be similarly replaced by this expression in the second equation $\sum_{i=1}^n w_i' x_i = t W$ which yields

$$\bar{x} W + \frac{1}{2}\mu \sum_{i=1}^n x_i(x_i - \bar{x}_0) = t W.$$

Consequently,

$$\mu = \frac{2(t - \bar{x})W}{\sum_{i=1}^n x_i(x_i - \bar{x}_0)} = \frac{2(t - \bar{x})W}{\sum_{i=1}^n x_i^2 - \bar{x}_0 \sum_{i=1}^n x_i}$$
$$= \frac{2(t - \bar{x})W}{n\left(\sum_{i=1}^n x_i^2/n - \bar{x}_0^2\right)} = \frac{2(t - \bar{x})W}{n \operatorname{var}(x)}.$$

Finally, replacing μ by this expression in equation (D2), we get the required formula for w_i'. The matrix of second derivatives is diagonal, with diagonal elements being equal to 2. Therefore, the solution (2.6) is a point of minimum.

Minimisation of variance

This is very similar to marginal weighting. The new function F is

$$F = \sum_i w_i^2 - \sum_{j=1}^m \lambda_j \left(\sum_i a_{i,j} w_i - B_j \right) - \mu \left(\sum_i w_i - P \right).$$

The partial derivatives of F are

$$2w_i - \sum_{j=1}^m \lambda_j a_{i,j} - \mu,$$

so that

$$w_i = 0.5 \left(\sum_{j=1}^m \lambda_j a_{i,j} + \mu \right).$$

The system (2.8) is then obtained if w_i is substituted by this expression in formulae (2.5) and (2.7). As in marginal weighting, the second derivative of F with respect to w_i is positive (it is equal to 2) and the matrix of second derivatives is diagonal. Hence, by the same arguments as above, the solution of (2.8) is a point of minimum.

Appendix E
Chapter 3: mathematical proofs

E1 Design effect and effective sample size

To get the design effect formula in Theorem 3.1, notice that the sampling variance is

$$V = \sum_s \lambda_s^2 \frac{p_s(1-p_s)}{(n_s)_e} = \sum_s \lambda_s^2 \frac{p_s(1-p_s)}{n_s/\text{DE}_s}$$

while the variance of simple random sampling is $p(1-p)/n$. Thus,

$$\text{DE} = \frac{\sum_s \lambda_s^2 [p_s(1-p_s)\text{DE}_s/n_s]}{p(1-p)/n}$$

$$= \sum_s \frac{\lambda_s^2}{n_s/n} \frac{p_s(1-p_s)}{p(1-p)} \text{DE}_s = \sum_s \frac{\lambda_s^2}{\mu_s} \frac{p_s(1-p_s)}{p(1-p)} \text{DE}_s.$$

The formula for the total effective sample size is then easily obtained:

$$\frac{1}{n_e} = \frac{\text{DE}}{n} = \frac{1}{n} \sum_s \frac{\lambda_s^2}{n_s/n} \frac{p_s(1-p_s)}{p(1-p)} \text{DE}_s = \sum_s \frac{\lambda_s^2}{n_s} \frac{p_s(1-p_s)}{p(1-p)} \text{DE}_s$$

$$= \sum_s \frac{\lambda_s^2}{n_s/\text{DE}_s} \frac{p_s(1-p_s)}{p(1-p)} = \sum_s \frac{\lambda_s^2}{(n_s)_e} \frac{p_s(1-p_s)}{p(1-p)}.$$

E2 Weighting effect

To prove Theorem 3.2, we consider $x_1, \ldots, x_n$ as independent identically distributed random variables. Because the weights are constant we obtain

$$\text{var}(\bar{x}_w) = \frac{\text{var}\left(\sum_{i=1}^n w_i x_i\right)}{\left(\sum_{i=1}^n w_i\right)^2} = \frac{\sum_{i=1}^n w_i^2 \text{var}(x_i)}{\left(\sum_{i=1}^n w_i\right)^2} = \frac{\sum_{i=1}^n w_i^2 \text{var}(x)}{\left(\sum_{i=1}^n w_i\right)^2}.$$

Therefore, $\text{var}(\bar{x}_w)/\text{var}(x) = (\sum_{i=1}^n w_i^2)/(\sum_{i=1}^n w_i)^2 = 1/n_c$. The design effect is, by definition, the actual variance $\text{var}(\bar{x}_w)$ divided by the variance of simple random sampling which is $\text{var}(x)/n$. Consequently,

$$\text{DE} = \frac{\text{var}(\bar{x}_w)}{\text{var}(x)/n} = \frac{n\,\text{var}(\bar{x}_w)}{\text{var}(x)} = \frac{n}{n_c} = \text{WE}.$$

The first property of the calibrated sample size has been proved in [10] but we give another, much shorter, proof. By the Cauchy–Schwarz inequality, $(\sum_{i=1}^{n} a_i b_i)^2 \leq (\sum_{i=1}^{n} a_i^2)(\sum_{i=1}^{n} b_i^2)$ for any real numbers (a_i), (b_i) with the equality if and only if there is λ such that $a_i = \lambda b_i$ for all i. (This inequality, known also as the Cauchy–Bunyakovskij inequality, is discussed in almost any textbook on functional analysis or Hilbert spaces.) Therefore,

$$\left(\sum_{i=1}^{n} w_i\right)^2 = \left(\sum_{i=1}^{n} w_i \cdot 1\right)^2 \leq \left(\sum_{i=1}^{n} w_i^2\right)\left(\sum_{i=1}^{n} 1^2\right) = n\sum_{i=1}^{n} w_i^2,$$

so that $n_c = (\sum_{i=1}^{n} w_i)^2 / (\sum_{i=1}^{n} w_i^2) \leq n$ with the equality if and only if all weights are constant.

To prove the second property, assume that $n = n_1 + \cdots + n_m$. We have to show that

$$n_c \leq (n_1)_c + \cdots + (n_m)_c.$$

It is enough to prove this inequality in the case of two summands because then the repetition gives the general case. In the case of two summands, we have to prove that

$$\frac{\left(\sum_{i=1}^{n} w_i\right)^2}{\sum_{i=1}^{n} w_i^2} \leq \frac{\left(\sum_{i=1}^{k} w_i\right)^2}{\sum_{i=1}^{k} w_i^2} + \frac{\left(\sum_{i=k+1}^{n} w_i\right)^2}{\sum_{i=k+1}^{n} w_i^2},$$

where $1 \leq k \leq n$. But this inequality is a particular case of a more general inequality

$$\frac{(a+c)^2}{b+d} \leq \frac{a^2}{b} + \frac{c^2}{d},$$

where $a, b, c, d \geq 0$. The last inequality is always true because

$$\frac{a^2}{b} + \frac{c^2}{d} - \frac{(a+c)^2}{b+d} = \frac{(ad-bc)^2}{bd(b+d)} \geq 0.$$

To calculate the maximum possible value of the weighting effect (for the third property), we first show that the maximum can be achieved only if all respondents have either the maximum weight w_{max} or the minimum weight w_{min}. Indeed, let us take a respondent with a weight w which is different from w_{min} and w_{max}. Let A (respectively, B) be the sum of weights (respectively, sum of squared weights) of *other* respondents. Then the weighting effect is computed by the formula

$$\text{WE} = \frac{n(B+w^2)}{(A+w)^2}.$$

We consider this expression as a function f of w, where $w \in [w_{min}, w_{max}]$. Simple calculations show that the derivative of this function is

$$f'(w) = \frac{2n(wA - B)}{(A+w)^3}$$

so that f achieves its minimum value at $w = B/A$. This implies, in particular, that its *maximum* value will be achieved either at $w = w_{min}$ or at $w = w_{max}$, independently of whether B/A is inside the interval $[w_{min}, w_{max}]$ or outside it. Therefore, the weighting effect will be increased if w is replaced either by $w_{\min}$ or by $w_{\max}$, whatever is appropriate. The same procedure can be repeated for all respondents so that each of them will have either the minimum or the maximum weight. Hence, we have proved the first part.

Now we prove the actual formula assuming that all respondents have one of the two weights $w_{\min}$ or $w_{\max}$. Assume that n_1 respondents have weight $w_{\min}$ and n_2 respondents have weight $w_{\max}$ so that $n = n_1 + n_2$ is the total sample size. The weighting effect formula then becomes

$$\text{WE} = \frac{n \sum_{i=1}^{n} w_i^2}{\left(\sum_{i=1}^{n} w_i\right)^2} = \frac{n(n_1 w_{\min}^2 + n_2 w_{\max}^2)}{(n_1 w_{\min} + n_2 w_{\max})^2} = \frac{n(n - n_2 + n_2 \theta^2)}{(n - n_2 + n_2 \theta)^2}.$$

We will treat n_2 as a variable t and consider the expression above as a function of this variable:

$$f(t) = \frac{n(n - t + t\theta^2)}{(n - t + t\theta)^2},$$

where t can have real values from $[0, n]$. It is again simple 'school' algebra to find the maximum value of this function. Straightforward calculations show that the derivative of this function is

$$f'(t) = \frac{n(\theta - 1)^2 (n - t(\theta + 1))}{(n + t(\theta - 1))^3},$$

so that the maximum will be for $t = n/(\theta + 1)$. The substitution of this value into the original formula for f will produce then the required maximum value $(\theta + 1)^2/(4\theta)$.

The calculations for the total calibrated sample size in formula (3.20) are the following: if respondent i in sample s has weight $w_{i,s}$ and the sum of weights in sample s is W_s then the new weight (after combining the samples) of the same respondent will be $\lambda_s w_{i,s}/W_s$. The sum of new weights is then equal to 1.0, so that

$$n_c = 1 \left/ \left[\sum_{s=1}^{m} \sum_i \frac{\lambda_s^2 w_{i,s}^2}{W_s^2} \right] \right. = 1 \left/ \left[\sum_{s=1}^{m} \lambda_s^2 \frac{\sum_i w_{i,s}^2}{W_s^2} \right] \right. = 1 \left/ \left[\sum_{s=1}^{m} \lambda_s^2 \frac{1}{(n_s)_c} \right] \right. .$$

Therefore, the weighting effect is

$$\text{WE} = \frac{n}{n_c} = n \sum_{s=1}^{m} \frac{\lambda_s^2}{n_s/\text{WE}_s} = \sum_{s=1}^{m} \frac{\lambda_s^2}{n_s/n} \text{WE}_s = \sum_{s=1}^{m} \frac{\lambda_s^2}{\mu_s} \text{WE}_s.$$

Now we prove the corollaries for the weighting effect in stratified random sampling. The first corollary is fairly obvious. The second corollary is based on the fact that the expression $x(1 - x)$ reaches its maximum at $x = 0.5$. Therefore, if $p = 0.5$, $p(1 - p)$ has the maximum possible value 0.25 and $p_s(1 - p_s)$ can never be greater than 0.25. Hence,

$$\text{DE} = \sum_{s=1}^{m} \frac{\lambda_s^2 p_s(1 - p_s)}{0.25 \mu_s} \leq \sum_{s=1}^{m} \frac{0.25 \lambda_s^2}{0.25 \mu_s} = \text{WE},$$

and the equality will be if and only if $p_s(1 - p_s) = 0.25$ or $p_s = 0.5$, for any s. Finally, to prove the third corollary, observe that in the case of proportional sampling we have $\mu_s = \lambda_s$ so that $WE = \sum_{s=1}^{m} \lambda_s^2/\mu_s = \sum_{s=1}^{m} \lambda_s = 1$ while

$$DE = \sum_{s=1}^{m} \frac{\lambda_s^2 p_s(1 - p_s)}{\mu_s p(1 - p)} = \frac{\sum_{s=1}^{m} \lambda_s p_s(1 - p_s)}{p(1 - p)} = \frac{p - \sum_{s=1}^{m} \lambda_s p_s^2}{p - p^2}.$$

By the Cauchy–Schwarz inequality,

$$p^2 = \left(\sum_{s=1}^{m} \lambda_s p_s\right)^2 = \left(\sum_{s=1}^{m} \sqrt{\lambda_s}(\sqrt{\lambda_s} p_s)\right)^2 \le \sum_{s=1}^{m} \lambda_s \sum_{s=1}^{m} \lambda_s p_s^2 = \sum_{s=1}^{m} \lambda_s p_s^2,$$

which proves that $DE \le 1$. The equality will be only in the case when the family $(\sqrt{\lambda_s} p_s)$ is a multiple of $\sqrt{\lambda_s}$ which can happen only if all p_s are the same.

The calculations for Example 3.4 are the following:

$$\frac{DE}{WE} = \frac{\lambda_1^2 p_1(1 - p_1)/(\mu_1 p(1 - p)) + \lambda_2^2 p_2(1 - p_2)/(\mu_2 p(1 - p))}{\lambda_1^2/\mu_1 + \lambda_1^2 \mu_2}$$

$$= \frac{c_1 p_1(1 - p_1) + c_2 p_2(1 - p_2)}{p(1 - p)},$$

where

$$c_1 = \frac{\lambda_1^2/\mu_1}{\lambda_1^2/\mu_1 + \lambda_2^2/\mu_2} \qquad \text{and} \qquad c_2 = \frac{\lambda_2^2/\mu_2}{\lambda_1^2/\mu_1 + \lambda_2^2/\mu_2}.$$

Notice that

$$c_1 = \frac{\lambda_1^2 \mu_2}{\lambda_1^2 \mu_2 + \lambda_2^2 \mu_1} = \frac{(1 - \varepsilon)^2 \varepsilon^3}{(1 - \varepsilon)^2 \varepsilon^3 + \varepsilon^2(1 - \varepsilon^3)} = \frac{(1 - \varepsilon)^2 \varepsilon}{(1 - \varepsilon)^2 \varepsilon + 1 - \varepsilon^3}$$

which is close to 0.0 so that the other coefficient $c_2 = 1 - c_1$ is close to 1.0. On the other hand,

$$p = (1 - \varepsilon)p_1 + \varepsilon p_2 \approx p_1$$

and hence $p(1 - p)$ will be close to $p_1(1 - p_1)$.

The calculations above mean that

$$\frac{DE}{WE} = \frac{c_1 p_1(1 - p_1) + c_2 p_2(1 - p_2)}{p(1 - p)} \approx \frac{p_2(1 - p_2)}{p_1(1 - p_1)}.$$

Finally, we have to prove Proposition 3.2. The statement that interval $[\bar{x} - ke, \bar{x} + ke]$ contains interval $[\bar{x}_{unw} - ke_{unw}, \bar{x}_{unw} + ke_{unw}]$ is equivalent to the following two inequalities:

$$\bar{x} - ke \le \bar{x}_{unw} - ke_{unw} \qquad \text{and} \qquad \bar{x} + ke \ge \bar{x}_{unw} + ke_{unw}. \qquad (E1)$$

These inequalities, on the other hand, can be rewritten as

$$\bar{x} - \bar{x}_{unw} \le k(e - e_{unw}) \qquad \text{and} \qquad \bar{x} - \bar{x}_{unw} \ge -k(e - e_{unw}).$$

These last relationships, however, mean that

$$|\bar{x} - \bar{x}_{\text{unw}}| \leq k(e - e_{\text{unw}})$$

or

$$U(\bar{x}) = \frac{|\bar{x} - \bar{x}_{\text{unw}}|}{(e - e_{\text{unw}})} \leq k,$$

so that the original statement is equivalent to this inequality. It is also clear that in the case of equality $U(\bar{x}) = k$ one of the inequalities in equation (E1) must become an equality so that either the left ends or the right ends of the intervals should coincide.

E3   Missing data

To derive equation (3.30), notice that

$$\tilde{x} - \bar{x} = \frac{\sum_{i=m+1}^{n} w_i f_i - \sum_{i=m+1}^{n} w_i x_i}{\sum_{i=1}^{n} w_i} = \frac{\sum_{i=m+1}^{n} w_i \epsilon_i}{\sum_{i=m+1}^{n} w_i} \cdot \frac{\sum_{i=m+1}^{n} w_i}{\sum_{i=1}^{n} w_i} = \tilde{\epsilon}\alpha.$$

Proposition 3.3 is, in fact, obvious under given conditions. The definition of effective sample size guarantees that the variance of $\bar{x}$ calculated as the variance of x divided by n_e as well as that the variance of $\tilde{\epsilon}$ is the variance of ϵ over $(n - m)_e$. The last assumption then allows us to replace $(n - m)_e$ by $(n - m)_c$. The variances of x and ϵ are then estimated by the usual statistical formulae. Finally, to deduce corollary 3.1, observe that the variance of x is $p(1 - p)$ where p is the 'true' proportion. Then, of course, p is approximated by $\tilde{p}$. The term $\tilde{\epsilon}^2$ is simply the second term in equation (3.35) and the last thing to prove is that the first term of (3.35) is $1 - R$. This is also easy to see: the squared values ϵ_i^2 can only be equal to 0 or 1 so that the average squared error will be equal to the sum of weights of respondents with error $= 1$ divided by the total sum of weights, which is the proportion of 'wrong prediction' or $1 - R$.

Appendix F
Chapter 4: mathematical proofs

F1 Difference between proportions

To prove formula (4.2), represent proportions $\hat{p}_1$ and $\hat{p}_2$ in the following form

$$\hat{p}_1 = \frac{1}{n}\sum_{i=1}^{n} x_i, \qquad \hat{p}_2 = \frac{1}{n}\sum_{i=1}^{n} y_i,$$

where x_i and y_i are identically distributed binary variables such that x_i, y_i are independent of x_j, y_j for $i \neq j$. Then

$$\mathrm{cov}(\hat{p}_1, \hat{p}_2) = \frac{1}{n^2}\sum_{i,j}\mathrm{cov}(x_i, y_j) = \frac{1}{n^2}\sum_{i=1}^{n}\mathrm{cov}(x_i, x_i)$$

$$= \frac{1}{n}\mathrm{cov}(x, y) = \frac{1}{n}(E(xy) - E(x)E(y)) = \frac{1}{n}(\hat{p}_{1,2} - \hat{p}_1\hat{p}_2).$$

When the proportions are derived from two overlapping samples or groups of a sample, it means that there are in fact three subsamples – the first sample without the second one, the second sample without the first one and the 'overlapping' sample. We assume that these three samples are independent from each other. To distinguish between binary variables from these samples, denote by x_i binary variables for respondents from the 'overlapping' sample and by y_j and z_k binary variables for respondents from *only* the first and second samples respectively. All variables, therefore, are assumed to be independent from each other. Then we obtain the following expressions for proportions:

$$\hat{p}_1 = \frac{1}{n_1}\left(\sum_i x_i + \sum_j y_j\right), \qquad \hat{p}_2 = \frac{1}{n_2}\left(\sum_i x_i + \sum_k z_k\right).$$

Hence,

$$\mathrm{cov}(\hat{p}_1, \hat{p}_2) = \frac{1}{n_1 n_2}\mathrm{cov}\left(\sum_i x_i + \sum_j y_j, \sum_i x_i + \sum_k z_k\right)$$

$$= \frac{1}{n_1 n_2}\mathrm{cov}\left(\sum_i x_i, \sum_i x_i\right) = \frac{n_0}{n_1 n_2}\mathrm{cov}(x, x) = \frac{n_0\hat{p}_0(1 - \hat{p}_0)}{n_1 n_2}.$$

249

Appendix G
Chapter 5: mathematical proofs

G1 Measuring a difference between two distributions

'Euclidean' distance

To show that the maximum value is 1, notice that

$$d_1^2 = \frac{1}{2}\left(\sum_{i=1}^{n} p_i^2 + \sum_{i=1}^{n} q_i^2 - 2\sum_{i=1}^{n} p_i q_i\right) \leq \frac{1}{2}\left(\sum_{i=1}^{n} p_i + \sum_{i=1}^{n} q_i\right) = 1.$$

This will be achieved only if $p_i^2 = p_i$, $q_i^2 = q_i$ and $p_i q_i = 0$, for any i.

'Symmetric' chi-square distance

The maximum value is 1 because

$$d_2 = \frac{1}{2}\sum_{i=1}^{n} \frac{(p_i + q_i)^2 - 4p_i q_i}{p_i + q_i} = \frac{1}{2}\left(\sum_{i=1}^{n}(p_i + q_i) - 4\sum_{i=1}^{n} \frac{p_i q_i}{p_i + q_i}\right)$$

$$= 1 - 2\sum_{i=1}^{n} \frac{p_i q_i}{p_i + q_i} \leq 1.$$

The equality will be if and only if $p_i q_i = 0$ for any i.

'Geometric' distance

The vectors $\bar{a}$ and $\bar{b}$ are on the unit sphere because their Euclidean norm (that is, distance from the centre of coordinates) is one. Clearly, they form a two-dimensional subspace in $\mathbb{R}^n$ so that it makes sense to talk about the angle α between them in this subspace. To express the distance in terms of probabilities, recall that the cosine of the angle between two vectors is equal to the product of their Euclidean norms times their *scalar product*. In our case, the norms are equal to one so that the cosine is equal to the scalar product (which is the sum of products of the corresponding coordinates):

$$\cos(\alpha) = \sum_{i=1}^{n} \left(\sqrt{p_i} \sqrt{q_i} \right).$$

Hence,

$$d_3 = \sin(\alpha) = \sqrt{1 - \cos^2(\alpha)} = \sqrt{1 - \left(\sum_{i=1}^{n} \sqrt{p_i q_i} \right)^2}.$$

The distance will achieve its maximum value of 1 when

$$\sum_{i=1}^{n} \sqrt{p_i q_i} = 0$$

or $p_i q_i = 0$ for any i.

The minimum value for d_3 is achieved when the sum $\sum_{i=1}^{n} \sqrt{p_i q_i}$ has its maximum value. By the Cauchy–Schwarz inequality,

$$\left(\sum_{i=1}^{n} \sqrt{p_i q_i} \right)^2 \le \left(\sum_{i=1}^{n} p_i \right) \left(\sum_{i=1}^{n} q_i \right) = 1,$$

with the equality being achieved if and only if the vectors $(\sqrt{p_i})$ and $(\sqrt{q_i})$ are multiples of each other. Because these are unit vectors (with non-negative coordinates), the equality can happen only if the vectors are the same. Hence, the maximum value for the sum $\sum_{i=1}^{n} \sqrt{p_i q_i}$ is one so that the minimum value for d_3 is zero, and it is achieved only if the distributions are the same.

G2   Strength of association between categorical variables

Cramer's coefficient

Notice that

$$\sum_{i=1}^{k} \sum_{j=1}^{l} \frac{(r_{i,j} - p_i q_j)^2}{p_i q_j} = \sum_{i=1}^{k} \sum_{j=1}^{l} \frac{r_{i,j}^2}{p_i q_j} - 1 = \sum_{j=1}^{l} \frac{1}{q_j} \sum_{i=1}^{k} \frac{r_{i,j}^2}{p_i} - 1.$$

Clearly, $r_{i,j} \le p_i$, so that

$$\sum_{j=1}^{l} \frac{1}{q_j} \sum_{i=1}^{k} \frac{r_{i,j}^2}{p_i} \le \sum_{j=1}^{l} \frac{1}{q_j} \sum_{i=1}^{k} r_{i,j} = \sum_{j=1}^{l} \frac{q_j}{q_j} = l.$$

To achieve the maximum value, the last inequality $r_{i,j}^2 / p_i \le r_{i,j}$ must become an equality for all i and j. Hence, $r_{i,j}^2 / p_i = r_{i,j}$ so that either $r_{i,j} = 0$ or $r_{i,j} = p_i$.

Entropy coefficients

To prove formula $E(P|Q) = E(P, Q) - E(Q)$, notice that

$$E(P|Q) = -\sum_{i,j} r_{i,j} \ln(r_{i,j}/q_j) = -\sum_{i,j} r_{i,j}(\ln(r_{i,j}) - \ln(q_j))$$

$$= -\sum_{i,j} r_{i,j} \ln(r_{i,j}) + \sum_{i,j} r_{i,j} \ln(q_j) = E(P, Q) + \sum_{j=1}^{l} \ln(q_j) \sum_{i=1}^{k} r_{i,j}$$

$$= E(P, Q) + \sum_{j=1}^{l} \ln(q_j)q_j = E(P, Q) - E(Q).$$

The formula $E(Q|P) = E(P, Q) - E(P)$ is proved similarly.

To show that $E(P, Q) \leq E(P) + E(Q)$, we will again use the Lagrange multipliers method. The function to maximise is

$$f = -\sum_{i,j} r_{i,j} \ln(r_{i,j}),$$

subject to constraints

$$\sum_{j=1}^{l} r_{i,j} = p_i, \quad i = 1, \ldots, k, \qquad \sum_{i=1}^{k} r_{i,j} = q_j, \quad j = 1, \ldots, l.$$

For our purpose, it is enough to show that the solution of this problem is $r_{i,j} = p_i q_j$. Indeed, if $r_{i,j} = p_i q_j$, the joint entropy $E(P, Q)$ coincides with $E(P) + E(Q)$ because

$$E(P) + E(Q) = -\sum_{i=1}^{k} p_i \ln(p_i) - \sum_{j=1}^{l} q_j \ln(q_j)$$

$$= -\sum_{j=1}^{l} q_j \sum_{i=1}^{k} p_i \ln(p_i) - \sum_{i=1}^{k} p_i \sum_{j=1}^{l} q_j \ln(q_j)$$

$$= -\sum_{i,j} p_i q_j \ln(p_i) - \sum_{i,j} p_i q_j \ln(q_j) = -\sum_{i,j} p_i q_j \ln(p_i q_j).$$

In other words, if the solution is $p_i q_j$, this will imply that the maximum value for $E(P, Q)$ is $E(P) + E(Q)$. It will also mean that the maximum value of $E(P, Q)$ will be achieved only when the variables are independent.

To find the solution, we introduce $k + l$ new variables $(\lambda_i)_{i=1}^{k}$ and $(\mu_j)_{j=1}^{l}$. The new function is then

$$F = -\sum_{i,j} r_{i,j} \ln(r_{i,j}) - \sum_{i=1}^{k} \lambda_i \left(\sum_{j=1}^{l} r_{i,j} - p_i \right) - \sum_{j=1}^{l} \mu_j \left(\sum_{i=1}^{k} r_{i,j} - q_j \right).$$

The derivative of F with respect to $r_{i,j}$ is

$$-(\ln(r_{i,j}) + 1) - \lambda_i - \mu_j$$

so that

$$r_{i,j} = e^{-1-\lambda_i-\mu_j}.$$

Let

$$A = \sum_{i=1}^{k} e^{-\lambda_i} \quad \text{and} \quad B = \sum_{j=1}^{l} e^{-\mu_j}.$$

The summation of the previous formula for $r_{i,j}$ by i and j separately gives us the following result

$$p_i = e^{-1}e^{-\lambda_i}B \quad \text{and} \quad q_j = e^{-1}e^{-\mu_j}A.$$

If we add these k equations for p_i, we obtain one extra condition: $1 = e^{-1}AB$ or $AB = e$.

Now we can get the solution. The last formulae for p_i and q_j can be rewritten in the form

$$e^{-\lambda_i} = \frac{e p_i}{B} \quad \text{and} \quad e^{-\mu_j} = \frac{e q_j}{A}$$

and hence we can use it as a substitution in the corresponding formula for $r_{i,j}$:

$$r_{i,j} = e^{-1}e^{-\lambda_i}e^{-\mu_j} = e^{-1}\frac{e p_i}{B}\frac{e q_j}{A} = \frac{e p_i q_j}{AB} = p_i q_j,$$

with the last equality being due to $AB = e$.

The last thing to show is that the solution we get is a point of maximum. To this end, notice that the second derivative of F with respect to $r_{i,j}$ is $-1/r_{i,j}$ so that its value at the solution is $-1/(p_i q_j)$. The matrix of the second derivatives is diagonal because the first derivative does not depend on other variables except $r_{i,j}$. All diagonal elements in the matrix are non-positive and hence the solution is a point of maximum.

G3 Cluster analysis for categorical variables

To prove formula (5.9), note that the 'old' entropies in the first and second clusters are computed as

$$E_{1,\text{old}} = -\sum_{i=1}^{k} \frac{U_i}{U}\ln\left(\frac{U_i}{U}\right), \qquad E_{2,\text{old}} = -\sum_{i=1}^{k} \frac{V_i}{V}\ln\left(\frac{V_i}{V}\right).$$

The 'contributions' of these entropies to the total sum $W_0 E_{\text{old}}$ are

$$U E_{1,\text{old}} = -\sum_{i=1}^{k} U_i \ln\left(\frac{U_i}{U}\right) \quad \text{and} \quad V E_{2,\text{old}} = -\sum_{i=1}^{k} V_i \ln\left(\frac{V_i}{V}\right).$$

When a respondent with value l of the variable is moved from the first cluster to the second, sums of weights U_l and U will be decreased by w while sums of weights V_l and V will be increased by w. Therefore, the 'contribution' of the 'new' entropy

$E_{1,\text{new}}$ to the new sum $W_0 E_{\text{new}}$ is

$$(U - w)E_{1,\text{new}} = -(U_l - w)\ln\left(\frac{U_l - w}{U - w}\right) - \sum_{i \neq l} U_i \ln\left(\frac{U_i}{U - w}\right)$$

while the 'contribution' of the second entropy $E_{2,\text{new}}$ is

$$(V + w)E_{2,\text{new}} = -(V_l + w)\ln\left(\frac{V_l + w}{V + w}\right) - \sum_{i \neq l} V_i \ln\left(\frac{V_i}{V + w}\right).$$

The 'contributions' of other clusters will be the same in $W_0 E_{\text{old}}$ and $W_0 E_{\text{new}}$ because they will contain the same respondents. This means that

$$W_0(E_{\text{old}} - E_{\text{new}}) = (U E_{1,\text{old}} + V E_{2,\text{old}}) - ((U-w)E_{1,\text{new}} + (V+w)E_{2,\text{new}}) = D_1 - D_2$$

where $D_1 = U E_{1,\text{old}} - (U - w)E_{1,\text{new}}$ and $D_2 = V E_{2,\text{old}} - (V + w)E_{2,\text{new}}$.

Hence, the required formula will be proved if we show that $D_1 = f_w(U) - f_w(U_l)$ and $D_2 = f_w(V_l + w) - f_w(V + w)$. The calculations for the first equation are shown below while the calculations for the second equation are very similar and we leave them as an exercise to the reader.

Note that

$$D_1 = -\sum_{i=1}^{k} U_i \ln\left(\frac{U_i}{U}\right) + (U_l - w)\ln\left(\frac{U_l - w}{U - w}\right) + \sum_{i \neq l} U_i \ln\left(\frac{U_i}{U - w}\right)$$

$$= (U_l - w)\ln\left(\frac{U_l - w}{U - w}\right) - U_l \ln\left(\frac{U_l}{U}\right) + \sum_{i \neq l} U_i \left(\ln\left(\frac{U_i}{U - w}\right) - \ln\left(\frac{U_i}{U}\right)\right)$$

$$= -f_w(U_l) - (U_l - w)\ln(U - w) + U_l \ln(U) + \sum_{i \neq l} U_i \ln\left(\frac{U}{U - w}\right)$$

$$= -f_w(U_l) - (U_l - w)\ln(U - w) + U_l \ln(U) + (U - U_l)(\ln(U) - \ln(U - w))$$

$$= -f_w(U_l) - ((U_l - w) + (U - U_l))\ln(U - w) + (U_l + (U - U_l))\ln(U)$$

$$= -f_w(U_l) - (U - w)\ln(U - w) + U \ln(U) = -f(U_l) + f_w(U).$$

Appendix H
Statistical tables

All tables in this Appendix are derived by using the corresponding programming subroutines from IMSL Libraries of Compaq Visual Fortran 90 (Compaq Computer Corporation), version 6.5.

For consistency, all tables use cumulative left-tailed probabilities. More precisely, the correspondence between a number a and a probability P in a table means that P is the probability that the corresponding random variable is less than or equal to a.

Table H1. Cumulative probabilities of the standard normal distribution

For a number x, the table gives the probability that the standard normal variable is less than or equal to x. For instance, the probability that the standard normal variable is less than or equal to -2.46 will be 0.0069; it is on the intersection of the row with -2.4 and the column with 6.

x	0	1	2	3	4	5	6	7	8	9
-3.0	0.0013	0.0013	0.0013	0.0012	0.0012	0.0011	0.0011	0.0011	0.0010	0.0010
-2.9	0.0019	0.0018	0.0018	0.0017	0.0016	0.0016	0.0015	0.0015	0.0014	0.0014
-2.8	0.0026	0.0025	0.0024	0.0023	0.0023	0.0022	0.0021	0.0021	0.0020	0.0019
-2.7	0.0035	0.0034	0.0033	0.0032	0.0031	0.0030	0.0029	0.0028	0.0027	0.0026
-2.6	0.0047	0.0045	0.0044	0.0043	0.0041	0.0040	0.0039	0.0038	0.0037	0.0036
-2.5	0.0062	0.0060	0.0059	0.0057	0.0055	0.0054	0.0052	0.0051	0.0049	0.0048
-2.4	0.0082	0.0080	0.0078	0.0075	0.0073	0.0071	0.0069	0.0068	0.0066	0.0064
-2.3	0.0107	0.0104	0.0102	0.0099	0.0096	0.0094	0.0091	0.0089	0.0087	0.0084
-2.2	0.0139	0.0136	0.0132	0.0129	0.0125	0.0122	0.0119	0.0116	0.0113	0.0110
-2.1	0.0179	0.0174	0.0170	0.0166	0.0162	0.0158	0.0154	0.0150	0.0146	0.0143
-2.0	0.0228	0.0222	0.0217	0.0212	0.0207	0.0202	0.0197	0.0192	0.0188	0.0183
-1.9	0.0287	0.0281	0.0274	0.0268	0.0262	0.0256	0.0250	0.0244	0.0239	0.0233
-1.8	0.0359	0.0351	0.0344	0.0336	0.0329	0.0322	0.0314	0.0307	0.0301	0.0294
-1.7	0.0446	0.0436	0.0427	0.0418	0.0409	0.0401	0.0392	0.0384	0.0375	0.0367
-1.6	0.0548	0.0537	0.0526	0.0516	0.0505	0.0495	0.0485	0.0475	0.0465	0.0455
-1.5	0.0668	0.0655	0.0643	0.0630	0.0618	0.0606	0.0594	0.0582	0.0571	0.0559
-1.4	0.0808	0.0793	0.0778	0.0764	0.0749	0.0735	0.0721	0.0708	0.0694	0.0681

(cont.)

Table H1. (cont.)

x	0	1	2	3	4	5	6	7	8	9
−1.3	0.0968	0.0951	0.0934	0.0918	0.0901	0.0885	0.0869	0.0853	0.0838	0.0823
−1.2	0.1151	0.1131	0.1112	0.1093	0.1075	0.1056	0.1038	0.1020	0.1003	0.0985
−1.1	0.1357	0.1335	0.1314	0.1292	0.1271	0.1251	0.1230	0.1210	0.1190	0.1170
−1.0	0.1587	0.1562	0.1539	0.1515	0.1492	0.1469	0.1446	0.1423	0.1401	0.1379
−0.9	0.1841	0.1814	0.1788	0.1762	0.1736	0.1711	0.1685	0.1660	0.1635	0.1611
−0.8	0.2119	0.2090	0.2061	0.2033	0.2005	0.1977	0.1949	0.1922	0.1894	0.1867
−0.7	0.2420	0.2389	0.2358	0.2327	0.2296	0.2266	0.2236	0.2206	0.2177	0.2148
−0.6	0.2743	0.2709	0.2676	0.2643	0.2611	0.2578	0.2546	0.2514	0.2483	0.2451
−0.5	0.3085	0.3050	0.3015	0.2981	0.2946	0.2912	0.2877	0.2843	0.2810	0.2776
−0.4	0.3446	0.3409	0.3372	0.3336	0.3300	0.3264	0.3228	0.3192	0.3156	0.3121
−0.3	0.3821	0.3783	0.3745	0.3707	0.3669	0.3632	0.3594	0.3557	0.3520	0.3483
−0.2	0.4207	0.4168	0.4129	0.4090	0.4052	0.4013	0.3974	0.3936	0.3897	0.3859
−0.1	0.4602	0.4562	0.4522	0.4483	0.4443	0.4404	0.4364	0.4325	0.4286	0.4247
−0.0	0.5000	0.4960	0.4920	0.4880	0.4840	0.4801	0.4761	0.4721	0.4681	0.4641
0.0	0.5000	0.5040	0.5080	0.5120	0.5160	0.5199	0.5239	0.5279	0.5319	0.5359
0.1	0.5398	0.5438	0.5478	0.5517	0.5557	0.5596	0.5636	0.5675	0.5714	0.5753
0.2	0.5793	0.5832	0.5871	0.5910	0.5948	0.5987	0.6026	0.6064	0.6103	0.6141
0.3	0.6179	0.6217	0.6255	0.6293	0.6331	0.6368	0.6406	0.6443	0.6480	0.6517
0.4	0.6554	0.6591	0.6628	0.6664	0.6700	0.6736	0.6772	0.6808	0.6844	0.6879
0.5	0.6915	0.6950	0.6985	0.7019	0.7054	0.7088	0.7123	0.7157	0.7190	0.7224
0.6	0.7257	0.7291	0.7324	0.7357	0.7389	0.7422	0.7454	0.7486	0.7517	0.7549
0.7	0.7580	0.7611	0.7642	0.7673	0.7704	0.7734	0.7764	0.7794	0.7823	0.7852
0.8	0.7881	0.7910	0.7939	0.7967	0.7995	0.8023	0.8051	0.8078	0.8106	0.8133
0.9	0.8159	0.8186	0.8212	0.8238	0.8264	0.8289	0.8315	0.8340	0.8365	0.8389
1.0	0.8413	0.8438	0.8461	0.8485	0.8508	0.8531	0.8554	0.8577	0.8599	0.8621
1.1	0.8643	0.8665	0.8686	0.8708	0.8729	0.8749	0.8770	0.8790	0.8810	0.8830
1.2	0.8849	0.8869	0.8888	0.8907	0.8925	0.8944	0.8962	0.8980	0.8997	0.9015
1.3	0.9032	0.9049	0.9066	0.9082	0.9099	0.9115	0.9131	0.9147	0.9162	0.9177
1.4	0.9192	0.9207	0.9222	0.9236	0.9251	0.9265	0.9279	0.9292	0.9306	0.9319
1.5	0.9332	0.9345	0.9357	0.9370	0.9382	0.9394	0.9406	0.9418	0.9429	0.9441
1.6	0.9452	0.9463	0.9474	0.9484	0.9495	0.9505	0.9515	0.9525	0.9535	0.9545
1.7	0.9554	0.9564	0.9573	0.9582	0.9591	0.9599	0.9608	0.9616	0.9625	0.9633
1.8	0.9641	0.9649	0.9656	0.9664	0.9671	0.9678	0.9686	0.9693	0.9699	0.9706
1.9	0.9713	0.9719	0.9726	0.9732	0.9738	0.9744	0.9750	0.9756	0.9761	0.9767
2.0	0.9772	0.9778	0.9783	0.9788	0.9793	0.9798	0.9803	0.9808	0.9812	0.9817
2.1	0.9821	0.9826	0.9830	0.9834	0.9838	0.9842	0.9846	0.9850	0.9854	0.9857
2.2	0.9861	0.9864	0.9868	0.9871	0.9875	0.9878	0.9881	0.9884	0.9887	0.9890
2.3	0.9893	0.9896	0.9898	0.9901	0.9904	0.9906	0.9909	0.9911	0.9913	0.9916
2.4	0.9918	0.9920	0.9922	0.9925	0.9927	0.9929	0.9931	0.9932	0.9934	0.9936
2.5	0.9938	0.9940	0.9941	0.9943	0.9945	0.9946	0.9948	0.9949	0.9951	0.9952
2.6	0.9953	0.9955	0.9956	0.9957	0.9959	0.9960	0.9961	0.9962	0.9963	0.9964
2.7	0.9965	0.9966	0.9967	0.9968	0.9969	0.9970	0.9971	0.9972	0.9973	0.9974
2.8	0.9974	0.9975	0.9976	0.9977	0.9977	0.9978	0.9979	0.9979	0.9980	0.9981
2.9	0.9981	0.9982	0.9982	0.9983	0.9984	0.9984	0.9985	0.9985	0.9986	0.9986
3.0	0.9987	0.9987	0.9987	0.9988	0.9988	0.9989	0.9989	0.9989	0.9990	0.9990

Table H2. Cumulative probabilities of the chi-square distribution

The table gives the chi-square statistic values corresponding to selected cumulative probabilities. The first column d indicates the number of degrees of freedom. For instance, for two degrees of freedom and for probability $P = 0.25$, the statistic value on the intersection of the corresponding row and column is 0.575. In other words, the probability that the chi-square variable with two degrees of freedom is less than or equal to 0.575 is 0.25.

	Probability										
d	0.025	0.05	0.10	0.25	0.50	0.75	0.90	0.95	0.975	0.99	0.999
1	0.001	0.004	0.016	0.102	0.455	1.323	2.706	3.841	5.024	6.635	10.83
2	0.051	0.103	0.211	0.575	1.386	2.773	4.605	5.991	7.378	9.210	13.82
3	0.216	0.352	0.584	1.213	2.366	4.108	6.251	7.815	9.348	11.35	16.27
4	0.484	0.711	1.064	1.923	3.357	5.385	7.779	9.488	11.14	13.28	18.47
5	0.831	1.145	1.610	2.675	4.351	6.626	9.236	11.07	12.83	15.09	20.52
6	1.24	1.63	2.20	3.45	5.35	7.84	10.65	12.59	14.45	16.81	22.46
7	1.69	2.17	2.83	4.26	6.35	9.04	12.02	14.07	16.01	18.48	24.32
8	2.18	2.73	3.49	5.07	7.34	10.22	13.36	15.51	17.53	20.09	26.12
9	2.70	3.33	4.17	5.90	8.34	11.39	14.68	16.92	19.02	21.67	27.88
10	3.25	3.94	4.86	6.74	9.34	12.55	15.99	18.31	20.48	23.21	29.59
11	3.82	4.57	5.58	7.58	10.34	13.70	17.27	19.67	21.92	24.73	31.26
12	4.40	5.23	6.30	8.44	11.34	14.85	18.55	21.03	23.34	26.22	32.91
13	5.01	5.89	7.04	9.30	12.34	15.98	19.81	22.36	24.74	27.69	34.53
14	5.63	6.57	7.79	10.16	13.34	17.12	21.06	23.68	26.12	29.14	36.12
15	6.26	7.26	8.55	11.04	14.34	18.25	22.31	25.00	27.49	30.58	37.70
16	6.91	7.96	9.31	11.91	15.34	19.37	23.54	26.30	28.84	32.00	39.25
17	7.56	8.67	10.09	12.79	16.34	20.49	24.77	27.59	30.19	33.41	40.79
18	8.23	9.39	10.86	13.68	17.34	21.60	25.99	28.87	31.53	34.81	42.31
19	8.91	10.12	11.65	14.56	18.34	22.72	27.20	30.14	32.85	36.19	43.82
20	9.59	10.85	12.44	15.45	19.34	23.83	28.41	31.41	34.17	37.57	45.31
21	10.28	11.59	13.24	16.34	20.34	24.93	29.61	32.67	35.48	38.93	46.80
22	10.98	12.34	14.04	17.24	21.34	26.04	30.81	33.92	36.78	40.29	48.27
23	11.69	13.09	14.85	18.14	22.34	27.14	32.01	35.17	38.08	41.64	49.73
24	12.40	13.85	15.66	19.04	23.34	28.24	33.20	36.42	39.36	42.98	51.18
25	13.12	14.61	16.47	19.94	24.34	29.34	34.38	37.65	40.65	44.31	52.62
26	13.84	15.38	17.29	20.84	25.34	30.43	35.56	38.88	41.92	45.64	54.05
27	14.57	16.15	18.11	21.75	26.34	31.53	36.74	40.11	43.19	46.96	55.48
28	15.31	16.93	18.94	22.66	27.34	32.62	37.92	41.34	44.46	48.28	56.89
29	16.05	17.71	19.77	23.57	28.34	33.71	39.09	42.56	45.72	49.59	58.30
30	16.79	18.49	20.60	24.48	29.34	34.80	40.26	43.77	46.98	50.89	59.70

When the number of degrees of freedom d is greater than 30, the chi-square variable χ^2 can be approximated as $(Z + \sqrt{2d - 1})^2/2$, where Z is the standard normal variable. Therefore, in this case the probability that $\chi^2 \leq x$ is approximated by the probability that $Z \leq \sqrt{2x} - \sqrt{2d - 1}$ which can be found from Table H1.

Table H3. Cumulative probabilities of the student's t-distribution

Similarly to Table H2, this table gives values of t-statistic for selected cumulative probabilities; d denotes degrees of freedom. For instance, there is 90% probability that the t-variable with seven degrees of freedom is less than or equal to 1.415.

	Probability									
d	0.6	0.7	0.75	0.8	0.85	0.9	0.95	0.975	0.99	0.995
1	0.325	0.727	1.000	1.376	1.963	3.078	6.314	12.71	31.82	63.66
2	0.289	0.617	0.816	1.061	1.386	1.886	2.920	4.303	6.965	9.925
3	0.277	0.584	0.765	0.978	1.250	1.638	2.353	3.182	4.541	5.841
4	0.271	0.569	0.741	0.941	1.190	1.533	2.132	2.776	3.747	4.604
5	0.267	0.559	0.727	0.920	1.156	1.476	2.015	2.571	3.365	4.032
6	0.265	0.553	0.718	0.906	1.134	1.440	1.943	2.447	3.143	3.707
7	0.263	0.549	0.711	0.896	1.119	1.415	1.895	2.365	2.998	3.499
8	0.262	0.546	0.706	0.889	1.108	1.397	1.860	2.306	2.896	3.355
9	0.261	0.543	0.703	0.883	1.100	1.383	1.833	2.262	2.821	3.250
10	0.260	0.542	0.700	0.879	1.093	1.372	1.812	2.228	2.764	3.169
11	0.260	0.540	0.697	0.876	1.088	1.363	1.796	2.201	2.718	3.106
12	0.259	0.539	0.695	0.873	1.083	1.356	1.782	2.179	2.681	3.055
13	0.259	0.538	0.694	0.870	1.079	1.350	1.771	2.160	2.650	3.012
14	0.258	0.537	0.692	0.868	1.076	1.345	1.761	2.145	2.624	2.977
15	0.258	0.536	0.691	0.866	1.074	1.341	1.753	2.131	2.602	2.947
16	0.258	0.535	0.690	0.865	1.071	1.337	1.746	2.120	2.583	2.921
17	0.257	0.534	0.689	0.863	1.069	1.333	1.740	2.110	2.567	2.898
18	0.257	0.534	0.688	0.862	1.067	1.330	1.734	2.101	2.552	2.878
19	0.257	0.533	0.688	0.861	1.066	1.328	1.729	2.093	2.539	2.861
20	0.257	0.533	0.687	0.860	1.064	1.325	1.725	2.086	2.528	2.845
21	0.257	0.532	0.686	0.859	1.063	1.323	1.721	2.080	2.518	2.831
22	0.256	0.532	0.686	0.858	1.061	1.321	1.717	2.074	2.508	2.819
23	0.256	0.532	0.685	0.858	1.060	1.319	1.714	2.069	2.500	2.807
24	0.256	0.531	0.685	0.857	1.059	1.318	1.711	2.064	2.492	2.797
25	0.256	0.531	0.684	0.856	1.058	1.316	1.708	2.060	2.485	2.787
26	0.256	0.531	0.684	0.856	1.058	1.315	1.706	2.056	2.479	2.779
27	0.256	0.531	0.684	0.855	1.057	1.314	1.703	2.052	2.473	2.771
28	0.256	0.530	0.683	0.855	1.056	1.313	1.701	2.048	2.467	2.763
29	0.256	0.530	0.683	0.854	1.055	1.311	1.699	2.045	2.462	2.756
30	0.256	0.530	0.683	0.854	1.055	1.310	1.697	2.042	2.457	2.750
40	0.255	0.529	0.681	0.851	1.050	1.303	1.684	2.021	2.423	2.704
50	0.255	0.528	0.679	0.849	1.047	1.299	1.676	2.009	2.403	2.678
60	0.254	0.527	0.679	0.848	1.045	1.296	1.671	2.000	2.390	2.660
70	0.254	0.527	0.678	0.847	1.044	1.294	1.667	1.994	2.381	2.648
80	0.254	0.526	0.678	0.846	1.043	1.292	1.664	1.990	2.374	2.639
90	0.254	0.526	0.677	0.846	1.042	1.291	1.662	1.987	2.368	2.632
100	0.254	0.526	0.677	0.845	1.042	1.290	1.660	1.984	2.364	2.626
110	0.254	0.526	0.677	0.845	1.041	1.289	1.659	1.982	2.361	2.621
120	0.254	0.526	0.677	0.845	1.041	1.289	1.658	1.980	2.358	2.617
∞	0.253	0.524	0.674	0.842	1.037	1.282	1.645	1.960	2.326	2.576

Table H4. Cumulative probabilities of the binomial distribution

The table gives cumulative binomial distributions for selected probabilities of 'success in one trial'. Notation: n is the number of Bernoulli trials, k is the number of 'successes' and the marginal 'column' probability is the probability of success in one trial. If a number q is in a (n, k)-row and in a column with probability p, it means that the probability for the corresponding binomial variable to have k or fewer successes in n trials is q. For example, if the probability of success in one trial is 0.25, the probability to have three or fewer successes in five trials is 0.9844.

		Probability									
n	k	0.05	0.10	0.15	0.20	0.25	0.30	0.35	0.40	0.45	0.50
3	0	0.8574	0.7290	0.6141	0.5120	0.4219	0.3430	0.2746	0.2160	0.1664	0.1250
	1	0.9927	0.9720	0.9392	0.8960	0.8438	0.7840	0.7182	0.6480	0.5748	0.5000
	2	0.9999	0.9990	0.9966	0.9920	0.9844	0.9730	0.9571	0.9360	0.9089	0.8750
4	0	0.8145	0.6561	0.5220	0.4096	0.3164	0.2401	0.1785	0.1296	0.0915	0.0625
	1	0.9860	0.9477	0.8905	0.8192	0.7383	0.6517	0.5630	0.4752	0.3910	0.3125
	2	0.9995	0.9963	0.9880	0.9728	0.9492	0.9163	0.8735	0.8208	0.7585	0.6875
	3	1.000	0.9999	0.9995	0.9984	0.9961	0.9919	0.9850	0.9744	0.9590	0.9375
5	0	0.7738	0.5905	0.4437	0.3277	0.2373	0.1681	0.1160	0.0778	0.0503	0.0312
	1	0.9774	0.9185	0.8352	0.7373	0.6328	0.5282	0.4284	0.3370	0.2562	0.1875
	2	0.9988	0.9914	0.9734	0.9421	0.8965	0.8369	0.7648	0.6826	0.5931	0.5000
	3	1.000	0.9995	0.9978	0.9933	0.9844	0.9692	0.9460	0.9130	0.8688	0.8125
	4	1.000	1.000	0.9999	0.9997	0.9990	0.9976	0.9947	0.9898	0.9815	0.9688
6	0	0.7351	0.5314	0.3771	0.2621	0.1780	0.1176	0.0754	0.0467	0.0277	0.0156
	1	0.9672	0.8857	0.7765	0.6554	0.5339	0.4202	0.3191	0.2333	0.1636	0.1094
	2	0.9978	0.9841	0.9527	0.9011	0.8306	0.7443	0.6471	0.5443	0.4415	0.3438
	3	0.9999	0.9987	0.9941	0.9830	0.9624	0.9295	0.8826	0.8208	0.7447	0.6562
	4	1.000	0.9999	0.9996	0.9984	0.9954	0.9891	0.9777	0.9590	0.9308	0.8906
	5	1.000	1.000	1.000	0.9999	0.9998	0.9993	0.9982	0.9959	0.9917	0.9844
7	0	0.6983	0.4783	0.3206	0.2097	0.1335	0.0824	0.0490	0.0280	0.0152	0.0078
	1	0.9556	0.8503	0.7166	0.5767	0.4449	0.3294	0.2338	0.1586	0.1024	0.0625
	2	0.9962	0.9743	0.9262	0.8520	0.7564	0.6471	0.5323	0.4199	0.3164	0.2266
	3	0.9998	0.9973	0.9879	0.9667	0.9294	0.8740	0.8002	0.7102	0.6083	0.5000
	4	1.000	0.9998	0.9988	0.9953	0.9871	0.9712	0.9444	0.9037	0.8471	0.7734
	5	1.000	1.000	0.9999	0.9996	0.9987	0.9962	0.9910	0.9812	0.9643	0.9375
	6	1.000	1.000	1.000	1.000	0.9999	0.9998	0.9994	0.9984	0.9963	0.9922
8	0	0.6634	0.4305	0.2725	0.1678	0.1001	0.0576	0.0319	0.0168	0.0084	0.0039
	1	0.9428	0.8131	0.6572	0.5033	0.3671	0.2553	0.1691	0.1064	0.0632	0.0352
	2	0.9942	0.9619	0.8948	0.7969	0.6785	0.5518	0.4278	0.3154	0.2201	0.1445
	3	0.9996	0.9950	0.9786	0.9437	0.8862	0.8059	0.7064	0.5941	0.4770	0.3633
	4	1.000	0.9996	0.9971	0.9896	0.9727	0.9420	0.8939	0.8263	0.7396	0.6367
	5	1.000	1.000	0.9998	0.9988	0.9958	0.9887	0.9747	0.9502	0.9115	0.8555
	6	1.000	1.000	1.000	0.9999	0.9996	0.9987	0.9964	0.9915	0.9819	0.9648
	7	1.000	1.000	1.000	1.000	1.000	0.9999	0.9998	0.9993	0.9983	0.9961

(*cont.*)

Table H4. (*cont.*)

						Probability					
n	*k*	0.05	0.10	0.15	0.20	0.25	0.30	0.35	0.40	0.45	0.50
9	0	0.6302	0.3874	0.2316	0.1342	0.0751	0.0404	0.0207	0.0101	0.0046	0.0020
	1	0.9288	0.7748	0.5995	0.4362	0.3003	0.1960	0.1211	0.0705	0.0385	0.0195
	2	0.9916	0.9470	0.8591	0.7382	0.6007	0.4628	0.3373	0.2318	0.1495	0.0898
	3	0.9994	0.9917	0.9661	0.9144	0.8343	0.7297	0.6089	0.4826	0.3614	0.2539
	4	1.000	0.9991	0.9944	0.9804	0.9511	0.9012	0.8283	0.7334	0.6214	0.5000
	5	1.000	0.9999	0.9994	0.9969	0.9900	0.9747	0.9464	0.9006	0.8342	0.7461
	6	1.000	1.000	1.000	0.9997	0.9987	0.9957	0.9888	0.9750	0.9502	0.9102
	7	1.000	1.000	1.000	1.000	0.9999	0.9996	0.9986	0.9962	0.9909	0.9805
	8	1.000	1.000	1.000	1.000	1.000	1.000	0.9999	0.9997	0.9992	0.9980
10	0	0.5987	0.3487	0.1969	0.1074	0.0563	0.0282	0.0135	0.0060	0.0025	0.0010
	1	0.9139	0.7361	0.5443	0.3758	0.2440	0.1493	0.0860	0.0464	0.0233	0.0107
	2	0.9885	0.9298	0.8202	0.6778	0.5256	0.3828	0.2616	0.1673	0.0996	0.0547
	3	0.9990	0.9872	0.9500	0.8791	0.7759	0.6496	0.5138	0.3823	0.2660	0.1719
	4	0.9999	0.9984	0.9901	0.9672	0.9219	0.8497	0.7515	0.6331	0.5044	0.3770
	5	1.000	0.9999	0.9986	0.9936	0.9803	0.9527	0.9051	0.8338	0.7384	0.6230
	6	1.000	1.000	0.9999	0.9991	0.9965	0.9894	0.9740	0.9452	0.8980	0.8281
	7	1.000	1.000	1.000	0.9999	0.9996	0.9984	0.9952	0.9877	0.9726	0.9453
	8	1.000	1.000	1.000	1.000	1.000	0.9999	0.9995	0.9983	0.9955	0.9893
	9	1.000	1.000	1.000	1.000	1.000	1.000	1.000	0.9999	0.9997	0.9990
11	0	0.5688	0.3138	0.1673	0.0859	0.0422	0.0198	0.0088	0.0036	0.0014	0.0005
	1	0.8981	0.6974	0.4922	0.3221	0.1971	0.1130	0.0606	0.0302	0.0139	0.0059
	2	0.9848	0.9104	0.7788	0.6174	0.4552	0.3127	0.2001	0.1189	0.0652	0.0327
	3	0.9984	0.9815	0.9306	0.8389	0.7133	0.5696	0.4255	0.2963	0.1911	0.1133
	4	0.9999	0.9972	0.9841	0.9496	0.8854	0.7897	0.6683	0.5328	0.3971	0.2744
	5	1.000	0.9997	0.9973	0.9883	0.9657	0.9218	0.8513	0.7535	0.6331	0.5000
	6	1.000	1.000	0.9997	0.9980	0.9924	0.9784	0.9499	0.9006	0.8262	0.7256
	7	1.000	1.000	1.000	0.9998	0.9988	0.9957	0.9878	0.9707	0.9390	0.8867
	8	1.000	1.000	1.000	1.000	0.9999	0.9994	0.9980	0.9941	0.9852	0.9673
	9	1.000	1.000	1.000	1.000	1.000	1.000	0.9998	0.9993	0.9978	0.9941
	10	1.000	1.000	1.000	1.000	1.000	1.000	1.000	1.000	0.9998	0.9995
12	0	0.5404	0.2824	0.1422	0.0687	0.0317	0.0138	0.0057	0.0022	0.0008	0.0002
	1	0.8816	0.6590	0.4435	0.2749	0.1584	0.0850	0.0424	0.0196	0.0083	0.0032
	2	0.9804	0.8891	0.7358	0.5583	0.3907	0.2528	0.1513	0.0834	0.0421	0.0193
	3	0.9978	0.9744	0.9078	0.7946	0.6488	0.4925	0.3467	0.2253	0.1345	0.0730
	4	0.9998	0.9957	0.9761	0.9274	0.8424	0.7237	0.5833	0.4382	0.3044	0.1938
	5	1.000	0.9995	0.9954	0.9806	0.9456	0.8822	0.7873	0.6652	0.5269	0.3872
	6	1.000	0.9999	0.9993	0.9961	0.9857	0.9614	0.9154	0.8418	0.7393	0.6128
	7	1.000	1.000	0.9999	0.9994	0.9972	0.9905	0.9745	0.9427	0.8883	0.8062
	8	1.000	1.000	1.000	0.9999	0.9996	0.9983	0.9944	0.9847	0.9644	0.9270
	9	1.000	1.000	1.000	1.000	1.000	0.9998	0.9992	0.9972	0.9921	0.9807
	10	1.000	1.000	1.000	1.000	1.000	1.000	0.9999	0.9997	0.9989	0.9968
	11	1.000	1.000	1.000	1.000	1.000	1.000	1.000	1.000	0.9999	0.9998

References

[1] American Association for Public Opinion Research (2004). *Standard Definitions: Final Dispositions of Case Codes and Outcome Rates for Surveys*, 3rd edn.

[2] Baker, K., Harris, P. and O'Brien, J. (1989). Data fusion: an appraisal and experimental evaluation. *Journal of the Market Research Society*, **31**, No. 2, 153–212.

[3] Bartholomew, D. J. (1961). A method of allowing for 'not-at-home' bias in sample surveys. *Applied Statistics*, **10**, 52–59.

[4] Bedrick, E. J. (1983). Adjusted chi-squared tests for cross-classified tables of survey data. *Biometrika*, **70**, No. 3, 591–595.

[5] Benford, F. (1938). The law of anomalous numbers. *Proceedings of the American Philosophical Society*, **78**, 551–572.

[6] Bethlehem, J. G. and Keller, W. J. (1987). Linear weighting of sample survey data. *Journal of Official Statistics*, **3**, 141–153.

[7] Breiman, L., Friedman, J., Olshen, R. and Stone, C. (1984). *Classification and Regression Trees*, Wadsworth International Group.

[8] Chow, S. L. (1996). *Statistical Significance: Rationale, Validity and Utility*, Sage.

[9] Cochran, W. G. (1977). *Sampling Techniques*, John Wiley and Sons, 3rd edn.

[10] Conway, S. (1982). The weighting game. *Market Research Society Conference Papers*, 193–207.

[11] Deville, J.-C. (1988). Estimation Linéaire et Redressement sur Informations Auxiliaires d'Enquêtes par Sondage. *Essais en l'Honneur d'Edmond Malinvaud*, ed. A. Monfort and J. J. Laffond, Paris: Economica, pp. 915–927.

[12] Deville, J.-C. and Särndal, C.-E. (1992). Calibration estimators in survey sampling. *Journal of the American Statistical Association*, **87**, No. 418, 376–382.

[13] Deville, J.-C., Särndal, C.-E. and Sautory, O. (1993). Generalized raking procedures in survey sampling, *Journal of the American Statistical Association*, **88**, No. 423, 1013–1020.

[14] Devroye, L., Györfi, L. and Lugosi, G. (1996). *A Probabilistic Theory of Pattern Recognition*, Springer.

[15] Digby, P. G. N. and Kempton, R. A. (1987). *Multivariate Analysis of Ecological Communities*, Chapman and Hall.

[16] Efron, B. (1979). Bootstrap methods: another look at the jackknife. *Annals of Statistics*, **7**, 1–26.

[17] Efron, B. and Tibshirani, R. J. (1993). *An Introduction to the Bootstrap*, Monographs on Statistics and Applied Probability 57, Chapman and Hall.

[18] Everitt, B. S. (1977). *The Analysis of Contingency Tables*, John Wiley and Sons.

[19]   Fuller, W. A., McLoughlin, M. M. and Baker, H. D. (1994). Regression weighting in the presence of nonresponse with application to the 1987–1988 Nationwide Food Consumption Survey. *Survey Methodology*, **20**, 75–85.

[20]   Gabler, S., Häder, S. and Lahiri, P. (1999). A model based justification of Kish's formula for design effects for weighting and clustering. *Survey Methodology*, **25**, 105–106.

[21]   Goodman, L. A. and Kruskal, W. H. (1954). Measures of association for cross-classifications, *Journal of the American Statistical Association*, **49**, 732–764.

[22]   Greenacre, M. J. (1984). *Theory and Applications of Correspondence Analysis*, Academic Press.

[23]   Greenacre, M. J. (1993). *Correspondence Analysis in Practice*, Academic Press.

[24]   Groves, R. M. (1989). *Survey Errors and Survey Costs*, John Wiley and Sons.

[25]   Groves, R. M., Dillman, D. A., Eltinge, J. L. and Little, R. J. A. (eds) (2001). *Survey Nonresponse*, Wiley.

[26]   Harris, P. (1977). The effect of clustering on costs and sampling errors of random samples. *Journal of the Market Research Society*, **19**, No. 3, 112–122.

[27]   Hill, T. P. (1995). A statistical derivation of the significant-digit law. *Statistical Science*, **10**, No. 4, 354–363.

[28]   Hill, T. P. (1998). The first digit phenomenon. *American Scientist*, **86**, 358–363.

[29]   Hoffman, D. L. and Franke, G. R. (1986). Correspondence analysis: graphical representation of categorical data in marketing research. *Journal of Marketing Research*, **XXIII**, (August 1986), 213–227.

[30]   Kalton, G. (1979). Ultimate cluster sampling. *Journal of the Royal Statistical Society, Series A*, **142**, No. 2, 210–222.

[31]   Kalton, G. and Flores-Cervantes, I. (1998). Weighting methods. In *New Methods For Survey Research, Proceedings of the Association For Survey Computing International Conference, Southampton, UK, 1998*, pp. 77–92.

[32]   Kendall, M. and Stuart, A. (1979). *The Advanced Theory of Statistics*, Griffin, Volume 2, 4th edn.

[33]   Keyfitz, N. (1957). Estimates of sampling variance where two units are selected from each stratum. *Journal of the American Statistical Association*, **52**, 503–510.

[34]   Kish, L. (1949). A procedure for objective respondent selection within the household. *Journal of the American Statistical Association*, **40**, 38–56.

[35]   Kish, L. (1965). *Survey Sampling*, John Wiley and Sons.

[36]   Kish, L. (1987). *Statistical Design For Research*, John Wiley and Sons.

[37]   Kish, L. (1987). *Weighting in Deft^2, The Survey Statistician June 1987*. The International Association of Survey Statisticians.

[38]   Kish, L. (1995). Questions/answers from The Survey Statistician 1978–1994. *International Association of Survey Statisticians, Section of the International Statistical Institute*.

[39]   Lee, E., Forthofer, R. N. and Lorrimor, R. J. (1989). *Analyzing Complex Surveys*, Sage.

[40]   Lehtonen, R. and Pahkinen, E. J. (1995). *Practical Methods for Design and Analysis of Complex Surveys*, Wiley.

[40a] Levine, M., Morgan, G., Hepenstall, N., and Smith, G. (2001). Single Source – for Increased Advertising Productivity in a Multimedia World (paper presented at The Advertising Research Foundation's '*Week of Workshops*' Chicago 2001). Available (2006) at http://www.roymorgan.com/resources/pdf/papers20011101.pdf

[41] Macfarlane Smith, J. (1972). *Interviewing in Market and Social Research*, Routledge and Kegan Paul.

[42] Market Research Society (1994). *The Opinion Polls and the 1992 General Election*, London: The Market Research Society.

[43] Morrison, D. E. and Henkel, R. E. (eds) (1970). *The Significance Test Controversy – A Reader*, Aldine.

[44] Moser, C. A. and Kalton, G. (1971). *Survey Methods in Social Investigation*, Heinemann Educational Books, 2nd edn.

[45] Politz, A. and Simmons, W. (1949). An attempt to get the not-at-homes into the sample without call-backs. Further theoretical considerations regarding the plan for eliminating call-backs. *Journal of the American Statistical Association*, **44**, 9–31.

[46] Quenouille, M. (1949). Approximation tests of correlation in time series. *Journal of the Royal Statistical Society B*, **11**, 18–84.

[47] Rao, J. N. K. and Scott, A. J. (1981). The analysis of categorical data from complex sample surveys: chi-squared tests for goodness of fit and independence in two-way tables. *Journal of the American Statistical Association*, **76**, No. 374, 221–230.

[48] Rao, J. N. K. and Scott, A. J. (1984). On the chi-squared tests for multiway contingency tables with cell proportions estimated from survey data. *Annals of Statistics*, **12**, No. 1, 46–60.

[49] Rothman, J. (1989). Data fusion and media research. *Data Fusion: Proceedings of a Market Research Development Fund Seminar, London*.

[50] Ryan, T. P. (1997). *Modern Regression Methods*, John Wiley and Sons.

[51] Shao, J. and Tu, D. (1995). *The Jackknife and Bootstrap*, Springer Series in Statistics, Springer-Verlag.

[52] Sharot, T. (1986). Weighting survey results. *Journal of the Market Research Society*, **28**, No. 3, 269–284.

[53] Sheth, J. N. (1977). *Multivariate Methods for Market and Survey Research*. The American Marketing Association.

[54] Skinner, C. J., Holt, D. and Smith, T. M. F. (1989). *Analysis of Complex Surveys*, Wiley.

[55] Soong, R. and de Montigny, M. (2004). No Free Lunch in Data Fusion/Integration. *Proceedings of the ARF/ESOMAR 'Week of Audience Measurement' Geneva*.

[56] Stephan, F. J. and McCarthy, P. J. (1958). *Sampling Opinions: an Analysis of Survey Procedure*, Wiley.

[57] Troldahl, V. C. and Carter, R. E. (1964). Random selection of respondents within households in 'phone surveys'. *Journal of Marketing Research*, **1**, No. 2, 71–76.

[58] United Nations (2005). *Household Sample Surveys in Developing and Transitional Countries* (publication no. E.05.XVII.6). United Nations.

[59] Ward, J. C., Russick, B. and Rudelius, W. (1985). A test of reducing call-backs and not-at-home bias in personal interviews by weighting at-home respondents. *Journal of Marketing Research*, **XXII**, (February 1985), 66–73.

[60] Zieschang, K. D. (1990). Sample weighting methods and estimation of totals in the consumer expenditure survey. *Journal of the American Statistical Association*, **85**, 986–1001.

Index